A NEW ORIENT

THE TAUBER INSTITUTE SERIES FOR
THE STUDY OF EUROPEAN JEWRY
Jehuda Reinharz, *General Editor*
ChaeRan Y. Freeze, *Associate Editor*
Sylvia Fuks Fried, *Associate Editor*
Eugene R. Sheppard, *Associate Editor*

The Tauber Institute Series is dedicated to publishing compelling and innovative approaches to the study of modern European Jewish history, thought, culture, and society. The series features scholarly works related to the Enlightenment, modern Judaism and the struggle for emancipation, the rise of nationalism and the spread of antisemitism, the Holocaust and its aftermath, as well as the contemporary Jewish experience. The series is published under the auspices of the Tauber Institute for the Study of European Jewry—established by a gift to Brandeis University from Dr. Laszlo N. Tauber—and is supported, in part, by the Tauber Foundation and the Valya and Robert Shapiro Endowment.

For the complete list of books that are available in this series,
please see https://brandeisuniversitypress.com/series/tauber

Amit Levy
  *A New Orient: From German
  Scholarship to Middle Eastern Studies
  in Israel*
Blanche Bendahan
Yaëlle Azagury and Fran Malino, editors
  *Mazaltob: A Novel*
Scott Ury and Guy Miron, editors
  *Antisemitism and the Politics of
  History*
Jeremy Fogel
  *Jewish Universalisms: Mendelssohn,
  Cohen, and Humanity's Highest Good*
Stefan Vogt, Derek Penslar, and Arieh
  Saposnik, editors
  *Unacknowledged Kinships:
  Postcolonial Studies and the
  Historiography of Zionism*

Joseph A. Skloot
  *First Impressions: Sefer Hasidim and
  Early Modern Hebrew Printing*
*Marat Grinberg
  *The Soviet Jewish Bookshelf:
  Jewish Culture and Identity
  Between the Lines*
Susan Martha Kahn
  *Canine Pioneer: The Extraordinary
  Life of Rudolphina Menzel*
Arthur Green
  *Defender of the Faithful: The Life
  and Thought of Rabbi Levi Yitshak
  of Berdychiv*
Gilad Sharvit
  *Dynamic Repetition: History and
  Messianism in Modern Jewish
  Thought*

*A Sarnat Library Book

# A NEW ORIENT

FROM GERMAN SCHOLARSHIP

TO MIDDLE EASTERN STUDIES

IN ISRAEL

## AMIT LEVY

*Translated by Ron Mordechai Makleff*

BRANDEIS UNIVERSITY PRESS

Waltham, Massachusetts

Brandeis University Press
© 2024 by Amit Levy
All rights reserved
Manufactured in the United States of America
Designed by Richard Hendel
Typeset in Minion Pro by Passumpsic Publishing

This book was published with the support of the Israel Science Foundation

For permission to reproduce any of the material in this book, contact
Brandeis University Press, 415 South Street, Waltham MA 02453,
or visit brandeisuniversitypress.com

Library of Congress Cataloging-in-Publishing Data
available at https://catalog.loc.gov/
cloth      ISBN 978-1-68458-203-7
paper      ISBN 978-1-68458-202-0
e-book     ISBN 978-1-68458-201-3

5  4  3  2  1

*To my grandfather, my teacher,*

SIMON ALVARES VEGA (1926–2008)

*societas, amicitia, veritas*

# CONTENTS

Acknowledgments      ix

INTRODUCTION      1

1: THE SCIENCE OF THE ORIENT      21
The Beginnings of Oriental Studies at
the Hebrew University

2: "WITH ITS BACK TO THE ORIENT"?      78
The School of Oriental Studies and the
Question of the Arab Intellectuals

3: ORIENT RENEWED      121
The Birth of Israeli Oriental Studies and
the Diplomatic Mission

EPILOGUE      174
"Truly, Jerusalem has one benefit:
Lying within the Orient."

Notes      185
Bibliography      261
Index      283

## ACKNOWLEDGMENTS

About a decade ago, at the outset of my graduate studies, I responded to a modest job offer: to be responsible for the sorting and cataloging of a small personal archive stored in a few containers at the National Library of Israel in Jerusalem. In hindsight, this was the beginning of a journey that encompassed an MA thesis, articles, lectures, countless discussions, a PhD dissertation, a Hebrew book, and ultimately—this book.

The patience and perseverance required for the collection, reflection, analysis, and writing that led to this book would not have been possible without the intellectual, material, and, at times, emotional support of many who accompanied me at various stages along the way.

To my two supervisors who guided me through my master's and doctoral work, Yfaat Weiss and Aya Elyada, I owe immense gratitude for the knowledge and skills they helped me acquire, for encouraging me to present and publish, and being willing to dedicate various resources for this purpose. All of this was done in an atmosphere that remained pleasant, focusing yet not suffocating, empathetic to the crises that occasionally arose, but always with constructive thoughts on how to overcome them. None of this should be taken for granted, and I am grateful for the privilege of their guidance in conducting this research.

My research was also supported by an advisory committee: Ami Ayalon, Reuven Amitai, and Liat Kozma. I thank all three of them for their useful comments on my research and for the interesting conversations we had. Additional gratitude is extended to Doron Avraham, Zvi Ben-Dor Benite, Arie M. Dubnov, Adi Gordon, and Ehud Toledano, who read this work in various stages and whose experience and knowledge contributed profoundly to its improvement.

I would like to express my gratitude to the institutions that supported me during the years of work on the book: the PhD Honors Program at the Jack, Joseph, and Morton Mandel School for Advanced Studies in the Humanities at the Hebrew University of Jerusalem; the Israel Science Foundation, Grants 633/12 and 1492/13; i-CORE *Da'at Hamakom*—The Center for the Study of Local Cultures in the Modern Jewish World; the Cherrick Center

X ::: ACKNOWLEDGMENTS

for the Study of Zionism, the Yishuv, and the State of Israel; the Institute for Jewish Studies and the Institute for Contemporary Jewry at the Hebrew University; the Nahum Ben Eli Honig Foundation; the Solomon and Penny Balaban-Glass Foundation; the *Studienstiftung des deutschen Volkes*; and the Leo Baeck Institute London.

A central academic home in recent years was the Franz Rosenzweig Minerva Research Center for German-Jewish Literature and Cultural History. I deeply appreciate the director of the center, Benjamin Pollock, for his amity and support, and the coordinators, Mor Hajbi, Naomi Goldman, Na'ama Seri Levi, and Audrey Fingherman, who tirelessly fought against bureaucratic obstacles for me.

The work of preparing the manuscript was made possible by the institutions that hosted me generously as a postdoctoral fellow: the George L. Mosse Program in History at the University of Wisconsin–Madison and the Hebrew University of Jerusalem; the Harry S. Truman Research Institute for the Advancement of Peace; the Bloom Graduate School and the Department of Israel Studies at the University of Haifa; and the Oxford Centre for Hebrew and Jewish Studies at the University of Oxford. Awards from the Middle East & Islamic Studies Association of Israel (MEISAI) and the Naomi and Bernard Frieden Fund at the Institute for Contemporary Jewry provided much-needed backing during that period. I am endlessly grateful for the support provided by the Richard Koebner Minerva Center for German History, its director, Ofer Ashkenazi—the first person to believe in this book—and its administrative director, Matthias Schmidt.

This book, therefore, marks the culmination of a fascinating research period, inevitably accompanied by disappointments and frustrations, but which were, however, dwarfed by the joys of discovery, connecting the dots, and formulating insights. Many days of enjoyable yet feverish archival work —often skipping meals inadvertently—were made possible with the active assistance of Ofer Tzemach from the Central Archives of the Hebrew University and Matan Barzilai and Stefan Litt from the Archives Department of the National Library of Israel. I am also grateful to the Central Zionist Archives, the Israel State Archives, the L. A. Mayer Museum for Islamic Art, Yad Chaim Weizmann, *Universitätsarchiv Frankfurt*, *Lautarchiv der Humboldt-Universität zu Berlin*, and the Library of the Hungarian Academy of Science for providing archival documents for my research.

In addition to the archival material, I had the privilege of engaging with several scholars who possess a deep familiarity with Israeli Oriental Studies or the discipline's founders, who were willing to share their experiences from the world beyond written documentation: Yohanan Friedmann, Israel Gershoni, David Heyd, Hagit and the late Natan Lavsky, Moshe Ma'oz, and Miriam Rosen-Ayalon. Special thanks are due to the late Jacob M. Landau, who hosted me for an unforgettable conversation; unfortunately, I cannot fulfill my promise to share the published research with him.

I presented chapters and excerpts from the book at multiple venues, and I would like to acknowledge the Institute of Asian and African Studies at the Hebrew University, whose members invited me, despite not being one of their own, to hear about their founding fathers. I am also grateful for the supportive research communities that I am proud to collaborate in: the Jerusalem DokKreis, and the two forums operating under the auspices of the Chaim Weizmann Institute at Tel Aviv University—for Israel Studies and for British Mandate Research. Their members provided me with valuable feedback and suggestions that contributed to the development of this work.

Ron M. Makleff did a wonderful job translating this book into English. His thoughtful and patient insight helped transform a book on German and Hebrew cultures into a flowing text for English readers, and I learned a lot from our translational dialogue, which was always good-spirited. Additionally, I extend my gratitude to Anat Schultz for her translation of an earlier version of the second chapter.

Scholarly generosity is not a trivial matter. Fortunately, I have encountered many instances of such generosity, and I am grateful to Walid Abd El Gawad, Hillel Cohen, Tom Eshed, Anna Kawalko-Holzer, Enrico Lucca, Shaul Marmari, Lee Rotbart, and Omri Shafer Raviv for the materials they labored to locate and agreed to share with me. Thanks to Jacob Barnai, Yuval Evri, Yoni Furas, Rebekka Grossmann, Mostafa Hussein, Ofri Ilany, Sarah Irving, Abigail Jacobson, Razak Khan, Sabine Mangold-Will, Yossi Mendelovich, Amos Noy, Or Pitusi, Itamar Radai, Orit Rozin, Assaf Selzer, Hila Shalem Baharad, Ghilad Shenhav, Yair Wallach, and Shira Wilkof for our enlightening conversations and their valuable advice. Heartfelt thanks go to Hanan Harif, Adi Livny, Yonatan Mendel, and Eli Osheroff. Our shared research interests made them not only ideal addressees for enthusiastic archival screenshots, but also dear friends.

Working with Sylvia Fuks Fried, editorial director of Brandeis University Press and associate editor of its Tauber Institute Series, has been an extremely pleasant experience. This book owes much to her support, understanding, and valuable advice, without which it would never have been xii ::: ACKNOWLEDGMENTS

published. I would also like to thank Sue Ramin and Eugene Sheppard; Ann Brash; and Katie Smith, for her meticulous copyediting. The translation of this book was made possible thanks to a generous grant from the Israel Science Foundation, no. 18/24. I am also indebted to the Hebrew University Magnes Press and its Managing Director Jonathan Nadav for facilitating a quick and smooth process of securing the rights to publish this updated English edition.

Thanks also to those who contributed to the research without even knowing it: to Jay Watson and Kevin Parker for their music, mae for their coffee, and the city of Lisbon for its delicious Pastel de Nata.

The most important thing is family. I wish to thank my in-laws, Irit and Motti Shaham, for their unwavering support of me and my family through-out the years of research; my beloved grandmother Rachel Vega (1931–2024), a truly remarkable figure; and my parents Dafna and Yehuda, from whom I inherited the passion for knowledge and, I hope, some of their humanity and kindness. Many pages would be needed to enumerate their myriad means of encouraging, assisting, and supporting me.

Ahinoam was born as I gathered materials for my master's thesis; Carmel was born during the archival research on which the book is based. Their wisdom and curiosity excite and inspire me. They bring joy to my heart. Without the significant place they occupy in my life, perhaps the book would have been published sooner, but the journey would have been far less enjoyable.

Lastly, my dear Moran. You did not ask to embark on this particular journey, yet you were and still are part of it. Thank you for everything, and a bit more.

# A NEW ORIENT

# INTRODUCTION

*Though it cannot be said that we are a nation primarily of the Orient—nevertheless, it is in the Orient that our origins lie and to there are we returning. (Shelomo Dov Goitein, 1935)*[1]

In April 1926, one year after the official opening of the Hebrew University in a festive and well-attended ceremony on Jerusalem's Mount Scopus, a new institute was inaugurated there somewhat more modestly—the School of Oriental Studies. Its founder and first director, the German-Jewish professor of Oriental Languages Josef Horovitz, travelled specially from the University of Frankfurt and delivered a lecture series marking the event. During this visit he also set an agenda for the institute—the first academic center of its kind in Palestine for the study of Arabic and Islam—and held meetings with his faculty. The latter were, during the institute's first decades, invariably Jews, and almost all were Orientalists trained at German universities, that is, those located within German-speaking Europe and where the primary language of instruction was German: among the institute's first seven faculty members, three filed their doctoral theses in Berlin, two in Frankfurt, and one in Vienna. Only one of the seven, a Jerusalemite, was born outside Europe; the remainder—apart from Horovitz, who remained in Frankfurt—relocated to Jerusalem over the course of the 1920s and 1930s. The tools acquired during their years of study at German universities framed these scholars' approach as they shaped the field and developed plans for research and instruction.

This was, therefore, a clear case of knowledge transfer, which, when it comes to science in historical context, amounts to the movement of ideas, expertise, research methods, technologies, and other units of knowledge between different groups, often crossing national or regional borders.[2] Once transferred, knowledge does not remain static or unchanged, of course: the social and cultural circumstances of its destination influence it deeply, as do the agents of transfer themselves—in the scientific case, that is, the scholars.[3]

This is the point of departure for the current study, which seeks to

## 2 ::: A NEW ORIENT

examine the history of Zionist academic Orientalism—referred to throughout this study as Oriental Studies, the term contemporary English speakers would have used—in light of its German-Jewish background as a history of knowledge transfer stretching along an axis from Germany to Palestine. The transfer, which took place primarily during the 1920s and 1930s, involved questions about the re-establishment, far from Germany, of a field of knowledge with deep German roots. Like other German-Jewish scholars arriving in Palestine at the time, some of the Orientalist agents of transfer did so out of Zionist conviction as *'olim* (immigrants making *'aliyah*, or literally "ascending" to the homeland) while others joined them later as refugees from Nazi Germany; both groups were integrated into the institutional apparatus of the Hebrew University thanks to their academic expertise. Unlike other fields of knowledge or professions, however, the transfer of Orientalist knowledge was unique in that the axis involved an essential change in the nature of its encounter with the Orient: from a textual-scientific encounter at German universities, largely disconnected from contemporary issues, to a living, substantive, and unmediated encounter with an essentially Arab region—and the escalating Jewish-Arab conflict in the background. Within the new context, German-Jewish Orientalist expertise was charged with political and cultural significance it had not previously faced, fundamentally influencing the course of the discipline's development in Palestine and Israel.

This study, then, delves into the development of the scientific discipline of Oriental Studies through scrutiny of the tension between the poles of the axis of knowledge—the European and the Middle Eastern—as demonstrated by the activities of the scholars of Oriental Studies at the Hebrew University, beginning in the 1920s with the founding of the Hebrew University School of Oriental Studies, to which I will be referring with the acronym HUSOS, and continuing into the 1960s. Inherent to this discussion are questions about how the environment of these scholars' training impacted their perspectives on their academic work; on the shifting roles of Orientalist expertise from Berlin and Frankfurt to Jerusalem; and on the nature of the tenuous seam running between science and politics and between academia and the state, in light of various social, cultural and political shifts.

The terms *Mizrahanut*—meaning "Orientalism," "Oriental Studies," or more broadly, "expertise in the Orient"—and *Mizrahan*—a (male) person who holds such expertise—began to appear in the Hebrew press largely around the time of, and in reports dealing with, the arrangements preceding the establishment of the Hebrew University.[4] In this book, which is based first and foremost on empirical findings, I will use the term much like contemporaries would have then: to describe an academic field of knowledge dealing with the study of the Orient and its historical, linguistic, religious, cultural, and social aspects. Moreover, in accordance with trends in the development of the discipline, the term will refer primarily to the study of Arabic and Islam; other fields of Oriental Studies research such as the study of the Far East or Assyriology held no significant foothold in university activity in the country during the years studied here.

As far as terminology is concerned, an important point needs to be addressed. In the English language, the term Orientalism has acquired an additional meaning, as a discourse that extends beyond the borders of academic work and emanates from a critical debate developing across the final third of the twentieth century.[5] I will delve into this criticism—most famously made by Edward Said—and its aftermath in the subsequent section of this introduction. In the meantime, it is important to stress that in employing the contemporary terminology, this book does not seek to divert the problems and negative connotations justly associated with the term Orient and its derivatives. Indeed, the book shows how some of the very historical figures being studied here, while they may have used the word "Orientalism" to describe themselves and their work, were already starting to problematize it long before the "Saidian" wave of the late 1970s.

This tension is further exacerbated by a significant translation gap. In contrast to the Hebrew, English possesses no terminological means of distinguishing between Orientalists (Oriental Studies scholars or experts, known in Hebrew as *Mizrahanim*) active in this academic field and the broader and more critical concept of Orientalism (*Orientalism* also in Hebrew, while those who engage in this discourse are sometimes called *Orientalistim*). To complicate things even further, in modern Hebrew the biblical word *mizrah* means both "East" and "Orient." Some scholars have sought clarification through use of the transliterated Hebrew word when discussing this scholarly field.[6] I have preferred to use terms easier on the eye of the English-language reader, and I will therefore refer from here on to the experts as Orientalists or Oriental Studies scholars, and to the field in which they were active as Oriental Studies.

This leads me to one final clarification. In order to focus on the process of academic knowledge transfer, and to attend to the decisive influence of its development within the university itself—the only one of its kind during

## 4 ::: A NEW ORIENT

the Mandate period and the State of Israel's first years—on the discipline as a whole, this study does not discuss the Orient experts operating on other fronts: in schools, newspapers, or diplomacy and security, except where their activities were linked to work being undertaken within the halls of the university. In other words, the focus of discussion here is Oriental Studies within the academy.[7]

This book, then, systematically examines the process by which Orientalism as a field of knowledge was transferred from Germany, and its consequences for the development of the field of Oriental Studies in Mandatory Palestine and, later, in the State of Israel. To this end, we turn first to the existing scholarly research discussing its various aspects: the Orientalist critique and the history of German Orientalism, or *Orientalistik*, the transfer of knowledge from Germany to Palestine during the British Mandate, and the field of Oriental Studies in Israel.

### CRITIQUE, COUNTER-CRITIQUE, TRANSFER, AND INFLUENCE: AN OVERVIEW
*German Orientalism, German-Jewish Orientalism, and Their Discontents*

Orientalism and European scholars of the Orient have been the subject of extensive historical and critical sociological study since the 1978 publication of Edward Said's *Orientalism*.[8] The literary scholar and critic's central claim was that Orientalism ought not be seen as a purely academic field of knowledge but rather "a style of thought based upon an ontological and epistemological distinction made between 'the Orient' and (most of the time) 'the Occident'" practiced by "a very large mass of writers, among whom are poets, novelists, philosophers, political theorists, economists and imperial administrators." Building on Foucauldian thought, Said argued that Orientalism be analyzed as a discourse, the only means of understanding the "enormously systematic discipline by which European culture was able to manage—and even produce—the Orient politically, sociologically, militarily, ideologically, scientifically, and imaginatively during the post-Enlightenment period"; and the importance of this discourse in European culture, which "gained in strength and identity by setting itself off against the Orient as a sort of surrogate and even underground self."[9]

In Said's view, Orientalism served imperial and colonial ends. This claim is framed as a paradigm and explored through a focus on three countries—

Britain, France, and the United States. Of German Orientalism Said wrote only briefly in the book's introduction, adopting an apologetic tone:

> There is a possibly misleading aspect to my study, where, aside from an occasional reference, I do not exhaustively discuss the German developments after the inaugural period dominated by Sacy [the late eighteenth and early nineteenth century] . . . Yet at no time in German scholarship during the first two-thirds of the nineteenth century could a close partnership have developed between Orientalists and a protracted, sustained *national* interest in the Orient. There was nothing in Germany to correspond to the Anglo-French presence in India, the Levant, North Africa. Moreover, the German Orient was almost exclusively a scholarly, or at least a classical, Orient.[10]

Said's biting critique of Orientalism prompted replies, of course, including some from the very Orientalists targeted in the book.[11] Among the central claims levelled against Said was the decision to ignore German Orientalism, which was more difficult to reconcile with the paradigm proposed in his book. Attempting not to shy away from the scholarly challenge posed by Said, but to research Orientalism without being beholden to the paradigm he established, gave rise beginning in the early 1990s to studies of Orientalist practice in other European countries such as Russia, Holland, and, of course, Germany.[12] Said's argument, skeptical of the very possibility of objectivity in the presence of colonial interests, prompted scholarly interest in the German case because it allowed the point to be turned on its head, opening the door for the possibility of scholarly objectivity in which politics were not involved. Historians dealing with German Orientalism argued that, since nineteenth-century Germany lacked any direct, significant colonial interests, study of the Orient—including the Middle East, Semitic languages, Arabic, and Islam—was driven in Germany by purely scientific interests rather than the pursuit of statist utilitarian ends. One representative of this approach is Baber Johansen, who argues that—apart from the political establishment's occasional involvement as an outside force either encouraging or discouraging Orientalist research—political involvement in academic research was not felt in Germany, certainly not on its content.[13]

Johansen's approach is also echoed by Sabine Mangold-Will, the first to intensively and systematically examine the development of Oriental Studies in Germany in the long nineteenth century, focusing on the study of Arabic, Islam, and the Middle East.[14] Mangold-Will considers the study of

## 6 ::: A NEW ORIENT

the Orient in Germany, at least through World War I, to have preserved a scientific tradition independent of political processes and completely devoted to deepening and widening the body of knowledge. For her, this was a scientific community that operated in a disciplinary framework free of an applied dimension.

Another scholar focusing on the nineteenth century is Susannah Heschel, who discusses various aspects of the consolidation of German-Jewish Orientalism. Heschel focuses less on questions about political-academic relations than on the prevailing social and cultural circumstances within Germany that prompted German-Jewish scholars to confront the "Orient," that is, Arabic and Islam: primarily the attempt to establish and even legitimize a European identity for Jews and Judaism—to de-Orientalize them, in other words—by turning the scholarly spotlight onto Islam, considered the "real" Orient.[15] John Efron, too, scrutinized the remarkable works of nineteenth-century German-Jewish Orientalists, finding that they differed from those of Christian Orientalists due to European Jews' feelings of otherness and rejection. Unlike Heschel, he argued that this prevented them from developing a colonial consciousness with regards to the Orient in general and Islam in particular, and his investigation originated primarily with an interrogation of the changing nature of Central European Jewry at the time. Moreover, the Jews could not ignore their unique connection to the Orient and the ways that rabbinical training made Islamic texts more accessible than they were to Christians.[16] Taking a minority opinion in the scholarship against the views expressed by Mangold-Will, Efron, Heschel and others, Lena Salaymeh sees the works of the Jewish Orientalists, emerging —if not out of direct colonial contact—nevertheless as a clear expression of cultural imperialism seeking to subjugate Islam to Judaism and wrest intellectual control over it from the Muslims themselves.[17]

The link between German Jews and the study of the Orient has also been discussed, or at least mentioned, in studies of the German roots of the field of Jewish Studies (*Wissenschaft des Judentums*). This is unsurprising considering, as we shall do in chapter 1, how the two fields overlapped in the German academic world. Christian Wiese's comprehensive study examines the development of Jewish Studies in Germany in the nineteenth and early twentieth centuries. At its center he asks whether Protestant theological research and Jewish Studies were engaged in a dialogue of equals or whether the former continued to adhere to its traditional supremacism, adopting a colonial discourse towards Jewish scholars. Woven into this discussion is Judaism's place among the Oriental religions, a matter of great interest to the Jewish founders of the field and a conceptual point of embarkation for Jews researching the Orient.[18] David Myers studied the Institute for Jewish Studies at the Hebrew University over the first decades after its establishment and analyzed the different ways in which its central figures navigated the Western (in many cases German) academic standards suffusing the roots of their field, on the one hand, and the attempt to forge a Jewish national identity on the other.[19] In his work, Myers emphasized the absence of a united scholarly front, but did find that, despite many attempts to distinguish Jewish Studies at the Hebrew University from contemporary European scholarship, in many cases these scholars maintained the latter's premises.

On the seam between the scholarship of Wiese and Myers rests the work of Ismar Schorsch on the history of Jewish Studies that draws parallels between the development of Jewish Studies and of Islamic Studies in the nineteenth century and considers the points of connection between them; adjacent to his work is a critical essay by Amnon Raz-Krakotzkin, in which Jewish Studies and the Institute for Jewish Studies are presented as mediating agents contributing to the assimilation of German Orientalism into Zionist thought.[20] Raz-Krakotzkin's central point, in the spirit of Said's thinking, is that German Orientalism—and German-Jewish academic Oriental Studies in particular—detached Judaism from its context in the Orient and presented it as European and rational, thus internalizing the Orient-Occident dichotomy; this was the tradition that accompanied Jewish Studies from its development in Germany. This tradition complemented the Zionist theological view seeing Palestine not as a concrete space but as a mythical Jewish one, infusing it with an isolationist view of Jewish history with the potential to become a national history. In this way, according to Raz-Krakotzkin, the founding of "a European entity in the East" was made possible even "while erasing the East itself."[21]

The studies described above have discussed the development of research on the Middle East in the context of German Orientalism, as well as the unique correlation between Jewish Studies and Oriental Studies in the German context. Still, they have attended primarily to the tradition rather than the actual practice of scholarly research, and largely avoided asking what factors—in the absence of political influence or practical applications—*had* shaped German Orientalism, and how. A partial response to this gap in the scholarship is found in the fundamental work of Ursula

8 ::: A NEW ORIENT

Wokoeck: characterizing the study of the Middle East as a conservative body of knowledge oriented towards philology and largely unchanged since the nineteenth century, she sought to refocus the discourse from the scholarly tradition to the scholars themselves and their institutional loci, the universities where they operated.[22] In her eyes, this conservatism was a product of the circumstances under which the field emerged as an independent discipline in an academic world emphasizing, first and foremost, the philological. Moreover, unlike the classical languages taught in school, the Oriental languages, and especially Hebrew, had to be taught and studied from scratch at the university level. In the absence of clear standardization in the field, scholars were obliged to "gear their main efforts towards the studies, research, and publications required for establishing and upholding their philological credentials, apart from fulfilling their obligations as language teachers."[23] Thus, even when they wanted to, they found it difficult to expand their studies beyond textual-philological concerns.

Wokoeck is ultimately in accord with the argument that examination of the Orient within the halls of the universities, remaining as it did primarily philological, did not emerge out of German political interests—scholars interested in studying the contemporary Middle East did so through non-university frameworks. Wokoeck goes to some length to emphasize that these frameworks did exist, first and foremost in the form of the Seminar for Oriental Languages (*Seminar für Orientalische Sprachen*, sos) founded in 1887 with the explicit goal of training students to conduct business and diplomatic relations with the Orient. Traditionally, the seminar's directors were professors with philological training, but unlike the university departments where they had been trained, the institution had an important political role in World War I, when its instructors and students assisted German propaganda efforts within territories belonging to the Ottoman Empire.[24]

Nearly contemporary with Wokoeck's work, Suzanne Marchand published a comprehensive study focusing on German Orientalism writ large —not only the study of the Middle East, that is—in the nineteenth and twentieth centuries and earlier.[25] We have seen how Wokoeck's investigation approaches Orientalism from a different angle than Said's generalist one, but Marchand is more direct in turning against his arguments: while she emphasizes that "in no way am I advocating a return to the pre-Saidian way of writing the history of oriental studies," she nonetheless explains that she set out to write "a critical history of the *practice* of oriental scholarship, one that treats the politics of the field, but does so without presuming that those politics were primordially and perpetually defined by imperialist relationships."[26] Marchand also rejects Foucauldian discourse analysis by noting that no single discourse comprised all of German Orientalism (to say nothing of European Orientalism as a whole), and that attempts to turn Foucault's theory—in Marchand's view a primarily philosophical one—into a generalizable tool of historical research does a disservice to both the research and to Foucault himself.[27] In general, the emphasis of Marchand's study is on unpacking the negative baggage loaded by Said upon the term "Orientalism." After all, when the first scholars became interested in the Orient, the field had not been a popular topic of discussion or study; other scholars reserved their interest for the European classical languages. To their credit, Marchand suggests, these scholars' deep-seated curiosity about the cultures and languages of the Orient and how these interacted with the Occident actually painted the Orient in a positive light.[28]

While Marchand's focus on practices dampens the cogency of any sweeping statements on the relation of politics to academia, since she judges each case on its own merits, her finding that only in a handful of contexts had political necessity dictated the character of university research on the Orient is nevertheless remarkable. Where Wokoeck attributed the character of German Orientalism to its institutions, Marchand found theological motivations significant, as texts from the Orient were applied to Christian questions. To judge by these prominent examples, contemporary research on German Orientalism would seem to be fundamentally opposed to Said's paradigm—yet ultimately in agreement with him that Orientalist academic research in Germany was not shaped by colonial interests and was carried out independently of questions of politics and policy.

## Knowledge Transfer and Its Impact: From Germany to Palestine

This book does not consider German, or German-Jewish, Orientalism as a whole, however, but instead explicitly examines its transfer as a field of knowledge from Germany to Palestine during the British Mandate period. Issues around knowledge transfer, cultural transfer, and influence along this axis have been discussed at length in the scholarship, in recognition of the central role played by Jews emigrating from Central Europe to Palestine in the development, especially during the 1930s, of the *Yishuv*, the Jewish community in pre-1948 Palestine. Yoav Gelber, who surveys German Jews' impact on various aspects of life in the *Yishuv* at length and in detail, writes

10 ::: A NEW ORIENT

that German immigration stamped a "collective mark . . . on the *Yishuv*," contributing to "the economic, scientific, social and cultural progress of Palestine."[29] And indeed, in addition to their influence on commerce and the economy, German Jews contributed to the development, among other fields, of medicine, law, education, welfare, and academic activity during the Mandate period.

Alongside Gelber's comprehensive work, various studies have focused on more specific disciplines: Doron Niederland, for example, examines the dynamic influence of German-Jewish immigrant doctors on the practice of medicine in 1930s and 1940s Palestine. Alona Nitzan-Shiftan distills the architectural field, and the arguments rumbling within it, down to an essential point: that there are often multiple influences and traditions rather than any single one. Eli Salzberger and Fania Oz-Salzberger investigate the case of the Israeli judiciary, noting that the formative traditions imported from Germany tended to be conservative. Yfaat Weiss also examines the legal context in her reading of the Israeli Law of Return and Citizenship Law in light of the Central and Eastern European experience and its patterns of thought. Rakefet Zalashik studies the influence of immigration from Germany on the institutionalization of the mental health field and characteristics of the psychiatric discourse in the country. Dani Schrire dissects the influence of German-Jewish folkloristics on the foundation of the field of folklore studies in Palestine and the complicated ways it established itself locally. Miriam Szamet, in her work on the Hebrew educational discourse in the *Yishuv* at the end of the Ottoman period and during the early Mandate period, sketches various multi-directional routes of knowledge transfer and influence that prompted the institutionalization and professionalization of Hebrew pedagogy. Shira Wilkof studies the meeting between German-Jewish legacies of urban spatial planning and the imperial apparatus of the Mandate period, and how this encounter shaped Israeli spatial planning after 1948.[30] The German scientific legacy, it would seem —even if the complex Israeli disposition towards Germany after 1945 may have obscured it—continues to beat at the heart of Israeli academia, as Dan Diner and Moshe Zimmerman have claimed.[31]

Yet among this rich body of scholarship, the question of German influence on Oriental studies in Palestine and Israel has in fact failed to attract adequate scholarly attention. While critical studies from the past two decades have examined Israeli Orientalism, they focus primarily on the connection, beginning in the late 1960s, between Israeli academia—especially

Introduction ::: 11

its departments of Oriental Studies—and the Israeli security establishment.[32] In addition, Arabic-language essays emerging out of ideological or religious discourses have analyzed newspapers and later Israeli Orientalist publications, seeking to prove that the discipline in Israel displays inherent anti-Arab and anti-Muslim bias.[33]

Other studies from recent years have discussed the activities of Jewish Orientalists—especially educators, journalists, political activists, and thinkers, both those born in Europe and in Palestine—operating outside universities during the late Ottoman period and under the British Mandate. Among these studies, the chapter Liora Halperin devoted to the use of Arabic among journalists, teachers, propagandists, and intelligence professionals in her book on the multi-lingual reality of Mandate Palestine's Jews is exemplary; as are Amos Noy's study of Jerusalemite intellectuals on the verge of the British Mandate, and their efforts to weave together the legacy of the Orient with the European Enlightenment, for example by studying local folklore; and the research of Abigail Jacobson and Moshe Naor on the political, social, and cultural role of non-European "Oriental" Jews, both Sephardi and Mizrahi, during the Mandate period as mediating influences between Jews and Arabs.[34]

Within the body of critical knowledge on Israeli Oriental Studies, Gil Eyal's book *The Disenchantment of the Orient* stands out as the first to engage in a significant critical discussion of the history of Orientalism in Palestine and Israel—as a field of knowledge but also as a political perspective.[35] Eyal, too, focuses on developments in relation to the security field, but does note the field's German roots and devotes several pages to the tension between political constraints and academic activity within the School of Oriental Studies, and the struggle over this institute's character prompted by demands from the *Yishuv*'s political establishment.[36] Eyal's claim, in a discussion too brief and short on archival sources to go beyond the general, is that academic self-isolation and adamant opposition to the subjection of research and instruction to the *Yishuv*'s political demands were characteristic of the institute's Orientalists; but rather than link this opposition to the German scientific tradition, he instead associates it primarily with their claims to expertise.[37] An additional study discussing the question of German influence on the field of Orientalism is that of Yonatan Mendel, who examines trends in the instruction of Arabic in Jewish high schools beginning during the Mandate period.[38] Mendel, who studies the status of the Arabic language in Israel, examines the German philological tradition

12 ::: A NEW ORIENT

that was the basis for Arabic study in the Mandate period in relative depth. Yet, like Eyal, he focuses primarily on the influence of security constraints on developments in the teaching of Arabic rather than the broader consequences for scholars of the change in how they encountered the Orient, beyond the specific subject of Arabic instruction that is his field of study.

Instead, the work of Eyal and Mendel is important for the purposes of this study because of the emphasis they place on the connection between German-Jewish Orientalism and the Zionist enterprise: corresponding, as we saw, with Edward Said, contemporary scholarship tends not to see a connection between academic activity and immediate colonial interests in the case of German Orientalism. At the same time, while critical studies of the past three decades have identified in the Zionist enterprise in Palestine obvious colonial characteristics, some have seen as an expression of colonialism remarkable for its dispossession and exploitation of the indigenous (in this case, Arab) population what others consider more indicative of "colonization within colonialism" or, in other words, the establishment of *Yishuv*-wide apparatuses by Jewish immigrants in a new land *sans* support or encouragement from the British—or indeed any other—colonial authority.[39]

The connection with German ideas is present in this aspect as well: numerous scholars have already shown how internal Prussian colonization— including the government's initiatives to purchase, distribute, and sell land so as to strengthen German possession of regions populated by a Polish majority—had an influence on the Zionist colonization enterprise. Noteworthy in this context is Derek Penslar, who examines Jewish social planning of rural colonization in late-Ottoman Palestine and how nineteenth-century German perceptions of "agrarian romanticism" shaped the worldviews and operational means of the planners of Zionist colonization; and Shalom Reichmann and Shlomo Hasson, who characterize the explicit influence of the German colonization enterprise in Poznań on the Zionist colonization enterprise before World War I.[40] Yfaat Weiss has analyzed the multifaceted place of the Central European spatial experience in shaping the Zionist worldviews of two central figures in the Brit Shalom association, Hans Kohn and Arthur Ruppin.[41]

We saw how Edward Said left the German case outside the scope of his study because it did not meet his pre-condition—that Orientalism emerges from urgent necessities of a colonial hue. The German Orientalist tradition in Palestine actually seems to meet that pre-condition: the Zionist enterprise did have imminent needs with regards to the Arab population and its language and culture, needs the recently arrived immigrant scholars of Oriental Studies, as experts who might provide solutions for them, were asked to accommodate. We have, then, a unique opportunity to examine the permutations of German Orientalism as it transitioned from a non-colonial context into one characterized, at the very least, by colonial elements; as we have seen, colonization was not in and of itself foreign to the Central European experience.

HUSOS, the institutional home of German-Jewish Oriental Studies in the country, has been at the center of several articles in recent years. In his writing about its foundational years and development, Menahem Milson did not directly address the aforementioned topics.[42] His article, published as part of a project undertaken in the 1990s to write the Hebrew University's history, surveys important landmarks in the institute's first decades. The article details, among other things, the institute's central research projects and provides brief biographies of its leading figures during these years. The connection between the institute's scientific activities and the political and security circumstances, is addressed in the article's final lines: "Two essential qualities of the founders continue to characterize the research and teaching in these departments at the Hebrew University: a deep respect for the written text, which inevitably dictates stringent language requirements; and a complete separation between scholarship and personal political bias."[43] This statement by Milson—professor of Arabic Language and Literature at the Hebrew University—seems to be written primarily as a response to contemporary critical discourse swirling about the discipline and its links to the political and security establishment.

The stated aim of a 1999 article published by another Hebrew University professor, the scholar of Islamic Studies Hava Lazarus-Yafeh, was to trace the transfer of the field of academic Orientalism to Palestine.[44] More than analyzing the transfer of the field of knowledge, the article effectively follows three figures who are central to this book as well—Josef Horovitz, S. D. Goitein, and D. H. Baneth—and their histories, adopting a somewhat pensive and nostalgic point of view; the article is primarily biographical rather than analytical, and in it Lazarus-Yafeh describes these three scholars' life stories with special focus on the ways in which their German background was expressed in aspects of their habitus. Other central figures are mentioned only in passing. More broadly, Shaul Katz's research on the history of the Hebrew University conceptualized the question of the institution's

14 ::: A NEW ORIENT

German nature by examining the activities of its various institutes—one of which was HUSOS—in their first years.[45] Katz determines that it was essentially German, but the goals of his article left no room for penetrating analysis of the ideas behind its origins or developments beyond the first years of operations.

Discussion in recent literature on the subject of Orientalist knowledge transfer from Germany has also dealt with another immigration target country—the United States. In her article on the Jewish Orientalist Ilse Lichtenstadter (1907–1991), who immigrated from Germany to the United States, Ruchama Johnston-Bloom seeks to indicate the meanings of tensions within the field of Islamic studies in the United States between the German philological approach and methodologies taken from the social sciences. Zachary Lockman also attends to this tension in his comprehensive essay on the development of academic Orientalism in the West, particularly the United States.[46] Johnston-Bloom illustrates how the German Orientalist legacy borne by Lichtenstadter was adapted to local trends in research, which were in turn influenced by political interests. By focusing increasingly on contemporary issues, she was able to find work as a researcher despite both the difficulties of immigration and the prevailing gender norms.[47] Johnston-Bloom's work on Lichtenstadter is of great importance in the context of Orientalist knowledge transfer, since she lays the groundwork for comparison between different immigration destinations; still, considering the unique political and demographic circumstances in Palestine, such a comparison can in no way replace an examination of the situation there.

The majority of scientific publications regarding the circle of German-Jewish Orientalists connected to HUSOS come in the form of the brief *in memoriam* accounts of their individual scientific achievements and life stories that are customary in the field. Thanks to increased historiographical interest in the topic in recent years, a number of analytical articles and chapters have been published on the leading figures among them. Josef Horovitz is the figure who seems to have enjoyed the most scholarly attention: Johnston-Bloom focuses on the impression made by Horovitz's years as a teacher of Arabic in British-controlled Aligarh, India, which shaped his anti-imperialist perspective as well as subsequent decisions involving the establishment of HUSOS in Jerusalem. Hanan Harif likewise connects this impression with Horovitz's ambivalence towards the Zionist enterprise, especially owing to its links with the British Empire. Sabine Mangold-Will, also analyzing the impact of the Aligarh period on Horovitz's outlook, examines the professional context for his political perspective, focusing on the institute's foundational memorandum that Horovitz formulated in 1925.[48]

This document, which I will discuss in detail in the chapters that follow, is of great importance for understanding the institute's disciplinary and ideological keystones. It is here that Horovitz declared his intention to include Arab lecturers in the institute's instructional staff, and to diverge from the accepted disciplinary path of German Orientalism in shaping the curriculum so as to reflect the Arab surroundings in which it was to operate.[49] Nevertheless, the document was only a first step in the process of launching Oriental Studies in Palestine. While Mangold-Will, like Johnston-Bloom and Harif, deals primarily with the initial, declarative stage that characterized Horovitz's involvement in preparations for the establishment of the institute, effectively the situation was far more complex. As this book shows, the practices engaged in by the institute's personnel after its establishment in Jerusalem did not always correspond with the original goals of Horovitz, who directed the institute from Frankfurt until his death in 1931.

Less attention has been paid to Horovitz's successors, especially on the questions at the center of this book. One study of note is Mangold-Will's study of Gotthold Weil, the immediate successor to both of Horovitz's positions. Like in her writing on Horovitz himself, her study of Weil also privileges political thinking and the declarative plane—in Weil's case, pan-humanist and anti-national—and is even less attentive to practices or dynamics between Weil and his colleagues in Jerusalem.[50] Among HUSOS faculty, Shelomo Dov Goitein has perhaps gained the most scholarly attention, in a series of studies examining his later years in the United States —when, after emigrating from Israel in the late 1950s, he established his reputation abroad as a leading expert on the Cairo *Geniza*—and the ways in which his studies expressed his ideological stance with regards to Judaism and Zionism.[51] Additional studies have noted specific issues in the Orientalist activities of other members of the first generation of HUSOS scholars —Yosef Rivlin, Martin Plessner and L. A. Mayer. While these studies have noted their links with the German Orientalist tradition in its new iteration shaped by the Zionist structures within which these scholars operated, they have not significantly pursued these links to examine the development of Zionist Oriental Studies.[52]

## 16 ::: A NEW ORIENT

### SCHOLARLY ARCHIVES AND KNOWLEDGE NETWORKS

This snapshot of the scholarly landscape presents a clear lacuna, therefore: no work has yet centered upon the transfer of German-Jewish Orientalism from Germany to Palestine by examining how the transformation of a textual encounter with the Orient into a living encounter with it shaped this academic field of knowledge. Moreover, considering as we have how the scholarly tradition was shaped in the ostensibly neutral German space, where a separation between the (German) scholars and the ("Oriental") object of research was possible, the leading trend in historical analysis of German Orientalism—that, as a rule, political considerations had no role in shaping professional practices—must be called into question. The few studies dealing with spatial questions in the development of German-Jewish academic Orientalism have focused upon the theoretical aspect: on the worldviews and desires adopted by the Orientalists. Yet these studies have hardly touched upon the scientific and political practices characteristic of the various Orientalists who immigrated to Palestine and shaped the character of HUSOS after its founding, effectively forming Zionist and Israeli Oriental Studies.

There is no diminishing the importance of declarations of principles and foundational documents. They provide a glimpse of the ideas, the cultural and political worlds, from which individuals and institutions embark upon their activities. Nonetheless, this book aims to divert the discussion not only from Germany to Mandate Palestine and Israel, but also from theory and discourse towards practice. That is, as Marchand puts it in her book, to the "knowledge-making practices of those individuals who counted as 'orientalists' in their cultural milieux;"[53] but also to practices, quite familiar to these Orientalists, that straddled the gap between politics and the academy, and which were accentuated in the case of Zionist Oriental Studies. Underlying this all is the understanding that the parallel, interwoven, and contradictory existence of these two aspects was the product of the living encounter with the Orient, a multi-lateral encounter of "transmutation of identities."[54]

This tracing of practices is carried out in this book primarily via archival documentation—correspondence, protocols, and memoranda—found in institutional archives and private estates deposited at various repositories in Jerusalem: The Historical Archive of the Hebrew University, the Archive of the National Library of Israel, the Central Zionist Archives, the Israel

State Archives, and the Archive of the Museum of Islamic Art in Jerusalem. Many of the documents found at these sites and presented and analyzed in the book's various chapters were only made available to researchers in recent years and are being exposed here for the first time. Other documents presented in the book were found in European archives—The Frankfurt University Archive, the Sound Archives of the Humboldt University in Berlin, and the Archive of the Hungarian Academy of Sciences. News reports and articles in Arabic-, Hebrew-, German-, and English-language newspapers from the period provided complementary information, enriched context, or filled holes in the archival record. Alongside these, the scientific publications of the figures in question were also examined, though our discussion focuses on questions of disciplinary transfer and coalescence rather than evaluation of the quality of its scientific products.

At the book's heart lie the pursuits of a group of individuals whose activities as creators of Orientalist knowledge took place primarily within a single institutional home—the School of Oriental Studies at the Hebrew University. This was a network of scholars who, beyond a biographical common ground that mostly remained rather broad, also shared professional values and a habitus.[55] The effectiveness of network analysis for the sketching of disciplinary history is emphasized especially in Wokoeck's research; she also points out the importance of academic institutions themselves in the development of the Orientalist discipline, which to some degree are the protagonists of her book.[56] Understanding the Orientalist discipline in Mandate Palestine and Israel demands an analytical framework that structurally integrates the following aspects: individuals in motion, or human actors, were one of the causes prompting its development, and the connections between them became an important driving force in the transfer of knowledge; yet this took place through interaction with "nonhuman" factors—such as academic and governmental institutions, texts, political episodes, research tools, and ideas. All these had a role in the development of the Orientalist field of knowledge and can be seen as part of a single network, broad and flexible, within which the interaction between the various bodies in question take place.[57]

This framework of analysis, known as Actor-Network Theory (or ANT), common in science and technology studies, enables the integration of biographical, disciplinary, material, and institutional elements into a historical discussion and the examination of reciprocal relations and sets of connections between the entirety of forces involved in the development of

18 ::: A NEW ORIENT

a field of knowledge, without making *a priori* assumptions about the dominance of any single one. Indeed, productive use of this approach has been made in recent years in research dealing with the history of disciplines and the history of academia discussing, among other things, questions of transnational knowledge transfer.[58] When it comes to the transfer of Orientalist knowledge, out of the use of Actor-Network Theory emerges recognition of the German universities where the scholars were trained, the manuscripts they studied, the Israeli Ministry of Foreign Affairs officials, Zionist ideology in its various hues, or the index cards used for philological documentation, to name a few examples discussed in this book—all were part of the tapestry that is Zionist Oriental Studies, and not external to it.

Within this analytical framework, this book seeks to observe the transfer of Orientalist knowledge from Germany to Palestine, focusing on the period between 1926, when the School of Oriental Studies was founded, and 1963, the year it completed a process of disciplinary expansion and became the Institute for Asian and African Studies, by which time most of its founding generation had already passed away or retired. While the tracking of the discipline's development will be chronological—for the field of knowledge cannot be detached from the political and cultural events occurring along the axis of time—it should be seen neither as a survey of the field's history nor as a series of biographies of the figures active in the field of Middle Eastern or Islamic studies in Israel.[59] Instead, the prism through which the development of the field will be studied in the book's three main chapters is the transfer of German Orientalist knowledge, corresponding to the three central organizing themes of Orientalism as German, as Zionist, and as statist.

At the center of the first chapter lies a discussion of the discipline's German nature in the years the Orientalist discipline was first shaped in the local academia—from the discussions preceding the foundation of an Orientalist institute within the steering committee of the Hebrew University, and until the 1940s. The chapter, which begins by laying out the stages of modern German Orientalism's development, seeks to trade the institute's vaguely German reputation for concrete characteristics manifested in its activities: the connection in German and German-Jewish academic worlds between Oriental Studies and Jewish Studies; the research tradition from which the immigrant scholars had emerged and its influence on the consolidation of the faculty in Jerusalem, and the sketching of the borders of inclusion; and the material aspects of the transfer of Orientalist knowledge to Palestine, specifically the transfer of books and manuscripts. Analysis of these characteristics allows the tracking of various sources of influence and paints a more complex picture than attributing to Josef Horovitz, with his chair in Frankfurt, exclusive purview over the institute's foundation and the making out of its path.

The second chapter conforms to the same chronological range but directs its glance away from Mount Scopus to focus, within the Zionist context of the *Yishuv*, on Oriental Studies' and Orientalists' local relationships. It exposes the political motives held by the university's leaders and its first Orientalists during the establishment of the HUSOS—for them, a tool to encourage intellectual affinity between Jews and Arabs and a means of mobilizing legitimacy from Arab and Muslim scholars for the Hebrew University, which had initially been greeted with skepticism in the local intellectual world. The German Orientalist legacy fostered relations between German-Jewish Orientalists and their Arab colleagues across the Middle East—opportunities which were seized upon and produced relationships of work and friendship—but, somewhat paradoxically, this commitment to that same legacy, within the Zionist institutional framework of the Hebrew University, actually hampered the formalization and consolidation of these relations. Much of the chapter is devoted to an episode that epitomizes this structural challenge: the institute's failed attempt to recruit an Arab faculty member, resulting for the first time in the appointment of a non-European, undertaken while nonetheless gradually departing from the political legacy of Horovitz, the institute's founder.

Unlike its two predecessors, the third chapter turns to another period of time: the state era, or the institute's first fifteen years following 1948. In the shadow of the difficulties brought on by the 1948 war and its aftermath, and considering the Hebrew University's gradual transformation into a statist university, the chapter focuses on processes of disciplinary expansion at the School of Oriental Studies—expansion of the topics, chronologies, and geographies covered—prompted by an attempt to institutionalize a previously informal set of connections with the Israeli Ministry of Foreign Affairs, colored by hopes that the latter might become a significant funder of the institute's activities. These processes were carried out under the leadership of Shelomo Dov Goitein and Uriel Heyd, German-born heads of the institute of different generations. Featured throughout the chapter is the relationship between the first generation, holding Orientalist training from German universities, and the second one—their students—graduates of the School of Oriental Studies in Jerusalem who were employed in applied Orientalist work for the Zionist diplomatic establishment while still receiving their scientific Orientalist training. It helps pinpoint the approaches of the two generations, since a closer examination shows that even the scholars of the first generation, supposedly conservative and classicizing keepers of the Germany tradition, were committed to the process of evolution, and to identify the consequences of a shift in the center of gravity of Oriental Studies across the globe after World War II, from Germany and continental Europe to the Anglo-Saxon realm, particularly the United States.

An examination of the different themes regarding the transfer of knowledge indicates that the German Orientalist heritage deeply influenced the development of Zionist and Israeli Oriental Studies, but rather than inevitable or natural, this should be seen as a downstream consequence of sets of relations—a kind of academic chain of transmission—between scholars at different stages of their careers and the institutions, methods and ideas circulating about them in Berlin, Frankfurt, and Jerusalem. Moreover, in Jerusalem there were political and ideological motives inherent to the development of the field from its very first day, explicitly so; even if these motives did not direct the day-to-day work of the scholars, they were certainly weighty considerations capable of coalescing the institute's professional path.

# 1 : THE SCIENCE OF THE ORIENT

## THE BEGINNINGS OF ORIENTAL STUDIES
## AT THE HEBREW UNIVERSITY

"It seems to me as if that subject, of my father's failed doctorate," writes the novelist A. B. Yehoshua of his Jerusalem-born Orientalist father, Yaakov Yehoshua, "formed a kind of veneration in our family, and primarily with my mother, of the *Yekim* [German-Jewish immigrants] as a well-ordered and disciplined world; the *Yeke* Oriental Studies scholars of Mount Scopus, to all of us, . . . were the ideal of the perfect researcher—and perhaps they really were." The elder Yehoshua had been a student of D. H. Baneth, one of the founders of HUSOS, "an extremely meticulous teacher, a strict *Yeke* harboring excessively scientific demands," who expected him to adapt "to the scientific severity characteristic of Berlin."[1] The demands proved too much for Yehoshua's father, who never completed the study that he was supposed to write under Baneth's supervision.

The historian of the Middle East Jacob M. Landau (1924–2020), who studied with those same "*Yeke* Orientalists" in the 1940s, said of his teachers that "what was considered right for Oriental Studies in Germany was considered right here as well. Of course, for the professors . . . Germany was the cultural model, and certainly for the Orientalist."[2] In fact, for the men and women of Israeli academia trained in the fields that emerged out of HUSOS—the study of Arabic, Islam, and the Middle East—Oriental Studies on Mount Scopus continues to stand as a symbol of the cultural connection with Germany and its habitus; or, to be more precise, a connection to Germanness.

Numerous studies have been devoted to the concept of Germanness as a political, social, and cultural characteristic of immigrant communities emanating from the German-speaking European world—both in the self-image of their members, and in the way others perceive them.[3] Within this inclusive term lies the idea of a collective Central European heritage—a deceptive idea since, as scholars have noted, "geography is neither fate nor essence."[4] Nevertheless, this chapter employs "Germanness" as a characteristic to be analyzed both because, as noted, Germany is popularly perceived as the origin of Oriental Studies scholars and the Orientalist knowledge they brought with them, and because most of the scholars studied in this book shared a sufficiently common geographic and personal background to enable careful use of the term, without falling into essentialization. In short, I wish to offer a somewhat more complex analysis of Germanness.

But what, actually, was the German Orientalist model? How was this abstract concept manifested in reality? What effect did the Germanness of Oriental Studies on Mount Scopus—for German universities produced the founders of HUSOS and the forefathers of the profession in Israel—have on the development of the discipline? In an article on the question of the Germanness of the Hebrew University in its first years, Shaul Katz proposed analyzing the German influence on the institution not only by examining the origins of its members, but also through the epistemological ideas and research agenda that guided their work, on the one hand, and the organizational and hierarchical structure within the university's departments, on the other. That study examined Germanness alongside two additional characteristics: Jewishness, that is, the degree to which its research ideals and organizational tendencies were influenced by the German-Jewish world of Jewish Studies, or *Wissenschaft des Judentums*; and localness, that is, the degree to which the scholarly practices and organizational tendencies of the scholars was a product of the Zionist presence in Palestine.[5]

Through these parameters Katz argued that the School of Oriental Studies, in its first years, was "German to the core" in its scholarship and especially in its organization, shaped as it was in the image of its founder and first director, Josef Horovitz.[6] This claim regarding the German essence of the institute is also reflected in a study of its first years by Menahem Milson, who characterized the founding generation—some of whom taught him there—according to their European birth, all but one, that is; all were also, save for Levi Billig, graduates of German universities; and all, except one, had an extensive background in Jewish Studies. After Billig's death, "Arabic and Islamic Studies became the exclusive domain of German-trained scholars. . . . This generation of scholars determined the character of the departments of Arabic and Islamic Studies for many decades to come."[7]

Nevertheless, it seems a more penetrating answer is needed on the Germanness of HUSOS, its first decades, and its characteristics. Though the official history of the institute indeed begins with the entrance of Horovitz, a lengthy prehistory led to that moment: the institute's emergence rested on the opinions of other Jewish scholars of Oriental studies from the German-speaking world and was anticipated by a protracted discourse on the relationship between Oriental Studies and Jewish Studies, two disciplines that enjoyed an unprecedented blossoming in nineteenth- and twentieth-century German-speaking Europe; scholars in these fields were profoundly involved in preparations for the founding of the Hebrew University. In addition, the assertion that HUSOS, the research conducted there, and its organizational form were "German" is insufficiently specific: a more rigorous analysis of these elements reveals a circle of scholars whose joint experiences as young scholars in Germany—from the early twentieth century through the 1930s, especially at the universities of Berlin and, later, Frankfurt—had a decisive impact on the institutional form of Arabic and Islamic studies in Jerusalem. In other words, the roots of the institute drew directly upon specific centers within Germany that represented a certain school of thought, rather than on some vague idea of the German essence. Moreover, this common background also impacted the ability of other Orient scholars not integrated in its circle to find a place at the Hebrew University.

The goal of this chapter, therefore, is double: on one level, its role is to fill a scholarly lacuna and reveal how knowledge on the Orient migrated from universities in the German-speaking world to the young Hebrew University, and the place of this knowledge in the foundation of HUSOS; and on another level, it seeks to deconstruct the convention of the institution's Germanness into its constituent parts in order to better understand the term's relevance and the ways it can be applied to the academic discipline of Oriental Studies at the Hebrew University during the Mandate period.

Before moving on to a discussion of the development of Oriental Studies in Jerusalem, the Oriental Studies experts, and the transfer of knowledge itself, a better historical definition of the field is necessary. To this end, the following pages offer a survey of this field, primarily as it developed in the period preceding the Hebrew University's establishment just after World War I: in other words, of modern German Orientalism, its branch of Arabic and Islamic studies that matured into an independent subfield over the course of the nineteenth century, and the integration of Central European Jews, especially Germans, into this disciplinary framework.

## GERMAN INHERITANCE: THE DEVELOPMENT OF MODERN GERMAN ORIENTALISM AND THE QUESTION OF APPLIED SCIENCE

At the root of one central explanation for the unique course of German Orientalism lies the geopolitical situation of Central Europe during the early modern period and in the conflicts set off by the Reformation. During the first wave of Spanish and Portuguese imperial expansion, German-speaking Europe was focused on the drama of the Reformation and the Schmalkaldic Wars. During the Thirty Years' War of the seventeenth century, Britain, France, and Holland competed with one another in overseas expansion while the Saxons, Bavarians, Prussians, and Austrians were busy fighting an intra-continental war of control and influence within Central Europe. This did not lead to the complete cutting off of contact with the Orient: many German speakers were involved, as merchants and experts, in building the Western overseas empires; and the Ottoman threat to Vienna, the capital of the Holy Roman Empire, continued until 1683, when the final siege of the Ottoman imperial soldiers was rebuffed. Yet in general, Central European scholarly interest in the Orient, and especially its languages, was born of local rather than global motives and was cultural, primarily religious.[8]

The Reformation was of course a seminal moment in shaping cultural and religious motives as well. In the preceding Middle Ages, European ecclesiastics had expressed much interest in Oriental languages—the Orient referring here primarily to Asia—as a means of spreading Christianity to its inhabitants. Insofar as Islam was considered at all, this was primarily as a competing religion to be fought.[9] But during the Renaissance, especially beginning in the late fifteenth century, Christian intellectual interest in one particular Oriental language—Hebrew, the original language of the Bible—emerged; the influential phenomenon known in the scholarly literature as "Christian Hebraism" spread over the course of the sixteenth century as a result of the Reformation, Martin Luther's call to return to the sacred texts (*sola scriptura*), and philological study of the Hebrew text to resolve theological disputes.[10] Such knowledge grew increasingly established during the Enlightenment period, when European thinkers, including Germans, began to reflect on the history of the Orient and its cultures and to collect information about them as a means of gaining new understandings of European history and culture. It was also at this point that "the Orient" emerged as a collective term including not only the lands of the Bible, but also India and the Far East.[11] At the beginning of the nineteenth century, Friedrich Schlegel (1772–1829) published his groundbreaking *Über die Sprache und Weisheit der Indier* (1808), in which he employed comparative linguistic research to claim that Indian peoples lay at the origin of European culture. His study was a landmark in the development of Indological research, an important branch of German Orientalism, particularly the study of Sanskrit.[12]

In comparison with developments in this field, the place of Semitic languages, including Arabic, is remarkable: they were taught primarily in theology faculties. Even when hosted within faculties of philosophy, their instruction was in the service of theology, which determined any appointments in the field. Oriental languages were generally considered an auxiliary science of theology; Arabic largely as a Hebrew dialect.[13] This situation began to change in the early nineteenth century, when, according to Sabine Mangold-Will, modern Orientalism was born.[14] A major impetus for this development was French rather than German: the linguist and Orientalist Sylvester de Sacy (1758–1838). In his academic work in Paris, de Sacy worked to disentangle Arabic studies from theology and to establish it as an independent discipline. Despite French colonial interest in modern Arabic, he emphasized the language in its classical form, preparing guides for language study—grammars and readers—that remained widespread long after their publication. Though De Sacy's stature owed much to his access to numerous manuscripts removed from the Middle East by scientific expeditions launched during the Napoleonic era, he never conducted research expeditions to the Orient himself. This distinguished de Sacy from other French Orientalists of the period, but his linguistic feats nonetheless attracted scholars from across Europe in spite of his patent disinterest in the practical applications of such scientific work.[15] Among his many students were young graduates of German universities—standout names included Heinrich Fleischer (1801–1888), who had studied in Leipzig, and Georg Freytag (1788–1861), who came to Paris after studying in Göttingen.

De Sacy's outsize impact on the development of modern German Orientalism was connected to the opening up of new employment opportunities in the German academic world precisely as German scholars came to study with him: during the first half of the nineteenth century, no less than twenty-six new chairs in Oriental languages were created at sixteen universities, as well as additional new *extraordinarii*, or extraordinary (non-chaired) professors in the field that could potentially become full chairs. Existing chairs

## 26 ::: A NEW ORIENT

moved from theology faculties to philosophy faculties.[16] Scholarship on the history of German Orientalism offers various explanations of the turn to the study of Oriental languages in universities, and typically identifies the impetus as other than political.[17] Mangold-Will believes that Orientalism's migration from theology to philosophy derived from the ideals of the Romantic movement, part of a wider process of non-theological knowledge creation in the spirit of the Humboldtian university.[18]

Ursula Wokoeck, on the other hand, proposes a complex institutional explanation of the discipline: in the framework of the reorganization projects launched at German universities in the first half of the nineteenth century, the stature of faculties of philosophy grew as centers for the training of *Gymnasium* (high school) teachers, with special emphasis on classical philology, a field then undergoing its own significant tribulations with the fading, by the end of the eighteenth century, of Latin's status as the academic world's lingua franca. Philologists refocused their work on grammatical analysis as a means of reading and teaching texts in additional languages, and classical philologists sought to demonstrate the legitimacy of grammatical analysis as a universal approach by implementing it on several languages—especially the Semitic languages, which might be compared with those known as Indo-European (a term born after the discovery of another Oriental language, Sanskrit, and its connections with European languages). Finally, the turn towards Oriental, and certainly Semitic philology, was facilitated by the reams of related knowledge already accumulated within theological scholarship, and the existence of theology students ensured ongoing demand for instruction in these languages even after the responsibility had passed to philosophy faculties.

The newfound need for scholars adopting this grammatic-philological approach to Oriental languages who could fill the new positions created particular demand for those who had undergone training in the subjects and methodologies of de Sacy in Paris, primarily in Arabic but also in other languages.[19] For example, Heinrich Fleischer had been one de Sacy's students in Paris between 1825 and 1828, as noted, after completing his doctoral studies in theology and classical and Oriental languages in Leipzig. He studied Arabic, Persian, and Turkish with de Sacy before returning to Leipzig, where he became a high school teacher. In 1835, he was appointed professor of Oriental languages at his alma mater.[20] This path of development explains the tendency of German Orientalism towards lexicographic and text-focused philological research. When historical discussions did ap-

*The Science of the Orient* ::: 27

pear, they mostly accompanied the publication and analysis of a new primary source.[21]

Fleischer was an especially influential figure in the history of German academic research on Arabic and Islam. He held his position in Leipzig for 52 years, where he trained generation upon generation of students who, spreading across Europe to dominate Arabic and Islamic studies in Germany, in turn celebrated his importance as a founding figure in the field.[22] He was also very actively involved in the foundation of a new learned society, the *Deutsche Morgenländische Gesellschaft* (German oriental society, or DMG).[23] Its foundation took place under conditions dictated by processes of disciplinary specialization: around the middle of the nineteenth century, a cleavage developed between the two primary branches of German Orientalism—the study of Sanskrit, and the study of Middle Eastern languages (Semitic languages, Persian, and Turkish). In addition to an overall decrease in the number of students, this split coincided with the awarding of new chairs to young scholars who would inhabit them for years to come. Scholars of Sanskrit (taught together with comparative linguistics) were somewhat better off thanks to its direct link with modern European languages.[24] In light of this situation, scholars of Middle Eastern languages founded the DMG in 1845 in an attempt to mobilize public and governmental support for research activities and disciplinary development; at the same time, those unable to find positions as professors worked as librarians at university libraries that had filled their shelves with Arabic, Turkish, and Persian manuscripts over the course of the nineteenth century.[25] Work in Orientalist libraries provided an important source of income for scholars of Arabic and Islam in Germany into the twentieth century as well, often supplementing irregular university teaching—an arrangement that also served to deepen the connection to text-based philological work.

In the 1870s came the time of Arabic and Islamic studies, in what Suzanne Marchand calls the "Second Oriental Renaissance."[26] In tandem with political developments—the foundation of the German Empire and Germany's advent as a rising power in Europe and beyond, which included attempts at colonial expansion in Asia and Africa—the number of students at universities rose once more, disciplinary specialization processes resumed, and faculties of theology continued to weaken. One result was that experts in Oriental languages were no longer expected to teach Hebrew and the Bible unless these were their specialties.[27] New positions were created at various universities, both full chairs and extraordinary positions, under the

28 ::: A NEW ORIENT

general heading of Oriental languages and for narrower specializations like Semitic languages (primarily Arabic, but also Hebrew), Egyptology, and Assyriology. Gradually, "Oriental languages" became synonymous with Semitic languages.[28]

Towards the turn of the century, another field known as *Islamkunde* (Islamic studies) emerged, though whether it was a coherent field prior to World War I is contested in the scholarly literature.[29] Here, in some ways, was the practical approach absent from text-focused philological Orientalist research: facing public criticism of the exclusively classical study of Semitic languages that thus contributed nothing to the colonial effort, practitioners of this subfield engaged questions of Middle Eastern history and culture after the age of Classical Islam, especially the modern era. This contrasted with the field's misleading name, which was selected in an effort to attract the attention of scholars and mobilize public support.[30] Nonetheless, the field failed to accrue sufficient academic support and was therefore never meaningfully institutionalized within university departments. It remained for the most part at their margins or at designated institutes. According to Wokoeck, its failure to take hold in the years preceding World War I, when other disciplines were in fact also taking a more practical approach, suggests that *Islamkunde* did not represent the direct influence of colonial interests on German university Orientalism.[31]

Following defeat in World War I, Germany's territory within Europe was considerably diminished and the short-lived German colonial project outside it was erased. Yet despite these geopolitical changes, German Orientalism demonstrated its practical wartime potential for a brief moment: a collection of popular-science ethnographic studies titled "Between Foreign Peoples: A New Ethnology" (*Unter Fremden Völkern: Eine neue Völkerkunde*), based in large part on a series of recordings made between 1915 and 1918 by a group of German researchers in the POW camps within Germany, funded by the Prussian Ministry of Education and Culture, and approved by Kaiser Wilhelm II.[32] The initiative to conduct a methodical study among POWs took shape early in the war; the POW camps controlled by Germany within Europe, which included many non-Europeans, already contained 625,000 foreign soldiers within half a year of the war's outbreak.

Linguists and anthropologists identified an opportunity in the imperial nature of the competing militaries: the chance to conduct systematic study among non-European populations without leaving the confines of Germany for research abroad. The military approved and oversaw the study after extensive efforts and petitions to higher military authorities. In all, 1,651 recordings were made as part of the project, documenting some 215 languages and dialects.[33] The initiative had several founders, but the Berliner linguist and educator Wilhelm Doegen (1877–1967) became its primary leader, and edited the eventual collection of articles, published without the typical academic apparatus and accompanied by pictures taken in the camp. In 1915, the Ministry of Education and Culture appointed him acting director of the Prussian Royal Phonographic Commission (*Die Königlich Preußische Phonographische Kommission*), which consisted mostly of professors from Berlin and Hamburg. Each member was assigned a field: music, ethnology, and various languages—Indo-European, Indian and Mongolian, African, and more.[34] The recordings themselves were produced by scholars at various stages of their career, including Orientalists; as we shall see, some used their work with the recording initiative to advance their academic careers.

Research was primarily conducted at two POW camps, the Halbmondlager (crescent camp) and Weinbergslager (vineyard camp) located in the Wünsdorf and Zossen regions near a local military base about fifty kilometers south of Berlin. They were founded with the initial goal of housing Muslim POWs: French and British soldiers from North Africa and India were sent to Halbmondlager—home of the first mosque in Germany— while Russian army soldiers from Asia were sent to Weinbergslager. The separation of Muslim soldiers from the other enemy soldiers was undertaken as part of the German propaganda effort and sedition strategy (*Aufwiegelungsstrategie*); they were held under comparatively better conditions than other soldiers and presented as guests of the Kaiser, who sought to improve Germany's reputation in the Muslim world in general, and to appeal to residents of its ally, the Ottoman Empire, in particular.[35] The Germans also hoped to foment rebellion among the Muslims under French and British control, forcing these powers to direct military resources towards the repression of rebellion and away from combat with the German military.[36] Thanks to their linguistic expertise, German Orientalists were involved in the preparation of propaganda materials, distributed primarily in the first camp, seeking to mobilize the POWs there to propagandize against and even wage combat on the armies to which they belonged.[37] The war, it seems, prompted a certain pragmatism even from supposedly neutral German Orientalism.[38]

Ultimately, this brief episode sharpens distinctions between German Orientalism and that of other European countries, especially with regards

## 30 ::: A NEW ORIENT

to the study of Arabic and Islam. In responding to Edward Said's book—both when it was initially published and in subsequent decades—scholars noted the error in his considering German colonial interests negligible compared to those of Britain and France. Even absent a direct colonial presence in the Orient, many Germans expressed interest in knowledge on the Orient, and increasingly so once Germany acquired colonial possessions in the later stages of the nineteenth century; certainly, cultural, economic, and political necessity prompted others to write about the region as well.[39] Nevertheless, one must distinguish between this desire for knowledge and the actual creation of scientific knowledge: in Germany, for structural reasons already noted, the latter was centered around universities, where the classical and textual focus was maintained; in other countries, primarily France and Great Britain, there was a much broader role for those located within the Orient and involved either in the mechanisms of imperial control or in influencing and contributing to their establishment.[40] Philological Orientalism existed there too, as indicated by de Sacy's endeavors, but the almost exclusive attention to classical knowledge was an overt and unique characteristic of Arabic and Islamic studies at German universities. The German study of POW camps was in fact exceptionally rare for its discipline.

This, then, was the status of Arabic and Islamic studies at German universities as it took shape during the final third of the nineteenth century: research of a primarily philological nature with roots in theology and a basis in primary sources, focusing on language and its analysis—though it made gestures at pragmatism during the war years.[41] As such, it drew Jews from Central (and later Eastern) Europe hoping to find their way in the academic world. While Arabic and Islamic studies were developing and new university chairs being founded, the field of Jewish Studies (*Wissenschaft des Judentums*) was maturing beyond their halls, within rabbinical seminaries in Breslau, Vienna, Berlin, and Budapest, where emphasis was also placed on philological work with sources. Jewish students at the rabbinical seminaries began to pursue university studies in parallel as doors were gradually opened to them over the course of the nineteenth century.

Within the university, these students could not approach Jewish Studies directly, for the Bible and the history of the Jews were still considered the domain of theology faculties, and remained so, to some degree, until the middle of the twentieth century. There were no chairs in Jewish Studies, but they could opt for Semitic languages and Islam, which overlapped somewhat with Jewish Studies because of the affinity between the languages, their shared medieval history, and the interwoven ideas found in Jewish and Islamic texts.[42] Their ranks included many students or protégés of Heinrich Fleischer, who saw in their knowledge of Hebrew and Aramaic an opportunity to advance and develop the discipline: it would be easier for them to embark upon the study of Arabic than their Protestant peers. He helped find them positions and provided venues in which to publish their research in the journal of the DMG, the *Zeitschrift der Deutschen Morgenländischen Gesellschaft* (ZDMG).[43]

Georg Freytag, after returning from Paris to take up a position as professor at the University of Bonn, also fostered Jewish students. Outstanding among these was Abraham Geiger (1810–1874); though better known for his contribution to Jewish Studies, early in his career Geiger published an influential essay titled "What did Mohammed take from Judaism?" (*Was hat Mohammed aus dem Judenthume aufgenommen?*, 1833) at Freytag's behest. Employing philological comparisons between the Quran and Midrashic and Talmudic literature, the essay argues that—rather than drawing upon early Christianity—the principles of Muslim religion and customs were an adaption of Judaism to fit pagan Arabs. This contradicted the widespread scholarly explanation accepted to that point by Christians unfamiliar with Talmudic sources.[44] Geiger's essay reverberated across the world of German Orientalism and beyond, earning praise and illustrating the contributions Jewish scholars with rabbinical training could make to the study of Arabic and Islam. An even more exceptional figure was that of Gustav Weil (1808–1889), a student of de Sacy's and a pioneering scholar of the history of Islam using Arabic manuscripts, who published a biography of the Prophet Muhammad in 1843.[45] With much hard work and the prestige of having studied with de Sacy behind him, Weil managed to find work as a *Privatdozent* (non-tenured instructor) at the University of Heidelberg, where he taught and held a position as a librarian; after numerous attempts, he was appointed professor there in 1861, a rare precedent for a Jewish scholar. His studies also found the origins of Islam within Judaism, and the former as a branch of the latter.[46]

The most influential Jewish scholar of Arabic and Islam in the generation after Geiger and Weil was among Fleischer's most exceptional students at the University of Leipzig, Ignác Goldziher (1850–1921). Born in Hungary, Goldziher never held a position at a German university, but alongside his prominence in the Hungarian academic world, he was a central figure in German Orientalist circles nonetheless. It would be difficult to exaggerate

## 32 ::: A NEW ORIENT

Goldziher's importance to the development of scientific research on the Islamic religion (*Islamwissenschaft*) or his contribution to German scholarly discourse. Like his predecessors, he too saw its deep connection to Judaism; in fact, he considered it a more pristine version of monotheism than contemporary Judaism that he believed, given certain reforms, could become universal.[47] From his home in Budapest, where he served as the secretary of the Jewish community and eventually earned a position as professor, Goldziher corresponded widely with Jewish and non-Jewish Orientalists across Europe and beyond.[48]

During the first decades of the twentieth century, therefore, Jews in the field of Arabic and Islamic studies at German universities already had an influential presence. The model common in the nineteenth century continued in this period as well: for the most part, Jewish students began their studies in departments and seminaries for Oriental and Semitic languages after receiving extra-university training in Jewish Studies, or they studied the two in parallel. In order to earn a living within an already-saturated market, at a time when Jews were still rarely employed as lecturers or professors, they often worked as librarians in one of the Oriental libraries. This was one of the reasons why Berlin—where the university housed the Prussian State Library and Abraham Geiger was among the founders of the *Hochschule für die Wissenschaft des Judentums* in 1872—became a focal point for this set of Jewish students. Around the turn of the century, German Orientalism began to develop in new, less philological directions, primarily through research trips to the Orient; during the nineteenth century this was not common practice among German university scholars, as the lack of a colonial apparatus made such journeys prohibitively expensive.[49] The practice was still novel in the first decades of the twentieth century, with scholars forced to fund themselves or secure external sources of funding, whereas Jewish students interested in Oriental Studies tended to pursue their training at the more established and traditional Orientalist centers, which were then working to preserve their dominance and often succeeded in doing so.

The text-centered philological tradition—from de Sacy through Fleischer, Freytag, and others to their many successors, including Goldziher—was the dominant factor in the Orientalist training of many Jews who entered the field. This climate was central to the education of nearly the entire first generation of Oriental Studies scholars in Jerusalem, which founded the field at the Hebrew University: Josef Horovitz, Gotthold Eljakim Weil, and D. H. Baneth in Berlin; Shelomo Dov (Fritz) Goitein and Yosef Yoʻel Rivlin in Frankfurt, where they were students of Horovitz's; and L. A. Mayer in Vienna.[50]

Before moving on to our subject itself, another aspect of the German legacy that goes beyond disciplinary characteristics must be pointed out. This is the separation principle formulated by Max Weber in his 1918 lecture on "Science as a Vocation" (*Wissenschaft als Beruf*), embodying the German professional ethos in the scientific field. In his speech, Weber explained that the role of university scholars is the production and dissemination of knowledge so as to provide tools for the elucidation and justification of certain viewpoints, emphasizing that "it is likewise true that politics has no place in the lecture room as far as the lecturer is concerned. Least of all if his subject is the academic study of politics . . . If you speak about democracy at a public meeting there is no need to make a secret of your personal point of view . . . The words you use are not the tools of academic analysis, but a way of winning others over to your political point of view. They are not plowshares to loosen the solid soil of contemplative thought, but swords to be used against your opponents: weapons, in short. In a lecture room it would be an outrage to make use of language in this way."[51] The role of the academic, Weber suggests, is to provide the means by which any issue might be clarified, in accordance with his field of specialization—but not to deal with his views on these issues.

In this way, Weber reflected the principle of separating science from politics that was so important to the German scientific and university ethos. After 1870 and the increase in the power of the state, university professors typically preferred to distance themselves from active involvement in politics or party affiliation and to pursue, if only declaratively, the nineteenth-century Humboldtian model of attending to science and research for their own sake rather than in service of the state, practical necessities, or defined political goals.[52] This principle developed alongside the Humboldtian university model itself and was also essential to the development of German-Jewish Orientalism, which emerged, as we saw, out of the German-Jewish engagement with Jewish Studies; in the construction of this field of *Wissenschaft des Judentums* (lit. "science of Judaism") in nineteenth-century Germany, emphasis was placed on the "science"—*Wissenschaft* in German—indicating scientific objectivity and the discipline's systematic nature, thus granting Judaism legitimacy and validity as a field of knowledge. The field's founders thus hoped to redeem Judaism from the severe crisis it en-

34 ::: A NEW ORIENT

countered in nineteenth-century Germany set against the background of political and social trends.[53] The search for a "pure" science, then, was part and parcel of German-Jewish Oriental experts' disciplinary achievements, accentuating the tension between politics and science in the field.

Weber's call for separation, notably, was normative rather than descriptive in the first place. In an open letter to the newspaper a decade before his lecture on "Science as a Vocation," he bemoaned that in Germany, academic freedom existed only so long as the political and religious views being expressed were acceptable to the authorities.[54] That university professors avoided dealing with politics was also a ratification of the political status-quo and, effectively, served as support for the policy of the government funding their positions and contributing to the stature and status of professors in German society.[55] In any case, one need accept neither Weber's call for separation between science and politics nor the chances of such a separation's success for his lecture to lend a framework for the analysis of Orientalist practices in Mandate Palestine and Israel that distinguishes between two realms: that of science and the professional-academic; and that of the political or ideological—which in this study are examined in light of the axis of immigration from Germany to Palestine.

## JUDAISM WITH THE ORIENT FOR AN ORIENT WITHOUT JUDAISM: PREPARATIONS FOR THE FOUNDATION OF THE SCHOOL OF ORIENTAL STUDIES
### The Goldziher Proposal

The endeavor to establish a Jewish university in Jerusalem, then under British control, was renewed in the wake of World War I. Following the initial approval to move forward with this plan at the Zionist Congress of 1913, the Zionist movement had purchased land on the remote Grey Hill estate on Mount Scopus, north of the Old City of Jerusalem.[56] A cornerstone-laying ceremony was held there in 1918; among the attendees were Zionist officials; General Edmund Allenby, the commanding general of the British forces in Palestine; and local Jewish, Christian, and Muslim dignitaries, including the Grand Mufti of Jerusalem, Kamil al-Husseini.[57] Originally imagined as an institution that would solve the problem of Eastern European Jewry, whose enrollment at universities was limited by anti-Semitic *numerus clausus* regulations, by this time the planned institution, now called the *Hebrew*

*University*, had become the flagship project of cultural Zionism. Zionist rhetoric compared it to the Temple itself.[58]

The university had a place, but it was still unclear what this place would be filled with. Under these circumstances, the Central Zionist Office in London established a Department for Education and Culture, headed by longtime Zionist organizer Shmaryahu Levin (1867–1935). A rabbi and political activist who was eventually forced to flee the Russian Empire due to his activism, Levin—a somewhat neglected figure in the English-language historiography on Zionism today—had experience leading Zionist educational causes.[59] Therefore, in 1919 he started working on a systematic plan for the university's organizational structure and scholarly content.

Attempting to recruit prominent names to the cause of the Hebrew University, Levin sent out letters seeking advice on university matters to established Jewish scholars and intellectuals, mostly from Europe.[60] As one of the most influential Orientalists in Europe at the time, and particularly in Germany, Goldziher was naturally among the scholars approached by Levin.[61]

It was in this capacity that Levin explained to his correspondent in Hebrew that, with the end of the war "our ancient hopes blossom and shine once more on the Oriental horizon," asking that Goldziher—as "one of the giants and standard bearers for the Hebrew science devoted to the rebirth of his people and its spirit"—aid in the "work of revival." Seeing the planned university as "Hebrew in every sense, its Hebrew character outwardly apparent . . . not only in terms of language but also in connection with the topics of study," Levin urged Goldziher to propose departments and chairs to be established at the university and the subjects that should be taught there: he asked that Goldziher explain, in other words, "how to make the Hebrew University—*Hebrew*," at least in comparison with European universities.

Replying in Hebrew, Goldziher made no explicit usage of the phrase "Hebrew University," but did provide his opinion about the university, or "general house of study" (*beit hamidrash hakolel*) soon to be established in the Holy City.[62] This institution, he explained from the outset, must rival any Western university in the variety, scope, and level of subjects it taught. The institution would be exceptional in that it would not be satisfied with these subjects alone, but, in Goldziher's vision, would include "wisdom tied to the land and to the university's purpose," including a) a department for the Science of Religion that would emphasize "the beliefs of the nations attributed to 'Shem the son of Noah' [the Semitic peoples] and the position of Judaism towards the beliefs of the nations," and teach "the rich and large literature emerging from matters surrounding our beliefs from the time of our sacred texts . . . until modern times [*hazmanim hame'uharim*]"; b) instruction and philological study of Oriental languages, since the university would inhabit a land where "Arabic is the language on the lips of the populace." Thus the students would be able to examine "our important literature written in the Arabic language and to publish the writings they find in the archives"; c) a department of Palestinian archaeology to include excavations revealing the history of the Jewish people and the establishment of study trips ranging across the country; d) the study of the history of the Jewish people from its beginnings until contemporary times in all countries, which should be framed as a separate major subject and not "as an offshoot of general history"; e) the study of "Jewish literature" of all kinds.[63]

Goldziher's letter is a revealing document shedding light on a number of aspects of this influential Orientalist's scholarly and religious understandings. Conspicuous from the outset is his call to set apart a department at the university for the study of Semitic religions, the role of which would be to study, in his words, the "history of our beliefs from the earliest times until the development of complete monotheism [*emunat hayehud hamuhlat*]."[64] Such a reading is rooted in a debate, which Goldziher engaged in with his first steps in the academy, over the controversial and influential essay "The General History and Comparative System of the Semitic Languages" (*Histoire générale et système comparé des langues sémitiques*, 1855) by the French Orientalist Ernest Renan (1823–1892). In this essay, Renan laid out his theory regarding the Semitic peoples and Semitism: the spirit, characteristics, and language of the Semitic race in general, including the Jewish people, he explained, emerged in the homogeneous, monotheistic desert. Thus, the entire Semitic race was fossilized and unable to adjust, change, or create; as such, it was inherently inferior to the Aryan race, which was consolidated within a polytheistic environment.[65] Renan's psycho-racial claim on the inferiority of the Semites became the foundation upon which nineteenth- and twentieth-century anti-Semitic theorizers would build.[66]

In 1876, some twenty years after the publication of Renan's essay, Goldziher—serving as secretary of the Jewish community in Pest (part of Budapest) after being denied a promised position at the Catholic University of Budapest for refusing to convert and suddenly thrust into the complexities of local politics—published his response to Renan in an essay in German titled "The myth among the Hebrews and its historical development" (*Der Mythos bei den Hebräern und seine geschichtliche Entwicklung*, 1876).

The Science of the Orient ::: 37

Goldziher's response, which prompted extensive criticism both when it was published and in subsequent years, stood out: unlike other critics, who confronted Renan with proof of the spiritual creativity of the Jews, Goldziher accepted the assumption that myths (and thus creativity) could emerge only out of polytheism. Instead, citing biblical and post-biblical texts as proof, he claimed that the Semites—the early Hebrews and Arabs—were themselves polytheistic: there was in fact a Hebrew myth, primarily because the ability to create myths is universal. Indeed, he believed no civilization at all could develop without myths.[67]

In 1919, when Goldziher sent his proposals to Levin, he was no longer the same frustrated young scholar. At 69, he was now a regular professor in Budapest, a member of the Hungarian Academy of Science, and among the most senior Orientalists in Europe, whose name in the field had been made by his studies of Arabic and Islam. The "Mythos," as he called it, was not among his primary concerns. Yet notably, here in the foundation of the Hebrew University he identified an opportunity to teach the consolidation of Semitic monotheism in a sustained and institutionalized manner. This was because Goldziher had continued to foster these ideas about monotheism over the years; but the lukewarm responses to his thesis from within the Jewish community had led him to focus on monotheism in another Semitic religion: Islam.[68] Goldziher saw in the study of Islam and its examination with the critical tools of religious studies a means to distill a purified and universal monotheism, one towards which the cultural and religious history of all humanity was leading: from mythos, to polytheism, and finally critical monotheism.[69] The Jewish ethics shaped by monotheism, he wrote to Levin, make up "the core of our existence to this day . . . the obligation we hold among the nations."[70] For him, therefore, the foundation of a Hebrew (i.e., Jewish) university offered a golden opportunity to give institutional heft to its monotheistic mission.

Goldziher's next recommendation concerned the teaching and philological study of Oriental languages, especially Arabic. In this context, his reasons are interesting and perhaps surprising. Goldziher is known to have opposed Zionism, believing that the vision of a universal monotheism ought to be advanced through Jews' integration in the emerging nation-states wherein they resided. He held this view, largely unchanged, until his death; but it may have softened somewhat, as suggested by his enthusiastic and businesslike response to Levin's letter.[71] Moreover, Goldziher enlisted the friendship and respect of scholars across the Arab world over the course

## 38 ::: A NEW ORIENT

of his life, so much so that the Egyptian Prince (later king) Fuad offered him a guest professorship at the University of Cairo.[72]

It is therefore remarkable that, when Goldziher mentioned Arabic among the possible advantages of building a Hebrew university in Jerusalem, his justification had nothing to do with any possible affinity that might result between Jews and Arabs—something he supported as part of his universalist monotheistic standpoint—but focused instead on utilitarian scholarly justifications having to do with research: at a university located in Jerusalem, in the Orient, that is, it would be easier to master the languages of the region, especially that of the majority population of the country, Arabic; and it should be learned in order to facilitate the study of Jewish literature written in that language. Moreover, Goldziher noted that delving into the philology of Oriental languages would prompt new revelations about "Ancient Israel" (*kadmoniot yisra'el*).

These justifications seem narrow, and though they recognize the existence of an Arab majority in the country, Goldziher does not so much as mention the possibility that learning its language might help improve relations with that majority.[73] The explanation may be that, when asked to explain what might set the Hebrew University apart as a Hebrew, that is, a Jewish university, Goldziher understood the university's Hebrewness as a platform for a better, more complete and scientific understanding of Judaism itself. He therefore did not address further possible consequences of the study of the Orient and its languages at such a university.

While his suggestions that the university deal with the country's archaeology and with Jewish literature were apt enough, the distinction Goldziher recommended making between general history and Jewish history stood out. He was raising a longstanding issue, one that would subsequently spark controversy at the Hebrew University once it had been established—and continues to do so at universities across Israel today.[74] The study of Jewish history mostly remained outside the halls of European universities during the nineteenth and early twentieth centuries, and Jewish scholars interested in the topic mostly did so within internal Jewish settings.[75] This was also the period when the study of "general history" was taking shape at universities, as the field became a modern academic discipline entertaining its own universal aspirations. Instruction and research on general history at various universities emerged not only out of a Eurocentric perspective but also one that emphasized the nation, especially with regards to the modern era. This was the popular model brought in by the German-Jewish historians Yitzhak Baer (1888–1980) and Richard Koebner (1885–1958) and their Russian-Jewish contemporary Avigdor Cherikover (1894–1958), all doctoral graduates of German universities who joined the Hebrew University during the first half of the 1930s.[76] Their desire to integrate Jewish history into general history was met with outright opposition from most of the faculty at the university's Institute for Jewish Studies, who feared the derogation of their own institute's status and preferred that—like all other topics dealing with Judaism and the Jewish people—this too be taught there: that is, separately from general history, which would effectively become a "history of others."[77] The latter view prevailed, and the subjects were indeed separated.[78]

When Goldziher formulated his proposals, of course, the establishment of the School of Oriental Studies was still several years away, so organizational politics were perhaps not his primary consideration. Why, then, did he find it important to separate Jewish history from general history within a national university—in contrast with the European model that took shape during his years in the academy? As noted, he arrogated to the Jewish people a key universal role as the heralds of monotheism to humanity. Perhaps, in stressing the need to prevent Jewish history from becoming "an entity clinging to general history," Goldziher hoped to prevent the inclusion within general history of a Jewish history inflected with nationalism —something that was frequently the case at European universities—from obscuring the uniqueness of the religion of the Jews, the role of which transcends the frame of the national.

Levin passed Goldziher's letter along to other figures, and there is evidence, albeit equivocal, that the scholar from Budapest also submitted a more detailed plan for an Orientalist institute to be founded at the Hebrew University, which was deposited at the offices of the Zionist leadership in London.[79] This plan, if it indeed existed, has not been preserved; Goldziher —who died in 1921—did not live to see the opening of the Hebrew University, and in later years his plan was never remembered among the foundations for the planning of the School of Oriental Studies.[80] The letter to Levin is significant in that it serves as crucial evidence for a direct and active link, during his lifetime, to the Hebrew University as an institution. Not all the suggestions in the letter related directly to "Orientalist" topics, but the deeper issues raised by them—the link between Judaism and Islam as Semitic religions, Arabic as the local language, the relation of Jewish history to other histories—all of which emerged out of Goldziher's experiences as

40 ::: A NEW ORIENT

an European Orientalist, would soon be raised in subsequent proposals for the foundation of an Orientalist institute and would trouble its personnel for many years more.

Goldziher's legacy takes its expression in other forms as well, first of all materially: after his death, the National and University Library in Jerusalem purchased his vast library of around six thousand books on the study of Arabic and Islam as well as rare prints from Egypt and Russia. Arranging the purchase from the Goldziher family was a complex affair requiring the intervention of scholars in both Palestine and Europe, Zionist operatives, and the British Foreign Minister, since other libraries and institutions (including one in Japan) were interested in purchasing the important library for themselves; Goldziher's books included comments and notations made in his clear and organized hand, increasing its research value. The Goldziher library was purchased with various donated funds at a bargain-rate price and transferred to Palestine in 1924.[81] Alongside further, smaller donations, it became the primary component of the library's Orientalist collection.

It would be difficult to exaggerate the importance of this library: a field based first and foremost on text-centered philological work, as the history of German Orientalism's development teaches us, relies on scientific editions and interpretations in order to carry on its everyday research and instruction.[82] Without it, in other words, the German university graduates who made up the School of Oriental Studies staff would have found the continuation of their scientific work impossible. Moreover, Goldziher was to them not only the library's former owner, but also a kind of forefather. They saw it as their responsibility to present his work to the learned Hebrew-speaking community, and translated several of his writings, first and foremost the well-known 1910 book *Lectures on Islam* (*Vorlesungen über den Islam*).[83] The Hebrew translation became an indispensable introductory text in Islamic studies in Israel for many years. The proposals in Goldziher's 1919 letter to Levin, meanwhile, represent an ideological facet of his legacy that has been forgotten over the years, expressing the wider context of his interest in the study of Islam and his influence on the development of the field at the university in Jerusalem.

## Jewish Studies, Oriental Studies, and the Humanities

Discussions regarding the character of the university and its constituent departments went on, without any real progress, after this correspondence with Goldziher (who was, as we saw, only one among several figures whom Levin approached for advice). One of the university's founders, the philosopher Hugo Bergmann, also pondered in late 1919 within the pages of *Ha'olam*, the official newspaper of the World Zionist Organization, how "the unique conditions of the Hebrew University would be reflected" in the humanities. "What place would be given to ancient languages, to Latin [*romit*] and Greek? What place for Arabic language and culture?"—though he proposed no solutions.[84] In early February 1920, in discussions of the Zionist General Council, a rather general plan for the formation of the university was approved, to include a "Hebrew Institute" and a "general course in the subjects of the humanities," without mention of an Orientalist institute of any kind.[85]

Initial operational discussions of the character of humanities at the university only began in 1922, when an assembly, and later a committee, was inaugurated to establish a faculty of the humanities. The committee included figures who had already been involved in various capacities in advancing the idea of the university: Ahad Ha'am, Eliezer Ben-Yehuda, David Yellin, Josef Klausner, and the scholar of Islamic archaeology and art Leo Aryeh Mayer (1895–1959), who was appointed secretary of the committee.[86] Mayer, born in Stanislaviv in Galicia, then part of the Austro-Hungarian Empire (today Ivano-Frankivsk, Ukraine), studied Oriental Art and Archaeology at the University of Vienna while undergoing rabbinical training at the town's Rabbinical Seminary. His doctoral thesis dealt with the construction of Muslim towns.[87] Where Mayer was shaped as a scholar is meaningful in the context of Orientalism: first because the geographical location of Austria as a borderland between Christian Europe and the Ottoman Empire meant that, unlike in other European countries that encountered the Orient as a result of colonialist expansion, Austria had some immediate connection with the "Orient"; moreover, the territories controlled by the Habsburgs to the East made their empire a multiethnic one; its capital, turn-of-the-century Vienna, attracted Slavs, Jews, and Muslims.[88]

Mayer later moved to Berlin, where he worked as a scientific assistant in the Oriental Department of the Prussian State Library and familiarized himself with the local Oriental and Jewish Studies milieux. From there he immigrated to Palestine in 1921 and within several months was appointed an inspector in the Antiquities Department of the Mandate Government.[89] He was the sole member of the committee to boast a comprehensive Orientalist training in a German university setting; this may explain his inclusion

42 ::: A NEW ORIENT

as secretary, but perhaps his work for the Mandate Government proved decisive on that score, or indeed the letter of recommendation with which he arrived in the country from Zwi Perez Chajes (1876–1927), Chief Rabbi of Vienna and head of its Rabbinical Seminary; Chajes had been involved in discussions held in Europe concerning the founding of the university since their early stages.[90]

As Hagit Lavsky has shown, members of the committee for the establishment of the faculty were concerned primarily with spurring progress in the field of Jewish Studies.[91] Still, their discussions also reflected the connection between Oriental Studies and Jewish Studies that had developed within the German academic tradition. The subject appears in the protocol of the first assembly, held in February 1922, which included the participation of Zionist scholars, operatives, and donors. It was entitled "Meeting for the Establishment of a Faculty of Oriental Studies of the Hebrew University in the Land of Israel." According to Menachem Ussishkin, chairman of the assembly, there were several reasons why, among the humanities fields, Oriental Studies became the focus: because so many individuals from the field inquired with the university's planners; because large sums would not be required to open such a department; because there was apprehension that—were the British to open a university in Palestine—it would precede the Hebrew University in this field; and, moreover, that no other field could boast of "competition by Jews with the faculties in other countries."[92] The Jerusalem-born Yellin laid emphasis, much like Goldziher, on the location of the university: "[We] are in the land of the Orient [*eretz hamizrah*] and, there being a desire across the world to teach the Orient, this must be all the more so in this country." Ben-Yehuda added that such a department could attract young Jews studying abroad and hoping to experience the subject "in situ."

Mayer's comment, meanwhile, that many experts in the field were figures of some stature within Jewish Studies, prompted the educator and Zionist activist Joseph Lurie—to ensure the quality of the research—to propose constraining the institute's plans in the early stages "and that teaching be limited to the subject of Judaism." The fundraiser (and donor) Saul Rosenblum was of a similar opinion, suggesting that on established subjects there was no point in competing with existing world universities, but that a potential relative advantage might come from "investigations in the study of Oriental Jewry, Hebrew philosophy, and so on," for which it would also be rather simple to raise support and donations.

*The Science of the Orient* ::: 43

These quotes inform us that, in the eyes of the participants in these discussions, Oriental Studies was a broad framework including Jewish Studies within it. Debate focused on whether to establish a faculty that would deal with this broader frame or focus solely on topics surrounding Judaism. In part, this duplicated the widespread model for various universities in Germany: we have seen how Hebrew, as a Semitic language, was taught within Orientalist departments. On the other hand, examination of Judaism as a research field was linked primarily to theology faculties, and Jewish Studies as a modern body of knowledge was taught in extra-university institutions such as rabbinical seminaries, often in response to Christian theological research.[93] Perhaps the participants saw in the establishment of the Hebrew University, as a matter of principle, an opportunity to give Jewish Studies their due by incorporating them into Oriental Studies, as German universities ought in fact be doing as well.

Rosenblum's comments proposing a focus on Jewish Studies, based as they were on his familiarity with donors and the topics they might be induced to support, would seem to indicate the direction of the Jerusalemite committee's discussion. This direction entailed a reversal of the original tendency—towards Jewish Studies as part of Oriental Studies—that had marked the university's early path, continuing after its official inauguration. And indeed, in a later discussion, about a year after the committee's establishment, David Yellin presented a new question: what of teaching "the study of Judaism and appending Oriental Studies to it, insofar as the latter are connected to the former."[94] At this point, the Reform rabbi and Zionist activist Judah Leib Magnes (1877–1948), a native of Oakland, California, who immigrated to Palestine in 1922, was already a participant in the discussions; he quickly became one of the dominant figures promoting the idea of a university in Jerusalem.[95]

The framing of the question reflects just how marginal the place of Oriental Studies was in the discussions: its role had shrunk to the teaching of the Semitic languages, including Arabic, within the broader framework of Jewish Studies—a mirror image of how Hebrew was taught within Oriental Studies at German universities. Subsequently, the committee decided that the Humanities Department, as it was then known, would include study of Arabic, Syriac, Assyrian, and Egyptian.[96] For the time being, no place was found for Islamic studies or Muslim history in the emerging structure.

In parallel to discussions in Jerusalem, additional committees were established in London, Paris, and the United States. For the most part, all were

44 ::: A NEW ORIENT

busy sketching out the borders of Jewish Studies at the university and determining the autonomy of the future institute; the central concern was how loyal it ought be to tradition, that is, how critical the institute's approach to the study of Judaism ought to be.[97] Eventually, hoping to put an end to the controversies between the different committees for the foundation of an Institute for Jewish Studies, a higher committee meeting was convened in London in July 1924, where representatives from all the committees gathered to reach final decisions about its structure: a research institute with Hebrew as the language of instruction hosting a limited selection of courses including Hebrew, Hebrew literature, philosophy, Jewish law, and Jewish thought, in addition to Arabic, which was to be taught under the aegis of Semitic languages. This led to the foundation of an institute in Jerusalem in late December 1924, of a limited scope; courses began in January 1925, though not all of the intended fields of study were launched immediately.[98] The higher committee meeting in London also included L. A. Mayer as one of the representatives from Jerusalem. While this meeting too hardly broached the Oriental Studies question, a decision was nonetheless reached to offer Eugen Mittwoch (1876–1942), Chair of Semitic Languages at the University of Berlin, the position of Professor of Arabic at the Institute for Jewish Studies for a period of one year.[99]

The choice of Mittwoch, a scholar of Islam specializing in Arabic and Turkish but also well-known for his pioneering works on Ethiopian languages, was a product of his considerable stature in the world of German Orientalism following World War I,[100] not to mention his involvement during the early 1920s in some of the earliest discussions in Europe regarding the development of the Hebrew University.[101] Whether or not an invitation was ever sent to Mittwoch, his candidacy was abandoned and he never ended up coming to Jerusalem.[102] Still, the committee participants' decision to name a senior Berlin Orientalist so closely identified with the contemporary world of German Orientalism, reflects their hope of fostering a program of Arabic at the Hebrew University that could meet the standards of that world.

*Initial Plans: Mayer, Margolis*

Proposals and ideas abounded during these formative years. Thus, although the committee in London eventually slotted Arabic into the Institute for Jewish Studies, the establishment of a separate Orientalist institute was

The Science of the Orient ::: 45

also considered as a potential future stage in the university's development. Magnes therefore prompted L. A. Mayer to prepare a memorandum proposing an institute for the study of Islam at the Hebrew University.[103] It was at that this time, too, that Mayer assembled a certain collection of fellows for the future institute—three young scholars of Arabic and Islam based in Palestine with Orientalist training from European universities.[104]

The first was Shelomo Dov Goitein (1900–1985) of Burgkunstadt, Bavaria, who had studied Arabic language and Islam at the University of Frankfurt and written his doctoral thesis on the topic of Islamic prayer. Goitein immigrated to Palestine in 1923, when he became a religion and history teacher at the Haifa Reali School.[105] Mayer recruited Goitein based on their previous acquaintance in early 1920s Berlin, when both had attended the lectures of the German-Jewish archaeologist Ernst Herzfeld and the Islam scholar and Prussian Minister of Education Carl Heinrich Becker.[106]

An additional Oriental Studies scholar was D. H. (David Hartwig Zvi) Baneth (1893–1973), born in Krotoszyn (then part of Prussia, now Poland).[107] Raised and educated in Berlin, Baneth was well-known in the circle of Jewish scholars of Jewish and Oriental studies there, thanks especially to his father, Professor Eduard Ezekiel Baneth (1855–1930), who taught Midrash and Talmud at the Higher Institute of Jewish Studies (*Hochschule für die Wissenschaft des Judentums*) in town. For his doctoral thesis at the University of Berlin, the younger Baneth wrote about the missives of the Prophet Muhammad as part of his studies in classical philology and Semitic philology.[108] His work at the library of the Higher Institute of Jewish Studies and the Prussian State Library, as well as his academic training, made him a natural candidate to found the Oriental department at the National and University Library following the purchase of Goldziher's library. Invited to take up the position of departmental librarian, he immigrated to Palestine in fall 1924.[109]

These European-born Orientalists were joined by Avinoam Yellin (1900–1937), the son of prominent Jerusalemite educator David Yellin (1864–1941). Unlike Mayer, Goitein, and Baneth, Yellin was born in Jerusalem; he was also the only one among them without a doctoral degree. He studied Arabic and Syriac during World War I, when his family was exiled by the Ottoman authorities to Damascus, and later made his way to Cambridge University to study Semitic languages and education. He wrote a master's thesis dealing with Arabic poetry written by Jews. With his pedagogical training, Yellin also worked as a teacher, and after returning from Cambridge served as the Assistant District Officer (for Jewish Affairs) at the Jerusalem Governorate

Office.[110] Mayer encountered Yellin, perhaps through this role, via Yellin's family pedigree, or thanks to Yellin's minor interest in archaeological excavations; in any case, his inclusion among the institute's faculty of fellows served to further link the individuals promoting the development of Oriental Studies at the Hebrew University to the Mandate regime, where Mayer also worked, in the Antiquities Department. The fellows—all of whom, as we saw, had European Arabist training—now began their preparations for the establishment of the Oriental institute and in laying out its curriculum and research agenda.

In the aforementioned memorandum formulated by Mayer—the first detailed document in the Hebrew University's history to directly address the structure of the forthcoming institute, found only recently in an uncatalogued archive at the National Library in Jerusalem—he emphasized that the institute would deal not only with the Arabic language, but would be built "upon a broad foundation of research on Muslim culture." Initially, Mayer proposed, the institute would be directed by the teacher for Arabic language—meaning that language instruction would not be coordinated through the Institute for Jewish Studies. Nevertheless, he added, direction of the institute would later be entrusted to a committee composed of "all the teachers of Islamic studies" once they joined the faculty.

This clarification, though ostensibly minor, anticipated a novel alternative to the accepted model for directing institutes and seminaries for Arabic, Islam, or Semitic philology at German universities. These had developed, not only for Oriental Studies but also in numerous other fields, in tandem with the scientific professionalization of various fields of knowledge and the expansion of state funding for universities beginning in the mid-nineteenth century. Under this model, each institute was headed by a single professor, an expert in the institute or seminary's field of study whose appointment required approval from the state apparatus. At that point he dictated the institute's topics of research and shaped its small group of fellows, enjoying almost complete autonomy from both the university authorities and the state itself.[111] There was another German model, that of institutes co-directed by a number of professors, each responsible for their field of expertise, but it was less common in the field of Oriental Studies, and was not employed at any of the Orientalist institutes in Berlin, Frankfurt, or Vienna.[112] Mayer provided no explanation of his preference that the institute be directed by committee, in contrast to the organizational approach he was familiar with from the sites of his training.

Alongside this organizational element, Mayer proposed that the heart of the endeavor would be studies conducted by the "institute's Fellows."[113] They would be appointed for a period of one or two years to examine a specific predetermined topic and take part in the administrative work of the institute. Topics of research would be general Islamic subjects ("fundamentals of research on Islam," without further elaboration) and those pertaining to the relationship between Judaism and Islam. Here Mayer did propose several examples, including: Jewish influence on Arabic literature; the compilation of the works of Jewish poets written in Arabic; Jewish dialects in the Arabic, Turkish, and Persian languages; synagogue architecture influenced by Islamic style; and the writing of a comprehensive essay on the history of Jews in the Islamic world. This level of detail on subjects straddling Judaism and Islam reflects what was still a deep connection between Jewish Studies and Oriental Studies, even if two fields of knowledge already seemed destined for separation. It is apparent that Mayer believed that the approach to Oriental Studies of the Hebrew University would have to serve, among other things, the study of Judaism and the Jews on the one hand, and on the other to establish the presence of a joint legacy of Jews and Muslims; at the very least he understood that Magnes, who saw the study of Arabic and Islam as a political opportunity to advance intellectual affinity between Jews and Arabs, expected as much.[114]

Other than the Fellows, Mayer noted, the institute would also include "non-collegiates [*außerordentliche Hörer*]" who would be granted access to the research materials located at the institute and could take part in the second focus of its activities: courses and lectures. The courses were to be taught by institute faculty, and though Mayer was light on specifics, he also proposed that the institute hold weekly lectures, open to the wider public, given by faculty as well as non-collegiates on questions to do with Palestine. He raised the possibility that teaching be conducted in Arabic as well, on the assumption that such a field might attract a large and varied crowd. As an example of a lecture subject, Mayer suggested "Palestine in the Sixteenth Century," a topic that "could prompt many nice lectures shedding light on the complete darkness obscuring that entire period." That complete darkness was essentially the lack of scholarly attention in research, and especially teaching by European Orientalists, to the history of Palestine after the Ottoman conquest of 1517.

In 1924, when Mayer formulated his memorandum, the study of Palestine by both Jewish and non-Jewish scholars trained in Europe was focused

## 48 ::: A NEW ORIENT

almost exclusively on earlier periods.[115] This was certainly related to the fact that four hundred years of Ottoman rule in the country had ended only several years earlier, but was primarily due to the common European paradigm, which held that the Ottoman conquest brought stagnation and isolation from a Europe just then renewing itself and striding towards modernity. This stagnation ceased, the argument goes, only in the late eighteenth century and the arrival of Napoleon's army in Egypt, which was followed by governmental reforms and harbingers of nationalism across the Ottoman world.[116] At the beginning of the twentieth century, historians of the Muslim world only rarely turned their attention to the modern era; when they did so, the research typically focused on broader questions relating to the structure of the Ottoman Empire, its rise and fall, and an ongoing emphasis on comparison with goings-on in Europe that inevitably placed Islam at the short end.[117]

Mayer's proposal, to address the early Ottoman period and study local rather than broader imperial issues, was thus a pioneering one based perhaps in the Habsburg context of his Orientalist training. This proposal suggests just how exceptional Mayer was on the scholarly horizon, certainly the Jewish one in which he operated—as an Orientalist who used philological tools but engaged with archaeology, art, and material culture; and as a Jewish archaeologist examining the Muslim periods in Palestine while most of his colleagues sought surviving evidence of a Jewish presence in Palestine during the preceding period in a bid to strengthen and establish the Zionist narrative.[118]

Mayer's proposals found their way into a further plan for the Orientalist institute proposed by the American-Jewish professor of biblical philology at Dropsie College, Max Leopold Margolis (Hebrew name: Mordechai Yom-Tov Margaliot, 1866–1932), who resided in Jerusalem during the 1924–25 academic year. Margolis, born in Merecz (then in the Russian Empire, now the Lithuanian town of Merkinė), was the only scholar to present a proposal for the institute who was not trained at a German university: his family emigrated to the United States when he was a child, and though he did study at the *Gymnasium* in Berlin, most of his academic training came at Columbia University (then Columbia College) in New York, where he earned the first doctorate awarded by the Oriental Department. Margolis was in Jerusalem primarily for reasons having nothing to do with the university: as an expert in the study of the Bible, he was invited to spend a year as a guest lecturer at the archaeological institute, The American School of Oriental Research.[119]

Since he was around, but knowing he had no interest in settling there, the university administration invited Margolis to teach Beginning Greek and to lecture on punctuation theory and Bible translation during the Institute of Jewish Studies' inaugural semester in early 1925, preceding the university's official opening.[120]

Margolis, though a scholar of neither Islam nor Arabic, nonetheless took administrative responsibility for the department of Arabic literature and culture at the Institute for Jewish Studies—as Magnes declared at its ceremonial inauguration—until the right professor could be found to head it.[121] As such, Margolis was in contact with L. A. Mayer, and provided him with a "temporary plan for the department of Arab Culture."[122] Margolis's brief plan mostly echoed Mayer's, whose suggestions to Magnes were clearly an influence on its writing. At the same time, there were several minor novelties: Margolis proposed that, in addition to studies of Jews in Arabic literature and Jewish poetry in Arabic, historical-geographical studies of Palestine "going beyond the borders of the Jewish community" according to Arabic and Turkish literature be undertaken; and that the lectures open to the wider public indeed discuss the state of the country in the sixteenth century, but also the Mamluk period preceding the Ottoman conquest.[123]

The most groundbreaking aspect of the plan, stated explicitly, was for the department to serve as a site of Jewish-Arab cooperation. The plan concluded with a further proposal that, alongside a full professor in the chair for Arabic Culture, there be an "Arab Muslim lecturer or Lektor [an instructor teaching his or her mother tongue]," and even suggested two possible candidates—as a lecturer, Ahmad Zaki Pasha, and as Lektor, Sheikh Sa'ud al-'Uri.[124] Nowhere were these names subsequently mentioned, but in principle the idea of recruiting an Arab faculty member would continue to accompany the development of Oriental Studies at the Hebrew University in subsequent years.[125] Aside from this aspect, Margolis's plan—like Margolis himself—did not leave a meaningful mark after the conclusion of his stay in Palestine and return to the United States. No disciplinary or organizational influence of the early twentieth-century American field of Orientalism was absorbed, in this way, by the forthcoming Orientalist institute.

## The Horovitz Plan and the Establishment of the Institute

As noted, this period was characterized by an abundance of proposals and lines of thought regarding Oriental Studies at the Hebrew University. Even

50 ::: A NEW ORIENT

before the opening of the Institute for Jewish Studies, Magnes set off for Europe in search of renowned scholars to aid in the foundation of the Hebrew University. This journey brought him to the home of the Jewish Orientalist Josef Horovitz (1874–1931) from Frankfurt; Magnes hoped to convince him to join the efforts to found a university. The two had first met at the beginning of the century, when—with Magnes the doctoral student living in Berlin and Horovitz the doctor pursuing his Habilitation—both maintained a scholarly interest in Semitic languages.[126] During these years, the two used to meet for communal lunches with other young Jewish intellectuals in Berlin, most of whom were also affiliated with the Higher Institute of Jewish Studies.[127] After Magnes completed his doctorate in 1902, the two parted ways: Magnes returned to the United States, while Horovitz became a lecturer at the University of Berlin.

At this point, his possibilities dictated by the limited number of positions available to Jews in Germany for the study of Arabic and Islam at the time, Horovitz embarked upon a unique career path. In 1905, he set off on a research trip to Egypt, Palestine, Syria, and Constantinople in the employ of the Italian Orientalist and politician Leone Caetani to search for Arabic manuscripts on historical subjects, and to evaluate how descriptions in the Arabic historical literature of the conquest of Palestine by the Arabs matched the geographic reality. This was his first journey to the Orient.[128] A short time later, Horovitz set off again, this time venturing still further: in 1907, he was invited to India to serve as Professor of Arabic at the Mohammedan Anglo-Oriental College, Aligarh, where he also became the government official responsible for Muslim inscriptions (epigraphs), most of which were in Persian.[129] These years in Aligarh deeply impacted his worldview, sharpening his critique of British imperialism.[130] He left the position in 1914 after appointment as professor at the University of Frankfurt, founded that year.[131]

The description of the chair created for him there was extraordinary— the Orientalist Chair in Semitic Languages and also of Targum and Talmudic literature. The opening of this unique chair, made possible by a donation from the Frankfurt-born Jewish-American banker Jacob Schiff (1847–1920), marked a defining moment in the history of Jewish and Islamic studies in Germany: for the first time, certain topics belonging to the field of Jewish Studies (beyond the study of Hebrew language) were taught within the university as part of the Orientalist field of knowledge and with no relation to Christianity.[132] In his scholarship, on which the chair now allowed him to focus, Horovitz addressed a variety of subjects, including Quranic studies (he planned to publish a scientific edition of the Quran with a modern interpretation), Arabic historical literature, and classic Arabic poetry.[133]

Now, Horovitz's stature as a leading professor in the study of Islam in Germany, with experience working at a university in the Orient, made Magnes's decision to approach his old friend an obvious one.[134] Though not initially sure that his efforts would be fruitful, Magnes succeeded in enlisting the professor from Frankfurt in the effort to establish an Orientalist institute in Jerusalem.[135] The involvement of this ground-breaking Orientalist marked a new direction in the development of Oriental Studies at the Hebrew University: Horovitz spent many years in the Orient after training in Berlin, unlike many others, not only for research expeditions but as an academic instructor, and later held a pioneering chair at the University of Frankfurt.

In April 1925, the Hebrew University's opening celebration was held in the Amphitheatre on Mount Scopus. Horovitz was invited to participate and served as one of a series of guest lecturers accompanying the occasion.[136] He was added to the university's Board of Governors and to its academic council, and Magnes came to consider him the leading candidate to lay the foundation for the Orientalist institute:[137] the two shared a similar worldview with regards to the relations between Jews and Arabs and the potential contribution of such an institute to advancing mutual understanding between the peoples.[138] During his time in Palestine, Horovitz presented —probably to the faculty of the Institute for Jewish Studies—a preliminary proposal for the structure of an "Arabic Department," as it was known in the meeting's protocols.[139] In the meeting Horovitz expressed opposition, despite Magnes's declarations some months earlier, to the idea that Arabic be taught within the Institute for Jewish Studies, and proposed another structure: an institute "of Jewish and Oriental Studies," of which one division would be a department of "Oriental sciences" composed of three chairs —one for the Ancient Orient (Assyriology and Asia Minor), one for Hellenism in Asia and in the Christian Orient, and the one for the Muslim world (including Arabic, Persian, and Turkish). Thus, Horovitz sought to reproduce the chair he headed in Frankfurt and to expand it—placing Oriental and Jewish Studies within a single frame not limited to Semitic languages alone but stretching across a vast chronological and spatial range.

Mayer, the old hand among the Orient scholars in actively developing plans for the opening of the university in general and the Orientalist institute in particular, meanwhile continued to reinforce his standing within

52 ::: A NEW ORIENT

the institution. In accordance with the Margolis plan, the members of the Institute for Jewish Studies asked him to submit a proposal for a research subject to write on;[140] when the summer semester began in April, he taught a course on "Muslim building in Jerusalem" as part of the curriculum of the Institute for Jewish Studies.[141] This topic, of building in Muslim cities, recall, had been the subject of his doctoral research at the University of Vienna. Other than courses in Greek and Latin, Mayer's lectures were the only ones in the curriculum not dealing with Judaism or Jews. They contrasted starkly with introductory lectures to the study of the formulation of the Mishnah or the internal organization of the Babylonian Talmudic academies. The subject of his lectures seems a kind of declaration of the university's principles (the summer semester was the first following the official inauguration) meant as a signal of intent to the scholarly public that an "Arabic Department" would be established, even if its structure was yet to be fully worked out.

While Mayer taught, giving at least one aspect of Oriental Studies an effective footprint at the university, Horovitz returned to Frankfurt after the university's inaugural celebration and laid out the final organizational infrastructure for the establishment of an Orientalist institute. In May, he delivered a detailed memorandum requested by Magnes, titled "Proposals for the Establishment of an Institute of Arabic and Islamic Studies in Jerusalem."[142] This memorandum was, in effect, the founding document of the future institute. From its title, we see that Horovitz had been able to sway the university administration in his preferred direction—not a department of Arabic under the auspices of the Institute for Jewish Studies but a freestanding institute of its own. Nevertheless, his success was only partial: he had intended, recall, for the study of Judaism and the Orient to take place under the roof of a single institute. His proposal began by expressing the hope that two institutes—for Arabic and Islam, and for Judaism—would eventually be combined, along with additional future institutes, under a Department of Oriental Studies.

While scholars have hardly paid attention to the plans prepared by Mayer and Margolis, Horovitz's has been discussed in a number of studies of both his own past and that of the institute.[143] These studies have placed especial emphasis on the precedent-setting recommendation to include Arab/Muslim scholars on the institute's faculty to teach Arabic language and literature, as well as a *sheikh* to take charge of traditional Islamic teachings.[144] It is also worth noting the plan's limitations: he believed the institute could only be headed by a scholarly expert in Arabic trained at a Western university. This would have cut off the path to head of the institute from those same Arab scholars Horovitz planned to recruit, as well as the local scholars with a different Orientalist training. In any case, Horovitz suggested later in the proposal, whoever the head was ought to have the authority to determine the subjects to be studied at the institute. He thus sought to maintain the most common single-headed organizational model for German research institutes; at the same time, he did recommend that one of the subjects studied be the history of Palestine during the Islamic period, and that L. A. Mayer be the faculty member in charge of that field.

Horovitz's plan also discussed the material aspects of the institute's opening for the first time. He floated a budget proposal to supplement the Goldziher library with additional collections and books, all to be bought in Europe.[145] Moreover, he suggested the names of Jewish Orientalists at universities in Europe and the United States who might head the institute. Remarkably, only four of the ten names listed—including his own—were born in German-speaking countries.[146] While it may be that Horovitz actually did so in order to limit the direct German influence on the institute, more likely he believed that the institute should be headed by a renowned Jewish Orientalist from a well-known university, and in 1925 very few Jews held professorships in subjects connected to the study of Arabic and Islam at German universities.

Horovitz noted, moreover, that not all the scholars mentioned were explicitly Arabists (he did not address elements of the study of Islam in their work) and were thus not all equally suitable candidates—that is, in his eyes, knowledge of the Arabic language was significant, more than other factors, in selecting a scholar to lead the institute. Yet Horovitz also regarded the suggested scholars who *were* associated with the study of Arabic texts as less than ideal candidates, because he doubted that they would agree to leave their positions and immigrate to Palestine. He believed the head of the institute ought to change their place of residence to Jerusalem rather than simply visit for a certain period of time. Having thus effectively eliminated most of the names he had himself suggested, he did finally recommend William Popper (1874–1963) from the list, a professor of Semitic languages at the University of California Berkeley who, as Horovitz noted in his favor, had lived in the Near East for one year. Popper was married to Tess, the sister of Judah Magnes. There is no indication that the university ever attempted to interest him in the position.[147]

54 ::: A NEW ORIENT

Following the delivery of the memorandum, Magnes and Horovitz met informally in London with Leo Kohn (1894–1961), the secretary of the Zionist Executive in London for Hebrew University matters, and the Berlinborn Jewish Orientalist Gotthold Eljakim Weil.[148] Weil (1880–1962) was awarded the doctoral degree in Oriental languages at the university in the city of his birth, specializing in Arabic grammar. He was then an irregular (*extraordinarius*) professor there, and the founding director of the Oriental Department of the Prussian State Library in Berlin. Like Magnes and Horovitz, he too belonged to the circle of Jewish scholars in Berlin at the turn of the century; his name was mentioned from time to time in the margins of discussions about the instruction of Arabic and Islamic studies in Jerusalem as someone who might be brought on board. Though he supported the idea of the university and was willing to mobilize in its favor, like most German Zionists, immigrating to Palestine seemed to him a bridge too far. He therefore never expressed any interest in immigrating to Palestine during the university's inaugural years or earning a position within it.[149]

The four men reaffirmed the decision to found the institute but reached a surprising organizational decision: the institute would not be directed by one person but rather by a committee consisting of Horovitz, Weil, Eugen Mittwoch, and William Popper (the only non-German on the committee). The decision was the result of the failure to identify a well-known professor who would agree to relocate to Jerusalem; the members of the committee, it was decided, would stay in frequent contact with institute staff and visit Jerusalem from time to time. In other words, this reversion to the rare organizational model of joint coordination of an institute resulted not from the delayed adoption of Mayer's proposal, but from the necessity of circumstances. At the meeting, the need to bring on board lecturers for Assyriology and Egyptology was also raised for the first time.[150]

Despite the conclusion of this four-way meeting, when the Board of Governors of the university eventually approved the establishment of the institute on the basis of the Horovitz plan, its members preferred to bestow the role upon one person. Although he had no plans to relocate to Jerusalem, Horovitz was selected to direct the institute alone—and to cultivate a future generation of "younger Jewish Arabists who are at present working in Palestine . . . whose work in the past at European universities has given indications of promise."[151] Plans for the opening of the institute moved on to the practical stage. In a memorandum written in English in early 1926 reporting on the decision of the Board of Directors, the institute was already referred to by its ultimate moniker: The School of Oriental Studies. This was the title, it was decided, under which Orientalist activities would take place, without the more limited modifiers "Arabic" or "Islam"; though Arabic and Islam would be under its purview for the time being, the name was a declaration of intent in the spirit of Horovitz's vision.

While Horovitz remained in Frankfurt, Mayer (who was not lecturing during the first semester of the 1925–26 academic year) took responsibility for the institute's facilities. He drafted a list requesting a lecture hall and a seminar room, additions to what had initially been the Goldziher library (in accordance with the list in Horovitz's plan), and further equipment to assist lecturing in his own field—Muslim archaeology and art—such as a magic lantern projector and materials for copying epigraphs by the squeeze paper method.[152]

When preparations were complete, Horovitz visited Jerusalem once more; as it turned out, it was his last visit. Instruction at the institute was inaugurated with a series of lectures and an intensive seminar given by the professor from Frankfurt stretching over four weeks in March and April 1926 to a small group of pre-registered students. In a press release, the university emphasized that only those with substantial knowledge of Arabic would be accepted.[153] Horovitz devoted his lectures to an essay written by the renowned ninth-century Muslim scholar al-Jahiz on the achievements of the Turks (perhaps implying a gentle slight to the British, conquerors of Palestine from the Ottomans), while the seminar dealt with the origins of Sufi Islam and its early development.[154]

Letters sent to the university by those interested in attending Horovitz's lessons, and the eventual list of seventeen auditors who took part, provide a glimpse of the potential makeup of the student body during the institute's early years, including its knowledge base, as they were asked to describe the origin of their Arabic knowledge. About half of the participants were either former students of Horovitz's or Orientalists trained at other European academic institutions, in particular the University of Vienna. The only woman to actually participate was Esther Agnon, wife of the Nobel Prize-winning author S. Y. Agnon, herself a onetime Horovitz student in Frankfurt.[155] The other half of attendees had studied Arabic at local teaching seminaries, primarily the Mizrahi Teacher Training College, which prepared students from the religious Zionist sector; some of them, like David Shalem Mahboub, Yehoshua Hoter Hacohen, and Avraham Shalom Shaki, described Arabic as their mother tongue. Students at the teacher training college were notably

56 ::: A NEW ORIENT

still only of high school age themselves, and had certainly never been privy to academic training anywhere else.[156] Only graduates of Western universities were allowed to participate in the seminar, while others were allowed to attend the lectures as passive listeners; these were held in English or German, while the text being examined was simultaneously translated into Hebrew by the active participants.[157]

Thus, in the most obvious distinction between the two groups of participants—the first having European academic training, and the other, including some non-Europeans, local pedagogical training—one may identify the two primary pools from which the fledgling institute could have drawn potential students: those seeking to deepen their academic grasp of Oriental Studies or perhaps even join the institute as research assistants or faculty; and those hoping to improve their knowledge of Arabic and Islam and therein perhaps gain a certain advantage over their colleagues in the quest for a job teaching at one of the Jewish schools in Palestine. To elaborate, one may already identify, at this stage, the distinction noticed by HUSOS faculty member S. D. Goitein nine years later, when he offered that "while an 'Orientalist' education is one thing, an education to do work in the Orient is another."[158]

Indeed, the document describing the requirements for acceptance to the institute, formulated in collaboration with Magnes upon Horovitz's arrival in Jerusalem, emphasized that it "was intended primarily to train researchers in Oriental Studies."[159] It was established to serve scholars trained in the European—and especially the German—academic tradition, and they were expected to fill the seats in the seminar room and lecture hall in accordance. The acceptance requirements themselves suggest this: those requesting admittance as auditors or participants in the seminars were required to be high school graduates with a corresponding level of knowledge in Greek and Latin (though it was decided that students could be accepted without these subjects and complete them at the university), "sufficient knowledge" of Arabic, and "sufficient knowledge to read an appropriate text (philosophy, history, etc.) on sight" in Arabic. Setting the appropriate threshold was left up to the teachers themselves, who were asked to examine the students' knowledge in Arabic before acceptance was confirmed.[160] The non-collegiate auditors, meanwhile, were only to be admitted to courses on the basis of recommendations from the instructors. In other words, the institute's faculty was asked to teach in an environment oriented towards research rather than training from the start, and to set standards in accordance with European university training. Of course, these conditions impeded potential students born in Palestine or neighboring lands, where there was no training of the kind to be had.[161]

After teaching and taking part in the shaping of instructional and research norms at the institute, Horovitz left Jerusalem and returned to Frankfurt, where he continued to hold his position at the university and harbored no intentions of relocating to Jerusalem. While Horovitz's position was officially described, accordingly, as "Visiting Director,"[162] this title did not capture the degree of his involvement; he continued to manage the institute diligently by means of daily correspondence with various figures at the institute and the university, through telegrams and meetings with visitors from Jerusalem to Europe, and was promised the final word on decisions made on the ground in Jerusalem.[163] The ongoing influence of Frankfurt on the institute's activities was therefore ensured.

## BERLIN-FRANKFURT-JERUSALEM: THE IMPACT OF IDEAS AND MATERIAL CONDITIONS

### The Research Projects

With his position as director, in the spirit of both his own proposal and the German institute model, Horovitz fashioned the institute's large scholarly undertakings. Within certain limitations—that the institute faculty had initially taken shape before he became involved, and the separation of the School of Oriental Studies from the Institute for Jewish Studies in opposition to his own approach, such that the research was not meant to be directly related to Judaism—Horovitz chose topics in which he had maintained an interest for years: the preparation of a comprehensive concordance of ancient Arabic poetry, from the pre-Islamic period until the end of the Umayyad period (the mid-eighth century); and the publication of the manuscript *Ansab al-Ashraf* by the ninth-century Muslim historian al-Baladhuri. Hava Lazarus-Yafeh, a student of the institute's founding members who joined its faculty herself in later years, retroactively made the accusation that Horovitz "determined—one might well say mortgaged —the scholarly agenda of the institute in Jerusalem to this very day."[164] Perhaps even more than the numerous organizational aspects, the work on these two projects reflected the institute's deep connection with the German legacy of philological Orientalism.

Behind the comprehensive concordance project lay Horovitz's idea that

58 ::: A NEW ORIENT

in the language of early Arabic poetry the original meaning of the words was retained; the preparation of a comprehensive concordance furnishing every appearance of a certain word in its textual context would supply a comparative apparatus that could be used in understanding the Quran, classical Arabic literature, and even writings in other Semitic languages (including the Bible). The concordance was prepared using index cards, each listing a word, its root, and the original form of its appearance, in the hope that poetry would perhaps "explain itself" and enable "true understanding of the meaning of its words."[165] This was a gigantic, Sisyphean task that weighed as heavily on the institute's budget as it did on the schedules of its faculty and students over the course of many years: by 1955, for example, it consisted of 360 custom-built drawers containing around 1,500 index cards each. Along with additional index cards in storage at the time, institute staff estimated that the total number reached 600,000, yet the project remained far from complete.[166]

Concordances, in the sense of a work that collects all the appearances of all the words appearing in a certain corpus in alphabetical order, began appearing in Europe in the thirteenth century, and were undertaken primarily for sacred texts, with the goal of serving as an aid to those studying the Old and New Testaments.[167] Concordances of various literary corpuses were first published in the nineteenth century, for example of the collected works of Shakespeare.[168] Yet literary concordances were not as widely used as those for holy scriptures, in part because their target audience and uses were not always apparent.[169] The concordance for Arabic poetry at the School of Oriental Studies, however, provided an answer to this particular problem: Horovitz planned to apply the results of the work as the basis for a future book on pre-Islamic poetry.[170] The institute employed research assistants whose entire role was the preparation of index cards for the concordance; the instructors too devoted part of their daily research routine to this demanding and seemingly endless philological effort. The concordance became closely associated with the institute's operations, a sign of its German heritage and of its director Horovitz as "a herald of German science."[171]

This German scientific legacy was present not only in the spirit but also in the material foundation of the second research project: the publication of a scientific edition of the biographical-genealogical book *Ansab al-Ashraf* (genealogies of the nobles) by the ninth-century historian Ahmad ibn Yahya ibn Jabir al-Baladhuri.[172] European Orientalists had long been interested in the text because it presented biographies of the Muslim elites

*The Science of the Orient* ::: 59

in Muhammad's times, arranged in genealogical order (according to family lines). A selection had already been published in 1883 on the basis of a partial manuscript found in Berlin. In 1902, at the annual International Congress of Orientalists in Hamburg, the German scholar of Islam Carl Heinrich Becker (1876–1933)—recently awarded his PhD from the University of Berlin—announced that he had located the full manuscript at a library in Istanbul. At the congress a decision was made, at Goldziher's urging, to support Becker financially so that he could publish a scientific edition of the manuscript.[173]

Eventually, various scholars undertook to assist Becker, including Josef Horovitz. The two had been familiar since their days together as students in Berlin under Eduard Sachau (1845-1930), professor of Oriental languages at the University of Berlin, under whose supervision Horovitz wrote his dissertation. Sachau is considered the founder of the Berlin school of Arabic studies (*Die Berliner Schule*); he was associated with another ambitious project to publish a foundational Muslim genealogical essay: *Kitab al-Tabaqat al-Kabir* (the major book of classes) by the biographer Ibn Sa'd (784–845).[174] The volumes of the scientific edition were published with the aid of his students, including Horovitz and Eugen Mittwoch, between 1904 and 1918.[175]

Horovitz and Becker emulated their teacher in their work on *Ansab al-Ashraf.* Copying the manuscript was a long and complex process: parts of it were copied by hand, in part with the help of Horovitz and Gotthold Weil, another student of Sachau's; Becker had the bulk photographed using very costly professional techniques.[176] Though the complete copied manuscript was ready for processing by 1912, work on it was delayed, due in part to the outbreak of the World War I. After the war, Becker pivoted towards a career in politics, becoming the Prussian Minister of Education and Culture (*Kultusminister*). He deposited the materials at the Oriental department of the Prussian State Library, where it was well known to Weil, its director and founder.[177]

The publication of *Ansab al-Ashraf*, then, was a goal shared by scholars of Arabic and Islam in Europe, particularly Berlin. When the School of Oriental Studies was established in Jerusalem, Becker proposed to Horovitz —at Weil's prompting—that the institute's faculty take upon itself to work on the manuscript.[178] The joint path of these three scholars, having met in Berlin at the beginning of the century, overlapped and influenced the scholarly path of HUSOS: after an exchange of correspondence with Weil and the

60 ::: A NEW ORIENT

Prussian State Library, the copies and facsimiles stored in Berlin were sent to Jerusalem in 1927.[179]

The role of the Orientalist research projects looks somewhat different when we consider another iteration of the cooperation between Sachau, Horovitz, and Weil, this one involving the Prussian government. All three were involved in the recording operation run by Wilhelm Doegen at POW camps during World War I: Sachau was responsible for the field of Oriental languages (*Orientalische Sprachen*) within the Prussian Phonographic Commission that directed the project. While he did not personally handle the recordings or other research in the camps, some of his students did, including Horovitz and Weil; though the two belonged to Sachau's Arabist Berlin school, however, this project hardly provided them with the opportunity to study any Arabic dialects, which were under the purview of other researchers. Instead, Horovitz recorded speakers of Hindustani and Balochi (both from the Indo-Iranian language family); and Weil encountered primarily speakers of Tatar, Turkish, and a few related languages such as Kyrgyz and Estonian (as well as one recording in Arabic, of a Muslim call to prayer by a Tatar soldier).[180] They also contributed articles to a volume edited by Doegen: Horovitz published an article titled "The Muslims in India" (*Die Indischen Mohammedaner*), whereas Weil published one article titled "The Tatars" (*Die Tataren*) and another short article on "The Jews" (*Die Juden*) about Eastern European Jews and Yiddish—though the Jewish soldiers from the Russian Imperial Army brought to the POW camp were not among his interviewees.[181] This article of Weil's, as well as Horovitz's on Indian Muslims, were written more on the basis of personal knowledge and historical documentation than the actual recordings, which were cited only in passing.

While there were various causes for these two young scholars' participation in the recording enterprise, it amounted to a direct professional contribution, founded in their academic training, to the war effort. Horovitz reached Germany, after the outbreak of the war, having been forced to leave India, then under British rule, as a citizen of an enemy state.[182] His deep opposition to the British regime in India, and perhaps also feelings of German patriotism, led him to cooperate substantively with the propaganda arm of the German Foreign Ministry, the NfO (*Nachrichtenstelle für den Orient* or Information Bureau for the Orient). Its primary role was to foment agitation and rebellions among the nations in the Orient under the control of Germany's wartime enemies and to spread pro-German pro-

*The Science of the Orient* ::: 61

paganda in local languages.[183] Horovitz had returned to Germany to take up his appointment to the chair in Oriental Languages at the University of Frankfurt, but being well-informed on issues surrounding Indian Muslims, he also offered his services to the foreign ministry.

According to recently published archival documentation, Horovitz supported the German initiative to encourage Indian Muslim soldiers at the front and in the POW camps to rise up against the British in the name of a pan-Islamic ideology. Horovitz prepared confidential reports on the topic for the NfO, and also provided practical assistance—he mediated prisoner exchanges between India and Germany; opened, sorted, and translated letters sent to Indians in exile in Berlin before they were sent along to their destinations by the German censors; and, of course, prepared propaganda materials.[184] Horovitz's work with the NfO and his involvement in the recording enterprise when the Chair in Frankfurt had already been promised to him, had a political basis, an ideological commitment that outlasted the war: in 1928, completely outside his fields of expertise on the Orient —which included Quranic studies and classic Arabic poetry—he published the book *Indien unter britischer Herrschaft* (India under British rule), proposing a political and social analysis of the state of India and its future that foresaw the collapse of British rule.[185]

For Weil, on the other hand, the recordings were a way of developing his career studying the Orient. Alongside Arabic, he had already begun to specialize in Turkish and Persian during his doctoral studies, giving him sufficient command of the Turkic language of Tatar; as his *Doktorvater*, Sachau knew Weil's abilities well and recommended him for the role of censor of letters sent from the Orient to Tatar soldiers in the Russian Imperial Army being held in Germany: every day, over forty letters went out in Tatar, which was at that point (and into the 1920s) written in Arabic letters.[186] Sachau believed that Weil was exceptionally well-suited for the role, which presented his former student with another advantage—service as a censor effectively released him from military service on the front lines.[187] Though Weil had been no specialist before the war, reading the letters solidified his stature as an expert in Tatar and Turkic languages more generally, and he was recruited to join the audio recording teams led by Doegen, taking detailed notes throughout.[188] According to a report he submitted to Sachau, who later presented it at a meeting of the Prussian Academy of Sciences, Weil filled forty-five notebooks over the course of four months with data on Tatar history, society, and language on the basis of his conversations

62 ::: A NEW ORIENT

with the soldiers.[189] It could well be that the presentation of his work in so prestigious a forum contributed to Weil's appointment to direct the Oriental department at the Prussian State Library and to a professorship at the University of Berlin a few years later.

Weil's work on Tatars did not end there, however. Based on the recordings, he published his book *Tatarische Texte* (Tatar texts) in 1930: poems, stories, descriptions, and proverbs from Tatar daily life, as told by the captive soldiers.[190] Each text appeared in both transliteration into the Latin alphabet and in the Tatar written language (in Arabic letters), alongside translation to German, footnotes within a scientific apparatus, and (anonymized) details on the speakers and their biographical and linguistic characteristics. Weil consulted the POWs themselves regarding the material he collected, and also sought the advice of Tatar scholars he met in Berlin before publication.[191] The publication of this book—a further element in the construction of Weil's reputation as a leading scholar of Turkish, a stage to demonstrate his linguistic abilities, and an inseparable part of his list of publications—would not have been possible had Weil not directed his talents towards political and security needs in the first place.

Horovitz and Weil provide precious little detail about how the recordings were actually recorded and the informants recruited. In an extant photograph from the time of Weil's work in the camp, perhaps taken by Wilhelm Doegen himself, Weil appears sitting at a table examining his notes along with a group of Tatar soldiers, whose expressions are calm and attentive.[192] A more complex picture emerges from other reports by anthropologists working in the camp: on the one hand, there were POWs who were grateful for the break in their routine; on the other, they encountered opposition from POWs who avoided or foiled attempts to question them.[193] To critical contemporary eyes, the inherently coercive nature of research conducted in a POW camp, no matter the intentions behind it, is glaring. Even if the POWs, in theory, maintained the right to refuse to participate and enjoyed reasonable living conditions, they remained in a vulnerable and subject situation, whereas the researchers were in control, enjoying the backing of the military forces in charge of the camp.[194]

Weil did nothing to obfuscate his work with the Tatar POWs, at least not at the time. In the introduction to *Tatar Texts*, he referred to the study being conducted in the camp; considering the widespread research carried out there and at other POW camps in Europe, it may very well be that, like other scholarly contemporaries, he saw no ethical issue with it.[195] Yet there is no indication that Weil's or Horovitz's students—in Berlin, Frankfurt, and especially Jerusalem—were familiar with the exploits of their teachers during World War I, to say nothing of how the political and military context might have manifested within their scientific research and Oriental expertise.[196]

Well-known to Horovitz and Weil's students, on the other hand, were the two Jerusalem-based research enterprises they helped establish. One of these students, S. D. Goitein, was particularly well-versed in preparing *Ansab al-Ashraf*. In a note published only after his death, Goitein explains the characteristics of the exacting philological work required to produce a scientific edition of the manuscript, which was slated to be published in some ten volumes. Typically, the philologist compares different iterations of the same text. But since there were no other complete manuscripts with which to compare the essay in question, the scholar is forced to survey the manuscript, searching for parallels within it (that is, for further uses of a certain phrase that may help shed light on its meaning) and subsequently do the same with other classical Arabic essays. The pace of work was very slow and, like the concordance, sapped a substantial portion of the institute faculty's time.[197] The first volume (the fifth chronologically) was only printed in 1936, after nearly a decade of work on the manuscript;[198] a further half volume was published in 1938, and its second half—as well as an additional two volumes—came many years later.[199]

The protracted work on these two scholarly enterprises was an unavoidable consequence of the concurrence between their ambitious nature and the institute's limited budget.[200] At the same time, the commitment to two fundamental research projects on this scale, both emanating from the heart of scholarly activity in Berlin and Frankfurt, contributed greatly to the institute's reputation as a site of Oriental Studies research on par with its counterparts in Europe, certainly in Germany.[201] Time and again, reports about the institute highlighted the concordance and the publication of *Ansab al-Ashraf*, emphasizing their connections to the world of German Orientalism.[202] In terms of the ideas and materials behind them, their image, and the character of the work on them, for years these research enterprises encapsulated the institute's German Orientalist roots in the most obvious manner.

## Teachers and Scholars

On the eve of its establishment, the institute's staff was very small, consisting of only three faculty. L. A. Mayer had already begun teaching in

64 ::: A NEW ORIENT

1925. His inclusion in the faculty of the institute was a foregone conclusion; the other teacher alongside him was D. H. Baneth, his colleague as faculty fellow. Baneth's field of expertise, as demonstrated by the limited publication record that preceded his immigration to Palestine, was in the writings of medieval Muslim and Jewish religious philosophy.[203] In accordance, during the semester initiated by Horovitz's visit, he taught a weekly seminar in which the students read the philosophical novel *Hai Ibn Yakzan* by the twelfth-century essayist and physician Abu Bakr Ibn Tufayl.[204] Mayer taught a class on Palestine under the Mamluk regime and a seminar discussing the scholarly literature on the origins of Islam. Goitein, another fellow, was still teaching at the Reali High School in Haifa at the time, and the prospect of him joining the institute was not on the agenda.

Mayer's expertise in history and Baneth's in philosophy left a lacuna in one principal field—Arabic literature. As noted, the position had been intended for Avinoam Yellin, another one of the fellows; his specialties included Arabic poetry, and he was an experienced instructor.[205] But Yellin was appointed Senior Inspector of Jewish Schools by the Education Department of the Mandate Government in 1925, and his candidacy seems therefore to have fallen by the wayside. Though he never became a member of the institute after its founding, he was present at Horovitz's inaugural lectures and remained close with HUSOS personnel until his murder in 1937 amidst the violence of the Arab Revolt.[206]

In Yellin's place, the London-based Secretary of the Zionist Executive Leo Kohn proposed the one of Yellin's classmates as a candidate, the English-born Levi (Lewis) Billig (1897–1936), who also held a master's degree from Cambridge.[207] Billig was interested primarily in research on the *Shi'a* according to early Muslim sources, and also had excellent command of Hebrew. This was emphasized in the curriculum vitae he passed along to Kohn—a reminder that the choice of candidates to teach at the institute depended not only on their scientific abilities and fields of interest, but also on their ability to lecture in the Hebrew language.[208] The university invited Billig to leave London in February, and thanks to an accelerated process facilitated by Kohn, by April he was already on a ship sailing for Palestine, arriving in time to meet Horovitz in Jerusalem during the latter's visit to the city to inaugurate the institute.[209] At the institute's faculty meeting in Jerusalem prior to Horovitz's return to Frankfurt, Billig was selected to head its research endeavors.[210]

The insistence on recruiting a young faculty member trained at an En-

*The Science of the Orient* ::: 65

glish university proceeded Horovitz's desire to form connections between the School of Oriental Studies and the English world of Oriental Studies, not only that of Central Europe.[211] Recall that Horovitz had encountered this world himself during his extended stay in India. It is also safe to assume that the recruitment of an English faculty member helped both to strengthen bonds with the university's supporters residing in London, and to enhance the institute's appeal in the eyes of the Mandate authorities.[212] Noteworthy too is the fact that the "institute" (*makhon*) was known only in English as a *School* of Oriental Studies; even before its establishment, the Jerusalemite institution had thus explicitly linked its name with that of the London University body then of the same name, later the School of Oriental and African Studies, or SOAS, which opened its gates in 1917.[213]

Unlike the School of Oriental Studies in Jerusalem, its British predecessor was founded with the clear goal of serving primarily as an imperial training institution to teach Oriental and African languages to government officials, officers, merchants, and missionaries. Still, the founders of the British iteration sought to integrate not only practical training but also research into its activities, an aspect which became increasingly central to its operations beginning in the 1930s.[214] Therefore, while the explicit goals of the identically-named institutions were quite different, and there is no real resemblance between the activities they conducted during the first decades of their existence, Magnes and Horovitz nevertheless clearly explored various avenues for establishing connections with the field of British Orientalism—not only the German one—during the Hebrew University's first years.

Alongside the three instructors—Mayer, Baneth, and Billig—research assistants also took part in the institute's operations, most of them boasting doctoral training in Oriental philology at German universities. Most prominent among these were the Frankfurt-born Walter Joseph Fischel (1902–1973), who held one doctorate in Political Science (*rerum politicarum*) from Frankfurt and another from Giessen;[215] Noah Braun (1892–1960), born in Krakow and awarded a doctorate by the University of Heidelberg;[216] Issachar (Bernhard) Joel (1900–1977), born in Hamburg, studied under Horovitz as a student in Frankfurt before returning to Hamburg, where he earned a doctoral degree in Semitic languages and became a certified rabbi;[217] and, later, Meir Moshe (Max) Bravmann (1909–1977), born in Eppingen in southwest Germany, who earned his doctorate in Semitic languages at the University of Breslau.[218] Some even worked without a salary

66 ::: A NEW ORIENT

for a time in hopes of finding a position at the institute or elsewhere at the university, in which they saw their professional futures.

These four research assistants never found tenured positions at the School of Oriental Studies, however. Despite appropriate training at German universities, none of them had filed their doctoral dissertations at one of the two primary Orientalist centers from which the institute's founders drew their inspiration: Berlin, and after 1914, Frankfurt. Of course, the circumstances of their personal lives and—as internal correspondence implies—estimation of their scientific capabilities also influenced their advancement. Nonetheless, that they remained outside the institute's plans suggests the importance in Jerusalem of these networks of connections emanating from Berlin and Frankfurt, two cities where, beginning at a certain point in the twentieth century, Jews were able to hold professorships in the field of Oriental Studies.

The incorporation in 1928 of two additional Horovitz students as instructors at the institute bolsters this impression. In 1927, the instructors asked that another research assistant be brought in to work on the concordance. Yosef Yo'el Rivlin (1889–1971) had just returned from Frankfurt after completing his doctoral work under Horovitz (on law in the Quran). Born in Jerusalem and also a student of David Yellin, among others, Rivlin was plugged into the cultural milieu of the Old *Yishuv*—the Jewish communities who lived in Palestine before the European-Zionist immigration waves that began in the 1880s.[219] Equipped with the appropriate philological training, Rivlin was offered a position as research assistant at the institute.[220] Meanwhile, having accumulated some experience teaching the institute's students—most of whom were graduates of teaching seminaries—Mayer, Baneth, and Billig identified the need for a preparatory course (*mekhina*) in order to improve the students' level in Arabic language and knowledge of Arab and Muslim history and culture if they hoped to meet the academic standards characteristic of European Orientalist training.[221] Rivlin—a childhood speaker of Arabic with experience as a teacher, training in Germany, and the personal acquaintance of Horovitz—was an excellent candidate for the role of Arabic instructor, as was Goitein, who had finally decided to leave the Reali School in Haifa and join the HUSOS faculty.[222] Both began teaching in 1928: Rivlin taught (literary) Arabic for beginners, and Goitein the history of Islam and Arabic grammar.[223] In subsequent years, they were fully integrated into the institute's faculty and began teaching regular classes as well.

The 1930s saw a gradual diminution of the direct connection with Germany. During the winter of 1931, Horovitz suffered a stroke and died at only fifty-six. The death shocked his students in Frankfurt and Jerusalem; after hearing word of his death, classes were cancelled in mourning for a day.[224] In a report to the university's board of governors, Billig described the immensity of this loss to the institute, now without the person who had skillfully guided the development of Oriental Studies at the Hebrew University thanks to his "administrative experience, his prestige in the world of scholarship, his perspicacity, and his consideration towards his colleagues."[225]

The administration of the University of Frankfurt decided, meanwhile, to award Horovitz's chair to his old colleague from Berlin, Gotthold Weil. When word reached the administration of the Hebrew University, it likewise invited Weil to succeed Horovitz in his role in Jerusalem, as head of the School of Oriental Studies.[226] Like Horovitz, Weil received the title of Visiting Director and remained in Frankfurt. On assuming the role, Weil clarified that he had no intention of diverging from the path charted for it by his predecessor, and applauded the research projects and the praise they were earning from scholars across Europe (Weil was, recall, personally involved in the work on *Ansab al-Ashraf*), as well as the promising teaching faculty.[227] For the time being, the institute's Berlin-Frankfurt-Jerusalem triangular axis of influence was to remain intact.

In early 1933, thanks to a generous contribution from the Jewish banker and collector Percival David of Bombay, the first endowed chair at the institute could be established, in the art and archaeology of the Near East. The chair made possible the awarding of a professorship to L. A. Mayer; he thus retired from his role at the British Department of Antiquities and dedicated himself to work at the institute.[228] His scholarly interests, unique within the landscape of research at HUSOS, thus found a final institutionalized form. To celebrate the granting of the chair, Rivlin, translator of the Quran into Hebrew, wrote seven comical *Suras* on the atmosphere at the institute. Yet news about the Nazi party's rise to power in Germany dampened the joy.[229] Indeed, the first days of Hitler's reign and the legislation of the Nazi race laws would profoundly impact the fate of Jewish scholars in Germany, and later across Europe, as well as the development of the Hebrew University of Jerusalem. Fifteen exiled European professors, refugees from their countries, joined the university between 1933 and 1939. Like early-career scholars and additional students, their integration into the university's fold was made possible by donations, from both individuals and Jewish organizations.[230]

68 ::: A NEW ORIENT

The refugees from Europe brought on board by the School of Oriental Studies were all trained at German-language universities; nonetheless, they expanded the fields of instruction and research at HUSOS.

"The Law for Restoration of the Professional Civil Service" (*Gesetz zur Wiederherstellung des Berufsbeamtentums*), legislated in Germany in April 1933, forced state employees not of "Aryan" extraction to retire. This prompted Gotthold Weil to lose his position at the University of Frankfurt in 1934.[231] After protracted negotiations with the administration of the Hebrew University, Weil decided to immigrate to Palestine, where he would become director of the National and University Library. In so doing he left his position as director of HUSOS but remained on the faculty as a Professor of Arabic as well as Turkish, which he had continued to research more deeply during his years in Berlin.[232] L. A. Mayer replaced him, the first director of the institute to actually reside in Jerusalem.[233]

Another immigrant scholar joining the institute was Hans Jakob (Hayim) Polotsky (1905–1991), born in Switzerland to parents from the Crimean Peninsula and raised in Berlin. Polotsky, by all accounts blessed with a great talent for languages, was especially interested in Egyptian, which he studied at the University of Berlin before completing his doctorate in Semitic languages at the University of Göttingen. After reaching Palestine he found a position as a junior lecturer of Egyptology;[234] this field, though closely tracked by the university leadership from the moment the institute was founded, had never developed thanks to two frequently overlapping difficulties: the challenge of convincing a renowned scholar to come to Jerusalem, and the lack of budgetary resources.[235]

Weil and Polotsky were refugees obliged to seek out alternatives to their planned academic careers.[236] They joined the faculty under different conditions than their predecessors at the institute, who had set out for Jerusalem fully intending to build their professional futures there.[237] Nevertheless, their joining the institute only continued to reinforce its connection to the German scientific legacy, certainly as seen from the outside. This legacy soon became the target of aspersions cast at HUSOS in these years by an investigative report known as the "Hartog Committee" (officially: The Survey Committee of the Hebrew University of Jerusalem).

The committee to examine the Hebrew University, led by the British-Jewish chemist Sir Philip Hartog (1864–1947), was established in 1933 by order of the Board of Governors, prompted by a certain tension regarding the balance of power within both the university administration and the board itself.[238] Hartog had extensive experience in academic management and reform within the British Empire: as academic secretary of the University of London; a member of the Board of the University of Calcutta, which had ushered in a general reform of the Indian higher education system in 1920; head of another commission bearing his name in 1929 that led to the reform of elementary education in India; as well as the vice chancellor of the University of Dhaka.[239]

The Hartog Committee Report on the Hebrew University was published in 1934 after its members spent several months in the country meeting various stakeholders, in the academy and elsewhere. It suggested a fundamental overhaul of the administrative structure of the university, including the restriction of Magnes's authorities, the formation of an Academic Senate, and a new Executive Committee. The report also addressed the situation within each of the university's various departments, including the School of Oriental Studies. Academic Oriental Studies was another field in which Hartog had experience, as one of the central driving forces behind the establishment of SOAS in London.[240] The Oriental Studies Institute in Jerusalem was also familiar to him from his term serving as President of the Friends of the Hebrew University in Britain, moreover, and he had even expressed support for HUSOS and its activities.[241] Nevertheless, the committee he headed considered significant changes to its operations necessary: it "has been and still is very severely criticized by many" not due to any disdain for its personnel but because it has "no other object in view than to give the students a picture of the Moslem civilization of the past." This was not enough to justify the existence of a special institute; the subject could be integrated into the general humanities.[242]

Members of the committee expressed certain doubts, which they presented as those of critical voices within the *Yishuv*, regarding the relevance of the institute's research endeavors or the study of Muslim archaeology and art to the reality of life in the Middle East. They called for both research and instruction at the institute to be broadened to include subjects touching on the study of the modern Middle East, as well as modern Arabic.[243] Put simply, the Hartog Committee suggested the institute infuse a more applied approach to its operations as distinct from the philological research that had characterized it to that point. This was the spirit of both London's SOAS and the Seminar for Oriental Languages (*Seminar für Orientalische Sprachen*, SOS), the latter being founded at the University of Berlin in 1887 with the express goal of training students to conduct business and create diplomatic

## 70 ::: A NEW ORIENT

ties in the Orient. Traditionally, the seminar was directed by professors with philological training, and well-known Orientalists taught there; Eugen Mittwoch was its director at one point.[244] Indeed, the SOS operated within the university, but was separate from academic Oriental Studies.

Responding directly to the report in the name of HUSOS, Mayer and Goitein suggested the addition of a course (comprised of lecture and practicum) taught by the Jewish Agency's Alfred Bonne (also spelled Bonné, 1899–1959), entitled "State, Society, and Economy in the Near East."[245] Bonne, born in Nuremberg, held a doctoral degree in Economics from the University of Munich and served as a member of the Jewish Agency's Institute for Economic Research; after immigrating to Palestine in 1925, he founded the "Economic Archives for the Near East," a database collecting information about the regional economy. His teaching at the university focused on economic issues—his field of expertise—and he did not join the institute full time, instead continuing his work at the Jewish Agency, where he became director of the Institute for Economic Research.[246] While Bonne was a product of German academia, he was also the first lecturer at HUSOS not primarily trained in the Orientalist-philological tradition, whose approach to the research topics did not emerge out of laborious textual analysis; in this sense he remained an isolated minority among the institute's other German expatriates.

Another product of the Hartog Committee Report was the recruitment of Isaac (Yitzhak) Shamosh, born in Aleppo, who in 1937 began teaching "Practical Arabic"—modern oral and written literary Arabic, writing skills, and translation. Shamosh, who did not yet hold a doctorate, was also brought in to teach only part time.[247] This was the final appointment to the HUSOS staff before the late 1940s; no new members or fields of instruction were added. The central research endeavors of the institute, the topics taught there, and the biographical and professional backgrounds of the majority of its members, were the most glaring proof of the influence inherited from the study of Arabic and Islam in Berlin and Frankfurt.

### Outside the Institute: Abraham Shalom Yahuda and Israel Ben-Ze'ev

This picture of the institute's members—of Ashkenazi origin, hailing from an explicitly German background in all cases but that of Billig, and for the most part previous personal acquaintance with Horovitz, from either Frankfurt or Berlin—in itself goes some way towards clarifying why the institute's faculty, across the ranks, included hardly any Jews of Sephardic or Mizrahi origin (which was true of the university's other departments as well). It dovetails nicely with the sociological analysis of the world of academia put forward by Pierre Bourdieu: when the old guard at an academic institution recruits those destined, after a course of training and professional development, to become their colleagues and heirs—they tend to choose those they feel comfortable with and similar to, not only in professional background but also their habitus, the particular world from which they have come to the institution.[248]

The historical context only adds to this: from the perspective of the founders and administrators of the Hebrew University, their young institution was in need of intellectual achievements that might secure its national and international stature, achievements that would not pale next to those of Western institutions, so that their university would not be suspected of "Levantinism," that is, of being a pallid and inferior Oriental replica of a Western cultural phenomenon.[249] As Adi Livny has shown, during the university's early years Magnes and others cautioned against the creation of a "Levantine" system of higher education in Palestine in no small part as a central argument against the establishment of competing institutions in Jerusalem.[250] Magnes, like Chaim Weizmann, Horovitz, and other decision-makers, matured and trained at Western academic institutions. Naturally enough, they hoped to acquire international—or rather, Western—prestige by filling university positions with others trained to standards suitable to this goal.

In this light, the cases of two Jerusalem-born scholars of Oriental Studies—who despite undergoing Orientalist training in Germany never joined the School of Oriental Studies—stand out: Abraham Shalom Yahuda (1877–1951) and Israel Ben-Ze'ev (born Wolfensohn, 1899–1980). Yahuda, born to a father of Baghdadi and a mother of German-Baghdadi origin, specialized in the Arabic language and its influence on Hebrew. He had been exposed since childhood to the learned Arabic and Hebrew milieux that flourished in late nineteenth-century Jerusalem, as well as its cosmopolitan intellectual elite. This introduction prompted him to travel to Europe to continue his studies at various German universities; his doctoral thesis was written under the influential Orientalist Theodor Nöldecke, Chair of Oriental Languages at the University of Strasbourg.[251]

Another one of Yahuda's teachers was Ignác Goldziher, who was in constant touch with his student. When, in correspondence no earlier than 1919,

Goldziher refused the university founders' offer to direct the Oriental Institute in Jerusalem, he instead offered Yahuda, who was already a professor of rabbinic language and literature at the University of Madrid.[252] Indeed, during discussions in the early 1920s about the composition of the Hebrew University, Yahuda's name was floated as a potential scholar in charge of Arabic language instruction and the Bible.[253] After corresponding on the matter with David Yellin and Eliezer Ben-Yehuda, Yahuda left Madrid in 1920 and returned to live in his hometown.[254]

Yet, as plans for the university's establishment materialized, Yahuda's position within them began to weaken, and he was not ultimately appointed to the role. In recent years, as scholars became newly interested in Yahuda, the decision not to appoint him to the position despite the initial intent has also been discussed, typically as an example representative of the exclusion of Sephardic and Mizrahi Jews from the Hebrew University's ranks.[255] It remains somewhat unclear what effective justification there was for Yahuda not to join the university faculty. Perhaps there were disagreements in negotiations over the nature of the position, and Yahuda ultimately turned down the position; in any case, negotiations over his employment ceased, and he left Jerusalem within several months.[256]

Yet in the eyes of Yahuda and his acquaintances from the Sephardic and Mizrahi milieux of Jerusalem, who published articles backing him in newspapers associated with their circles, like *Do'ar Hayom* and *Hed Hamizrah*, Yahuda's political stances were the essential factor: positions on Zionism, the Arab Question, and Jewish regional integration that had their roots in his being Jerusalem-born rather than a European immigrant. It was Yahuda who advanced this argument himself, fusing his personal story with the emergence of the university as an entirely foreign, Western entity refusing to integrate itself in the Orient. The university administration, he explained in the late 1920s, chose to ignore the locally-born "and gives precedence to students who have only just completed their studies in Europe," whereas even those few locals who managed to make inroads at the institute, "were made subordinate to teachers who have just arrived in the country and are inferior to them in both knowledge and their ability to teach effectively."[257]

The tale of Israel Ben-Ze'ev, twenty-two years Yahuda's junior, can be seen in many ways as a continuation of the latter's. Descended from an Ashkenazi family that immigrated to Palestine in the early nineteenth century, his course of training also incorporated both local and German institutions. He studied at the Arab Teachers College in Jerusalem, Dar al-Mu'allimin (later:

The Arab College) and completed his doctoral dissertation at the University of Cairo, in Arabic, on Jews in the Arab world during the advent of Islam; in fact, the renowned writer and literary scholar Taha Hussein, one of his examiners, wrote the introduction to the book published on its basis.[258]

Yet Ben-Ze'ev did not content himself with the Cairene doctorate: in the early 1930s, the Prussian Education and Culture Ministry—then headed by Carl Heinrich Becker—approved his request to study for an abbreviated period in Germany and complete an additional doctorate in Semitic languages on the seventh-century Yemenite Jewish convert to Islam, Ka'b al-Ahbar, on the basis of sources from the *hadith*. He crossed paths with HUSOS while studying in Germany: initially he became a student of Josef Horovitz's in Frankfurt, but after the latter's sudden death he moved to Berlin to study under Gotthold Weil, among others, during the brief period after Horovitz's death and before Weil's relocation to Frankfurt.[259] Upon completing the doctorate in 1933, he returned to Egypt and taught at the University of Cairo and the Dar al-'Ulum, the local teacher training seminary; but he longed for Jerusalem, where he hoped to earn a position at HUSOS—this was apparently the reason for his travelling to study with Horovitz in Frankfurt and complete his second doctorate in the first place.[260]

While in Egypt, Ben-Ze'ev made sure to stay in direct touch with both the Hebrew University and the Jewish Agency.[261] His professional future in Cairo seemed less than promising, as no tenured teaching position was likely to be made available to him in Egypt. When a position supervising Arabic instruction in Jewish schools was created by the Jewish National Council, it was offered to Ben-Ze'ev—he was an experienced teacher with proven fluency in Arabic and philological training from a German university on good terms with Jewish Agency personnel—and in 1939 he left Egypt with his family to return to Jerusalem. He remained in the supervisor position until his retirement in the 1960s without ever successfully earning a position at the Hebrew University.[262]

Ostensibly, Ben-Ze'ev possessed all the appropriate attributes to become part of the HUSOS faculty: extensive and fundamental knowledge of the Arabic language, German Orientalist training from the former heads of the Jerusalemite institute, and a wide network of contacts in the Egyptian intellectual world that, as the following chapter illustrates, was of the utmost importance in achieving the political ambitions that stood behind the institute's founding. Nevertheless, he was left on the outside looking in. A. S. Yahuda claimed that—like in his own case—with Ben-Ze'ev, who

74 ::: A NEW ORIENT

was in many ways his protégé, the reason was the arrogance of the institute faculty: either German or somehow associated with Germanness, they felt themselves superior to those born in Palestine: "You, who have tasted the bitterness and blows of Mount Scopus's ministers," he wrote to Ben-Ze'ev, "your pinky is thicker than the very waist of the Goiteins and the Baneths and their whole crew that gazes down upon the locals as people deficient of the 'scientific' purity inherited from Germany."[263] Indeed, at various opportunities, a number of institute and university personnel did express negative opinions of Ben-Ze'ev and his talents, especially on the basis of their familiarity with him as supervisor of Arabic language studies.[264] For his part, Ben-Ze'ev labelled them derisively as "the wise men of Mount Scopus, most of them bereft of creativity, intellectual featherweights who [have not published] a piece of research worthy of the name."[265] Yahuda and Ben-Ze'ev, then, were two dominant personalities who identified with the people of the Old *Yishuv* and subsequently became symbols, in their own eyes and others', of the exclusion of locals from the School of Oriental Studies, relegating them to "the margins (or entirely outside) of the newly formed academic milieu in Jerusalem."[266]

## A GERMAN IMAGE: ON THE CHARACTER
## OF THE GERMAN LEGACY

A photograph taken by the Hebrew University's public relations department in 1963 shows HUSOS faculty members Martin (Meir) Plessner and Meir Jacob Kister standing one alongside the other. Plessner—pipe in mouth and bowtie round neck—gravely examines a document presented to him by Kister. Behind them stand row after row of square drawers: the drawers of the Concordance Room, which rise above the figures in the photograph and run on past its edges. Kister is holding a single index card soon to find its place in one of these drawers.

Born in Posen (then in Germany, now the Polish town of Poznan), Plessner (1900–1973) completed his doctoral dissertation in Breslau, later arriving in Frankfurt, where he planned to develop his academic career under the tutelage of Horovitz and Weil. The Nazi rise to power scuttled these plans, and he immigrated to Palestine, but the circumstances of his arrival delayed his incorporation into HUSOS; he taught Arabic at the high school level for many years before earning an appointment as professor in the Department of Arabic Language and Literature in 1955.[267] In the eyes

*Martin Plessner (right) and M. J. Kister in the Concordance Room, January 6, 1963. Courtesy of Braun Werner / Hebrew University Photo Archive*

of his students and colleagues at the institute, Plessner's manner of dress, his etiquette, and his overly strict approach in and out of class—that is, in his habitus, but also in his philological studies on the history of Islamic science—were a relic of the German world that birthed the School of Oriental Studies in Jerusalem.[268] Kister (1914–2010) on the other hand, though born in Galicia, belonged to the next generation of lecturers at the institute, who had received their training on the Orient not at German universities but as students at the Hebrew University. Though he never studied directly with Plessner, Kister was trained by others of his academic generation, the HUSOS faculty members of the 1940s: Baneth, Goitein, Mayer, and Polotsky, as well as an older Weil. He said they hailed "from the German school excelling in pedantry and precision."[269]

This impression of erudite philology was also a product of the fields taught and studied at the institute. Indeed, save for rare exceptions, their courses dealt with early Islam and texts in classical Arabic. A list of courses and sections proposed by HUSOS for the 1948–49 academic year illustrates this clearly: it included the Theory of Arabic Writing and Readings in Sources for Muslim Art (Mayer); Exercises on the Historical Essay *Futuh al-Buldan* by al-Baladhuri and Introduction to Turkish Language (Weil);

76 ::: A NEW ORIENT

Introduction to Studies in the Muslim Orient and Persian Prose (Goitein); Readings in the Writings of the Poet Abu Tammam and the Historian al-Ghazali (Baneth); Chapters in Arabic Grammar, Geʿez, and Introduction to Egyptian Language (Polotsky); and Readings in the Quran (Rivlin).[270] These courses are mostly on advanced topics; throughout the Mandate period, recall, the university offered master's and doctoral degrees but no bachelor's.

Students entering the institute knew both its research initiatives and its library well. Some had even been research assistants in the preparation of the concordance. These, at least, certainly fit the image of German toil. In the studies of individual institute instructors, however, one finds subjects that—while not foreign to the world of German research—fit rather less comfortably within the classical philological spirit: Mayer, we know, had already moved towards the study of art and archaeology soon after arriving in Palestine; Goitein developed a research interest in Yemeni language and folklore;[271] and Baneth's primary field of research was in Jewish-Arabic philosophical writings at a time when the institute itself did not address Jewish subjects at all. One should distinguish, then, between the habitus of Germanness and a professional Germanness, and between expressions of Germanness within the institutional setting and those outside it.

Even within the framework of the institution, as this chapter has shown, an examination of the specific sources of that "German legacy" discloses set of more subtle characteristics. It began with the meeting in early twentieth-century Berlin between the Jewish students of Eduard Sachau (alongside Carl Heinrich Becker), part of the Berlin school of Arabic studies trained in philological editing and publication work that influenced their eventual research agendas as well as the creation of HUSOS's large research initiatives. Most were also students at the Higher Institute of Jewish Studies, and therefore fused Oriental Studies with Jewish Studies. Even Josef Horovitz, who was not one of those to study at the Higher Institute, did nevertheless found the first chair that officially combined Oriental Studies and Jewish Studies. From that perch, he trained numerous students, some of whom were among the first instructors and scholars at HUSOS.

The shape of this German—or rather Berliner—tradition was not a given or a foregone conclusion, nor was it a monolith. In discussions about the establishment of the Hebrew University and the shaping of the humanities there, various scholars—including the father of Islamic Studies, Ignác Goldziher—proposed various approaches to Islam within a university that

*The Science of the Orient* ::: 77

was, first and foremost, Hebrew; underlying this was a desire to buttress the field of Jewish Studies, which in Germany was taught primarily in extra-university settings. The shape eventually taken by these studies at the university had everything to do with the organizational circumstances and the scholarly (and, as I show in the following chapter, political) ideology of Josef Horovitz, Magnes's old Berlin acquaintance.

Moreover, and in contravention of the picture painted by the existing scholarly literature, Horovitz did not arrive in a land unsowed. L. A. Mayer —a Galician Jew and product of the University of Vienna, with scholarly interests mostly quite distant from the HUSOS founder—deeply impacted the formation of Oriental Studies at the Hebrew University; his centrality at the university and to HUSOS during the years of the British Mandate reflects another scholarly aspect of Germanness that had to do with his training in the Vienna of the multiethnic Habsburg Empire. Whereas HUSOS's philological research projects were born in Berlin and Frankfurt, Mayer's work —which the institute often materially provided for—though itself philological, was far more local; Yosef Rivlin, too, represented a connection to the local. Meanwhile, Avinoam Yellin and, later, Levi Billig afforded a different connection—scholarly and, in the case of Billig, one of habitus—to the British Empire, within which and with the support of which the university was established. In any case, the School of Oriental Studies was certainly not "staffed by professors who were brought from Germany" by Magnes, as one study claims.[272] On the other hand, an examination of its faculty does reveal that those with origins outside the German-speaking world mostly failed to find their place within its research and teaching endeavors during the Mandate period. This had to do not only with the core subjects taught at HUSOS, which demanded the type of training received by students of Semitic or Oriental philology at German universities, but—no less—belonging to networks of connections that had taken shape back in Europe.

So far, discussion has surrounded the German legacy within the confines of lecture hall and library. Yet the transfer of Orientalist knowledge from Berlin and Frankfurt to Palestine took place within a wider context: the Zionist context out of which emerged the idea of the Hebrew University of Jerusalem. The following chapter continues to examine HUSOS during the Mandate period, but focuses on the political mission leaning upon the scientific work of its scholars: the laying of foundations for intellectual affinity between Jews and Arabs.

# 2 : "WITH ITS BACK TO THE ORIENT"?
## THE SCHOOL OF ORIENTAL STUDIES AND THE
## QUESTION OF THE ARAB INTELLECTUALS

Even in the early stages of its planning, the founders of the Hebrew University saw it as a Jewish cultural center that would address the Arab population as well. "My hopes for the university are high—surely Arabs too will enter, and perhaps they will join its ranks not only as students but also as professors, making our university the true site of political rapprochement."[1] When Chaim Weizmann presented the idea of the university in his speech before the Eleventh Zionist Congress (September 1913), he explained that "a university where space is made for the Arabs and the Turkish shall pave the road to the friendly relations we anticipate between ourselves and the surrounding nations."[2] During the ceremony marking the laying of the university's corner stone in 1918, granted, Weizmann declared it inconceivable that a Jerusalemite university not be Jewish, and that it was meant first and foremost for Jews, and yet added that the university would "gladly welcome members of all races and religious affiliations," quoting from Isaiah 56:7 regarding the universal stature of the Temple: "For my house shall be called a house of prayer for all peoples."[3]

Weizmann may have chosen these words in accordance with a British request addressed to him several months earlier, preceding his speech at the reception for the Zionist delegation (*Va'ad hatzirim le'Eretz Israel* headed by Weizmann) held on Mount Scopus, not to agitate the non-Jews: to emphasize in his speech that the university would be open to all, and especially to "our Palestinian neighbors."[4] Still, he would echo the idea seven years later, at the opening ceremony held on Mount Scopus on April 1, 1925: "But a University is nothing if it is not universal. It must stand not only for the pursuit of every form of knowledge which the mind of man embraces, but also for a commonwealth of learning, freely open to all men and women of every creed and race. Within the precincts of these Schools political strife and division cease . . . Our University would not be true to itself or to Jewish traditions, if it were not a house of study for all peoples and more especially for all the peoples of Palestine."[5]

Among the crowd hearing Weizmann's universalist vision was the rector of the Egyptian University (later the University of Cairo) Ahmed Lutfi al-Sayyid (1873–1963) who, in response to the Hebrew University's invitation, represented the Egyptian government at the request of its Prime Minister.[6] Owing to Lutfi al-Sayyid's public and official stature, his participation prompted outraged responses from the local Palestinian Arab populace —much as it did in his own country. A day before the ceremony, when the university made public the scholar's arrival, an unsigned editorial in the Jaffa-based *Filastin* attacked him: in agreeing to participate in an event, the sole aim of which is "political propaganda, since contemporary science does not use the dead Hebrew language . . . Professor Ahmed Lutfi al-Sayyid cedes the scientific prestige in which his Palestinian brothers had held him."[7] In response to harsh criticism lobbed at Lutfi al-Sayyid back in Egypt as well, the scholar published a clarification in the Egyptian press after his return, explaining that he and the Egyptian government believed that the invitation had come from a scientific institution with no connection to politics; only upon arriving in Jerusalem had he discovered that the event served as cover for Zionist propaganda, and that the language of studies at the university was to be Hebrew.[8]

The Lutfi al-Sayyid episode, which predated the School of Oriental Studies, effectively incorporates numerous aspects of the issue at the center of this chapter: the scientific and personal connections between the scholars of HUSOS and Arab and Muslim scholars and intellectuals, in light of the Hebrew University's universal vision; the expertise of its German-Jewish scholars of Oriental Studies; and the Jewish-Arab conflict during the British Mandate. The previous chapter described the process by which HUSOS was founded and how instruction and research there were established. The current chapter focuses not on the research and instruction themselves, but how these served as a platform for the creation of working relations and friendships with Arab and Muslim scholars in Palestine, neighboring Middle Eastern states, and beyond. These connections were the manifestation of one of the central goals of the institute's establishment, as formulated many times by its founders and pioneers: encouraging intellectual affinity between Jews and Arabs.

In an effort to understand how the German Orientalist heritage and the intensification of research into Arabic language studies, Islam, and Muslim history impacted the professional and personal relationships between Jewish and Arab scholars, in this chapter I will examine the vision, within the university framework, of affinity between the peoples while at the same time seeking to legitimize its very existence both within the Arab world and beyond; trace the scale and nature of these relations on the basis of archival sources and historical newspapers, employing a number of prominent examples; and through analysis of the sequence of events leading to the failure of one of the central initiatives at the time of the institute's founding —recruiting an Arab faculty member—explain why, in the final analysis, thanks to the Zionist context out of which the Hebrew University emerged and, to some degree, also the German scientific criteria upheld by HUSOS faculty, the institute was unable to realize the vision of Arab-Jewish affinity proclaimed at its founding.

Though the question of Arabs and Muslims and their place within the university was broached in the earliest conversations regarding its establishment, the first operative steps on the subject took place in the 1920s, in internal correspondence and debates among the various committees planning the structure of the university. At a meeting convened by Menachem Ussishkin in April 1922 to examine the "foundation of a faculty of Oriental Studies," the participants—including Ahad Ha'am, Eliezer Ben-Yehuda, Josef Klausner, and L. A. Mayer (the only explicit Oriental Studies expert present)—presented their thoughts regarding the establishment of an Orientalist department within the university. Rather than the academic content of the department's activities, the discussions focused on the actual necessity of its opening. One of the participants, the prominent German-Jewish scholar and Zionist activist Heinrich Loewe (1869–1951), commented that "this department is also necessary for the purpose of creating a bridge between the Jews and the Arabs. It will provide the opportunity to show the extent of Jewish wisdom and prove that there is, on the one hand, an opposition between the Semitic spirit and the European one, and on the other that there are sides to Jews and Arabs that are identical."[9]

Why this discussion had been convened in the first place is clarified in a letter sent by Hugo Bergmann to Chaim Weizmann several months previous, in early January 1922. A troubled Bergmann warned Weizmann that the British government favored the opening of a British university in Jerusalem, towards which a reasonable first step would be the opening of an Orientalist research institute to include, among other positions, a Professor of Arabic and a Professor of Hebrew.[10] Bergmann was apprehensive that such a move might harm the standing of the soon-to-be-founded Hebrew University and create unwanted competition. He therefore recommended that they "begin immediate work on the creation of an Oriental Department . . . [and] publish at once the announcement of the opening of such an institution in the autumn," emphasizing that "the supporters of the English College plan oppose our university in that it will be accessible only to Jews. It seems to me that now is an opportune moment to state that an Arabic Chair with Arabic as the language of instruction is to be opened."[11]

The words of Loewe and Bergmann quoted here represent the two faces of the institute's political purpose: to establish a bridge to the Arab-Muslim intellectual world on the one hand, and to repudiate the notion that the Hebrew University was exclusively Jewish on the other. One of the standard-bearers for the prospect that the Orientalist institute at the university might help advance such mutual understanding, both before and after its establishment, was the chancellor and later president, J. L. Magnes;[12] an important ally in this approach to the role of the institute was its founder and first director, Josef Horovitz. Horovitz's commitment to the idea of Jewish-Arab affinity was well-known, and the Jewish Agency even considered approaching him, as an expert on Arab affairs, to lead the institutional effort to build the relationship between the Zionist movement and Arab and Muslim countries.[13] For him, this commitment was of different origins than it was for the university's chancellor, who in a speech memorializing Horovitz addressed the idea that the latter "was not a Zionist" but hoped "that above all quarrels and disputes a deep understanding of Semitic origins might help in the creation of humane relationships."[14]

In recent years, scholarship has examined the nature of Horovitz's views: based on his experience as a professor at the Mohammedan Anglo-Oriental College, Aligarh (between 1907 and 1914), and the friendly relations he formed with Muslim scholars there, the German-Jewish Orientalist developed an anti-imperial approach, opposed British rule in both India and Palestine, and supported joint Semitic organizing against the British.[15] In an article published in Germany, he opined that inviting Lord Balfour to the recent opening ceremony of the university had been a bitter mistake sure to associate the university with the British authorities and undermine the establishment of relations with the Arab world, but hoped that the founding of an Orientalist institute might be some consolation.[16] Horovitz also laid out the ideological motive behind the establishment of the institute in a 1928 letter:

The idea was to establish a school for the study of the East, its languages and literatures, its history and civilization, and in which more especially the Arabic and the Islamic world were to be considered. The school was to undertake work connected with these subjects and to serve as a center for all those who are interested in engaging in the pursuance of these studies. It was hoped that the work to be undertaken would be such as to be appreciated by savants of the Arabic-speaking countries; and that in its own way, i.e., by showing that there was a ground of intellectual interests common to Jewish and Arabic scholars, the Institute might also help to promote the good feeling between these two communities."[17]

The pioneering scholars of the institute, who were partners in shaping its image, also saw in its activities an opportunity to foster Jewish-Arab common cause and affinity between the two peoples. In their eyes, the emphasis was not only on the research itself, but also on instruction, which would help diminish the foreignness of the two peoples, especially from the Jewish and perhaps primarily the European-Jewish perspective. Even before the establishment of the institute, L. A. Mayer expressed hope that "with time, this institute will become a meeting-place for Arabs and Jews interested in the history of Arab culture."[18] D. H. Baneth, in a letter to the university administration, addressed the question of Arabic language studies at the School of Oriental Studies, explaining that "a fair and in-depth knowledge of the language as well as the religious and secular culture of the Arabs is necessary to prepare the hearts of our young generation to find the correct approach to the people in whose midst we reside."[19] Levi Billig declared that "in the School of Oriental Studies we hope to advance the study of Arabic and also to disseminate an understanding of Arabic culture, which is so foreign to Jews brought up in the west or among Slavs."[20]

In an unsigned memorandum the institute often distributed in its early years (written by the institute's instructors and approved by Horovitz), the pursuit of intellectual affinity was in fact tied to the history of relations between the Jews and the Arabs: "The university . . . is entirely free to pursue its own policy of rapprochement with the Arabs. It is felt that understanding of common cultures leads to mutual sympathy, such as existed between Jews and Moslems in the Middle Ages, and that if Jews and Arabs met first of all in the intellectual, cultural and social spheres of life, a betterment of political relations might also result."[21]

The parallel with relations between Jews and Muslims during the Middle Ages was raised again in a letter written by Baneth and Billig that once more emphasized the institute's role in dispelling this foreignness of Arab culture among the Jews. The French Catholic Orientalist Louis Massignon (1883–1962) had sent the university a proposal: in order to advance reconciliation and find common ground between Jews and Muslims in Palestine, the Hebrew University should publish medieval essays written in Judaeo-Arabic—except that, instead of the Hebrew letters of the original writings, they now be transliterated into Arabic letters.[22] The effort to achieve inter-religious mutual understanding was significant for Massignon, who devoted much of his life to encouraging relations between Christians and Muslims, in Europe as well as in Arab countries and other countries of the Orient.[23] Baneth and Billig, who were asked to respond to the proposal on behalf of the institute in Jerusalem, were not enthusiastic:

> Perhaps we should ask whether the idea itself, desirable though its intention might be, is built on a faulty premise. Were we of a mind to assimilate among the Arabs and to adopt their tongue for ourselves in the future, the Arabic writings of medieval Jews might have served as a basis for cultural understanding between the Jews and the Arabs. Seeing as we now desire our Hebrew culture and not the Judaeo-Arabic one, it would be irrational to boast to the Arabs of the Arabic culture of the Jews of the Middle Ages. In our opinion, the better means of achieving mutual understanding is to disseminate knowledge of the Arabic culture of the actual Arabs amongst our own people, as it is the culture of the people who live together with us.[24]

The stance implied by this excerpt of Baneth and Billig's letter is instructive because it incorporates the complexity experienced by those who had come to Jerusalem and begun to act, research, and teach there: the Zionist structure seeking to create the central Zionist vision, shared by Baneth and Billig, of a Hebrew culture that meant, among other things, the relinquishment of previous identities or histories connected to diasporic Jewish existence outside of Palestine;[25] relinquishing such identities, in the view of these two, meant ignoring neither Arab culture nor Arab existence—but these were now external to contemporaneous Jewish culture.

Shared by the founders and first faculty of the School of Oriental Studies, then, was the notion that the institute had a role extending beyond its scientific tasks and perhaps even exceeding them in importance: to advance mutual understanding between Jews and Arabs, or Muslims. This through the intellectual winning of hearts on the Arab and Muslim side—by means

84 ::: A NEW ORIENT

of the research initiatives, which would prove the institute's authentic interest in Arabic and Islam, and the sophisticated scientific capacities they applied to these fields—and the educational winning of hearts on the Jewish side, that is, by enriching students' knowledge of the history, language, and culture of the Muslim peoples. It is unsurprising, then, that Mayer, Billig, and Baneth (as well as Walter Fischel, the research assistant) were members of the Brit Shalom association, and others, including S. D. Goitein, were counted among its supporters and friends.[26] This association, founded in 1925, included a great many members from Central Europe, especially Germany. Accompanied by a sense of anxiety for the fate of the Zionist project in Palestine in light of its encounter with the Arabs, it was established out of the desire to influence both the Zionist movement and the Arab world, hoping "to pave the way for understanding between Jews ['ivrim] and Arabs ['aravim] for forms of common life in the Land of Israel on the basis of complete equality of the political rights of both nations, with broad autonomy, and the forms of their common work for the benefit of the development of the country."[27]

Horovitz has a special place in the history of Brit Shalom: while visiting Jerusalem for the inauguration of the university, he gave a lecture at Arthur Ruppin's house on "The Arab-Islamic world's stance on Zionism." According to the anti-imperial stance Horovitz presented in his lecture, while the attitude towards Zionism was not necessarily negative, there was an expectation in the Arab world that "the Jewish people returning to its land shall see itself as part of the Oriental world, not as the representative or standard-bearer of the West."[28] Some claimed that the impression left by Horovitz's talk prompted the attendees' decision to found Brit Shalom; others attributed a somewhat lesser role to the lecture, and on the basis of various accounts of the event, Aharon Kedar, who researched the association's history, concluded that Horovitz served "at most as an important catalyst."[29] Even given this secondary role, there was clearly a deep connection between the faculty of HUSOS and the Brit Shalom association.[30] This connection, when juxtaposed with the gap between the Hebrew present and the Judaeo-Arabic past as presented by Billig and Baneth, illuminates a significant inherent obstacle to achieving the vision of rapprochement pursued by the leaders of the Hebrew University: if their aspiration was to create links with contemporary Arab and Muslim scholars, how was the early institute's exclusive concentration on the study of the classical Arab culture of the Middle Ages meant to serve this end?

One of the essential virtues of the founders' legacy, claimed former HUSOS student and future director of the institute Menahem Milson in his article on the institute's early years, was their "separation between scholarship and personal political bias."[31] Milson, presumably, wished to emphasize that no improper considerations were involved in the scholarly method of his teachers and his teachers' teachers in the analysis of a certain text or historical phenomenon. But political tendencies certainly did have an impact on a preceding stage, that of selecting the research corpus upon which the institute would focus its energies. Magnes said as much of the twin research endeavors taken on by the newly-founded institute: compiling the Concordance for Ancient Arabic Poetry, and the publication of the ninth-century Arabic essay *Ansab al-Ashraf* by al-Baladhuri, both of which I discussed in the previous chapter. These research projects, he wrote, "have nothing directly to do with Judaism, and they were chosen purposely in order to show that the Hebrew University was concerned with the study of Islam and of Moslem peoples and their literature on their own account. It is one of the fondest hopes of the Hebrew University that it may serve as a great center of Arabic learning."[32] Indeed, these research initiatives provided the prime, though not the sole basis for the efforts of the institute and its scholars to form those connections with Arab and Muslim scholars —Palestinians, Egyptians, Syrians, and others.

## SCHOLARLY LOVE: RELATIONS BETWEEN THE SCHOOL OF ORIENTAL STUDIES AND THE ARAB AND MUSLIM INTELLECTUAL WORLD

The relations between scholars cannot be discussed in isolation from the wider imperial context. As far back as Antiquity, empires were already spaces containing a multiplicity of ethnic and religious groups without firm borders separating them, enabling the free movement of people, the formation of relations, and the mutual interchange of a variety of ideas, a diversity that was maintained as the empire expanded.[33] This imperial characteristic of mobility persisted into modern times; the British Empire, within which networks of scholars flourished in the nineteenth and twentieth centuries, was no exception. In Palestine, the Ottoman imperial space had previously provided opportunities for intellectual interactions and connections as well, including those between Jewish Zionists and Arabs.[34]

Following the Ottoman defeat in World War I, Palestine became part of

# 86 ::: A NEW ORIENT

the British imperial space. Under the auspices of the new ruling authority, the Hebrew University was established on Mount Scopus, attracting Jewish scholars, including some locals but mostly European-born individuals. The British regime, with its own independent imperial interests, was an active player in local politics, and its intervention had an influence, at times pivotal, on the university's decision-making.[35] These were the circumstances under which professional relationships—and some true friendships—developed between the Oriental Studies scholars of HUSOS and the Arabs and Muslims whose scholarship, thought, and writing intersected with the topics that stood at the center of the institute's activities.[36]

In the sociological analysis of academia and knowledge formation, this type of networked relationship is known as the "Invisible College": a group of intellectuals sharing a common interest in a similar scholarly field, whose members are engaged in formal (joint scientific publications) and informal (correspondence or meetings) means of advancing their joint professional goals, even when any institutions with which they may be affiliated are geographically distant from one another.[37] The geographical question was, as noted, a relatively minor one within the imperial zone of the Middle East. More challenging were questions about the nature and level of the relations' formality, which I will explore in detail later in this chapter.

As for the connections between the scholars of HUSOS and their colleagues in the Middle East and beyond, recall the unique conditions within which this Invisible College operated beginning in the mid-1920s: a (mostly immigrant) Jewish community steadily growing under the auspices of the imperial regime, perceived by the local Arab community as a mounting political, economic, social, and cultural threat. As a Zionist intellectual project of unprecedented scope and consequence for Palestine, the Hebrew University was another element of this threat. And yet, both archival evidence and contemporary media reports depict a widespread network of connections during the British Mandate. It can perhaps most easily be sketched by way of three primary circles: the textual circle, the ethnographic-archaeological circle, and the student circle. Shared research interests were the basis for these circles' formation and prompted the emergence of a number of initiatives. The same political, cultural, and institutional conditions that followed from the Hebrew University's place within the Jewish-Arab conflict meant that most of these initiatives never matured beyond their preliminary stages —and most of the relationships tended to remain informal and, therefore, difficult to maintain.

## The Textual Circle

The most expansive set of relations with Arab and Muslim scholars represented, to some degree, just what Horovitz and Magnes hoped to create when shaping the institute's identity and its scientific tasks. The focus on textual research promoted the formation of common cause with Palestinians, Egyptians, and Syrians who were themselves scholars of literature and Islam. Perhaps the most senior and influential scholar with whom connections were made in this field was the author and literary scholar Taha Hussein (1889–1973), one of the cultural icons of twentieth-century Egypt. It was natural enough, seeing as he published academic scholarship on Arab culture and Islam (in addition to fiction), for the institute to seek out a connection with Hussein, who was the first dean of the Faculty of Humanities and later rector of the University of Alexandria as well as director of the Arabic Language Academy in Cairo.[38]

Hussein's relations with Hebrew University scholars are demonstrated by pieces of both direct and indirect archival evidence, in personal diaries and other texts, in both Hebrew and Arabic. The Anglo-Jewish jurist and Hebrew University official Norman Bentwich (1883–1971) included a remark by Hussein in his early biography of Magnes as proof of the latter's good relations with leaders of Egyptian universities: that Magnes was "the most conciliatory person he ever met."[39] Hussein was to some degree or another familiar with the undertaking of the Hebrew University, and though the archives have not preserved any correspondence between him and the scholars of the School of Oriental Studies, this particular connection did produce formal expression, a rarity: in 1947, an article by S. D. Goitein on the life and activities of Ignác Goldziher appeared in the literary monthly founded and edited by Hussein, *al-Katib al-Misri* (The Egyptian writer).[40] It begins by describing how Goitein wrote the article in Arabic especially for the monthly.[41] Though rare, this publication reflected Hussein's aspiration that his journal serve to bring the cultures and literatures of Egypt and the West closer together, and was only possible in the first place thanks to the Jewish Harari family of Cairo, whose donation funded its publication.[42]

To the Arab intellectual world, especially those focused on the study of Islam, the figure of Goldziher was no stranger: during his visits to the Middle East he befriended numerous scholars, especially during his long visit to the region in 1873–1874. Though sent as an emissary to the Middle East with funding from a Hungarian Ministry of Culture pursuing its own

88 ::: A NEW ORIENT

colonial aspirations—to learn the spoken language, familiarize itself with Arabic bureaucracy, and secure manuscripts—he preferred the company primarily of scholars and reform-minded clergy, forging warm relations with them that helped him deepen his familiarity with Islam (and to enjoy the then-rare privilege of entering Al-Azhar University as a non-Muslim).[43]

Further evidence of HUSOS scholars' unmediated connection with Hussein (and another Arab intellectual) emerged years after his death in an interview with the Palestinian writer Ishaq Moussa al-Husseini, who received a doctoral degree in Semitic languages from the University of London before teaching in the 1930s and 1940s at the Arab College in Jerusalem, a teacher's seminary that was the town's only institution of higher education for Arab men.[44] In the introduction to an interview with him in the early 1940s, al-Husseini recounts how he wrote a critical allegory titled *Memoirs of a Hen* (*Mudhakkirat Dajaja*), which he sent to Taha Hussein in the hopes of having it published in the press he directed. Initially, Hussein refused, claiming the book was political in character. The writer then passed his manuscript on to D. H. Baneth; there is no archival evidence for his link with al-Husseini, so it is difficult to know the circumstances that led his essay to end up with Baneth. In any case, Baneth examined the manuscript and determined, in a response letter, that the book had not even the slightest hint of the political or a connection with the Jewish people (that is, any kind of analogy to the Arab-Jewish conflict—as Hussein may have assumed), and this letter was sent along to Hussein. In the wake of this letter, Hussein agreed to publish the book with his press and even added an introduction, which made no mention of Baneth.[45]

The potential value of relations with Hussein, and his cultural and political weight, were apparent to all, both within the HUSOS faculty and beyond. Hussein spent August–October 1942 in Jerusalem instead of vacationing in war-torn Europe. He took advantage of the rather protracted visit to write one of his books.[46] Hussein also broadcast a series of radio lectures on the subject of Egypt and its culture on the British radio station *Sharq al-Adna* (*Near East Broadcasting Station*, NEBS), which broadcast from Jaffa in Arabic.[47] Officials within the Political Department of the Jewish Agency found out about his planned visit, along with several other unnamed Egyptian, Syrian, and Lebanese authors. On September 24, Eliyahu Sasson (1902–1987), head of the Arab Bureau of the department, reported: "At my request, Professor [L. A.] Mayer and [Isaac] Shamosh visited them. They escorted four [of the visiting authors] on a tour of the university. At my request,

Shamosh proposed that they visit a number of Jewish sites—industrial, medical, and more. They agreed."[48] Hussein Fawzi (1900–1988), dean of the Faculty of Natural Sciences at the University of Alexandria and a novelist, also joined the tour.[49]

Sasson's involvement was neither a coincidental nor an isolated incident. As a youth in Damascus, the city of his birth, he had been educated alongside Muslims and Christians, developing an Arab national consciousness but also a Zionist one, which spurred him into activity in various political settings and to extensive journalistic writing in Arabic and Hebrew.[50] Regional developments in the wake of World War I led to his arrival in Palestine in 1927, in the hopes that he could advance his political vision from there: to find a solution based in Jewish-Arab dialogue founded upon equal rights, under an independent regime free of any British presence—a very similar approach to that that of Josef Horovitz, though based on rather disparate life experiences. At first, he focused on journalism, and in 1934 joined the Political Department at the initiative of Moshe Shertok (Sharett), who was appointed to head it after the assassination of Haim Arlosoroff the previous year. Shertok assigned Sasson to lead the Political Department's writing and publication activities.[51] His writing in Arabic was mostly devoted to debating with opponents of Zionism. Gradually, his activities with the Political Department came to focus on intelligence tasks.[52] His attempt to leverage Hussein's visit was part of a broad trend at the Political Department, which sought to forge connections with Arabs from neighboring countries in hopes of convincing them of the justice of the Zionist path, and was simultaneously an attempt to provoke conflict between different Arab countries and persons by demonstrating one or another as a supporter of Zionism.[53]

No evidence from his visit to Mount Scopus is extant in the archive of the Hebrew University, but Hussein hinted at it in a speech given in 1965 (while serving as president of the Egyptian Arabic Language Academy) before the Arabic Language Academies conference in Cairo: "At one of the foreign universities, and I do not want to name it because you all consider it deplorable, . . . I observed the preparation of a historical dictionary and saw many index cards, thousands of them, with words and quotations in Arabic from the various periods. It is not proper that they should precede the Arabs in this achievement."[54] Hussein was referring to the Hebrew University; the index cards he mentioned were almost certainly those of the concordance, even if his description failed to capture the precise nature of

90 ::: A NEW ORIENT

the classical project. Though this remark does not directly address the type of work being done at the Hebrew University, his words certainly reflect respect for it. Nor was it mere chance that one of the highlights of the trip to Mount Scopus was a visit to the concordance card catalog—which of course had been launched, among other things, as a basis for turning towards the Arab intellectual world.[55]

In any case, Magnes's continued efforts to form connections with Egyptian academic institutions during the Mandate period relied upon the research enterprises of HUSOS, whose staff were at times called upon to serve this cause.[56] Billig, for example, suggested that Magnes pursue a relationship with Muhammad Ahmed Gad al-Mawla (1883–1944), whom Billig and Horovitz had met in Oxford in 1928 at the Seventeenth International Orientalist Congress through Maulvi Abdul Haq (1870–1971), a Muslim professor from Hyderabad and among the pioneers of the town's Osmania University.[57] Presumably, Horovitz made his acquaintance while living in India in the early twentieth century. Gad al-Mawla was the Arabic language supervisor for the Egyptian Ministry of Education, and he attended the congress as a representative of his government.[58] In conversation with him, Billig and Horovitz learned that the Egyptian government was planning to fund the composition of an Arabic-Arabic dictionary in Cairo. They proposed informally—since they were unsure "about the scientific worth of the Cairo scheme" (without elaborating upon their doubts on this score)—to open up the concordance materials in Jerusalem to those involved in the project, thus saving them much labor. Billig concluded, emphasizing the importance of cooperation: "It would be satisfactory if we established relations with the learned world of Cairo, which is looked up to by Moslems in Palestine." This initiative never materialized, for reasons that remained obscure to the Hebrew University.[59]

One more member of this textual circle—another man of stature within the cultural and political arena of his region and beyond—was the Syrian scholar Muhammad Kurd Ali (1876–1953), friendly enough with Taha Hussein that the two actually gave a joint lecture series during the 1930s.[60] Like his colleague from Cairo, he headed a parallel Arabic Language Academy for years, which he founded himself in 1918 in Damascus, the town of his birth.[61] Alongside his activities advancing the Arabic language, Kurd Ali published studies on regional and Muslim history and was involved in political activity, editing and writing newspapers and magazines, first and foremost the newspaper he founded, *al-Muqtabas*.[62] In the case of Kurd Ali

"With Its Back to the Orient"? ::: 91

as well, who visited Palestine several times, it is informal archival documentation that attests to his links with HUSOS and its personnel.[63]

In 1930, the journalist and Oriental expert Tuvia Ashkenazi met Kurd Ali in Damascus and relayed to the Jewish Agency that he expressed interest in advancing scientific cooperation between the Hebrew University and the Arabic Academy in Damascus.[64] The report was passed along to the Hebrew University, which responded that "His Highness Kurd Ali is well-known to us, as he has visited here [in Jerusalem] and is a close friend of Prof. Horovitz."[65] The letter also noted that Horovitz himself was a member of the Arabic Academy in Damascus—and as such his name still appears on its website today.[66]

Kurd Ali's relationship with European—particularly German—Orientalism was complicated: on the one hand, he levelled criticism at the attitude towards Islam, the Arabs, and Arabic culture in certain Western studies, even voicing this criticism at the International Congress of Orientalists held in Leiden in 1931; on the other, he was friendly with a number of European Orientalists and expressed admiration for their work.[67] One of the most remarkable Orientalists with whom Kurd Ali kept in contact was Ignác Goldziher, who had, he said, "no equal before or since."[68] The two met in Budapest in 1914: Goldziher consulted on a professional matter with Kurd Ali, introduced him to the vast library which, as the previous chapter illustrated, came to Jerusalem after the death of Goldziher, and even invited him over for dinner at his home. Kurd Ali was tickled that "a Jew is teaching a troop of Christians about the book of the Muslims."[69]

In any case, Kurd Ali was also on good terms with German-trained Oriental experts living in Jerusalem: Shaul Hareli of the Political Department reported meeting Kurd Ali in Damascus in 1936 or 1937.[70] He recalled that Kurd Ali "inquired after the Orientalists of the Hebrew University and heaped praise upon Prof. Mayer, who would visit him frequently, 'but who' —he added—'has apparently strayed from the path, because he has not come to see me for two years.'"[71] He also took the opportunity to commend the research of HUSOS: "You have done something big and beautiful, continue with it unflinchingly . . . if not for you, who knows what would have been the fate of that wonderful manuscript of al-Baladhuri."[72] Kurd Ali was also curious about the publication of the Hebrew translation of the Quran by HUSOS faculty member Yosef Yoel Rivlin. Hareli, an emissary of the Political Department, was disappointed that Kurd Ali refused to talk about politics, preferring instead to continue speaking about the publication of

92 ::: A NEW ORIENT

the works of al-Baladhuri: "Do not forget to tell Dr. [*sic*] Mayer that I am still alive and anticipate his visit. Send my regards to all those working on the Baladhuri manuscripts."[73]

Despite Kurd Ali's—perhaps somewhat wry—expression of disappointment, his friendship with Mayer survived the Arab Revolt of the second half of the 1930s. In September 1941, Kurd Ali came to Jerusalem to give a series of radio lectures on the Palestine Broadcasting Service's *Jerusalem Calling* (in Arabic: *Radio al-Quds*), the official trilingual radio station of the British Mandate, during the month of Ramadan.[74] Mayer and Goitein attended the reception held in honor of the Syrian scholar's arrival.[75] There is no evidence that Kurd Ali visited Mount Scopus, but he certainly browsed at least one of the products of the institute's research: in March of that year, Kurd Ali sent Goitein a letter thanking him for sending the first published volume (sequentially the fifth) of *Ansab al-Ashraf* published as part of the institute's research initiative.[76] The two had known each other since at least 1932, when Goitein travelled to Damascus to work at the Zahiriyya Library, which was under the auspices of the Arabic Language Academy; there he met Kurd Ali, who greeted him with, in Goitein's words, an "exceedingly pleasant demeanor."[77] About a decade later, when Kurd Ali received Goitein's book, he praised the quality of the work, asked that the institute send the Arabic Academy copies of all further volumes it published in Arabic, and offered to send the academy's publications in exchange. Goitein apologized, explaining that apart from the *Ansab al-Ashraf* volumes, the remaining volumes of Arabic literature were printed in Hebrew letters; he therefore saw no reason to send them.[78] Goitein's answer might have been different had HUSOS taken up Louis Massignon's proposal years earlier and devoted its resources to the publication of Judaeo-Arabic essays in Arabic letters.

The reception for Kurd Ali in 1941 (at which Mayer and Goitein were present, as noted) took place at the home of his host in Jerusalem, the Palestinian writer, poet, and scholar of literature and philosophy Issaf Nashashibi (1882–1948),[79] who was inspector of Arabic language instruction at Arab schools under the British Mandate government for a decade and a familiar figure in the Arab cultural milieu of Jerusalem and well beyond: his luxurious house in the Sheikh Jarrah neighborhood served as a library and a venue for social meetings.[80] One learns something of Nashashibi's stature for the scholars of HUSOS from the fact that, upon his death in January 1948—with the civil war in Palestine already raging—room was made for a brief notice in the Hebrew newspaper *Davar* to mention his "cultural connections with Jewish scholars of Oriental Studies."[81]

Hailing from a large, influential, and well-connected Jerusalemite family, Nashashibi hosted events at his large family home, which may have been the setting where he first made the acquaintance of the Jewish scholars and cultural figures noted by the editors of *Davar*. The only archival evidence for this connection consists of a draft letter that Baneth planned to send in response to Nashashibi's essay *The Eternal Hero Salah al-Din and the Eternal Poet Ahmed Shawqi*, which he had sent to Baneth and eventually published in 1932.[82] In his letter, Baneth addresses Nashashibi's discussion on the question of genius using Max Nordau's writings on the concept;[83] Baneth rejects Nashashibi's conclusion that there were no Jewish poets or cultural figures of genius, and suggests examples of Hebrew texts from various periods that must be read in the Hebrew original if one is to take the measure of their genius.[84] The draft letter, inundated with erasures, additions, and corrections, indicates that, as usual, Baneth thought long and hard about how to formulate his objection precisely without hurting the author's feelings.[85] His emphasis on the Hebrew language recalls the aspiration he and Billig formulated in their 1926 letter, where they aligned their purpose at the university with the creation of a new Hebrew culture.[86]

Hussein, Kurd Ali, and Nashashibi—three prominent figures in the textual circle of associates around HUSOS scholars—all contributed articles to the Egyptian weekly *al-Risala*, published in the 1930s, where Hussein was an early associate editor. According to the scholar of twentieth-century Egyptian intellectual history Israel Gershoni, this weekly sought to foster an Arab-Islamic identity and Arabic cultural unity and frequently examined Islam and early Islamic history, but at the same time advanced modernist and reformist approaches to Islam, rejecting orthodoxy and supporting liberal democracy; it "held a western orientation." The weekly symbolized a broader intellectual tendency in the Egypt of the 1930s: the integration of Islam and liberalism.[87]

The extensive common ground HUSOS scholars found with the intellectuals active in connection with this weekly is therefore understandable. Such an approach to Islam did not contradict its analysis under the German Orientalist tradition. As a matter of fact, Ignác Goldziher, for example, saw in Islamic studies an opportunity to implement a historicist reform of religion (primarily with regards to Muslim law).[88] To a certain degree, such an outlook parallels the processes out of which Jewish Studies emerged in

94 ::: A NEW ORIENT

nineteenth-century Germany: Jewish scholars' attempt to navigate their encounter with the renewing world of science, and in effect to pour Judaism into modern scholarly molds while emphasizing the need for research of an objective scientific nature and a systematic approach to the discipline that might grant validity and legitimacy to Judaism as both a field of knowledge and a cultural and historical phenomenon.[89]

## The Ethnographic-Archaeological Circle

Alongside the textual circle of associations that crossed the borders of Mandatory Palestine was an additional circle that, while rooted in the local Palestinian context, had a cosmopolitan nature: the ethnographic-archaeological circle. While the textual circle rested on the intellectual activities of all the institute's scholars, the connections of the ethnographic circle emanated primarily from the scholarly interests of L. A. Mayer. Because he focused on material archaeological findings from the Muslim era, Mayer's publications resonated and prompted positive responses from Arab countries, especially Egypt, in no small part because they strengthened the historical aspect of the national narratives taking shape at the time.[90]

Moreover, after arriving in the country in 1921 and up until his appointment as a professor in 1933, Mayer worked in the Mandate's Antiquities Department. Founded in Palestine immediately after the transition to British civil rule in 1920, the department's role was to manage, document, and maintain the existing historical sites and to coordinate research by the various archaeological societies hoping to carry out digs in Palestine. While management positions in the department were mostly held by administrators from Britain, local Jews and Arabs also reached senior roles.[91] Over more than a decade of work in the department, Mayer became part of the British-oriented Jerusalemite intellectual and cultural milieux, within which he formed relationships with numerous Palestinian Arabs.[92] Mayer was the only scholar from the School of Oriental Studies, at least insofar as the archive lets on, ever invited to lecture at the Arab College in Jerusalem, the only Palestinian higher education institution at the time, and to publish in its periodical.[93]

Mayer's close friend, and the Palestinian in many ways at the center of the ethnographic circle, was the doctor Tawfiq Canaan (1882–1964). Canaan, whose father was the founder of the Lutheran Church in Beit Jala, had an interest in Palestinian archaeology and ethnography and published research in the field. Canaan was known to the Jerusalemite public, primar-

"With Its Back to the Orient"? ::: 95

ily for his work at the Leprosarium Jesus Hilfe, the home for those suffering from Hansen's disease, in Talbiyeh; he was a specialist in skin medicine. Not only prominent in the Arab nationalist movement in Jerusalem, Canaan —thanks both to his family's Lutheran affiliation and because he married a Jaffa-born German woman, Margot Eilander—was also closely connected to the German-speaking world.[94]

The relationship between Canaan and Mayer belongs within a wider collection of scholars—Christians, Muslims, and Jews from Palestine and beyond working within the fold of the Palestine Oriental Society.[95] Founded in 1920 by the American Assyriologist Albert Clay (1866–1925) during a visit to Palestine as a joint initiative of foreign archeological institutions, the organization's leading force was the American archaeologist William Albright (1891–1971), who directed the American School of Oriental Research in Jerusalem during the 1920s and 1930s and was active in the archaeological field in the country for many years. Under Albright's leadership, until 1948 the Society published the *Journal of the Palestine Oriental Society* (JPOS), in which a good proportion of the research on the archaeological, folkloric, geographic, and philological aspects of Palestine was published by local Jews (27 percent) and Arabs (15 percent).[96] Canaan stood out among the seven Palestinian Arabs involved in the activities of the Society and the publication of its periodical (a group that included Khalil Totah, Elias Haddad, Omar al-Salih al-Barghouti and Stephan Hanna Stephan, among others), serving as its secretary for many years and eventually succeeding Albright as president.[97] Generally, the articles published by Arab-Palestinian scholars in JPOS focused on ethnography—culture, tradition, and folklore. On the other hand, the Jewish scholars touched specifically upon biblical texts and associated topographies; Mayer's articles, reflecting an explicit interest in Muslim art and archaeology, were outliers.[98]

Hence, when Mayer was invited to lecture at the YMCA in Jerusalem on "Muslim Dress" in medieval Palestine, Egypt, and Syria, he was introduced by Canaan—a member of the YMCA board—as "the greatest European authority on this subject in the East."[99] This description is fascinating: Mayer, who immigrated to Palestine as a Zionist together with his parents in 1921, was presented neither as a Jew nor as a local, but rather a "European authority." Perhaps explicitly assigning this European foreignness to Mayer—who, according to one *in memoriam* indeed "may have absorbed some British manners"—made it easier for Canaan, a sharp critic of the Zionist movement, to nevertheless maintain good and warm relations with his Jewish

96 ::: A NEW ORIENT

colleague, with whom he collaborated on an initiative to found a museum for the folklore of Palestine.[100]

In his YMCA lecture, Mayer rallied support for the plan, promoted at the time by Canaan and director of the Palestine Department of Education for the Mandate Government Humphrey Bowman (1879–1965), to found a museum of national costumes. This initiative expanded in scope, enlisted British support, and took shape in the years subsequent to Mayer's 1931 lecture. The efforts were motivated by alarm that modernization would decimate the traditional material culture of the *fellahin* and Bedouin that had inhabited the land for centuries;[101] according to the historian Salim Tamari, the modernization process in Palestine was accelerated in an effort to meet the substantial needs of the Ottoman army during World War I, when Palestine became "one major construction site."[102] In the eyes of Canaan, the *fellahin* —in their material culture and folklore—were the living quintessence of all the cultures the country had ever known.[103] Their disappearing culture urgently needed to be preserved.

Thus, in 1935, the British High Commissioner Arthur Wauchope agreed to sponsor the museum, named the "Palestine Folk Museum," and a committee was formed to plan its establishment. Alongside Baumann and Canaan, the committee was composed of the mayor of Jerusalem, the French and American consuls, president of the Hebrew University J. L. Magnes, Yitzhak Ben-Zvi, Khalil Totah, and others. The museum also had a steering executive committee on which, unlike the founding committee, Mayer was the only academic included.[104] The museum opened a year later, in 1936. On display were costumes, in accordance with the original initiative, but liturgical and household objects were shown alongside them, as were instruments, weapons, and agricultural equipment. The museum struggled financially since it and was established on the basis of membership fees and donations; in particular its supporters had difficulties finding the museum a permanent home. The collection of around 1,600 items was initially put on display in Muristan within the Old City (on a plot held by the Lutheran Church), and moved to the tower of the Jerusalem Citadel (also known as the Tower of David) in 1941.[105] Its activities waned and came to an end by early 1948 but, after the war's impact on the Old City that year, they were not resumed in either West or East Jerusalem.[106] The friendship between Canaan and Mayer made a significant contribution to the museum's opening, but was unable to overcome the tectonic shifts prompted by the war.

Another ethnographer in contact with HUSOS, and especially with Mayer, was the journalist and historian Aref al-Aref (1891–1973), a supporter of the Palestinian national movement who would later become mayor of Jordanian Jerusalem. Al-Aref was a politically controversial figure, as the unique course of his life would attest: as a youth he published an article criticizing the Zionist movement, soon becoming editor of Jerusalem's first Arab-nationalist newspaper, *Suriya al-Janubiyya* (southern Syria).[107] Nonetheless, he participated in joint Jewish and Palestinian evening courses in Jerusalem in the late 1920s, the purpose of which was to teach the Jews Arabic and the Palestinians Hebrew.[108] These lessons were cut short when in 1920 al-Aref was accused by the British of disseminating words of incitement, both within his newspaper and on horseback, before a crowd at the Jaffa Gate, allegedly provoking the Palestinian violence of the 1920 Jerusalem Riots.[109]

Al-Aref fled Palestine with Hajj Amin al-Husseini and remained in Syria, where they took part in political activities to advance the Palestinian national cause. Later, they moved on to Transjordan, where they were granted pardons by the British High Commissioner and were allowed to return to Jerusalem. At this point the two parted ways, and al-Aref—after the British refused a request to resume publication of his newspaper—was offered a position within the British Mandatory Government, becoming a district officer in various towns in Palestine, including Jenin, Nablus, and Jaffa, and later Beersheba, Gaza, and Ramallah. It would be difficult to argue that al-Aref's views were completely transformed. To be sure, during the 1936–1939 Arab Revolt, he managed largely to keep the peace in Beersheba and was proud of this success; at the same time, he remained in contact with activists from the Arab national movements, even maintaining secret relations with groups opposed to the British.[110] In any case, the Zionist leadership received reports that al-Aref would support an agreement between the Jews and the Arabs;[111] his complaints were directed primarily at the British.[112] He participated himself in public meetings between Jewish and Arab journalists in the 1940s and called for the enhancement of mutual understanding.[113] As noted, al-Aref was also a historian and ethnographer alongside his political activity and work. The Jewish public in Palestine was familiar with him thanks to two books he wrote on the history of the Bedouin, based largely on material collected when he was district officer for Beersheba, which had already been translated into Hebrew by the mid-1930s.[114]

This expertise led to the only documented case of an Arab scholar giving

98 ::: A NEW ORIENT

a lecture at the Hebrew University during the years of the Mandate: in late 1940, the university advertised a lecture series on "The Arab Orient" intended for the general public. Alongside lectures by HUSOS instructors Mayer, Baneth, Goitein, and Rivlin, the first lecture in the series stands out, given by Aref al-Aref on "The Life of the Bedouin."[115] Al-Aref indeed gave his lecture on Bedouin customs at the Hebrew University in May 1941 before a large crowd; he delivered it in Hebrew.[116] By way of introduction, al-Aref explained that his friend L. A. Mayer had invited him on behalf of the institute to give the lecture, but that "I initially hesitated to accept because I was unfortunately not endowed with the learning and wisdom to match this honorable crowd that frequents the Hebrew University, which is justifiably considered the pinnacle of Jewish science and culture in the East."[117] Before moving on to the subject of his lecture, al-Aref apologized that his Hebrew was sufficient only for everyday conversation, and that he would be reading his pre-written lecture aloud.

The archive of the Hebrew University provides no further evidence of the preparations leading up to this lecture, but the fact that it took place at all attests, once again, to the depth of intellectual ties maintained by HUSOS scholars within a broad, nation-bridging community of scholars. For Mayer, such connections were formed not only through the institute's activities, but also thanks to his other interests and his governmental connections; this was likewise the case with Goitein, who encountered many Palestinian Arabs through his work in the Mandate Government's Department of Education. He causally met colleagues and others he knew through shared acquaintances in Jerusalem as a matter of course, as documented in his journals.[118] The prospect of such common encounters in Mandate Jerusalem—at times arising from the mere fact of residing in the same neighborhood—also contributed, of course, to the strength of the connections.[119]

Oriental expertise, as we have seen, was the basis for the emergence of these relationships; figures within the *Yishuv* took note of and sought to attach this expertise to their own attempts at promoting contacts between the populations in Palestine. Yet the generalizing assumption about Oriental Studies scholars' ability to serve as mediators between Hebrew and Arabic did not take into account the fact, which also became an obstacle, that this expertise was, for most of them, textual: in one case in the middle of the 1930s, Dr. Noah Braun, a longtime research assistant at the institute, was asked to serve as interpreter at an event organized by the writers and translators Immanuel Olsvanger and Asher Beilin. The project originated with an idea of Olsvanger's to form an extra-institutional framework for Jews and Arabs to meet. Moshe Shertok lent his support behind the scenes, without revealing any link between the initiative and the Jewish Agency, and secured a year of funding from the head of the Executive Committee of the Hebrew University, Shlomo (Salman) Schocken.[120]

Following a number of preliminary discussions, the event was held in early January 1936. Around eighty Jews and Arabs were invited, and Beilin gave introductory remarks. According to the report delivered to Shertok by Eliyahu Sasson and Shaul Hareli (who were present), Braun "translated the speaker's lecture into flawed Arabic," giving the impression that he had said the country belonged to the Jews more than it did to the Arabs. As a result, one of the Arab attendees protested and an argument broke out between him and Braun, the interpreter, who claimed to have said nothing of the sort and refused to retract his translation. Finally, the dissenter and four others left angrily. After the clamor, Sasson (in Arabic) and Hareli (in Hebrew) managed to calm things down and the event continued.[121] But the damage had been done, and the initiative of Olsvanger and Beilin was short-lived.

## The Student Circle

This chapter began with the vision, expressed by Ussishkin and Weizmann, that Arab students would also attend the university. A number did indeed study at HUSOS during the British Mandate, mostly Palestinians and Egyptians. Details on these students are exceedingly sparse in the university's archive, and in any case there were only a handful since, to study there, they had to be proficient in its language of instruction; however, those who documented their time at the university typically recalled a positive learning experience, and maintained some degree of contact with their teachers. Hamdi Bakr al-Nubani (1915–2009) from the Sheikh Jarrah neighborhood liked to call himself the first Arab to study at the Hebrew University where, after graduating from the Arab College, he continued his studies under Mayer, Billig, and Goitein, among others. His father, Sheikh Bakr al-Nubani, was friendly with a number of Hebrew University scholars, including L. A. Mayer. He criticized the actions of the Mufti during the Arab Revolt and was subsequently murdered, prompting Magnes—fearing for the younger al-Nubani's safety—to recommend he cut short his studies at the university.[122] Thanks to his proficiency in Hebrew, al-Nubani worked as a Hebrew-to-Arabic translator; among other projects he translated the

100 ::: A NEW ORIENT

*Mishnah* into Arabic.[123] According to the university's registers, only one other Palestinian-Arab studied at the School of Oriental Studies from its establishment until 1938.[124]

In addition to the Palestinian students, HUSOS was home to a number of students from other Arab countries over the course of the 1940s. The most well-known was the Cairo-born Hassan Zaza, who studied Hebrew and Semitic Linguistics (a field taught at the time within HUSOS) between 1942 and 1944.[125] Zaza moved on from Jerusalem to complete his doctoral studies in Paris before teaching at the Arab University of Beirut and King Saud University in Saudi Arabia.[126] Another student who began his studies in Cairo was Muhammad Salim al-Rashdan (1918–2001), a native of Salt in Transjordan who came to Jerusalem for pedagogical training and studied Semitic Linguistics in parallel at HUSOS, where he completed a master's degree in the mid-1940s.[127] Al-Rashdan also worked as a research assistant in the concordance project.[128] He went on to become a teacher and school principal, and eventually returned to Jordan. Many years after passing through the Hebrew University's halls, al-Rashdan attested to the institute's reputation, noting that it was recommended for the study of Semitic linguistics, and spoke with praise of his teachers there.[129] After his studies he became a political activist siding with the Arab national struggle in Palestine and published poetry on the topic in Arabic newspapers in Palestine and elsewhere; he was even attacked for this once in a brief item in the Revisionist newspaper *Hamashkif*.[130]

Students also moved in the opposite direction: the relative ease of travel from Palestine to the countries to its north, even after the division of the Ottoman realm into French and English territories following World War I, made possible a deliberate policy, primarily in the 1930s, of sending HUSOS students on exchanges at the American University of Beirut (AUB). Founded in 1866, the presence of Jewish students at this university became routine after the turn of the century: during the 1930s, for example, Jewish students regularly made up 10 to 12 percent of the overall student body.[131] Among them were both European- and locally-born Jewish students from Palestine, as well as Jews from other Arab countries, alongside the Christian and Muslim majority. There were relations of personal friendship between students of different religions, but disagreements and arguments erupted at times between Zionist students at the university and groups of non-Jews, especially during episodes of violence in Palestine; Jewish students so inclined could join the Kadima association at the university. Founded in 1908, it be-

"With Its Back to the Orient"? ::: 101

came increasingly involved with Zionist activities over the years, organizing events to mark the anniversary of the Balfour Declaration, for example.[132]

For Jewish students studying Arabic and Islam whose mother tongue was not Arabic, studying at the AUB was a golden opportunity to improve their knowledge of the modern literary language. At the university, aligned with the Protestant tradition and administered by Americans, most courses were in English; but Muslim topics were taught in Arabic. Thus, upon Goitein's initiative and with his dogged encouragement, at least five exceptional HUSOS students set off for short courses of study in Beirut, mostly in the first half of the 1930s.[133] One of them, David Ayalon, attested many years later that he enjoyed good personal relations with many Arab students, and also recalled his Arabic-speaking teachers fondly, although during his visit, he informed Goitein that the academic level was not uniform.[134] Other students recalled that friendly relations between Arab-Palestinians and Jewish students in Beirut were limited, and in any case did not survive the return from Beirut to a politically-charged Palestine.[135]

In any case, connections with students and other local figures also had an additional, intelligence, element: in at least two cases—Eliahu Epstein (later Elath) and Aviva Tourovsky (later Landman)—students are known to have engaged with local entities and collected intelligence on events in Lebanon and Syria for the Political Department of the Jewish Agency alongside their studies, receiving compensation towards their living expenses. The connections forged by Epstein during his years in Beirut (1931–1934) continued to serve the Political Department years after he returned to Palestine and became a regular official in its organization; while Tourovsky, who specialized in the study of the Arab national movement, made connections with, among others, the leaders of the Maronites.[136] This bond between HUSOS students and the Political Department would later prove crucial in establishing the institute's relationship with the Jewish Agency and—after the founding of the State of Israel—with various government ministries. In the meantime, it demonstrates that even friendships between students, at least when the Hebrew University was their home institution, could be loaded with political baggage and consequences that extended beyond shared interests or scientific curiosity.

These three circles—the textual, the ethnographic, and the student—paint a clear picture of intellectual affinity that extended at times into genuine personal friendship. In deciding to focus on classical subjects that would at-

102 ::: A NEW ORIENT

tract the Arab and Muslim intellectual communities, Horovitz and Magnes made a well-informed wager—and, considering the German Orientalist tradition that shaped the institute, a predictable one—that paid off, and the Invisible College of Oriental expertise permeated the borders of Mount Scopus; the recruitment of L. A. Mayer to the institute made inroads with scholars of Palestinian culture; and its focus on literature and linguistics attracted Arab students (albeit only a few) interested in these topics, while Jewish students of the institute travelled to Beirut to deepen their knowledge of the Arabic language and at the same time form still more connections with a learned crop of students there. Nevertheless, what the circles of scholarly association—unlike those of the students, which were by nature more temporary and less impactful in the first place—had in common was that they remained mostly informal: the Jewish-Arab conflict, in the shadow of which these invisible links of respect and affinity were formed, prevented them from becoming formal and long-term connections.

## INVISIBLE AND EXPOSED: INTELLECTUAL AMITY AND THE FAILURE TO INSTITUTIONALIZE

By the time Taha Hussein visited Mount Scopus in 1942, the scandal of Ahmed Lutfi al-Sayyid's participation in the Hebrew University of Jerusalem's inauguration ceremony—including the criticism he received, and the apology he was forced to publish—was a distant, if still unpleasant, memory. This contentious precedent was, presumably, among the factors that prompted the Egyptian consul in Jerusalem in the early 1940s, Mahmoud Fawzi, to ask that Taha Hussein not publicize the visit in the Arab world;[137] Hussein Fawzi, who accompanied Taha Hussein during his visit to the Hebrew University, revealed as much some decades later—once the peace agreement between Egypt and Israel had already been signed.[138] Hussein was fielding criticism in Egypt and beyond as it was because of the liberal tack he followed, and was accused more than once of collaborating with the Zionist movement.[139] Despite having a positive view of the visit, therefore, the Egyptian Consul General downplayed its existence.

Several months later, during a conversation with Eliahu Epstein that was relayed in a secret report to the Political Department of the Jewish Agency, the consul regretted "that despite his [Taha Hussein's] progressive views and belief in the usefulness of cooperation between Jews and Arabs, he had little choice but to completely avoid this question owing to pressure from

"*With Its Back to the Orient*"? ::: 103

local Arab functionaries." The consul explained to his interlocutor that, "no matter the personal outlook of the official representative of Egypt, or the representative of any other Arab country in Palestine, on the benefits of interacting with the Hebrew *Yishuv*, he must consider the position of the Arabs of Palestine, who are sure to see in every serious attempt by the Arab state representative to break the wall of non-cooperation dividing Jews and Arabs in Palestine as an act of solidarity [with Zionism]."[140] The Political Department had long been familiar with this Egyptian perspective regarding the university: the two institutions had cooperated in inviting Egyptian and Lebanese representatives to the ten-year anniversary celebration of the university's inauguration in 1935. The university had suggested inviting Taha Hussein for a visit and lecture, only for the Cairo Friends of the Hebrew University's association to balk: "It is currently impossible to invite Arab intellectuals from Egypt to lecture in Jerusalem. They fear the Arabs of Palestine will be a bad influence on them."[141] In any case, this was not the only instance in which the visit of a Muslim scholar was kept from the public eye at the request of HUSOS personnel,[142] who displayed a heightened sensitivity to the immediate political consequences of the publication of such intellectual cooperation in the local Palestinian press.[143] In fact, attentiveness to the wider context of these consequences was ultimately detrimental to the central attempt to realize, in concrete terms, the political vision upon which the institute's academic activities were based: the effort to recruit an Arab lecturer to the faculty.

## *The Question of the Arab Lecturer*

The goal of recruiting an Arab or Muslim lecturer to the HUSOS faculty, as noted previously, was older than the institute itself, motivated by the goal of promoting amity between Jews and Arabs as well as that of enhancing the university's international legitimacy. Most dedicated in pursuit of this goal was Josef Horovitz, who saw the study of Arabic and Islam at the Hebrew University as an opportunity to create intellectual bonds between the peoples. He alluded to this matter in the founding memorandum, written at Magnes's invitation in 1925, in which he outlined a plan for the establishment of the institute.[144] While he insisted that the director of the institute be an expert in Arabic trained in Europe or America, since "there is no scholar from the Orient [*orientalische Gelehrte*] with complete mastery of modern scientific methods," Horovitz emphasized that an Orientalist insti-

104 ::: A NEW ORIENT

tute in Jerusalem—even one founded on European methods—could not simply replicate those institutes from which it emerged: "Here, unlike in the West, Arabic plays not merely the role of a 'classic language.' Like in Egypt and in Syria, even though not to the same degree, modern Arabic [*Schriftarabisch*] is also in Palestine a tool to convey the expression of contemporary intellectual life; a total separation of scholarly research on the Arabic language and its literatures from contemporary literary production in Arabic would be then neither natural nor desirable. This connection can be saved in the best way by adding an Arab scholar to the teaching staff. He would be obliged not only to deliver his lectures in Arabic, but also to give seminars on spoken and written modern Arabic." In addition to an Arab member of the faculty, Horovitz suggested recruiting a Lektor (one providing foreign language instruction in their mother tongue) apprised "of European methods of instruction," to teach beginner Arabic courses. He also raised the further possibility of subsequently hiring "one or more of these old-style Arab Sheiks [*einen oder mehrere arabische Schaichs der alten Art*]," who would teach about various fields of Islamic theology.

Horovitz did not address the nationality or religion of the faculty member or Lektor in the document, but the two names he did mention for the former position—Muhammad Kurd Ali and Taha Hussein—indicate that he had in mind intellectuals active in the Arab literary life of the 1920s; later, in correspondence with Levi Billig, he wrote that (Issaf) Nashashibi would also make a good candidate for the position, explaining that his role would be to give lectures about Arabic literature, especially modern literature, and exercises in spoken and written Arabic.[145] Horovitz recognized the additional instructional value a professor for whom Arabic was a living language provides a university; in fact he had already felt this way during his time in Aligarh.[146] Still, he expressed doubt that the intellectuals he had named would agree to come teach in Jerusalem, even if the material conditions were satisfactory. The same memorandum, in fact, also hints at the limitations of intellectual amity: there is no mention of Hussein or Kurd Ali directing the institute, a job for Western scholars only. Even taking these limits into consideration, however, at least considering the German Orientalist tradition in which Horovitz was trained, this proposal represents a revolutionary precedent. There were already university students arriving from Asia and Africa in late nineteenth- and early-twentieth century Germany, but those who taught did so only as Lektors.[147]

Doubt continued to eat away at Horovitz after the proposal was submit-

"With Its Back to the Orient"? ::: 105

ted, and two months later he wrote to Magnes that "there is no chance of any suitable candidate for the post of a professor of Arabic coming forward at present."[148] Moreover, when Horovitz came to Jerusalem in the spring of 1926 to mark the opening of HUSOS and hold meetings with its coalescing faculty (Mayer, Baneth, and Billig), they agreed not to appoint an Arabic teacher for the time being;[149] he suggested that an Arab scholar be appointed the following year, but emphasized that this "must not be done prematurely; the appropriate timing will be decided by the staff in Palestine."[150] This reservation notwithstanding, among Horovitz's suggestions for how to spend the institute's potential budget surplus that year was applying the sum to recruit "a lecturer of Arabic, i.e., an Arab by birth."[151] For the faculty in Jerusalem, conditions certainly seemed to have ripened for such a move, and Billig wrote to Magnes that "the coming of an Arab lecturer would add a new aspect to the Institute; it would be a step forward, and (may I add) a step that in the minds of some of the students is already overdue."[152] Baneth, too, after his first semester teaching at the institute, identified the need for an Arab lecturer who could improve the students' knowledge of Arabic, and—in a letter to the university administration concerned with those students at the institute preparing to teach at Jewish schools in Palestine—related this to another need, the opening of a preparatory program, or *mekhina*:

(A) a preparatory program providing the institute's students with precise knowledge of the Arabic language is needed. An elementary knowledge of Arabic can be expected of those accepted to the institute; but experience dictates that the country's schools mostly do not provide a fair knowledge of the intricacies of Arabic grammar, and therefore, a full course of grammar with advanced exercises must be given again.

(B) philological knowledge on the situation of Arabic language and literature in the past is not sufficient for a teacher. He must have a living connection with the present. For this, the institute requires an Arab Lektor to speak Arabic with the students and enunciate the phrases properly for them, accustom them to writing Arabic essays, introduce modern Arabic literature to them, and, *en passant*, familiarize them with the outlook and customs of the contemporary Arab.[153]

With this recommendation, Baneth combined the role of the Arab professor with that of the Lektor proposed by Horovitz—the Lektor would also

106 ::: A NEW ORIENT

be the one to teach modern literature and provide a link to the Arab intellectual world of the twentieth century. The recommendation connects two central driving forces of the institute's activities: on the one hand, the desire to preserve the academic standards to which Baneth and the other institute faculty were accustomed, with their European (mostly German) Orientalist credentials—hence the need for a preparatory program—and on the other, an aspiration to realize through the person of an Arab lecturer the political role of the institute as an Orientalist body within the Hebrew University of Jerusalem. Billig, too, suggested the addition of general courses primarily aimed at students from Hebrew-language schools in Palestine, "local products," who "have been taught their Arabic by native lecturers [speakers]. They come to us with little or no knowledge of the history, the political constitutions, the literature and the religious development of the Moslems."[154] Visiting Frankfurt in early 1927, indeed, Baneth met Horovitz and was able to convince him to support the idea of a preparatory program.[155] Horovitz suggested S. D. Goitein for the role of the preparatory instructor.

It swiftly became apparent that the need for a preparatory program and the search for an Arab lecturer might contradict one another. In May 1927 Magnes wondered whether Horovitz believed that, in light of the limited budget, "this preparatory program ought to be preferred to the appointment of a Muslim teacher," and a month later Horovitz responded that he agreed to put off the question of the Arab lecturer until the following year at least.[156] Even before confirmation from Horovitz, Goitein had already submitted a plan for the Arabic preparatory program to "correct and complete the natural and temporary disadvantages of the high schools in Palestine." They were missing "the scientific training included as part of a humanistic education abroad," as well as "any perspective or precise knowledge regarding the history of the Muslim Orient." The plan for the preparatory program included lectures on the history of Islam and the Muslim nations until 1517 (the year of the Ottoman conquest of Palestine), grammar lessons, reading of classical texts, and translation and grammar exercises; it was included in the budget proposal prepared for the 1927–28 academic year.[157] After several more months of discussion, Goitein and Rivlin (another former student of Horovitz's, see above) were invited to serve as instructors in the preparatory program.[158] In addition to their philological training in Germany, both were experienced high school teachers, which presumably favored their selection.

The idea of the Arab or Muslim lecturer was not abandoned, but it became clear to Horovitz and Magnes that, to make it a reality, additional funding beyond the existing budget would have to be found. Magnes explained to Horovitz that private donors would prefer to fund the establishment of a new chair rather than bring in an Arab lecturer;[159] but in late 1927, an institutional fundraising opportunity presented itself to Magnes through his correspondence with Nicholas Murray Butler (1862–1947), president of the Carnegie Endowment for International Peace. Founded in 1910 with the ambitious goal of ending war in the world, the American foundation earmarked a significant portion of its funds for donations to various educational initiatives.[160] Butler explained to Magnes, who was inquiring about potential support for the operations of the School of Oriental Studies, that the Endowment would consider supporting specific aspects of the institute's policy aiming to encourage international friendship and amity.[161] The institute's faculty was thus asked "to draft informational materials for the university administration . . . on aspects of your work that may be considered efficacious in promoting amity between Jews and Arabs and strengthening the peaceful relations between the two peoples through scientific aid."[162] Among the suggestions floated was work on the Concordance of Ancient Arabic Poetry, "which would eventually be used by Arab scholars as well."

The application submitted to Butler in July 1928, which included letters from Magnes and Horovitz (glorifying the institute's work in hopes of convincing the foundation), also detailed proposals for the expansion of the School of Oriental Studies, first and foremost the addition of a Muslim lecturer to the academic faculty.[163] Referring to "a Moslem lecturer" rather than an Arab lecturer, it perhaps sought to emphasize the links between religions, and not just nations, which the institute hoped to advance with the help of the Carnegie Endowment's contribution, thus shading its mission in a more universal hue. Yet to Magnes's great disappointment he received word in a brief October 1928 message that, due to a lack of resources, the Endowment's board of directors had decided not to cooperate on the plan presented by the Hebrew University.[164]

As far as the archival record reveals, this was the primary substantial attempt to advance the matter of the Arab lecturer at the School of Oriental Studies. Billig did write to Magnes in early 1929 that he hoped an Arab lecturer would be added to the institute's faculty soon;[165] but the subject never came up again in subsequent correspondence, including communications with Horovitz through his death in 1931. No further applications were submitted to raise funds for the hiring, nor were any concrete proposals for

108 ::: A NEW ORIENT

a relevant lecturer ever raised. Perhaps the archival silence on this matter had to do with the political shockwaves that swept through Jerusalem, in particular after the Palestine Riots of summer 1929, and so deepened the fault-lines between Jews and Palestinians. Following the riots, Magnes and many other Brit Shalom members became increasingly convinced that a solution to the conflict on the basis of Arab agreement was necessary, and began to distance themselves from the Zionist leadership;[166] yet for most of the Jewish public, as well as the Arab-Palestinian leadership and public opinion, the riots were a landmark moment for radicalization, as the two sides to the conflict coalesced and consolidated their views in opposition to one another. The riots also prompted mounting identification with the Palestinian cause in the wider Arab and Muslim worlds.[167] Considering the responses garnered by the Egyptian Lutfi al-Sayyid's visit four years before the riots, it should be said that public cooperation with the Hebrew University had not been looked upon kindly by Arab public opinion even before the violence of summer 1929. Still, whatever small chance still existed that an Arab intellectual could be found who would agree to join the institute's faculty was washed away by the riots.

Meanwhile, the need for a lecturer who was a native speaker of Arabic only grew. In the late 1920s and early 1930s, various forces within the *Yishuv* criticized the institute for remaining essentially "European" and hardly reflecting in its teaching and research the fact of its presence in the heart of the Middle East. Particularly acerbic critics in the Hebrew press in Palestine included Abraham Shalom Yahuda, who was not included in the university's plans and accused it of neglecting "all of those Palestine-born students with sufficient knowledge of Oriental languages . . . and preferring students fresh from their completed studies in Europe";[168] and the Orientalist, journalist, and Palestine Workers' Party (*Mapai*) operative Michael Assaf (1896–1984), born in Lodz. Assaf protested: "We are located in the physical, geographical Orient. And for this and other obvious reasons are we drawn towards the politico-cultural, socio-cultural, and spiritual-cultural Orient. And yet we are mute, truly mute: we are without the Arabic tongue." For this reason, he explained, "the School of Oriental Studies, founded in a Zionist Jerusalem, cannot exist in the image and character of an institute in Berlin, Paris, or New York. In Jerusalem this institute must stand shoulder-to-shoulder with the most practical subjects." Rather than the "petrified Orientalism" currently taught there, Assaf called for HUSOS to teach a "living Orientalism," for it "must, and only it—through the sea of hateful propaganda against us—can breach the Arab world with a living touch. This will be possible through Arab teachers, who will be easy to find for such roles [of teaching the everyday rather than the classical language]."[169] Assaf's article, published in 1933, echoes many of the claims made by Horovitz and other institute faculty, but where they saw a solution in the tempered integration of modern Arabic literature and intellectual cooperation, Assaf called for the School of Oriental Studies to be transformed into a practical training center.

The question of the institute's practicality and relevance was raised all the more forcefully in the Hartog Committee Report of 1934. In their report, which drew upon the external voices criticizing the institute, members of the committee called for a change to the focus of research and teaching at the institute: "Jewish Palestine is surrounded on all sides by the Moslem world, a thorough knowledge of which is of the greatest importance for the economic and political development of the country. For this purpose it is not the study of pre-Islamic poetry, nor the study of old Arab historians that matters, but the study of the living Islamic world."[170] The committee believed the School of Oriental Studies ought to resemble schools in Paris, Berlin, and London, "in which the student is made to know the living and not only the dead Orient."[171] In their eyes, blame lay with the late Horovitz,

> who was an excellent Islamic scholar, and especially wished to develop the Islamic side and, by so doing, to establish the reputation of the University in Islamic countries. His plan was accepted by others, who . . . also had the idea that Arabs would look favorably upon the University because of its devotion to Islamic studies. It is always dangerous to allow politics to interfere with education. Whatever one may think about the means that might lead to a better understanding between Jew and Arab, so necessary for the building up of Palestine, it is now quite evident that no Arab will change his political views on the Jewish question because of the preparation by the Hebrew University of a Concordance of Ancient Arabic Poetry.[172]

The committee's conclusion was unequivocal: the institute should take a more practical direction, adding "a professorship or readership in modern Arabic language and literature and a lectorship in Arabic language." The desired impact, according to the report, was that graduates of the institute be fully competent in modern Arabic. In pursuit of this goal, "we see no objection to engaging Arab scholars."

The committee's evaluation of the institute as a "school" to be modeled after its European counterparts reveals different perceptions of the essence of European, and particularly German, Orientalism. The European model to which the report's conclusions point is, in effect, the precise inverse of the European model Michael Assaf opposed in his criticism, though their demands had been the same; Assaf had in mind the university-based research institutes, while the committee members envisioned a training center similar, for example, to London's School for Oriental and African Studies (SOAS) or Berlin's *Seminar für Orientalische Sprachen* (SOS). Yet while in Berlin the seminar was distinct from the university's Department of Oriental Studies, the Hartog Committee hoped one body founded at the Hebrew University could combine the two functions.

The committee's report was received with ambivalence at the School of Oriental Studies. By 1934 Horovitz was no longer director, having passed away in 1931. It fell to L. A. Mayer, appointed shortly after the report was delivered, instead of Horovitz's replacement Gotthold Weil, to formulate the official response to the committee's reproach. In his candid response, Mayer not only revealed how the institute took exception to the criticism, but also laid out a different perspective on the political reality in Palestine and the role of the institute: "During the first and financially best years of the School the difficulties were not so much on the financial as on the political side. It was exceedingly difficult to find any Moslem scholar of repute and integrity of character willing and capable of filling such a post. For that reason a Moslem lecturer was not appointed there and then, and Dr. Rivlin was asked to teach the subject."[173] He concurred, in the name of the entire School of Oriental Studies staff, that "politics should not be allowed to interfere with education," and that the concordance project would not lead to political change; at the same time, he explained that the institute was obliged "to see that our graduates in Islamic studies be considered by the Arabs as educated in this subject, and no student who masters, for example, the Palestinian dialect, but is not well versed in the Arabic classics, will be considered by our neighbors as a man who knows the language."

Mayer, whose connections with Arab scholars were among the most extensive of all the institute's faculty, hereby admitted that there was no hope for Horovitz's vision, the very dream of intellectual rapprochement that served as the basis for the institute's work. He understood that, whether or not leading Palestinian, Egyptian, and Syrian scholars valued the work of the School of Oriental Studies and maintained personal connections with its members, the complex political reality was far stronger. Moreover, the extent to which real effort was put into the search for an Arab or Muslim lecturer in the first place is entirely unclear—in effect, the university archive contains no evidence that the institute ever officially approached Taha Hussein, Muhammad Kurd Ali, or Issaf Nashashibi on the matter, the candidates Horovitz had at one point suggested—but Mayer's comments indicate that the list was always going to be limited to scholars who would meet the Orientalist standards set by graduates of German universities.

Not by chance did both the committee report and Mayer's response touch on the involvement of politics in teaching, a reflection of the professional ethos that largely characterized the self-image of German academia in the nineteenth and early twentieth centuries. Under this ethos, formulated by Max Weber in his lecture "Science as a Vocation," academics were to leave their political views outside the lecture hall.[174] Mayer's response makes clear that he—and, presumably, the institute's other faculty members—felt that their work did not diverge from the principle presented by Weber: even if there were political imperatives involved in the choice of research topics, these had no impact on either the conclusions of the research or the corresponding teaching material. Remarkably, the committee was effectively demanding the very thing it opposed: that research and instruction be influenced by "practical" motives that themselves, after all, emerged out of the political and social situation in Palestine.

As an alternative to the Arab lecturer, Mayer mentioned the Jerusalem-born Yosef Rivlin for whom Arabic was not a native language but a familiar one since childhood. It seems that Rivlin, from an Ashkenazi family with roots in the Russian Empire, did not satisfy the chorus of critics, however, which was joined in 1936 by the institute's own students, worried that the selection of topics was not sufficiently practical. In February that year, "All HUSOS Students"—or "all but one," according to a handwritten addendum to the typed signature—passed along a letter to the Executive Board of the University, the rector, and all the teachers at the institute.[175] Two years after the completion of the Hartog Committee Report, which prompted no changes to the field of Arabic studies at the institute or to the chronological period taught there, the students, too, wondered about its primary goal:

The university administration has pointed out at several junctures that, in addition to its scientific role, the university is also obliged to serve the essential needs of the *Yishuv* and the Zionist movement, imposing on our institute an important role in our national reality. In

# 112 ::: A NEW ORIENT

accordance with this recognition, we see two primary directions for the role of the School of Oriental Studies:

A) training of scholars and teachers.

B) providing a comprehensive education in Oriental Studies as preparation for official jobs in the Jewish and governmental civil service, for public functionaries, the press, etc.

The said role seems to us to demand an institute consisting of these three departments:

A) Arabic language (Classical, Modern and, if possible, also colloquial Palestinian). Whereas today only the Classical language is taught systematically. It defies logic that, after completing four years of study at this institute, graduates are able neither to write a regular article or letter in Arabic nor to speak with an Arab.

B) The history of the Arab and Muslim peoples, their religion and literature until the present. Whereas today the history taught here reaches only the year 1517.

C) The political, economic, and sociological problems of the Near and Middle East in our times. The vital need for students to gradually complete [the aforementioned article] (b.) first in order to accumulate systematic knowledge on this subject goes without saying.

The letter lays out a series of demands on the basis of this analysis, including "the expansion of modern Arabic language instruction through the addition of a teacher whose mother tongue is Arabic (several hours per week)," and "learning of the colloquial Arabic language by systematic practice in speaking Arabic." While the students' criticism resembles that of Michael Assaf and of the Hartog Committee, the justifications differ. The students saw HUSOS neither as a means for drawing the peoples closer together, nor as a body that must remain neutral, but rather as an institution meant to serve the Zionist movement as a training center. This differing perspective owed in part to their generational position as young people educated mostly in Palestine, within a society undergoing militarization, in the midst of escalating conflict.[176] The students hit upon the distinction proposed by S. D. Goitein in his 1934 article in the newspaper *Davar* between "an 'Orientalist' education" and "education to do work in the Orient";[177] but while he had suggested a bifurcation into two programs within the institute—similar, though not identical, to the Berlin model—the students proposed a comprehensive reorganization.[178]

Though the letter aroused resentment, both the institute and the university administration realized that, as the lack of an Arab teacher was constantly attracting criticism, a solution would have to be found. In April 1936, Mayer made a remarkable proposal to the Standing Committee of the Academic Senate to invite Muhammad Kurd Ali for a lecture series on "Arab Style" as a visiting lecturer, and the committee in fact raised the possibility of offering Kurd Ali a permanent appointment.[179] The proposal, which belied Mayer's response to the Hartog Committee Report, failed to catch on and quickly fell by the wayside. In its place, Mayer began to promote another proposal, which was approved by the Executive Committee at the end of 1936—the appointment of a teacher of "Practical Arabic."[180]

This step, which also carried budgetary implications, was at least in part a consequence of the murder of Levi Billig in his room in the Talpiyot neighborhood of Jerusalem on August 21 of that year, in one of the first waves of violence stemming from the Arab Revolt of the years 1936–1939. The emotional tempest at the university following this episode is evident in the eulogies given at Billig's funeral. Magnes decried the "irony of fate that the cruel bullet had hit this particular man . . . He devoted his strength to Arab science and to understanding Islam and is known by many Arabs." Billig had been found shot dead in his room by Goitein, who declared that "the earth will never be able to disclose the bloodshed, which will not be disclosed or forgiven except with the blood of the one who spilt it . . . Now is not the time to cry. We are in the thick of battle, and soldiers in battle have not the leisure to cry." Yitzhak Ben-Zvi, who also eulogized Billig, attacked the Palestinian national movement—as a "criminal movement that wraps itself in a shroud of freedom"—as well as Arab intellectuals: "What have they done—those who feign compassion? They are, after all, close with the victim. Yet have they uttered a single word of condemnation?"[181] In fact, condemnations of Billig's murder did appear in the Palestinian press, though some expressed doubt that his killers had indeed been Arabs.[182]

Billig's murder and the violent episodes of those years (Avinoam Yellin, who was close with institute staffers, was murdered in 1937 as well), must have done even more to convince the Orientalists that there was no hope of hiring a permanent Arab lecturer. Among their students, some believed —even before Billig's murder—that public opinion would never have accepted it in any case: "Of course, this is the desired goal: to have people who

114 ::: A NEW ORIENT

have mastered the Arabic language, who will be able to teach in the schools, to carry out negotiations in Arabic, write in newspapers in Arabic, serve in government officialdom, and so on. But all of this can be sufficiently provided by those teachers who are here now, as well as Jewish teachers of Oriental extraction, rather than from Arabs. Bringing in Arab teachers . . . would not be effective at this moment, and would only increase the uproar in our camp, especially seeing as there are Jewish teachers trained to teach, lecture and write in Arabic."[183]

With all this in the background and Billig's chair so tragically vacant, the decision came to hire a Jewish lecturer. Mayer put it this way to the Standing Committee of the Academic Senate: "A well-spoken instructor with Arabic as a mother tongue is required, a good teacher, though not necessarily a specialist in the same subject [of Arabic]. The need is for a preparatory course [*mekhina*] instructor."[184] Initially there was talk of employing two teachers for a probational period, and among the candidates considered for the position was the Beirut-born author, translator, and thinker Esther Moyal, who corresponded on the matter in Arabic with S. D. Goitein (who was put in charge of contacting candidates).[185] Yet the only one eventually brought to Jerusalem, invited at Michael Assaf's suggestion, was Isaac (Yitzhak) Shamosh (1912–1968).[186] At the time of his invitation to Jerusalem, Shamosh lived in Aleppo, Syria, where he had been active in the Jewish community from a young age and published articles on various topics in the Arabic press. While studying and earning a certification to practice law at Saint Joseph University of Beirut, Shamosh gained experience teaching at a school in northern Syria. Attesting to the quality of his Arabic were his studies at the Department for Arabic Language and Literature at the Syrian University of Damascus and a prize in the literary competition held by the periodical *al-Hadith*, to which he had submitted an essay on the topic of ancient and modern Arabic literature.

Shamosh initially arrived for a two-month trial course between April and June 1937. He was invited to "take charge of beginner and advanced classes in practical Arabic language, primarily spontaneous Arabic as spoken by educated Arabs in their home countries on the radio, at the university, and so on," as well as "writing exercises and correcting the style of the students."[187] From this description, the intention was clearly not colloquial Arabic, but rather modern literary Arabic, in both speech and writing—the same *Schriftarabisch* mentioned in Horovitz's memorandum of 1925. Goitein wrote to Shamosh before his arrival, asking him to prepare "weekly one-hour lectures on any subject he liked, for example: Arabic literature since the World War." In a letter to the rector, which was not passed on to Shamosh, Goitein made clear that "these were not meant to constitute academic study." Clearly, Shamosh was not being brought in as a regular lecturer, and after a successful trial period, the institute decided to add him to the faculty as a "Lektor in Practical Arabic."[188] The university was therefore obliged to arrange immigration papers for Shamosh. Since his work at the university did not amount to a full-time position, and in order to arrange for him to support his family—who had moved to the country with him—Arabic writing work for the Political Department of the Jewish Agency was arranged for Shamosh. He was eventually given less of this work than was promised, however, and there were frequent disputes over his salary, prompting Shamosh to threaten more than once to quit and leave the country.[189] Shamosh, in any case, was the only faculty member at the time who worked in parallel for the Political Department; this became more common with the second generation of HUSOS faculty members.

Shamosh's arrival achieved the faculty's goal and answered the demands of the students. Goitein informed the university administration that "the instructors who have visited Mr. Shamosh's classes and also the students, insofar as I was able to inquire, have been very pleased with his lessons and his work in general."[190] Six years after Shamosh joined the HUSOS faculty, Mayer praised him for "successfully and devotedly [teaching] one of the most essential subjects in the humanities faculty," for "the instruction of Arabic language and literature at the Hebrew University could in no way be complete without it."[191] Mayer continued, noting that "Practical" Arabic instruction was also useful to the Jewish National Council's Education Department, which was in need of high quality Arabic teachers, and to the Jewish Agency, which sought university graduates capable of speaking Arabic. He added:

> The need for instruction of this kind was identified as soon as the institute was founded, but finding the right person was very difficult. We were looking to find a graduate of higher education with Arabic as a mother tongue, excellent style in spoken and written Arabic, and precise in his language in the best Arab intellectual tradition, with close connections to the intellectual traditions of the Arab world, and pedagogical talent. After searching for several years, we found Mr. Shamosh, who meets all these requirements: born in Aleppo, a uni-

116 ::: A NEW ORIENT

versity graduate, a characteristic Arabic writer involved in the intellectual life of the Arabs, especially well-informed regarding modern Arabic literature, very precise in his language, and an experienced schoolteacher.

The hiring of Shamosh lived up to expectations, then, and "there is no comparing [student] achievements in 'Practical Arabic' before the outset of Mr. Shamosh's work with those now that he has been teaching for several years."

Just over a decade after Horovitz's death, the situation described here by Mayer was leagues removed from the founder's intentions. In 1942, Palestine was awash with anxiety regarding World War II, and memories of the Arab Revolt were still fresh. Shamosh enabled the university to meet the moment's demands: he embodied what was at that moment a reasonable compromise between German philological standards ("a graduate of higher education," "precise in his language") and the demand from students and other critics for a lecturer who was a native speaker of Arabic, especially since the efforts to locate the initial target hire—an Arab or Muslim lecturer—had sputtered long ago, apparently even before they began in earnest.[192] In this sense, Shamosh was part of what Abigail Jacobson and Moshe Naor define as "a hybrid group that bridged . . . the gaps between the Arab and Jewish identities": educated Sephardic and Mizrahi Jews in Palestine who mediated between the old and new *Yishuv*, as well as between Jews and Arabs, through their knowledge of political, cultural, and social aspects of both sides.[193]

Jacobson and Naor's use of the term echoes the theoretical writings of Homi Bhabha on the concept of hybridity and the critical application of his concept to the study of Zionist history by such scholars as Yehouda Shenhav and Gil Eyal.[194] The aspiration of Zionist society, Eyal explains, was to "purify" the Arab-Jews, using them to help sketch the border between Jews and Arabs, defining them as either Jew or Arab; that is, to eliminate their hybridity and thus hone "Jew" and "Arab" into mutually exclusive categories.[195] The Hebrew University of the 1930s and 1940s was in need of Shamosh's hybridity: he was the closest available replacement for an Arab lecturer, both as a teacher of Arabic and as a specialist in the world of contemporary Arabic literature. He remained through the early 1950s the only native speaker of Arabic teaching at the institute.[196] In accordance with Eyal's explanation, Shamosh's hybridity was also "purified" in his new role: the idea that he might mediate the world of modern Arabic literature was little more than an unrealized excuse—Goitein, after all, noted that Shamosh's literature lectures were not considered academic instruction—and in the eyes of the institute's instructors and students, Shamosh's primary virtue was not the content of his courses but his impressively articulate literary Arabic, and the effort he made to inculcate this capacity in his students.[197]

In 1938, after Shamosh's employment had already been made full and official, a man from Haifa named Hassan Amin al-Habash wrote to the Hebrew University. Identifying himself as a *sheikh*, he submitted his candidacy for the role of lecturer in Arabic literature and history.[198] Al-Habash, citing his academic credentials as a graduate of al-Azhar University, expressed a desire to teach "Advanced Arabic and Arabic Poetry" at the Hebrew University, which he had heard about while in Cairo.[199] Reply from the university came that there were no positions available at the School of Oriental Studies at the time.[200] Though al-Habash proposed meeting then-rector Hugo Bergmann or perhaps university administrator David Werner Senator during occasional visits to Jerusalem, the meeting never came to pass— primarily for technical reasons, but perhaps also owing to a lack of interest on behalf of the university's leading figures.[201] The arrival of Shamosh, then, made the necessity of an Arab lecturer redundant.

## THE BORDER LINE: DREAMS OF AFFINITY, ZIONIST REALITY, AND GERMAN STANDARDS

In early December 1946, the journalist and Jewish Agency official Alexander Lutzky (later Dotan, 1911–1971), subsequently of the Israeli Ministry of Foreign Affairs, sent a report to the Arab Bureau of the Jewish Agency's Political Department after having a conversation with Ahmed Samih al-Khalidi (1896–1951), director of the Arab College in Jerusalem.[202] Among other topics, the two discussed the Hebrew University, and Lutzky relayed al-Khalidi's recollection that, "Dr. Magnes laid the impression before him [al-Khalidi] that the university was to serve the entire Near East, and seeing as the university stands with its back to the Orient, he [al-Khalidi] wondered [*tamah*] about this idea. In which language does the university intend to serve the Arabs, in Hebrew? Why should the language of instruction at the university not be English? Why, if the Arabs in Beirut and Cairo have acceded to this as the language of instruction, should the Jews not do so here? . . . He believes the Jews want to create a chauvinistic culture relegating the Arabs to 'tree-chopping and water-pumping' *fellahin*."[203] Lutzky

118 ::: A NEW ORIENT

added in his report that he responded by explaining to al-Khalidi the trademark Zionist stance that the Jews were in fact providing the Orient with a scientific and technical service. There was nothing novel about this claim, which had accompanied Zionist-settler discourse from the outset;[204] al-Khalidi's biting remarks are another story, however, in retrospect even more than at the time of their speaking. They put a mirror before the university leadership and HUSOS faculty, their declarations, and the steps they did (or did not) take during the Mandate to actualize their vision of Jewish-Arab affinity within the Hebrew University.

HUSOS was to be a preeminent means to this end. Its founders hoped that, through the institute's research projects and the fields of knowledge to which it would be devoted, a bridge to the Arab and Muslim intellectual world could be built and well-founded cooperation established. In individual terms, this hope proved fruitful: the institute's Oriental Studies experts forged warm and friendly relations with leading Palestinian, Egyptian, and Syrian scholars on the basis of their research and shared fields of interest.

Yet, almost invariably, these connections remained informal. The political circumstances behind the establishment of the Hebrew University, that is, an explicitly Zionist project enjoying the declarative—though not the regular financial—support of the British authorities, were plain to see both for intellectuals and the wider Arab public in Palestine and the neighboring countries. The escalation of the Jewish-Arab conflict beginning in the late 1920s only exacerbated and sharpened this obstacle. Indeed, hardly any initiatives to foster fraternity between Jewish and Arab scholars of Arabic and Islam found official and public expression—the most glaring example being the failed attempt to recruit an Arab lecturer to the HUSOS faculty. It might have been possible, considering the institute's already limited budget, to take the potentially massive symbolic step of recruiting such a lecturer had the leadership been willing to make certain compromises with regards to the scientific standards that had defined their own studies and training —for example by forgoing the establishment of a preparatory program (at a stage when the chances of locating a candidate willing to teach on Mount Scopus were still somewhat higher). That being said, the young institute, like the entire university, was in fact still struggling at this stage to establish its scientific bona fides and its scholars, of course, had no way of knowing the fate that awaited Mandatory Palestine.

Pressure from the *Yishuv* and the university itself, as well as the gradual realization that the nature of the Jewish-Arab conflict would prevent the institute's research projects from achieving their political aims, meant that—when the institute took on another endeavor—this was aimed not at the Arab and Muslim world but rather Jewish society in Palestine: the preparation of an Arabic-Hebrew dictionary. The profound involvement of the Jewish Agency in the production of the dictionary, providing the material basis and the framework for employing the institute's students working on the project, was meant first and foremost to serve Jewish teachers of Arabic in schools and night classes by furnishing them with "the fundamental tool in the teaching of any language," as its authors described it in their funding application to the Political Department.[205] Numerous copies of the 1937 first edition of the dictionary (a selection of foundational words drawn from the Arabic daily press) were distributed among Arab diplomats and scholars, earning praise in thank-you notes and in several Arabic newspapers;[206] nonetheless, a one-way Arabic-Hebrew dictionary implies a certain declaration of intent. It assists the study of Arabic for beginners and especially the translation of Arabic into Hebrew—particularly of excerpts from the press, in the case of the dictionary produced at the institute—but it remains basic, its connection with classical Arabic is exceedingly weak, and it is unable, indeed was never intended to serve, as a base for connections between scholars.

Recall that journalists, activists, linguists, and educators from the *Yishuv* outside the HUSOS or Hebrew University frameworks formed relations with Arab educators and political activists—Palestinians, Egyptians, and others, especially when it came to the teaching of Arabic.[207] Being active outside the strict institutional framework of the university freed them from the two types of burden borne by scholars within the institute: the obligation to create systematic academic knowledge up to the standards of European universities, and the need to serve as a representative of the expanding Zionist intellectual project on Mount Scopus. Thus, for example, while Taha Hussein was visiting the university in secret in 1941, members of the *Hashomer Hatzair* group were engaged in half a year of intensive Arabic study with a Christian Arab teacher from Haifa, conducted while living in the Druze community of Isfiya, where frequent conversations with the residents were part of their course of study.[208]

Over the course of the 1940s, HUSOS faculty, who had lost colleagues and students to the escalating conflict, grew more realistic in their view of their discipline's capacity to precipitate political change and improve relations between Jews and Arabs, producing in at least some a kind of pessimism that bordered on true dread. In a 1945 letter to Michael Assaf, D. H. Baneth described an experience in the bookstores of the Old City of Jerusalem that left him shaken. He sensed an attitude of sharp hostility on behalf of the merchants: "Nothing like this has ever happened to me, even during the worst times," he wrote. Later, Baneth encountered a threatening group of youths. "My experiences indicate to me that the situation is very tense . . . and I guessed that grave events await at our doorstep," Baneth concluded, citing various reports in the contemporary press. He begged of Assaf: "If, according to the information you possess, there is real cause to fear an eminent outbreak, the press will be obliged, in my opinion, *to awaken our public somewhat from its complacency* . . . the average citizen will be completely surprised; and, if he is prepared with caution, he may manage to act in time to protect life and property."[209] Assaf, a Mapai operative, passed the letter on to the Political Department of the Jewish Agency.

Baneth was writing as an honestly concerned citizen with vivid memories of the previous waves of violence in Jerusalem—he even wondered "whether the situation was prompted specifically in the season of Nabi Musa," perhaps remembering that the 1920 Jerusalem Riots, which took place before his immigration to Palestine, broke out after the Muslim prayer marking the Nabi Musa festival that year. But his letter is also a harbinger of a new stage in the emergence of a relationship between HUSOS and the political decision-makers of the Zionist establishment and the future State of Israel; 1948 was the foundational moment of this stage, in which HUSOS and Israeli Oriental Studies scholars were obliged to operate within the new framework of a statist university; its activities were expected to operate in accordance with the needs of the young Israeli state. For HUSOS, this meant deepening its ties with government ministries, in particular the Ministry of Foreign Affairs (the state-era successor of the Political Department of the Jewish Agency) and, later, with the security establishment. With the sealing off of the borders and the momentous geopolitical shifts undergone in the region, there remained little point to fostering an intellectual affinity that was in any case impossible under the new circumstances, and would now no longer be formed with neighbors but residents of enemy territory.

# 3 : ORIENT RENEWED

## THE BIRTH OF ISRAELI ORIENTAL STUDIES
## AND THE DIPLOMATIC MISSION

In a December 1948 press release, seven months after Israel's declaration of independence, the Hebrew University announced a new appointment: L. A. Mayer of the School of Oriental Studies would serve as "honorary advisor to the Department of Muslim Affairs adjoining the Ministry of Religion of the State of Israel." In this role, Mayer, "as an authority in matters within the purview of this department," would advise the government regarding Muslim religious buildings damaged during the war and their restoration. Mayer's expertise in Muslim structures—the topic of his dissertation at the University of Vienna—was being mobilized for statist ends. Mayer's appointment, the press release announced,

> is another example of the assistance the State of Israel is receiving in the great tasks that stand before it from the university's scholars and scientists. The teachers, graduates, and students of the School of Oriental Studies of the Hebrew University in particular provide invaluable service to the Government of Israel in accommodating the Muslim population within the country and in laying the foundations for good future relations between the two communities ['edot]. They work not only in the special department founded for this purpose at the Ministry of Religion but also in the Middle Eastern department of Israel's Foreign Ministry, where they make up the majority of the employees.[1]

The previous chapter illustrated how, for its founders, improving relations between Jews and Arabs had been one of the goals of the School of Oriental Studies since its opening. This declared goal remains in place within the press release, but the surrounding context that had emerged was fundamentally different: the diplomatic, educational, and cultural needs of the State of Israel, as manifested in the activities of the new government ministries, now topped the agenda.

Over the years, HUSOS personnel remained attentive to surrounding developments: the deteriorating political situation, the external criticism, and their students' expectations from a training in Oriental Studies. During the Mandate, this awareness had not prompted any far-reaching changes to the institute's research activities or the subjects taught there, and its classic textual-philological emphasis was maintained. Work on the large research endeavors continued, even after the institutions where they first emerged —the universities of Berlin and Frankfurt—expelled Jewish scholars from their ranks and began to work in service of the Nazi regime.[2] Students at the institute continued to learn primarily about the early days of Islam, early poetry, and literature, using classical sources, alongside a few courses and practicums that were added to the catalog in the wake of the Hartog Report.[3]

After 1948, this situation began to change fundamentally. The entire university underwent an organizational and spatial overhaul as Judah Magnes, the president with whom it had been so closely associated since its establishment, died during a visit to the United States devoted to preventing the implementation of the partition plan and its consequences; and the hostilities in Jerusalem cut Mount Scopus off from the Israeli-controlled western portion of the city, isolating it in a demilitarized exclave under international supervision.[4] As a result, the university was unable to continue its activities on the Mount Scopus campus, which was hastily abandoned. For the School of Oriental Studies—the "favorite child" of Magnes, who shared founder Josef Horovitz's vision of building affinity between the peoples through the study of Arabic and Islam—Magnes's demise certainly represented a symbolic blow. But the severance from Mount Scopus, which remained within the Israeli portion of the exclave but was inaccessible for routine work, isolated within the heart of Jordanian-controlled territory, was even more grave. Instruction at the institute, and definitely research, were based almost exclusively on materials held in its library and rooms on the Mount, to say nothing of the concordance cabinets. Although the university's activities indeed resumed swiftly in various buildings scattered across the city, like many other university departments, the institute set up in the close quarters of the Terra Sancta compound, where its personnel were forced to adapt to unprecedented material constraints.[5]

For the university, adapting to the crisis of 1948 meant establishing a new "budgetary formula" that ensured the ongoing and indeed significantly-expanded funding of its activities, in exchange for subordinating instruction and research at the university to the needs of the state.[6] HUSOS was no exception. Its two dominant directors—first S. D. Goitein, and later Uriel Heyd, the first Jerusalem-trained scholar of Oriental Studies to head the institute—pursued relationships with various government ministries. First and foremost, as suggested by the press release regarding Mayer, was the Israeli Foreign Ministry: by offering an academic answer to the ministry's diplomatic missions, the institute attempted to secure its financial support in undertaking a chronological, geographical, and thematic expansion of research and instruction at the institute.

Studies that have analyzed the connection between Israeli Oriental Studies and the Israeli state have focused on "security" contexts—especially with regards to Arabs in Israel and the neighboring Arab countries—and on how scholars of Arabic, Islam, and the Middle East have related to the military and the security apparatus's intelligence community, as well as the bureau of the advisor on Arab affairs at the Prime Minister's Office.[7] These studies incorporate sociological perspectives and observations on the contemporary world of Oriental expertise, but the historical surveys they put forth make apparent that institutionalized collaboration in this field between academia and the state was established primarily beginning in the second half of the 1960s, with the dismantling of the military rule of Arab areas within Israel and decision-makers' resulting need for a body of knowledge to replace daily contact with the Palestinian population; and after 1967, in studies that would help give direction to Israeli policy in the territories that had been occupied.[8] To that point, collaboration had generally been the work of individuals with Oriental Studies training, in particular students of HUSOS during the 1950s and early 1960s.

The centrality of the security establishment's links to developments in Israeli Oriental Studies beginning in the mid-1960s is undeniable. Yet the forging of these relations, and the willingness of Orient experts at the very heart of research academia to accommodate governmental necessity from within their institutions, originated in the establishment of another relationship of central importance: one dating back to 1948 between HUSOS and the diplomatic establishment. Despite the significant impact of this relationship on the discipline from 1948 until the middle of the 1960s, it has not been the subject of thorough scholarly examination. Seeing this effort to establish and fortify relations with the Foreign Ministry as a central motive for the development of Oriental Studies during the state period, what we might call "statist Oriental Studies," the bulk of this chapter is therefore an analysis tracing the institute's disciplinary expansion process through

124 ::: A NEW ORIENT

Goitein and Heyd, the figures that led it. Unlike the internal dynamic that had prevailed since the institute's founding, and certainly between Horovitz's death and the end of the Mandate period, the consecutive terms of these two HUSOS directors were characterized by centralization; their voices are the most apparent in the period's archival record, although they largely enjoyed the full backing of their colleagues in Oriental Studies.

In what little writing there is on the history of the institute during these years, its expansion is mentioned briefly as a self-evident product of the establishment of the State of Israel.[9] Yet this expansion, and the particular direction taken in answering the diplomatic efforts and needs of the Foreign Ministry, was not a foregone conclusion. This chapter seeks, for the first time, a parallel examination of the ideological and the functional motives for the expansion of the institute as articulated in archival documentation from the period and in the accompanying writings of Goitein and Heyd.

The chapter will demonstrate that HUSOS expansion was executed under their leadership on the basis of an ongoing dialogue with the Foreign Ministry, part of an attempt to provide both direct and indirect responses to the diplomatic needs of the State of Israel, but that it was also guided by their own fields of interest as scholars. Under Goitein, the institute turned to the study of the modern Middle East, including Turkey and Iran, and its personnel took part in the establishment of the Israel Oriental Society and its journal, *The New East;*[10] Heyd, whose familiarity with the Anglo-American world of Oriental Studies research helped him lay the conceptual foundations for the institute's disciplinary expansion, brought into focus an Orient beyond the Middle East and an Africa beyond North Africa. This process culminated in the change of the institute's name, now known as the "Institute of Asian and African Studies." Moreover, this chapter emphasizes that it was not the younger generation of scholars alone who constructed this relationship with the Foreign Ministry and mobilized in pursuit of its goals, though some of them had certainly joined the institute as instructors after years working in the Political Department of the Jewish Agency and its state-era successor, the Foreign Ministry. On the contrary: the institute's founding generation, those of the classic German training that ostensibly sealed itself off in the ivory tower, were full and enthusiastic partners in these processes.

## THE GOITEIN ERA: POSTWAR RECOVERY AND
## CHRONOLOGICAL AND THEMATIC EXPANSION

In the spring of 1949, amidst the challenges of severance from Mount Scopus, L. A. Mayer announced his intention to retire as director of the institute after fourteen years. For part of that time he had also served, among other roles, as dean of the Humanities Faculty and even, between 1943 and 1945, rector. The university's Executive Committee selected S. D. Goitein to succeed him in the role.[11] The departure of the British brought an end to Goitein's position with the now-closed Education Department of the British Mandate, enabling him to devote himself to the responsibilities of a head of institute. Upon assuming the role, Goitein took a number of steps to address the new era facing the institute, as well as the entire university: the statist era.

According to Uri Cohen and Adi Sapir, who study developments at the Hebrew University after the establishment of the State of Israel, until 1948 the university had been administered under the unique model of a "diaspora university"—that is, alongside some support from the Jewish Agency and the British Government, the bulk of its budget came from donations solicited by various "Friends of the Hebrew University" associations across the world, especially in the United States.[12] This model, without any significant dependence upon a state entity, bred an ethos of administrative and intellectual autonomy at the institution. Having navigated the economic struggles of the World War II years, the university's leaders planned to expand but struggled to raise funds abroad during the political and security travails of 1947–1948, and once the state was founded the government set a low exchange rate on foreign currency. These factors left the university facing a grave economic crisis and in real danger of bankruptcy.[13]

In light of this danger, the first years after the state's establishment were marked by prolonged negotiations between the government and the Hebrew University meant to ensure its ongoing budgetary viability. This cagey process culminated in 1952 after the appointment, supported by Prime Minister Ben-Gurion, of the archaeologist and historian Benjamin Mazar (originally Maisler, 1906–1995) to the dual role of president and rector of the university.[14] As compensation for its funding, writes Adi Livny, the university subordinated research—and, conspicuously, instruction—to the needs of the state, "systematically and on a wide scale": applied research

126 ::: A NEW ORIENT

serving the Zionist movement had predated the state-era university, but this trend now grew to include the social sciences and humanities; as for teaching, the university began to certify at scale the professionals necessary for the nation-building project—both professional training (in law, medicine, or social work) and preparation for public-sector office. This meant, in accordance, that for the first time the university would run a bachelor's program.[15] While it continued to receive donations from abroad that greatly assisted its development, and the influence of the "Friends of" associations was far from negligible, a deep connection was nevertheless formed between the university and the statist idea.[16] At the core of this idea, advanced by Ben-Gurion in contrast to the split that characterized the Zionist movement in the pre-state *Yishuv*, stood the statist demand for loyalty and identification with the central political and cultural authority, while demonstrating a civic conscience and responsibility.[17]

Recall that Goitein was selected to direct the institute in 1949, during the challenging transition from an ethos of autonomy to committed statism. Well aware of both the challenges arrayed before him and the university administration's expectations, he posed several budgetary demands as conditions for taking up the role ("*sine qua non* conditions," he called them) that would enable the institute to continue and expand its activities. In doing so, he sought to lessen the spatial and material constraints of the first years after the displacement from the campus on Mount Scopus in 1948 and the abrupt move to the Terra Sancta compound within the downtown campus. In his letter he demanded, among other things, a designated reading room for the institute's library and an adjoining seminar and practicum room; the appointment of a secretary for the institute; and the provision of a budget to publish research by institute faculty and guarantee its ongoing administrative coordination.[18] Yet the most urgent task, inherited when taking up the position and a first test of the institute's new rapport with the ministries of the Israeli government, was to find an immediate solution to the loss of access to the library on Mount Scopus.

### The "Abandoned Property" Books

In 1948, like in 1926, the work of the institute's scholars, the courses they taught, and the assignments they gave to their students were all text-based. Therefore, the severance of the institute from the books that remained on Mount Scopus prompted a true crisis demanding immediate solutions. A number of potential sources for books emerged at HUSOS faculty meetings: first of all, certain books from the National and University Library were nevertheless gradually making their way to the western portion of the city, or could be located in other libraries scattered across the city; other books could be brought from the scholars' private collections.[19] Finally, a substantial complement to the institute's library was provided by Abandoned Property books, as they were generally known: the thousands of books from public and private libraries and private Palestinian homes, primarily from Jerusalem but also including other towns like Jaffa and Haifa, belonging to people who had fled or were forced to leave their homes during the wartime hostilities in 1948. The government granted the university the authority, through the library, to look after these books: its task was to salvage the abandoned books from plunder, to collect, and to preserve them; a memorandum prepared by Curt Wormann (1900–1991), the library's director, noted that the books would subsequently be returned to their rightful owners, were they to appear.

In recent years, the gathering of the Abandoned Property books has been a focus of scholarly interest and debate, with some condemning the university and the library for conducting a systematic plunder of cultural property under the pretext of urgent salvage.[20] In contrast with contemporary discourse on this episode, records of the meetings and correspondence of the personnel of HUSOS on the subject at the time are remarkably matter-of-fact: at no point did they weigh in on the ethical aspects of collecting the books.[21] The matter at hand was whether the Abandoned Property books could serve the researchers and students in continuing their courses properly, and the university administration did indeed grant the institute permission to establish its own library and transfer some of these books to its own rooms; it also held a list of all the Arabic Abandoned Property books held by the National and University Library, among which the institute's instructors were free to browse.[22]

Even before this, the National and University Library in tandem with HUSOS had entrusted abandoned Arabic books of potential value for Orient scholars, primarily to Martin Plessner, a contemporary of Goitein's whose academic career in Germany had been cut short by the Nazi rise to power.[23] Extensive labor had been invested, in fact, in sorting and listing the books coming from the Haifa home library of Muhammad Nimr al-Khatib (1918–2010), the Muslim cleric and member of the National Committee in Haifa and the Arab Higher Committee during the war, which contained

128 ::: A NEW ORIENT

thousands of books of value to the work of the institute.[24] Nimr al-Khatib left Haifa in early 1948 after being wounded in a failed assassination attempt by undercover agents of the Haganah, the main pre-state Jewish paramilitary organization.[25]

The task of sorting through these and other abandoned books paved Plessner's path into the institute: he had been unable to find a position there after immigrating to Palestine in the 1930s, and worked as an Arabic teacher in Haifa and Jerusalem, all the while seeking a way to return to a university setting and maintaining contact with his German-born acquaintances and colleagues on Mount Scopus. Not even Plessner—a dominant figure in the dovish Ihud association and an outspoken critic of Zionist policy and the Government of Israel—ever expressed qualms about using these books that presented him an opportunity to join the university: he became the institute's librarian first and later began teaching, eventually receiving an official position as a university employee and becoming a professor in the field of the history of science in Islam.[26]

With new purchases and gradual transfers of books from the library on Mount Scopus, HUSOS and National and University Library personnel managed in subsequent years to supplement the institute's library. Once it was capable of hosting the institute's day-to-day work, the subject was no longer a concern for Goitein and the other instructors. They turned their efforts towards bringing the index cards of the concordance down from the hill campus:[27] work on the project continued in West Jerusalem, but without the entirety of the material the labor was less effective. These materials, like those connected with the second research endeavor—publication of the volumes of *Ansab al-Ashraf*—were still on Mount Scopus in 1956, with no clear prospect for when they might be transferred.[28]

As mentioned, any search for voices of opposition to the use of the Abandoned Property books is bound to be disappointed with the correspondence and protocols of HUSOS personnel, or even their subsequent recollections. Apart from the librarian Eliyahu Ashtor, who was part of the collection team put together by the National and University Library and proposed that a portion of the books be "bestowed" upon the library as reimbursement for the effort, neither did any of the Orient scholars address what should happen with these books in the event that their owners demanded their return.[29] Within the prevailing military, political, and social whirlpool, at the time this question seems simply not to have concerned the scholars, for whom use of the books was a necessity without which it would have been impossible to conduct ongoing instruction and research at the institute. In any case, these books would not have reached them without authorization and active assistance from government ministries, which in at least one case preferred the university over other entities interested in them: the Nimr al-Khatib library had initially been intended for the Arabic library established in Jaffa from abandoned books personally collected in various towns by Israel Ben-Ze'ev, then supervisor of Arabic instruction at the Education Ministry; but at the university's request, senior Ministry officials decided that the books go there instead, consulting Ben-Ze'ev only after the fact.[30] This move can be seen as a portent for the coalescing collaboration between the institute and the state.

## The Modern Middle East

As well as a tactful solution to the institute's book problem, Goitein also sought to ease its troubles by re-drawing the borders of the academic field of Oriental Studies on a scale surpassing anything since HUSOS's founding in 1926: expansion of the periods studied and the addition of new subjects of research, to accompany an institutionalizing of collaboration with governmental bodies. After all, back in the 1930s Goitein himself had pointed out the need for another kind of training, alongside the institute's existing emphasis on scientific research: training people of action seeking "to do work in the Orient."[31] Indeed, Goitein fused these two aspects throughout his career in Palestine, both before and after his appointment to head the institute: active in the public realm as the holder of an office in the Education Department of the Mandate government, on the one hand, he was a scholar and lecturer at the institute on the other.[32]

The most dramatic change Goitein sought to implement was the establishment of a new department for the study of the modern Middle East. As I showed in the previous chapters, HUSOS had drawn criticism for its shortcomings in this field; in fact, though students in the mid-1930s had demanded the university administration incorporate modern Middle Eastern history—from 1517 until the twentieth century—into the curriculum, their demands had not been met in any systematic fashion. Now, Goitein felt the conditions had finally ripened to go through with the step: "Though this need was already felt some time ago," he set out to convince a meeting of the Faculty of Humanities, "there were doubts about the propriety of positioning the developments of recent times as a subject of scientific study, but

130 ::: A NEW ORIENT

the recent events in our country and our surroundings have accentuated their necessity, even bringing developments to a certain inflection point that enables scientific study."[33]

Goitein presented his proposal to open a new department within the faculty—entitled "The Contemporary Middle East"—to various ranks at the university, from the Faculty's Curriculum Committee to the Standing Committee of the Senate.[34] His correspondence regarding this department illuminates how he sought to establish and institutionalize the institute's collaboration with the Foreign Ministry specifically by combining forces to hire two HUSOS graduates on the ministry's staff: David Ayalon and Uriel Heyd. Both had been outstanding students of the institute during the 1930s who had been sent for several months of studies at the American University of Beirut at Goitein's urging. The pair's life circumstances, quite distinct, reflect the paths taken by students in the Mandate period who found themselves in need of further income as they completed their dissertations at the institute. There was certainly no guarantee of a professional future within the university—in effect, HUSOS had not completed a single full hire since Isaac Shamosh joined the faculty in 1937—but the focus of their scholarly interests touched upon new fields that departed from the chronological, geographical, and thematic subjects at the heart of the institute's scholarship and teaching, thus opening alternate employment horizons before them.

David Ayalon (until 1948, Neustadt, and in early documents also David Haglili, 1914–1998) was born in Haifa and raised in Rosh Pina by parents who had emigrated from Russia. Arabic was familiar to him from the setting of his childhood. Under the guidance of L. A. Mayer, his studies at the institute specialized in the subject of Mamluk military society. In parallel, after completing his MA, Ayalon found work in research jobs, propaganda, and later teaching in the Arab Bureau of the Jewish Agency's Political Department. Progress writing his dissertation was delayed when, during World War II, he enlisted in the British military in a combat role (though he never left Palestine), and also owing to his extensive involvement in the preparation of the Arabic-Hebrew dictionary published in cooperation with the university.[35] He finally submitted his study on the Mamluks in 1946.

Unlike Ayalon, Uriel Heyd (in German—and early in his career—Heydt, 1913–1968) was born in Cologne, Germany. He began to study law and economics there, but left for Jerusalem in 1934 after the Nazi rise to power and opted for Oriental Studies at the Hebrew University, inspired by his uncle, the linguist Kurt Levy.[36] His studies focused on Ottoman rule in Palestine during the eighteenth century, and at the urging of Gotthold Weil he familiarized himself with the Turkish language. He, too, volunteered for the British military after completing his studies, briefly working as a translator to Arabic and Hebrew. Subsequently, during the war, he travelled to Istanbul University to study Turkish language, literature, and history, and upon his return put to use the Turkish language knowledge he had amassed: first as a translator and editor on the Turkish broadcasts of "Jerusalem Calling" and later as part of the Political Department of the Jewish Agency, where he joined Ayalon. In 1946, Heyd was relocated to the Agency's offices in London, where he completed his doctorate on Ziya Gökalp, one of the progenitors of Turkish nationalism in the nineteenth century. He also capitalized on his time in London to study Persian and Urdu at SOAS.[37] He moved to Washington in 1948, serving as First Secretary to the Ambassador of Israel to the United States, Eliahu Elath (formerly Epstein, 1903–1990), also a former HUSOS student and graduate of the American University of Beirut.

Goitein's move was therefore planned not only to prompt the Foreign Ministry to recognize the contribution of HUSOS training to the state-building project, but also to fund the establishment of a new department by paying the salaries for the additional necessary positions, which were intended *a priori* for institute graduates employed by the ministry. He presented the new department as an alternative to the short-lived training institute founded by the Political Department late in the Mandate period. In this effort, Goitein sought to enlist an influential partner at the Foreign Ministry: Executive Director Walter Eytan (Ettinghausen, 1910–2001). Before his position running the ministry, Eytan had been in charge, within the framework of the Political Department, of founding and directing the Institute for Further Studies (*Hamosad Lehishtalmut*), popularly known as the "School for Diplomats."[38] Founded at the behest of Moshe Sharett (formerly Shertok), director of the Political Department, the institute was a first attempt to systematically train the emergent state's clerical workforce, inspired by the British ideal of the civil service. After a rigorous admissions process, the first class began its studies in November 1946, which were to last a year and a half. Among the lecturers included in the curriculum were scholars from the Hebrew University, such as Ben-Zion Dinur, Richard Koebner, and Roberto Bachi, as well as Goitein and Alfred Bonne of HUSOS. However, with the outbreak of the war, its ranks thinned as cadets began leaving one after the other to mobilize in support of the war

132 ::: A NEW ORIENT

effort.[39] Finally, in February 1948 the institute closed its doors, which never reopened. The first cohort of the School for Diplomats was also its last.[40]

Goitein's overture to Eytan was based on personal familiarity with the training institute and the necessity of finding a replacement for it, and came in the wake of conversations involving L. A. Mayer, who was still HUSOS director at the time. In March 1949, Goitein formulated an official letter to Eytan explaining that institute personnel had long hesitated to delve into twentieth-century political history, fearing they would be unable to distinguish "propaganda from a scientific lecture."[41] This situation changed, he went on, with the establishment of the State of Israel and the achievement of political independence for the Arab countries, which "effectively ended a historical era" that could be engaged with scientifically. Goitein tied this explanation in with his proposed alternative to the School for Diplomats: "It would be illogical to give such a course of study at the university without the Foreign Ministry having a hand in its creation," he wrote, "especially since it will no doubt educate a good number of future candidates for the state's foreign service." Even taking into account the rhetorical context of their writing—an attempt to enlist the addressee and his ministry in a process of both short- and long-term financial significance—Goitein's words were without precedent. For the first time in the history of the institute, a government body was being invited to take part in the establishment and molding of a scientific discipline.[42]

With characteristic practicality, Goitein explained that Mayer's original plan may have been the establishment of a Chair in the Contemporary History of the Middle East, but that the matter depended upon the eventual answer to the larger question of governmental support for the university; as noted, the university was in the midst of its budgetary crisis, and the eventual scale of government support for it remained unclear. Goitein was therefore proposing an initial solution that had already been raised in previous conversations with Eytan, which was the real reason for the writing of the letter in the first place: bringing David Ayalon to the university for a year of research and teaching in Jerusalem while continuing to receive his salary from the Foreign Ministry. Ayalon was not chosen at random: he had taught the history of the Middle East from the year 1000 until the twentieth century during his months of activity at the School for Diplomats.[43] Eytan acceded to the proposal, even adding "that it would be advisable to refer those seeking to complement their studies in preparation for diplomatic service to the Hebrew University, and we shall do so in the future."[44] With the Foreign

Ministry's promise to fund Ayalon as an adjunct lecturer in hand, Goitein was able to convince the faculty, the Standing Committee, and the Executive Committee to approve the establishment of the new department. The ministry's involvement was emphasized during these discussions, including its commitment to grant approval for the proposed curriculum.[45]

The plan for the new department, established as a secondary program exclusively chosen in conjunction with one of the institute's other departments, was focused on subjects appropriate for training in diplomatic work: the political history of the Middle East, with an emphasis on the first half of the twentieth century; economy and society in the Middle East; Arabic literature and journalism; modern literary and colloquial Arabic; and modern Persian and Turkish. It was decided that Ayalon would teach courses such as "European Powers and the Arab Orient," Egyptian history since the nineteenth century, and "Arab Asia in the Twentieth Century." Alongside these courses, the departmental curriculum included preexisting courses by the veteran lecturers in the institute's other departments, including: Economy and Society (Alfred Bonne), Modern Arabic Literature (Isaac Shamosh), and Turkish (Gotthold Weil). Goitein's knowledge of Persian allowed him to take on instruction of both the language and the existing introductory course on "Foundations for the Emergence of the Contemporary Arab Orient"; as befitting a scholar whose training and scholarly focus did not include contemporary history, his teaching thus drew primarily on earlier periods.[46]

This paved Ayalon's path into the ranks of the institute faculty, part of the new department slated to open during the 1949–50 academic year. Remarkably, it was at this point, during the summer before the launch of the academic year, that a dispute burst forth—an ostensibly marginal but actually fundamental one—between Ayalon and the institute faculty. Ayalon preferred that the department be named "The Modern Middle East," rather than "Contemporary," a request unanimously denied at an institute meeting. Goitein explained to Ayalon that "such a change would amount to a change in the subject's direction and content." He added that the faculty members asked that Ayalon "not linger unnecessarily in your lectures on the period before World War I," though he would have a certain flexibility until the proper balance could be found.[47]

Despite the unequivocal decision of his future colleagues, including his former teachers Mayer and Goitein whose work to establish the department had been intended, at least in part, to create a position for him

134 ::: A NEW ORIENT

—Ayalon refused to give in on this demand. The requested name change seemed to him essential, in fact: his lectures aimed to place significant weight on the history of the Middle East as early as the sixteenth century. In retrospect, Ayalon considered his insistence on this matter justified, in spite of his junior position, because he—a former HUSOS student—knew what the students entering the department would be expecting: "The Contemporary Middle East [bahove, lit. 'in the present'], to be told about the ongoing issues."[48] With the term "Modern" (bazman hehadash, lit. "in the New Era," probably operating from a translation of the German Neuzeit), Ayalon hoped to signal to those interested in the "present" not to expect the study of current events. Since Mayer, Goitein, and Baneth taught about the Middle Ages, he explained, if he were brought in to lecture only on late modernity, this would create a "vast empty gap" in between the two periods, prompting a focus on "ongoing events and prognostication. . . . Without this [historical contiguity]—everything would collapse."[49] Ayalon considered the term "Modern" to include the missing period beginning in the late sixteenth century. We might add that, even as a student, Ayalon had been drawn more to study of the Mamluk period, whereas his work on the nineteenth and twentieth centuries had developed primarily as part of his role in the Political Department of the Jewish Agency.[50] His insistence paid off, and—after he threatened not to join if the name was not changed—the institute faculty agreed to his demands. The new department was therefore inaugurated during the 1949–50 academic year. The final course catalog has Ayalon teaching a course on the modern history of Egypt and "Arabic Asia"; he also voluntarily initiated an additional course on Jordan.[51]

The disagreement between Ayalon and his former teachers, primarily Goitein, exposes complexities that undermine the dichotomy common in the research scholarship regarding intergenerational relations at the institute and their impact on the development of Israeli Oriental Studies. According to this bipartite division, the first generation of Oriental Studies scholars tended to focus exclusively on classical subjects and presented a formidable obstacle to any external demand to change the curriculum, whereas it was their students, of the second generation, that brought the winds of change to HUSOS and set aside fears about committing to state demands and fostering the more practical elements of their discipline.[52] Yet here, on the essential question of selecting the period of instruction, it was Ayalon who insisted on a certain distance from issues bordering on the contemporary, whereas Goitein encouraged him to deepen them.

Though they did display pragmatism at various opportunities, the association of the first generation with a tendency towards the classical in selecting the proper period for research and instruction is not without merit. It stems, in part, from their response to the Hartog Committee in the mid-1930s.[53] The institute—which had, recall, nearly the same composition in the 1930s as in the early statist period—never fully implemented the committee's conclusions, which called for explicitly practical elements to be added to the curriculum. HUSOS had instead sufficed with adding "Practical Arabic" lessons and hiring Alfred Bonne of the Jewish Agency, who was brought in to teach courses on the connection between economy and society in the Middle East. Now, some fifteen years later, the trend was reversed.

This shift in the stance of institute veterans prompts a number of explanations. The first is the historiographical explanation provided by Goitein himself in his correspondence with Eytan: the political developments of 1948 marked the end of an era, which might now be subjected to historical research. Yet neither is this explanation sufficient, since it provides no justification for the insistence on the twentieth century in particular. Perhaps focusing on late modernity rather than events adjacent to the Middle Ages ensured that no juxtaposition would ensue between the new subjects and those overseen by institute veterans.[54]

The circumstances of the new department's establishment were prominent in all this: the first collaboration of its kind between the institute and the Foreign Ministry, with aspirations to take part in the training of Israeli diplomats. The institute and the university hoped to strengthen this collaboration, perhaps even including a chair funded by the ministry. For this purpose, it would be necessary to shape a preliminary curriculum, the emergent shape of which fit the needs of diplomatic training, and appealed to the Foreign Ministry. A focus on the twentieth century was a key element of this, and a name reflecting that emphasis would certainly suit the purpose. In any case, even if the considerations were utilitarian, the stance of the faculty veterans of the first generation—Ayalon would later name Goitein, Baneth, and Mayer as those opposed to him on this score—attests to the fact that, while their training had been classical and philological and their scholarship did not broach contemporary historical and political issues, they were the ones eager to incorporate the latter in the curriculum offered by the School of Oriental Studies.[55]

Goitein saw the recruitment of Ayalon to the teaching faculty, despite the latter's disagreements with faculty veterans about "the Modern Era," as

136 ::: A NEW ORIENT

a successful experiment in the improvement of relations between the institute and the Foreign Ministry, which could now be expanded and built upon. "It would be no exaggeration," he wrote to Eytan,

> to say that the students at the School of Oriental Studies showed more interest in this new topic than in any other [course of] study offered there. . . . This was due not only to the novelty of the topic, but through the devotion and enthusiasm of David Ayalon, the depth and precision of his learnedness, and the brilliant combination of historical knowledge and expertise on the present in which he excels. Truly, Ayalon is the exemplary product of the "joint education" of the Hebrew University on the one hand and the Political Department [of the Jewish Agency] on the other.[56]

"[F]or the sake of the young generation we both must help prepare for its roles and for the sake of the entire country," Goitein wrote, the Foreign Ministry must help establish a Chair for the Modern Middle East. He proposed, moreover, that the ministry grant scholarships to some of the department's students.

Throughout this period, the faculty veterans, primarily Goitein and Mayer, were hard at work developing the second branch of the new department—Turkish and Iranian Studies. Uriel Heyd, for whom the position was intended, was then still on diplomatic duty in Washington, and the two older scholars wondered if he might spend time in Turkey and especially Iran before joining the institute, in order to gain a deeper familiarity with both, and with modern Persian. It was important in their eyes that "the man to deal with the *contemporary* Middle East be oriented in it not only through the literature and the passing personal contact that comes with living in an Oriental setting for some time," as Goitein wrote to Heyd himself.[57]

Here too, Goitein intended to make the most of the new opportunities offered by the budding collaboration with the Foreign Ministry: unable to promise him a stipend from the Hebrew University to cover the expenses necessary to reside in these countries for a time, Goitein encouraged Heyd to take the initiative and ask his superiors at the ministry for postings to the diplomatic missions in Ankara and Tehran—to positions enabling him to conduct research in parallel. He clarified to a skeptical Heyd, who did not see how he could divide his time between diplomatic work and academic research, that this was the only way to find stable employment at the institute—even if it meant a delay of several years in taking up his academic

*Orient Renewed* ::: 137

position.[58] Heyd did as Goitein ordered and made the most of a chance opportunity: as a Turkish speaker, he was sent by the Foreign Ministry to advise the Israeli Legation in Ankara headed by Eliyahu Sasson, and was effectively a full partner in its establishment.[59]

Despite opposing the Partition Plan and the granting of UN membership to Israel, Turkey recognized the State of Israel in the spring of 1949 as part of its campaign to establish closer ties with the West, and the United States in particular; the Foreign Ministry hoped this recognition might present an opportunity to forge a strategic alliance between Israel and the non-Arab countries of the Middle East.[60] Heyd's practical and scholarly experience made him a fitting candidate for the task of establishing the Israeli mission. After completing his work in Ankara, during which he was able to make connections with scholars and scientific institutions, Heyd was set to move to Tehran as a "Special Representative," and establish the Israeli Consulate there; however, the journey was cancelled in light of the political situation in Iran, which was experiencing a period of regime instability. Heyd, still an employee of the ministry, was left waiting in Israel.[61]

With Goitein preparing the ground for Ayalon to be brought on as a full university employee, and waiting for Heyd to be available after his mission, a blow to his long-term plans was struck: the Foreign Ministry informed him, in a tone too laconic for him to ignore, that "there was no financial possibility" of establishing a Chair in the Modern Middle East with ministry funds.[62] In retrospect, though this was not the final word on the involvement of the Foreign Ministry in the institute's development, this letter did mark an end to any possibility of its direct and ongoing funding of a chair at the Hebrew University. It seems to indeed have lacked the budgetary capacity to do so: not only was the idea that the new department would replace the School for Diplomats off the table, Foreign Minister Sharett had been unable to secure the necessary funding from the government to establish any kind of training institution whatsoever.[63]

Goitein did not hide his disappointment with the Foreign Ministry's response, but turned his efforts inwards to focus on convincing the various university committees to secure Ayalon's position and to create one for Heyd.[64] Like most attempts to create a position out of thin air, let alone in times of acute budgetary crisis at the university, much convincing was required from the director of the institute, though the Senate and its Standing Committee did eventually approve the creation of the positions.[65] Ayalon's year of successful experience and the escalating student demand for the new

138 ::: A NEW ORIENT

department were contributing factors; and on the budgetary front, Professor of Turkish and Arabic Gotthold Weil would be reaching retirement age in 1952, thus freeing up the position he held—a half-time position upon his arrival in Palestine in 1935 and full-time since completing a term as director of the National and University Library in the middle of the 1940s.[66]

Unsurprisingly, the new department, established in part thanks to years of student demands, quickly gained popularity.[67] Due to the high number of students—nearly a hundred in the 1953–54 academic year—Heyd and Ayalon added another former HUSOS student, Gabriel Baer (1919–1982), as a teaching assistant.[68] Born in Berlin, Baer was the youngest German-born scholar on the institute's staff, having arrived in Palestine with his family as a young man after the Nazi rise to power in Germany and enrolling in the Reali School in Haifa. Like Heyd and Ayalon, he, too, studied for a period at the American University of Beirut, but left the Hebrew University in the early 1940s to become an Arabic teacher and journalist in Jerusalem and Haifa.[69] He did not seek a position at the Political Department of the Jewish Agency, but joined the military in 1948 and served as an intelligence research officer. After Baer's discharge from the military, he completed his master's studies, preparing him to work as a teaching assistant. That Baer's path was unique for those of his generation is also evident from his doctoral dissertation, written while working at the institute; it was advised by the scholar of the Middle Eastern economy Alfred Bonne and dealt with agrarian reform in nineteenth- and twentieth-century Egypt.

Goitein's push for a new approach went beyond the historical side to include the field of language: instruction in colloquial Arabic. Unlike the previous addition to Arabic studies at the institute—bringing Isaac Shamosh on board in 1937 as a teacher of practical Arabic, that is, of conversation and writing skills in modern literary Arabic—the Palestinian dialect was now on the table ("the Arabic spoken in *Eretz Israel*," as Goitein called it).[70] The opportunity presented itself thanks to the expansion of the teaching faculty and the decision to integrate colloquial Arabic lessons in the "Basic Studies" program—general courses in the Humanities included in the bachelor's degree curriculum, under the influence of the American collegiate model.[71] In one instance, Goitein proposed finding "an Arab man or woman" to teach the subject, thus reviving (without mentioning it) the late Josef Horovitz's proposed inclusion of Arab members in the institute's faculty, including a Lektor with Arabic as his mother tongue. This idea was never brought up again, and no explicit explanation was given.[72]

Nonetheless, with Shamosh's support and after consulting the HUSOS faculty, Goitein pursued the appointment of Moshe (Musa) Piamenta (1921–2012), who had completed a master's degree at the institute in the 1940s.[73] Hailing from an old Moroccan-Jerusalemite family, Piamenta's childhood in the Nahalat Shim'on neighborhood adjacent to Sheikh Jarrah meant he spoke fluent Arabic, which Goitein saw as a major advantage: Goitein placed immense value on the correct accent and pronunciation, in both Arabic and Hebrew.[74] Much like the dynamic that led to Shamosh's appointment in the 1930s, here, too, the initial idea to recruit an Arab instructor was swapped out for the hire of a Jew with Arabic as a mother tongue.

Goitein had little difficulty convincing the university committees this time: he had reduced the other HUSOS faculty members' hours of instruction in Basic Studies, freeing up budget for a part-time hire of the new instructor beginning in the 1951–52 academic year.[75] For the first time since Shamosh's recruitment, and the second time in total since the establishment of the institute, a scholar with non-Ashkenazi origins had joined the HUSOS staff. Though Piamenta's addition was not discussed as an integral part of the establishment of the Department of Modern Middle East, and was not tied to the creation of Heyd and Ayalon's positions, it should be seen as part of the same process.

Skepticism of studying colloquial Arabic had, until that point, long been based on the perception that knowledge of classical and literary Arabic ought to be established first on the basis of written texts; this was befitting of the institute's forte in scientific training of a philological nature. Even after the inclusion of everyday literary Arabic—"Practical Arabic," as it was known both at the institute and elsewhere—colloquial Arabic was still excluded. Only in the late 1950s did the American linguist Charles A. Ferguson coin the related social linguistics concept of diglossia to distinguish within a certain language between a low variant acquired as a mother tongue, in this case colloquial Arabic, and a high, literary variant acquired artificially through schoolroom instruction as the proper form, and enjoying greater stature. The fundamental distinction he identified, from which the preference for literary Arabic both written and spoken follows, also determined the approach to Arabic at the university and in the Hebrew-language education system, before and after 1948.[76] At this point, however, the institute found itself needing an answer for students interested in practical training rather than scientific specialization. Colloquial Arabic courses were now open both to students in Basic Studies and bachelor's students at the School of Oriental Studies beginning in their third year—in other words, the latter still had to establish their knowledge of literary Arabic first as a basis for the colloquial language.[77]

An overtly practical aspect was therefore successfully added to the institute. Though the Foreign Ministry may not have funded the chair like Goitein (and, surely, the university leadership) had hoped, its relationship with HUSOS, which had existed since the time of its iteration as the Political Department, became stronger and more established in the subsequent years.[78] The ministry's involvement would be felt in further ways, as I discuss later in this chapter. Just how instrumental its influence was, however, is made clear by the fate of other initiatives Goitein hoped to advance—in which he had a personal scholarly interest—touching upon a subject that had been absent, at the institutional level, from the institute's activities: the history and ethnography of Jews from the Islamic world.

## The Study of Jews from the Islamic World

One of the central initiatives Goitein pushed as an HUSOS project was the study of the language and folklore of Jews from the Islamic world. There was a relatively solid methodological and organizational basis for this: his own work. Though he had studied Quranic prayer under Horovitz's supervision in Frankfurt and was responsible in Jerusalem for the preparation of one of the *Ansab al-Ashraf* volumes, after arriving in Palestine he became intrigued by the Mizrahi Jewish communities living in Palestine, especially the Yemenite Jews. Like many European observers, he saw these Jews as representing an authentic Jewish way of being.[79] He began studying the language and way of life of the Yemenite Jews, the "Most Jewish and most Arab of all Jews" as he put it, and established himself as an important researcher in that field during the 1930s and 1940s.[80] When he was appointed director of HUSOS, Goitein sought to institutionalize the arrangement he had already implemented, which included research assistants, Yemenite-Jewish informants, and others he had recruited, under a new HUSOS research initiative. In light of the mass immigration from Yemen, he saw this initiative as an opportunity to research Yemenite-Jewish heritage, "to save it from oblivion and inscribe it in the scientific record, preserving the results for posterity."[81] The project did earn a one-time budgetary allowance from the university, but the administration asked Goitein to find external sources of funding to continue it.[82] No such sources were found.

*Orient Renewed* ::: 141

Nevertheless, the research enabled by this limited funding, as well as the personal research activities of a number of HUSOS faculty and students — specific bits of which received funding from the Ministry of Education — amounted to an apparatus Goitein described to the education minister as "the department for the study of Judaism in the Islamic lands," though this was seemingly not a formal, institutionalized department. Apart from the study of Yemenite Jewry, Goitein also mentioned among the research activities of this department the collection of studies conducted on Jews from Libya, Iraq, and Kurdistan.[83] Except for the studies of Yemenite Jewry, in most cases the preliminary studies presented by Goitein in this letter never came to fruition within the framework of HUSOS activities, and this initiative, which never received ongoing, official support in the first place, ended up being short-lived.

A further initiative in this direction, which never made it past the planning stages, was Goitein's attempt to integrate the history of Jews in the Islamic world as a subject in the university's course catalog. The place of the School of Oriental Studies with regards to both the Hebrew University and the state in its early years, is actually better understood through an exploration of this failure and the contributing circumstances behind it; so, too, is Goitein's role as its leader. Indeed, Goitein's initiative was driven by shifts in his own research interests in this case as well: it was in the late 1940s that he became interested in the history of the Jews of the Mediterranean basin in the Middle Ages.

The central corpus of texts that was used to study this branch of history is the Cairo *Geniza*, which Goitein had first encountered during a visit to Hungary during the first ceasefire of the war in 1948.[84] Looking back, he attested to the complete transformation this encounter had upon the character of his work and the course of his life.[85] This was also the beginning of a more general change in the character of research on the Jews of Mediterranean lands in the Middle Ages, marked by a turn in focus from the religious and literary creations of these communities to their social and economic histories. Goitein's scholarly engagement also had its ideological roots: he believed that the classical *Geniza* period (the tenth through thirteenth centuries) presented a model of Jewish-Arab communal life that should be emulated, to some extent, in planning the future of the State of Israel and the Jewish people.[86]

Within the university framework, Goitein's initial goal was to integrate the history of Jews from the Islamic world as a field not under the umbrella

142 ::: A NEW ORIENT

of the School of Oriental Studies, but rather the Department for the History of the Jewish People.[87] Faculty at the Institute for Jewish Studies, which encompassed the activities of this department, opposed this objective. Their aversion resulted from the widespread Eurocentric perception of the history of these Jews—especially after their "Golden Era" in Spain—as a secondary field within Jewish history; they also entertained personal doubts about the candidate Goitein proposed to teach the field, Eliyahu (Eli) Ashtor.[88]

By age, Ashtor (born Eduard Strauß in Vienna, 1914–1984) belonged to the institute's second generation, but unlike his contemporaries, his Orientalist training was completed in Europe, at the University of Vienna, which awarded him his doctoral degree in Arabic Language and History; he even studied at the local rabbinical seminary, much like some of the institute's old guard, but his studies were cut short with the annexation of Austria to the Third Reich in 1938. Goitein felt a sense of personal responsibility towards Ashtor: it was in part with his aid that Ashtor managed to receive immigration papers, escape Austria, and join the National and University Library in Jerusalem as the librarian responsible for Oriental Studies (a role which involved him in the collection of Palestinian books in 1948). In parallel, he studied towards a second doctoral degree in the Department of Islamic Culture. Ashtor's primary scholarly focus, in addition to the study of the Mamluk period's economic aspects, was the history of the Jews in Egypt and Syria; he published a book in Hebrew on this topic in 1944 based in part on sources from the Cairo *Geniza*. This improved his standing in the eyes of Goitein, who saw in him an eminently appropriate candidate to teach and conduct research in the field.

In light of the Institute for Jewish Studies's unequivocal opposition, Goitein composed an alternative proposal for the establishment of a new department devoted to the topic within HUSOS, its courses to be open to students in the Department for the History of the Jewish People. The new department's purpose, as Goitein formulated it at the beginning of his proposal, was "to train its students to recognize and research the history and culture of the Jews in Islamic lands through the ability to independently read Oriental sources and through knowledge of one of the dialects that was or is spoken by these Jews."[89] According to the plan, the department's offerings would include required courses on "Judaism in the Age of Emergent Islam"; Jews of the Islamic world through the First Crusade; the history of the Jews in the Orient from the First Crusade until the Ottoman occupation of Palestine (1516); the history of the Jews in Spain and North

Africa; readings in literary texts—philosophical, religious, and others; and a course titled "'Oriental Communities' in Our Time." The required courses proposed by Goitein are a good reflection of the change he hoped to bring about with regards to the scholarly tradition at the institute and its German roots: the explicit emphasis suggested in the core courses was historical, including the Mamluk period, rather than the classic text-centered philological tradition.

In addition to this historical emphasis, the inclusion of "'Oriental Communities' in Our Time" also stands out. Goitein's use of the category "Oriental communities" (*'edot hamizrah*)—as well as its placement between quotation marks in the title—indicates a certain awareness of the term's complex nature: this was one of those categories that—much like the use of "Sephardi" or "Mizrahi"—artificially molded Jews originating across the Islamic world into a single concrete, sociologically-generalizable group. "Oriental communities" was born out of the reality created on the ground by the Zionist movement: groups of different origins meeting one another, and encountering those from other ethnic backgrounds.[90] The sociologist Yehouda Shenhav claims that the use of such categories in establishment Zionist discourse (both before and after the founding of the state) defined all the Jews of the Islamic world "as holders of a homogeneous and unitary identity, effectively blurring the differences between them."[91] Presumably, Goitein invoked the category of "Oriental communities" for practical reasons: the need for a term in common parlance that was concise enough to include in a curriculum meant for a large audience of discussants. At the same time, the quotation marks indicate a certain discomfort with the phrase.[92] The draft curriculum itself shows that Goitein preferred the phrase "Jews in Islamic lands"; the homogenous category of "Oriental communities" fit awkwardly into his understanding, as a scholar at least, of the ethnic differences between these groups and their distinguishing characteristics.

The explanatory detail and the various elective courses offered thus reflect an attempt to appeal to as large a student population as possible, such that the course of study could be shaped around a historical ("The History of the Jews in Spain and North Africa"), literary ("Persian-Jewish Literature"), or ethnographic ("'Field Work' with one of the communities living in Israel") emphasis. The ethnographic element had roots in the German academy as well as the research and cultural activities practices of both German and Eastern European Jews,[93] but it had no institutional foothold within the Humanities Faculty in Jerusalem during the 1940s or the 1950s.[94]

144 ::: A NEW ORIENT

Still, the ethnographic study of Jews from the Islamic world was not completely foreign to the School of Oriental Studies. Goitein himself, after all, had studied the Yemenite Jews and advocated the study of other Jewish communities arriving in Palestine. In 1929, the institute's first Lord Plumer Prize was awarded to the anthropologist Erich Brauer (1895–1942) to advance his ethnographic study of Yemenite Jewry.[95] As the previous chapter illustrated, L. A. Mayer exhibited a particular interest in ethnography through his collaboration with the Palestinian ethnographer Tawfiq Canaan and in his activities with the Palestine Oriental Society. The historian and geographer Samuel Klein (1886–1940) of the Institute for Jewish Studies worked on the ethnography of Palestine, among other topics.[96] Nonetheless, as we saw, the bulk of research in this field in the 1940s and 1950s took place beyond the hallowed halls of the Hebrew University. No scholars followed in these footsteps of Klein's at the Institute for Jewish Studies after his death, in no small part because its dominant personalities considered ethnography marginal relative to the central status of historical research; as the Institute for Jewish Studies sought to center its research upon text rather than territory, ethnographic research was neglected.[97]

After a roiling discussion at an undocumented faculty meeting, this proposal of Goitein's was rejected as well, and a large majority opted, alternately, to establish a "program" rather than a department, to be based solely on existing courses in the departments of HUSOS, to which "a course in the history of the Jewish people in the Islamic lands based primarily in Arabic sources" would be added, which Ashtor would indeed be appointed to teach.[98] There may have been a certain echo of historical and literary elements here, but the ethnographic field—the one in which Goitein maintained a personal scholarly interest, of course—received not a mention in the new program.

The primary impact of this decision to examine neither contemporary Jews of the Islamic world nor their recent past seems to have been to leave this body of knowledge—within the halls of the Hebrew University—to the exclusive purview of sociologists. The Sociology Department at the Hebrew University received its essential spur to action in 1949 with the appointment of Shmuel Noah Eisenstadt (1923–2010) as chair. In comparison with the approaches of those who preceded him in conducting sociological research at the university—Arthur Ruppin and Martin Buber, despite the profound differences between them, were both oriented towards German scientific and political thought—Eisenstadt offered an empirical-analytic approach founded in American scientific methods.[99] The Hebrew University administration asked him to fashion a "modern" department of sociology. His empirical approach, alongside the need to establish the relevance of the new department, gave rise to close cooperation with state authorities; this was reflected in scholarship that aimed to meet certain challenges the Israeli establishment encountered in shaping its contemporary policy on various topics, first and foremost the absorption of Jewish immigrants from the Islamic world.[100] Under Eisenstadt's leadership, the Sociology Department carried out sustained observational studies among immigrant populations; on this basis, it offered practical solutions to problems stemming from cultural difference. Thus, unlike a decimated European Jewry and its culture, contemporary Jews from the Islamic world became the responsibility of sociologists and immigrant absorption experts; that is, they became a social issue to be solved.[101]

Thus, in attempting to establish widespread institutional representation for his own research interests, Goitein was far from successful. The initiative had clearly been his, and no other members of the institute were visibly involved; this made it a lesson in the limitations of his power within the framework of the Hebrew University and the potential horizon for development on offer there. Moreover, while Goitein had enjoyed the favorable winds of both government cooperation and widespread student demand for the process of integrating modern Middle Eastern history into the institute's programs, no such winds prevailed in this set of activities—government offices were certainly more interested in the applied sociological approach, and since delving deeper into this field was unlikely to open any professional opportunities, the institute's students made no demands that it be taught.[102] This makes no less remarkable Goitein's efforts to break with the institute's preceding line—in the spirit of Magnes and Horovitz and the selection of subjects that were not "Jewish"—and not only turn to the study of Jews but also employ methods that had not previously been an integral part of the institute's work. His insistence on this highlights once again that the School of Oriental Studies' German heritage should not be seen as a monolithic, unchanging inevitability.

## The Israel Oriental Society and The New East

Novelties and additions to the ongoing activities within HUSOS were not the only fundamental change brought by 1948. Under Goitein's leadership, the

146 ::: A NEW ORIENT

institute's faculty—more determined than ever to establish collaboration with bodies outside the university that might be translated into budgetary sources—took part in establishing an association that, while it enjoyed the institute's patronage, did not belong directly to the university: the Israel Oriental Society and its flagship activity, the publication of its periodical *The New East*.

As early as 1945 at the Political Department of the Jewish Agency, Uriel Heyd had suggested establishing a "scientific society" separate from the Agency itself, which would publish an English-language monthly providing news about events in Middle Eastern countries that would benefit from "precision, objectivity, and perfect editing," granting the Agency "a chance to present a most important circle of readers with whatever articles we would like on Palestine and neighboring countries."[103] But Heyd's general idea was made operational only in late 1948 and 1949 at the behest of Goitein, the "living spirit" behind the establishment of the new learned society.[104] In the history and sociology of education, modern learned societies are defined as relatively open organizations that serve to disseminate knowledge, exchange knowledge, and create research networks within a discipline, a sub-discipline, or a specific field by holding conferences and meetings and publishing books and journals as well as recognizing and financially supporting its members for their achievements and public representation of the discipline or field.[105] The previous chapter illustrated that such societies existed in Palestine before 1948: some provided Jews, Arabs, and Europeans with a joint forum to share their research, while others were exclusively Zionist-Jewish.[106]

The new learned society was officially launched at a founding assembly held in May 1949, following months of preparations involving, among others, Goitein, Mayer, and the Foreign Ministry staffer Alexander Dotan, there on behalf of the minister Moshe Sharett.[107] The name chosen for it, the Israel Oriental Society (*Hahevra Hamizrahit Hayisra'elit*), was almost identical to the Palestine Oriental Society in which L. A. Mayer had been a leading member and with which other institute faculty had collaborated during the British Mandate. Yet the ostensibly symbolic transition from "Palestine" to "Israel" was, of course, fundamental. The Palestine Oriental Society ceased to exist after the establishment of the State of Israel as a result of political and demographic developments and changes in the nature of foreign institutions' involvement in research within the country.[108] The Israel Oriental Society was a completely new institution.[109] While the former included Jewish and Arab members working together, as we saw, the latter's council and committee did not include a single non-Jewish member when established.[110]

Another element distinguishing the new society from the Mandate-era one was that its officials, and especially its (forty-person) council, included not only outright scholars but also governmental officials, diplomats, journalists, politicians, and even one military official. The selection of council members attested to the founders' hopes regarding the character of the society: linking the university's scholars of Oriental Studies to the experts and those with a personal and professional interest in developments in the Middle East. This was a different type of learned society, one consistent with the statist era. According to Eyal Clyne, the Israel Oriental Society functioned as an intentionally liminal space between academia and the state where scholars of Oriental Studies could make connections with governmental figures without staining the purity of their academic authority. In other words: the Israel Oriental Society was a place in which to meld science and politics, so that the university itself could remain free of such mixing.[111]

Jacob M. Landau, who served as secretary at the society's first meeting, recalled anecdotally years later how one participant in a smaller discussion of mostly university scholars had raised the possibility of calling the organization "The Orientalist Society" (*Hahevra Hamizrahanit*), and Baneth had responded forcefully that the name must be "The Oriental Society" (*Hahevra Hamizrahit*), in accordance with its German equivalent—the *Deutsche Morgenländische Gesellschaft*, or German Oriental Society (DMG).[112] Baneth's determination offers a fascinating parallel (though, due to the chronological and geographic distance, a tentative one): since its founding in 1845, the DMG, too, had included diplomats, officials, and military personnel alongside both university-affiliated and independent scholars;[113] and its founders, who were professors, also sought to channel Prussian political interest in the Middle East, which was aroused in the 1840s, to marshal public support and governmental financial support for the research and development activities of the Orientalist discipline.[114]

At the same time, one ought to emphasize that the DMG was established within an unique learned context—as part of the effort, at the time, to free German Orientalism from the theological field and to prop it up as an independent discipline, and to provide an answer, at the national level, to the foundation of Oriental associations in France and Great Britain.[115] No comparable challenge stood before Israeli Oriental Studies, and there

148 ::: A NEW ORIENT

is no indication that the circumstances of the DMG's founding consciously guided the decision to found the Israel Oriental Society. Nevertheless, the first generation of HUSOS scholars, with their German training, knew the DMG as a dominant and fertile group in the Orientalist world from which they emerged. In both the mid-nineteenth-century German and the mid-twentieth-century Israeli cases, it seems—despite the different contexts —that scholars of the Orient sought to strengthen their connections with governmental and other forces harboring interests in the Orient, and to solidify public legitimacy for their activities, in the hope that these connections might ensure the material future of the field.

The founding assembly of the Israel Oriental Society gathered in Tel Aviv—initially the center of government activities and later of the Foreign Ministry, rather than in Jerusalem, home of the university—under the leadership of Goitein and Michael Assaf. Assaf, the Orient expert, journalist, and Mapai activist, was in regular contact with the Orient scholars of the Hebrew University and occasionally critical of the institute, as attested by his engagement with their affairs during the 1930s.[116] The assembly made decisions about what form the society would take and what institutions it would include: Goitein was elected president, Assaf his deputy, and Mayer an honorary president; the members of the society's council and committee were also selected, with both including academics, diplomats, educators, and other governmental officials.[117] In addition, a set of regulations was ratified, including details on its goals, primarily "to stimulate interest, disseminate knowledge, encourage original study of the Orient in its entirety, and to foster cultural and friendly relations with the peoples of the Orient," before emphasizing that "the society is an independent and apolitical body."[118] In the spirit of statism, while the society did not belong to any government institution or particular party, apart from membership fees and payments for activities it initiated, the bulk of its budget came from government bodies—the Foreign Ministry, the Ministry of Education, and the Jewish Agency.[119]

The voices of these funding bodies and other institutions were certainly audible: the first meeting of the society's council was held in December 1949 in the home of the cabinet secretary of the Israeli Government, Ze'ev Sherf. Apart from the host and the founders Goitein, Assaf, and Dotan, participants included member of Knesset Yitzhak Ben-Zvi, Israel Defense Forces (IDF) chief of staff Yigael Yadin, justices Nathan Bar-Zakay (Bardaki) and Emmanuel Matalon, Israel Ben-Ze'ev, United Workers Party (*Mapam*) of-

*Orient Renewed* ::: 149

ficial Aharon Cohen, *Ha'aretz* publisher Gershom Schocken, and deputy executive director of the Ministry of Education Yehuda Leib Benor.

Discussion at the meeting primarily considered how the society's affiliated publications might properly be distributed more widely, particularly the journal it had only just begun putting out, *The New East*. Ben-Zvi and Ben-Ze'ev believed the focus should be on publications in Hebrew rather than foreign languages. Schocken proposed that the society serve as a clearing house to help articles find their way into newspapers and periodicals, so that news about the Orient might be disseminated broadly and not just to "a narrow circle dealing with issues of the Orient." Yadin, on the other hand, was in favor of publishing in foreign languages, but mentioned another role he attributed to the society's publications—as a back-channel by which to pass information to the leaders of Arab countries: "Everything that is written in Israel on the neighboring countries, is pounced upon there and translated by the intelligence [services] right away . . . These things will soon reach the Arabs." Yadin suggested writing articles with "a certain orientation," like an article on the importance of the southern Negev region to the State of Israel, and concluded as the IDF representative at the meeting: "The Army would like to receive hundreds of iterations and distribute the quarterly [*The New East*] among the officers. The quarterly could also give expression to military organs, [and] to arrange seminars for officers."[120]

Indeed, the dissemination of news and knowledge became the primary activity of the society: as an entity mediating between lecturers—academics and non-academics alike—who were members of the society, and various bodies and the wider public;[121] and as a publisher, primarily of *The New East*, the first issue of which went out in October 1949, edited by Yaacov Shimoni of the Foreign Ministry. It included an introduction by Society president Goitein, written in Hebrew and carrying an identical name to the title of the journal. In an English table of contents for the issue, this introduction was titled, unlike the journal, "The New Orient"—which attests to the confusing interchangeability of the two terms in Israeli eyes. The issue also included an article by Michael Assaf on Arab integration in the State of Israel, and three more articles written, without any academic apparatus, by Foreign Ministry personnel: Shimoni prepared an analysis of the political situation in Syria; Pessah Shinar, a former HUSOS student and the official in charge of research on North Africa at the ministry, wrote about "Italy's colonies on the international stage";[122] and Shmuel Ya'ari surveyed the present state of railways in Syria and Iraq as well as plans to develop them in the

150 ::: A NEW ORIENT

future. Foreign Ministry personnel added brief press overviews on developments in countries in the region. The issue concluded with a number of book reviews. This basic combination was maintained, for the most part, in subsequent issues—numerous contributions from Foreign Ministry staff, alongside an article or two in each issue by scholars from HUSOS.[123]

The Israel Oriental Society (today the Middle East and Islamic Studies Association of Israel, MEISAI) and its periodical *The New East*, therefore, represented a new route, apart from university research and instruction, by which to strengthen relations with state institutions, and the Foreign Ministry in particular—one which, in this case, also entailed various opportunities for funding.[124] In addition, the institute's veteran faculty—who, unlike their students, had never worked in the Jewish Agency's Political Department, the Foreign Ministry, or the newspapers—now had an opportunity to engage in newsworthy topics and outside the purview of their direct university role, and to establish their expertise vis-à-vis a wider audience.[125]

Naturally but also ironically, the institute's expansion in all its aspects exacerbated the most obvious physical challenge posed to its teachers and students—a lack of space. During the university's severe budgetary crisis in 1951, the university administration had mobilized the institute for the purposes of an appeal to the government. Goitein wrote a strongly-worded letter addressed directly to Rector Schwabe, who forwarded it to various ministers—including the Finance, Labor, and Education ministers. The letter described difficulties at the institute, which received no more than a single room, which was in poor shape, and did not shy away from the odd dramatic phrase ("we are in a situation of prolonged death," "I am ashamed in front of my students and cannot stand to show myself to them").[126] This letter was part of the ongoing effort to increase the scope of government support for the university. Indeed, several months after its sending, the government decided—conditional upon increased involvement in the decision-making process around the university's future—to double its budgetary allocation.[127] Over the course of 1952, the institute received additional rooms for its use within the confines of the university's temporary seat at Terra Sancta.[128]

This is another example of Goitein's place in the chain linking the university to the government. The accumulation of initiatives he led, some involving other institute faculty members but under his definite leadership as director, add up to a critical mass of evidence allowing one to see him as the father of Israeli Oriental Studies. The incorporation of the history of the modern Middle East in the curriculum, as well as the establishment of the Israel Oriental Society and the regular dissemination of its *The New East* were steps that transformed the field locally and institutionalized a set of relationships between HUSOS and the government. The institute being a university body in a statist era, this was not achieved solely through indirect means but rather directly, especially vis-à-vis the Foreign Ministry. In parallel, Goitein engaged in building up the institute's workforce, folding the development of the discipline in with the personal development of former HUSOS students and their integration within its teaching and research apparatus in permanent positions. These students were members of a new generation trained, in the spirit of the distinction Goitein made in the 1930s, in both academic expertise on the Orient and in preparation to work in the Orient—in diplomacy, journalism, and the military.[129] Although there were also initiatives that failed to progress as he hoped, the charismatic and active Goitein became practically the face of Israeli Oriental Studies and the leading architect of collaboration with the government during the state's first decade.

## THE HEYD ERA: RISE OF THE SECOND GENERATION AND THE GEOGRAPHICAL EXPANSION OF ORIENTAL STUDIES

Goitein's dominant directorship of the School of Oriental Studies, wide-ranging involvement in the development of various aspects of higher and primary education in the country, and his parallel commitment, expressed at various opportunities, to the Zionist project—all led to widespread surprise when his long research stay in Philadelphia became a second and final episode of emigration. Though he consistently described this as a temporary move, Goitein effectively transplanted himself to the United States in the summer of 1957, at age fifty-seven—first to Philadelphia and, later, to Princeton, where he lived until his death—in order to delve into the study of Cairo *Geniza* documents.[130]

His departure left an understandably large void at HUSOS.[131] Uriel Heyd was appointed to fill the directorship, on Goitein's recommendation, after he gave notice before setting off that he was leaving the role.[132] For the first time the institute in Jerusalem would be led by one of its own graduates, in a moment of symbolic intergenerational handoff: the institute's directors had

152 ::: A NEW ORIENT

to that point held doctorates from Berlin, Vienna, and Frankfurt. A point of similarity represented another layer of symbolism: despite the distinction in age and biography, like his predecessors Heyd, too, was born in Central Europe and raised with German as his mother tongue. He had already earned the rank of professor before being appointed director, evidence of his swift rise within the institute; correspondence regarding his appointment included no reservations from the institute faculty or university administration. He had been involved in developments at the institute dating back to the foundation of the state, operating in a kind of pincer movement with Goitein, who was constantly engaged administratively in pushing initiatives for expansion and in forging the connection with the Foreign Ministry, while Heyd—described by one of his students and colleagues as a "man of vision"—provided the university, at two separate junctures, with the more profound disciplinary justifications for these shifts.[133]

### The Conceptual Infrastructure

In the fall of 1948, while serving as secretary of the Israeli Embassy in the United States, Heyd sent a document from Washington proposing the establishment of the study of the modern Middle East at the Hebrew University.[134] David Werner Senator, acting director of the university after the death of Magnes, had requested this document from Heyd following a meeting in New York during Senator's visit.[135] In its introduction, also sent to L. A. Mayer (at the time still director of HUSOS), Heyd noted that he had pondered the subject since his years as a student at the university, and had discussed the proposal with Orient scholars and others interested in the modern Middle East in Palestine, England, and the United States. All considered the plan important and feasible. He added, based on personal experience, that there was ample interest in the field among the younger generation of academia in the country, suggesting that there was local demand that the proposal would meet, which was in accordance with trends in the study of the Middle East and Islam in the Western world.

Indeed, following World War II and amidst the emerging Cold War at the close of the 1940s, the field had undergone significant change in the Anglo-American world. This was especially true in the United States, which had become the leading power of the Western bloc, taking the lead from the states of Western Europe. The American government saw North Africa and the Middle East, in the process of decolonizing, as sites of strategic importance. Yet the scholarly body of knowledge on the area was lacking: even following World War I, the vast majority of Oriental Studies scholars at American universities continued to study classical and philological topics.[136] Out of this need was born the area studies approach, according to which knowledge creation should be divided by area rather than discipline, with all those interested in studying a specific area, across the humanities and social sciences, collaborating in the production of knowledge that could serve government decision-makers. One of the leading fields, which various universities developed according to this approach, was Middle East Studies or Middle Eastern Studies. Parallels between Israel and the United States have their limits: unlike the expectation (achieved only in part) of governmental funding at HUSOS, in North America this field initially developed not through public funding but with the contributions of private donors and foundations.[137]

In accordance with the developments he was personally observing in America, Heyd—intimately familiar with both HUSOS and the diplomatic challenges of the State of Israel—proposed a new definition of the role of Israeli Oriental Studies within the document. The State of Israel, he said, "is rebuilding the center of Jewish national life in the midst of Oriental, mainly Islamic, nations." In order "to integrate in the Middle East, the people of Israel"—a phrase that assumes the Jewishness of the country's residents —"need a deep understanding of the history," culture, and "contemporary developments" in neighboring countries. "Academic research and instruction in this field will go far in prompting understanding and cooperation between Israel and its neighbors."[138] The institute's pioneers some twenty years earlier spring immediately to mind, with their expressions of hope that instruction and research would advance understanding between Jews and Arabs—except that Heyd was referring now to new state entities, rather than to peoples and religions; and if Horovitz and Magnes believed that the knowledge produced by the large research endeavors at the institute would serve as a field of joint interest or a subject of conversation of sorts that might aid the formation of relationships with the Arab intellectual world, for Heyd knowledge about the modern Arab and Muslim world in and of itself would enable the State of Israel to make a connection with it.

Heyd offered a further, parallel justification that was common in the Zionist arsenal: as the peoples of the Middle East experienced significant developments not only of an economic and social but of a religious and cultural nature, the entire modern world stood to benefit from Israel

## 154 ::: A NEW ORIENT

"interpreting these developments to the West," thereby "fulfill[ing] its historic mission as a bridge between East and West."[139] Israel's geographic location, he specified, provided it with a comparative advantage over farther-away institutions in Europe and the United States; but the Hebrew University would nonetheless conduct research on these subjects "by Western scientific methods, which are often lacking in the research work done by natives of these countries," that is, by local Arab scholars.

As the previous chapters have shown, arguments about the benefits of the institute's combination of Western methodologies and its presence in the region had been in circulation since HUSOS's earliest days, as were complaints within the university and the *Yishuv* that it took insufficient advantage of this benefit. Heyd's words applied these regular remarks to a new field of research that his teachers at the institute, most of whom were trained in the German philological tradition, hardly touched upon in their personal research, the courses they taught, or the institutional research initiatives. He emphasized this himself when writing that the School of Oriental Studies engaged primarily with classical Islam and Arab history before the Ottoman conquest in 1517. Therefore, he found it to be missing important fields: systematic instruction on tendencies in modern Islam, secularization and Westernization, religious minorities in the Middle East, and modern literature studies in languages other than Arabic. Heyd's justifications led to his central plea: a new chair should be established within the School of Oriental Studies for the history of the Middle East since the sixteenth century and for modern Islam, and courses on these subjects should be added, to become an "integral part" of the university's plans to engage in the training of civil servants, journalists, economists, and teachers. Heyd, in effect, repeated almost precisely the demands of the institute's students in the mid-1930s, who expected it to not only mold scholars and teachers, but also provide "a comprehensive Orientalist education" to those entering the local job market in relevant professions, whether within the civil service or elsewhere.[140]

Not coincidentally, Heyd's claims were interwoven with those made by Goitein during these years as director of the institute. Heyd may have sent the document, but he was still in touch with his former teachers, who encouraged him to sustain this initiative for the development of modern Middle Eastern studies.[141] While Goitein primarily prepared the ground for the bureaucratic efforts awaiting within the university, Heyd—familiar from his time in England and the United States with institutions studying the Orient and the personalities active within them, and well-informed of course on the prevailing demands of diplomacy—provided him with the disciplinary justifications for the move, and perhaps also represented the university's interests within the Foreign Ministry. The cooperation between Goitein and Heyd from the outset of the institute's expansion illustrates an important point, to which we shall return: the institute's older, German-trained generation, and their former students—the younger generation of instructors—were of one mind with regards to the direction the discipline of Oriental Studies ought to take in the wake of the state's founding.

Several years later, after leaving the Foreign Ministry and joining the HUSOS faculty for the 1951–52 academic year, Heyd elaborated upon the ideas expressed in his letter to Senator. He was invited to give a methodological "introductory lecture" of a historiographical nature laying out the new subject being included in the institute's work and the challenges involved in its research and instruction. Unlike the memorandum drafted several years earlier, or Goitein's letters on the subject, which were intended for governmental eyes, it was delivered in an academic setting, at an event honoring Gotthold Weil's seventieth birthday and arrival at retirement age.[142] The lecture was later published in a celebratory booklet by the university, indicating the subject's importance in the eyes of administrators at both the institute and the university. It also illustrated the young, junior Heyd's centrality within the institute; a historiographical opening lecture in Oriental Studies had been published for the first time in 1933, after L. A. Mayer delivered one to mark the establishment of a Chair in Near Eastern Art and Archaeology.[143]

The primary points of Heyd's systematic and well-reasoned lecture are well worth reiterating, since—unlike the main justifications given to that point, which dealt with the potential political payoff Heyd was certainly aware of—the lecture engaged in particular with scientific justifications for the development of the field and offered a pioneering critical perspective. After recalling that, as a student, he had "been of the opinion that it would be very advantageous to expand the studies at our institute to include knowledge of the modern Orient," he began by laying out and then refuting several common arguments against Modern Middle East Studies. The first had to do with the recency of the developments in question ruling out any possibility of treating them objectively. Heyd pointed out that this was a question of concern to historians of all world regions, but rejected its relevance since "our department is in no way limited to the contemporary

156 ::: A NEW ORIENT

Middle East"—a claim echoing Ayalon's successful struggle to determine the department's name and his aversion to hewing too close to current events. Its goal, rather, was "to reveal the forces that shaped the image of the Orient in modern times."[144]

The second argument Heyd set out to refute was that, since the countries of the Middle East had become "a stage for encounters between the great powers" beginning in the early nineteenth century, their history should be discussed within the framework of the histories of those powers and not as an independent field.[145] Heyd did not dispute that the fate of the countries of the Orient in the nineteenth century had been settled in European capitals, but explained that, alongside the political history indeed tied up with these powers were the socio-cultural histories internal to the countries of the Orient, the sources for which were in Oriental languages. The Western scholar "without training in Oriental Studies who approaches the socio-cultural problems from a western point of view and with European concepts" was denied the tools necessary to correctly understand the processes and forces active in the region, tools the scholar of Oriental Studies, well-versed in its languages, did hold.[146]

It was here, however, that Heyd believed the central problem lay: despite the linguistic advantages at their disposal, Oriental Studies scholars showed no interest in the modern Middle East, since they associated "the modern Middle East, especially socially and culturally, with the degeneration of the classical Muslim tradition, and the typically rather superficial mimicry of western civilization." According to Heyd, this "negative approach" of European scholars of the Orient had to do with the centrality of Arabic and other Oriental languages to Oriental Studies in the West for such a long period; since European Orientalism had emerged out of "linguistic tradition . . . scholars interested in Muslim history turned their attention primarily to periods known for their sources of outstanding literary value, that is, to the era of classical Islam. Recent centuries . . . were considered a period of the general ossification of Islam."[147] In other words, "European Orientalism was, typically, more interested in the cultural creations of the Orient's peoples than in these peoples themselves . . . such a stance necessarily seems unjust and hurtful to those from the Orient. . . . There is a condescension in the aforementioned stance held by western scholars, which kept many of them from examining the social and cultural history of the modern Middle East."[148]

Heyd's piercing words on the very world of Oriental Studies from which he had emerged, and its ideas concerning the Orient's degeneration and stagnation, were unprecedented—certainly for the School of Oriental Studies. Heyd had levied in 1952 what, during the 1960s and especially after the publication of Said's 1978 *Orientalism* would become a widespread critique of the field, albeit in gentler form and, of course, from the historiographical perspective of someone belonging to the discipline, and not employing Foucauldian discourse analysis.[149]

In opposing the focus on language, Heyd was challenging widespread tendencies in the world of research, but not necessarily opposing those of his instructors who studied historical subjects: Mayer and Goitein, who led the effort to integrate him into the institute's faculty and represented a more inclusive line with regards to the history of the Islamic world in the first place. As chapter 1 illustrated, Mayer's advocacy for the integration of lectures on the history of Palestine in the sixteenth century into the HUSOS curriculum predated the institute's establishment; whereas Goitein, beginning in the late 1940s, became increasingly committed to researching the social history of the Jews of the Islamic world in the Mediterranean. In this sense, Heyd followed his teachers' path more than he rebelled against it.

Heyd's lecture went on to present a comparative survey of the state of the field in the West—primarily in England and the United States, and making not the slightest mention of developments in Germany in his time—as a basis for presenting the new department.[150] He explained that study of the modern Middle East was split in England among the various general departments (history, economics, law, and so on), with no dedicated department to itself; while the area studies approach had gained popularity in the United States since World War II, but with the "teaching of so many subjects tied together only by a common 'area,' the territory, comes the danger of superficiality, of course."[151]

In Heyd's telling, the institute's instructors sought the middle ground between these approaches, and as such proposed the following separation: the history and culture of the Islamic peoples would be taught together, common practice in classic Oriental Studies as well since studying them required knowledge of Oriental languages; geography and economics in the present, which can also be researched without knowledge of these languages, would be taught within the general departments; whereas the study of language and literature would stand on its own. The Modern Middle East would be, therefore, an explicitly historical department with geographical, demographic, and economic questions serving as background for the

158 ::: A NEW ORIENT

understanding of subjects taught and no more, while language study—not only of Arabic, but also Persian and Turkish—would serve there as auxiliary tools aiding the understanding of historical sources.

It was at this point that Heyd faced the challenge that Goitein described nicely in the 1930s, and continued to accompany the institute in its relations with students and critics: how to meet the needs of both "those preparing for practical work" and "those interested in scientific work" within a single institutional framework.[152] His answer was that those in the former could study towards a BA in the department while those in the second group, if they were interested in pursuing an MA in the department, would have to enter the Department of Muslim Culture (the new name of the Islamic Culture Department) in parallel, which was concerned with the period of classical Islam.[153] Combining modern and classical studies would ground knowledge of the modern Middle East in a thorough understanding of its historical depth; Heyd described it as a first attempt of its kind ("to my knowledge") that could protect the institute from any "blurring of the line separating science from opinion [*publitzistika*], journalism, and politics."[154] Insistence upon an ethos of division between science and politics such that none be suspected of crossing this line, was not therefore the terrain of the founding generation alone, with its German training. It also trickled down to the generation of their students.

Heyd concluded his lecture by addressing what was unique about studying the modern Middle East from Jerusalem in particular. Delving into this subject, he explained, would offer understanding of an important but previously unresearched period in the history of Palestine, an opportunity to study the history of the Jews of the Middle East, a familiarity with the Arab and Druze minorities in the State of Israel, and above all else, the chance to improve relations between Israel and neighboring countries, on the basis of greater scientific familiarity with developments there. In addition, Heyd pointed to a number of the Hebrew University's advantages over other Western institutions: its location in the region would encourage sustained scholarly engagement in the subject; daily proximity and contact "with people of the Orient [that] vaccinates us against that romanticized idealization of the Orient to which many European scholars succumb"; and the fact that students would not be encountering Arabic for the first time in their lives, but rather arriving with foreknowledge from their school days.[155] This same tone criticizing the image of the Orient in Western scholarship that was often raised in Heyd's lecture appeared once more in its incisive final lines:

"If—as I do believe—the Hebrew University is to fulfill an educational purpose as well, study of the modern Middle East will have its fair share to contribute. Here we could learn to avoid the same condescension of many westerners towards he of the East, 'the native,' backward in his technical knowledge and organizational capacity. For some time now—perhaps increasingly so in recent years—the dangerous tendency to adopt from Europeans this dismissive view of our neighbors has been apparent in our camp, a stance that is as inferior morally as it is foolish from the perspective of our future in this region."[156]

Heyd's lecture was apparently not published in an English translation and did not resonate widely. Although the points he raised were similar to those expressed in subsequent decades by other prominent scholars, his name is not among those in the literature on the origins of the critique of Orientalism.[157] Nonetheless, his analysis emphasizes a complex duality: Heyd's teachers and, by extension, he himself as their student, emerged out of the German Orientalist tradition, which Edward Said had opted not to place at the center of his critique because he believed it was a classical tradition focused almost invariably on research, and not motivated by any national interest.[158] And here, seemingly, the department of which Heyd was among the architects under the umbrella of HUSOS managed to combine statist necessity with academic work to a unprecedented degree—that is, to establish a relationship defined by Said as a key element in the development of the Western Orientalist approach of seeing the Orient as inferior. Yet Heyd, for whom the national mission was certainly front of mind, also chose to conclude his lecture by pointing out the fundamental failure of such an approach. The lecture remains a rare programmatic document that is illustrative not only of his approach to the profession, but of the challenges that would face Israeli Oriental Studies in the subsequent decades.

Just as Heyd was central in laying out the ideas at the base of the institute's expansion, he was also heavily involved in its practical aspects after being appointed director. The number of students grew every year and the existing corps of instructors at the institute was insufficient, especially after Goitein's departure. True to his stance regarding the institute's role, Heyd approached the university administration seeking to expand its two purposes—"to make our unique contribution to the scientific study of the origins of the Orient and its culture," and "to meet the state's demand for people of action knowledgeable of contemporary regional issues."[159] This development would include, over the course of his first years in the position, the reorganization of the institute's departments. Under Goitein, Semitic Linguistics and Egyptian were moved to the Department of Linguistics, founded by Hans Jakob Polotsky within the Faculty of Humanities but outside the umbrella of the institute. The School of Oriental Studies was left with only three departments: the two older departments—Arabic Language and Literature, with its Classical and Modern tracks, and Islamic/Muslim Culture—and a combined department called "The History of the Islamic Lands," within which students could choose to specialize in either the Middle Ages or the Modern period.[160]

A perusal of the curriculum of the combined department brought to the faculty council for discussion in 1959 reveals that it included no courses on twentieth-century matters. When HUSOS faculty were asked about this, David Ayalon explained in lockstep with his decade-old stance that "the fundamental question . . . is what to teach at the university—things of passing value or things of prevailing value. The region is undergoing constant change and such constant change cannot be taught."[161] The treatment of contemporary problems in the Middle East at the university—and not just within the Israel Oriental Society, where the matter was led by Foreign Ministry personnel—was left unanswered within the institute itself.

Alongside organizational change, the approaching retirement of most of the founding faculty generation—Mayer, Baneth, and Rivlin (the older Weil had already retired several years earlier), alongside Goitein's departure to the United States—meant that new research and instructional manpower had to be developed. To this end, Heyd developed an approach with the backing of the university administration: he concluded agreements with students on the verge of completing their master's degrees as to what their future specializations would be during their doctoral studies, in exchange for offering them future positions at the institute in this field of specialization.[162] In addition he expanded and solidified the positions of the institute's current instructors in the older fields as well: among others he was able to create a secure position for Yehoshua (or Joshua) Blau (1919–2020), who had begun to teach Arabic during Goitein's era but only on a partial scholarship, and add another HUSOS master's graduate to its ranks, the veteran Arabic teacher from Haifa Meir Jacob Kister (1914–2010), who had taught many outstanding institute students (and later lecturers) as high school students.[163] Heyd was also chosen to serve as Vice President of the Israel Oriental Society, and effectively ran its affairs. In all administrative matters,

Heyd was Goitein's clear successor. Like his predecessor, and perhaps even more so, he took steps to guarantee the institute's budgetary future and its expansion through collaboration with the Foreign Ministry.

## The Institute of Asian and African Studies

Just before departing his position, Goitein inquired with the university administration regarding the possibility of developing East Asian studies, in particular the study of China and Japan, within the framework of the School of Oriental Studies. The response he received from Academic Secretary Edward Poznansky was less than enthusiastic, noting that the institute must continue building the existing fields that had been established there several years earlier.[164] Nevertheless, as Goitein's replacement, Heyd insisted on prolonging these efforts. As a veteran of both the Political Department of the Jewish Agency and the Foreign Ministry, he understood the importance of intensifying the study of East Asia, if only from the diplomatic perspective: in 1944, he had prepared a survey of the subject "The Muslim-Hindu Problem in India."[165] In spite of the university administration's doubts, Heyd found an influential partner in advancing the initiative: secretary of the Friends of the Hebrew University in Great Britain, the attorney Walter Zander (1898-1993).[166] Zander corresponded with Poznansky himself and succeeded in placating his skepticism;[167] and in the spring of 1958 gathered the more experienced faculty—Goitein, Baneth, and Mayer—as well as Heyd, at a meeting in London to discuss the future of the institute. The goal of this meeting, according to Zander, was to think in an operative fashion about expanding the institute's activities with the aid of the Friends of the University (that is to say, relevant fundraising would be conducted)—such that the curriculum could also include Asia and Africa, because with the Arab boycott, the states beyond the immediate surrounding circle were "the real neighbors of Israel."[168]

Zander's statement here articulated the Israeli foreign policy that emerged over the course of the 1950s. In an effort to create alliances that might break the Arab boycott, strengthen Israel's legitimacy and support within international institutions, and pave the way to economic relations, Israel reached out to the countries beyond the immediate circle of its neighbors, most of whom had gained their independence in recent years.[169] Early attempts were made with Turkey and Iran; as noted, these were the first countries added to the expanding discipline of Oriental Studies in Jerusalem, and

162 ::: A NEW ORIENT

the focus of Heyd's research specialization. Subsequently, efforts were focused on Asia until 1956. Israel hoped to establish connections with India, China, Japan, and other East Asian countries like Burma, Thailand, and the Philippines. These efforts bore only limited results in the first place, and Israel's involvement in the Sinai War, considered proof that Israel was an ally of the Western imperial powers, caused further damage.[170] Beginning in 1957, the main thrust of relation-building moved to Africa, where decolonization processes had begun to wind to a close. Economic and agricultural links, aviation routes, and military training emerged vis-à-vis many countries on the continent—the first being Ghana, followed by additional sub-Saharan countries—and by the early 1960s Israel maintained embassies in thirty-three African countries.[171] Its fundamental stance regarding relations with Asia and Africa was overt and publicly-known, expressed in numerous public pronouncements of leading governmental and foreign service personnel.[172] Zander was well aware of this fact when he decided to call a meeting on the subject of establishing Asian and African studies at the institute.

Perhaps unsurprisingly considering their previously expressed stances, Goitein and Heyd were enthusiastic about the suggestion. Mayer and Baneth, on the other hand, the only ones present who had been full faculty members at the School of Oriental Studies from the outset, expressed some pessimism, even disillusionment, at the idea that Asian and African studies would bring about any kind of affinity or mutual understanding. As Mayer put it, suggesting disappointment at the institute's limited achievements as a vehicle for encouraging Jewish-Arab affinity during the Mandate years: "Knowledge did not necessarily create sympathy."[173] Alongside these reservations, both were also troubled by the fact that, while the institute had earned a reputation for itself in the field of Arabic and Islamic studies, in the study of Asia and Africa it would have difficulty competing with older institutions in the Western world that had years of experience in the study of these fields.

One of those institutions was the London-based SOAS, where courses in Asian and African languages had been included from its first years as an institution for professional training, and offerings in the history of various African and Asian countries beyond the Middle East were being expanded by the mid-1930s.[174] Also invited to the meeting was the Anglo-Jewish scholar of Oriental Studies Bernard Lewis (1916–2018), professor of Near and Middle Eastern History at SOAS, where he was then establishing his stature as

*Orient Renewed* ::: 163

a historian specializing in modern Turkey, among other subjects.[175] Based on familiarity with his home institution and its peers across the world, Lewis discussed various academic, preparatory, and political purposes for expansion, and recommended focusing efforts on African studies, a less-developed field in Western universities than the study of India and China. His recommendation was disregarded, and Asian Studies was opened in parallel to African Studies; still, this consultation demonstrates how Oriental Studies scholars in Jerusalem hoped to emulate the Anglo-American world of activities in their own expansion of the field.

Asian and African studies, it should be emphasized, were not completely foreign to German Orientalism. India was an old object of research at German universities, with an increasingly established Indological branch active in Germany beginning in the early nineteenth century that even surpassed the stature of Semitic philology for a certain period. The establishment of the first German chair in Sinology at the University of Berlin in 1910, moreover, was a development serving clear colonial interests, especially as Germany took control of the Chinese city of Qingdao between 1898 and World War I. Still, rather than modern subjects, these fields were characterized by a focus on the ancient world, religions, and, of course, languages, which not infrequently prompted criticism from contemporaries as well.[176]

Colonial interests also sparked the development of African Studies, primarily at the SOS (*Seminar für Orientalische Sprachen*, see chapter 1) and at the Hamburg Colonial Institute (*Hamburgisches Kolonialinstitut*, HKI), which reported directly to the German Colonial Office.[177] While these institutions may not have been part of Orientalist departments, they certainly emphasized language instruction as well, especially with regards to African Studies.[178] Eugen Mittwoch—the German-Jewish Orientalist involved in early discussions around the establishment of the Hebrew University who was for a time a candidate to serve as professor of Arabic at the Institute for Jewish Studies—was a pioneer also in his specialization in Ethiopian languages (part of the Semitic language family), which he had taught as part of his appointment to the Chair in Semitic Languages at the University of Berlin. Mittwoch bolstered his knowledge of these languages as early as 1905, when he took under his wing a scholar invited to Berlin by the local German colonial mission in Ethiopia to teach Amharic at the SOS.[179]

The study of Asia and Africa being discussed in the context of the School of Oriental Studies, however, had been shaped only marginally by the German Orientalist tradition. Numerous documents in the archive of

164 ::: A NEW ORIENT

the Hebrew University demonstrate the gradual emergence of the institute's expansion process, prompted by Zander, who also contacted Eliahu Elath —the Israeli Ambassador in London at the time—and forwarded a detailed memorandum to university president Mazar.[180] Following Zander's meeting with institute personnel, he also established an external committee composed of scholars from SOAS and other academic institutions in England, with the intent of helping shape the plan to expand HUSOS, concerning not only the topics and personnel but also material questions, especially the creation of a satisfactory library.[181]

Zander, who emphasized the diplomatic importance of developing Asian and African studies, also sent the memorandum to Prime Minister Ben-Gurion, who had expressed support for the initiative in accordance with his view that the State of Israel must "accelerate its existing progress in the establishment of closer links with the Asian and African peoples," a mission to which the "study of African and Asian culture, and particularly Indian history, literature, religion, and philosophy" would contribute, in addition to their educational and humanistic value.[182] With this backing, Zander began to solicit donations, contacting the Israeli ambassador to the United States, Abba Eban, to enlist him in the task of seeking out American donors as well.[183] Heyd, for his part, focused on selecting the appropriate personnel to recruit, turning to young Jewish scholars who had connections to the Hebrew University but had specialized in the relevant subjects at foreign universities, and invited them to come teach at the institute.[184]

The institute's expansion plan continued to develop into the early 1960s. Following the meetings in Jerusalem and London, committees at the Hebrew University formed two plans, one for Asian Studies and one for African Studies. Both focused primarily on master's degree studies, offering new courses as well existing ones from various university departments (not only from the institute itself), and offered students the opportunity to focus upon specific sub-topics. The Asian Studies curriculum included language courses, and others on religion, history, and society; in African Studies, on the other hand—due in part to the lack of historical research literature— the same aspects were included alongside a more liberal dose of subjects from the social sciences, such as geography and sociology. In both cases, the institute's contribution was largely in the fields of history and religion, especially Islam.[185] The preparation of both curricula, with their integrative nature, would indeed seem to be influenced by the American area studies approach.

As we saw, Bernard Lewis suggested in his meeting with the institute's veterans that African Studies lacked a historical literature on the subjects relevant to HUSOS. In his role as chairman of the African Studies Committee, Shmuel Noah Eisenstadt from the Department of Sociology therefore asked the founder and director of the Africa Department at the Foreign Ministry, Netanel Lorch, for assistance in locating material. With the help of various Israeli missions in Africa, Lorch and his deputy composed a list for the university of newspaper and magazine titles published in various African countries, as well as relevant scholarship.[186] After the university's efforts to secure external funding for the program through the Rockefeller Foundation fell through, the Foreign Ministry stepped in and established a fund for the development of African Studies.[187] Foreign Ministry personnel continued to correspond with the university regarding the curriculum and passed along reports from representatives in Africa regarding academic conferences and scholars with whom the faculty should be in contact.[188]

In 1962, the two programs were already operational, administered by temporary committees. They included classical Chinese and Sanskrit—perhaps the principal survivor from among the early twentieth-century fields of interest at the German university in Asian and African Studies; the history of China, Africa, Southeast Asia, and the Maghreb; courses on social and religious issues on the two continents; and studies in Indian philosophy. HUSOS master's graduates were now located at various universities abroad specializing in additional fields relevant to the study of Asia and Africa. Within the institute's older departments, Heyd continued to develop the study of Turkey and Iran—subjects, including Persian and Turkish, on which he taught himself. He especially encouraged his students to study Ottoman sources, and published numerous studies on the legal, political, religious, and historical aspects of Ottoman and Turkish history.[189] Here, too, Heyd was careful to make occasional mention of not only the academic, but the diplomatic efficacy of engaging in these subjects.[190]

In light of this broad range of offerings, he approached the university administration with a symbolic, if weighty request: to change the name of the School of Oriental Studies to "The Institute of Asian and African Studies" (*hamakhon lelimudey asia ve'afrika*). This request also entailed the subordination of Asian and African Studies to the institute, though courses that fundamentally belonged to other disciplines (like geography, sociology, or European history) would remain under the auspices of their departments.[191] In his 1952 lecture, Heyd had questioned the area studies

166 ::: A NEW ORIENT

approach and proposed a more moderate version of them; as these subjects were brought under the institute's purview, this more modest version of the model seems to have been maintained, as the courses remained connected to their home disciplines.

Heyd incorporated within the name change request the two aspects that characterized his activities in Oriental Studies—opposing condescension and patronizing the cultures being researched and attention to the vantage points of the peoples creating those cultures—and meanwhile expressed his commitment to the needs of the State of Israel: "The term 'Orient' [*Mizrah*, also translated 'East'] is dated, to say nothing of 'Middle East.' Seeing the region from a European viewpoint is illogical for those of us residing in the region and damages the pride of its peoples (Turks, etc.) who do not want to be included in the 'Orient' or Indians and others who identify 'Orientalism' with a western imperialist approach . . . At this time, as the State of Israel seeks to enrich its relations with the peoples of Asia and Africa, it is most advisable, therefore, to choose a name that will be acceptable to these peoples and which facilitates collaboration with them."[192] Heyd noted that many institutes across the world—in both the United States and Russia—were already avoiding generalizing usage of the term "Orient," opting instead for the specific names of the relevant regions.

The name change request was discussed in the Standing Committee and passed with nearly no opposition. While the physicist Ernst Alexander feared that "by changing the name we are abolishing the institute's original purpose," Benjamin Mazar—having recently left his role as university president—responded that the change actually projected the institute's development beyond an emphasis solely "on the surrounding region."[193] Though this exchange was between two members of the faculty not affiliated with HUSOS, it accurately reflected the deeper political processes that prompted the institute's expansion. A more significant reservation was raised among the committee members with regards to the organizational implications of the proposal—that is, whether Asian and African Studies would belong to the institute or to another organizational unit, and what faculty would be responsible for it. The argument among them concluded with a decision to affirm the name change, which Heyd noted was "urgent and determines our outward appearance." Upon further discussion, the Standing Committee decided that the existing programs would continue to be run by temporary committees, but would be inserted under the institute's umbrella. Once departments were founded on this basis within the institute, each would be administered by two heads, one from the Faculty of the Humanities and one from the Faculty of the Social Sciences. The inclusion of these new departments, a concluding report emphasized, would in no way alter the character of the existing ones.[194]

The Academic Senate granted its final approval to the proposal at the end of 1962;[195] and on January 6, 1963, the university held a press conference in which Uriel Heyd announced the establishment of the Institute of Asian and African Studies.[196] The English-language press release that was sent in parallel, unlike the Hebrew announcement, made no mention of the anticipated benefit to the State of Israel, but did nevertheless contain its own glaring diplomatic-propagandist undertone: the new name, it said, was meant to reflect the university's desire to include Asian and African countries outside the Middle East within studies at the institute, a decision "prompted not only by the recent emergence of these countries on the international scene but also by the great and ancient civilizations of some of them, which undoubtedly form important subjects of study."[197]

That same year, Heyd's term as director of the institute ended after seven years (including one on sabbatical). His replacement was also his contemporary, David Ayalon.[198] Thirty-seven years after its establishment, the institute—now of Asian and African Studies—would be headed by a native-born scholar of the Orient for the first time. Ayalon did not embark upon additional far-reaching changes at the institute but engaged "only in completing" things left unfinished, as he put it.[199] Heyd had left him with an institute wiped clean in a reform based on an established research ideology, which meanwhile anchored its relationship with the Foreign Ministry still further.

GENERATION GAP? THE FLORENCE CONFERENCE
(1958) AND GENERATIONS OF ISRAELI
ORIENTAL STUDIES

The intervening period between the founding of the State of Israel and the official transition from "Oriental Studies" to "Asian and African Studies" discussed in this chapter was also the primary period during which two generations of scholars actively overlapped there: the first and founding generation that had established it as an institution for the production of knowledge on the Orient and academic training; and the second generation, composed of the institute's students in the 1930s, which relied upon

168 ::: A NEW ORIENT

the Arabist expertise learned there to make inroads in the *Yishuv's* job market during the 1940s—and who made their return as lecturers and researchers after 1948, as the institute came to define its focus more broadly and was able to create new positions.[200]

In his seminal article "The Generational Problem," Karl Mannheim sought to characterize the concept of the generation as a sociological category.[201] Rather than biological age, he claimed, the common ground for a certain generation was generational consciousness. This emerged out of shared social experiences in members' formative years, which were reflected in historical events. In this sense, despite biographical differences between the active figures within each generation, there was one clear difference: those of the first generation earned doctoral degrees in their twenties in Europe, almost exclusively in Germany; while most of the second generation did so in Jerusalem, and at a more variable age.

In terms of Oriental Studies, there were certainly those among this second generation whose scholarship remained primarily classical—Hadith scholar Meir Kister is perhaps the most glaring example of this—but most of the others pivoted into fields that were not at the heart of the training their teachers had received.[202] According to Gabriel Baer, a member of this second generation, "While a cultural urge had brought the Orientalists of the 1920s and 1930s [the first generation] to the profession in no small part as a complement to a classical, Jewish education and thanks to their advantage over colleagues in western countries of knowing Hebrew, those of the younger generation of Orientalists since the 1940s have used the profession to seek meaningful answers to the surrounding reality within the Middle East, and believed this meaning would be better sought in modern and contemporary history than in the culture of classical Islam."[203] Despite the differing impulses that inspired the two generations, conflicts between them—when they occurred at all—took place behind closed doors or were recorded in private diaries, never finding their way into protocols, correspondence, or publications in the press. The argument between Ayalon and his teachers regarding the name of the new department did not create a significant or lasting rift between them. In light of this harmonious impression, one episode involving both generations of Orient scholars, as well as the Foreign Ministry, stands out: an event that aroused a public firestorm in 1958, known in the press as "The Florence Affair."

In early October that year, mayor of Florence Giorgio La Pira (1904–1977) convened the "Mediterranean Conference" in the town. The conference's goal was to bring together individuals from Mediterranean countries to discuss various regional problems, specifically the Algerian War of Independence and the Israeli-Arab Conflict.[204] The conference was planned by La Pira together with his friend Joe (Yosef) Golan (1922–2003), the advisor on Arab affairs for the World Jewish Congress (WJC); Golan maintained ties with figures in various Arab countries, principally in North Africa, with which Israel had no diplomatic relations. La Pira and Golan forwarded an official invitation to the Israeli Foreign Ministry, which rejected it, however.[205] Some have suggested that the ministry refused because Golda Meir, Foreign Minister at the time, was said not to appreciate Golan's independent diplomatic initiatives.[206] The invitation's refusal may have been influenced by personal animosity, but it did not represent a departure from Israel's general foreign policy during the 1950s, which, after the failure of the Lausanne Conference (1949), centered on a preference for direct dialogue with neighboring countries rather than attempts at international mediation and patronage.[207] In effect, Israel's steps on the stage of international diplomacy, including the pro-Western approach to the inter-bloc struggle, were those of a state recognizing that the enmity of its direct neighbors was not likely to dissipate anytime soon.[208] There was precious little faith to be found within Israeli foreign policy circles at the chances of an international conference as ambitious as the Florence Conference.

Following the Foreign Ministry's refusal, the conference organizers chose to pass individual invitations along to a number of public figures—mostly members of Mapam—and to Martin Buber, who was unable to attend due to the death of his wife. In his place Buber suggested his Hebrew University colleague Martin Plessner of HUSOS, who was asked to give a lecture on the shared values of Christianity, Judaism, and Islam. Plessner accepted the invitation and prepared the lecture.[209] Under Italian diplomatic pressure, the Foreign Ministry decided at the last minute to send a delegation that would serve as a counterweight to the private invitees, primarily Plessner.[210] In contravention of early agreements, the delegation included a number of formal officials: Reuven Barkat, director of the Political Department of the Histadrut (Israel's national trade union center, traditionally identified with Mapai), and two Foreign Ministry personnel—Maurice Fischer, deputy director, and Reuven Shiloah (formerly Zaslani), the diplomatic advisor to the Foreign Minister and a close associate of Ben-Gurion. They were invited at the suggestion of the Israeli ambassador in Rome, Eliyahu Sasson, who also travelled to Florence to assess the diplomatic damage.[211] They were

# 170 ::: A NEW ORIENT

joined by Mapam representatives who had been invited privately, as well as representatives from *Ahdut Ha'avoda* (Labor Unity Party).[212] The group was topped off by one more participant, who was a neither politician nor diplomat: Uriel Heyd.

Heyd's inclusion in the delegation seems an attempt to provide a counterweight to Plessner's Oriental expertise and academic stature. Plessner was known on the public stage as a peace activist and member of Ihud opposed to the Ben-Gurion's statist line. He was attending the conference as a private person, and pronounced himself not committed to the State of Israel's official stance.[213] Heyd, on the other hand, attended as a director of the School of Oriental Studies who had expressed his obligation to the state and to the needs of the government, as demonstrated by his statements regarding the role of the discipline of Oriental Studies at the Hebrew University; he was also identified with the Foreign Ministry, where he had served in a number of roles before joining the university. Superficially, though Plessner had never been among Heyd's instructors (the two began teaching at the institute around the same time), this appeared to be a moment of intergenerational conflict.

The composition of the delegation led to a complex diplomatic affair: due to the Arab delegations' opposition to the unexpected presence of official government representatives from Israel, the invitations of Fischer and Shiloah from the Foreign Ministry were rescinded; in response the entire delegation, including Heyd and the Mapam members who had been individually invited, decided to leave. The only one who refused to do so was Plessner, even after being explicitly asked to do so by Barkat; though in the meantime he agreed not to attend the opening session.[214] After additional discussions with the conference organizers, on which Sasson reported in detail to the Ministry in Jerusalem with urgent telegrams, a compromise was reached: Fisher and Shiloah would remain at the conference as observers with no speaking privileges. Withdrawal of the delegation was averted.

In refusing to walk out with the rest of the delegation, Plessner nevertheless drew the wrath not only of the Foreign Ministry personnel, but also politicians and editorialists in Israel, who were outraged by the "disgrace" the episode's conclusion had inflicted upon Israel's image.[215] He was maligned in the press, described as a "bizarre" (*timhoni*) professor; some even wrote in the press calling on students to express their opposition in his courses.[216] He was attacked in governmental meetings as well, and in a discussion on the Knesset floor on the subject; Ben-Gurion made thinly-veiled references to him when addressing the Israeli decision to participate in the conference "even if a number of Jews of a certain kind were slated to participate . . . Though the brown-nosing [*majufes*] Jews have been reduced in number in our days, we have not fully ejected this 'race' from our midst."[217]

The hatred for Plessner, moreover, threatened to bleed through the public discourse onto the university itself. At the charged meeting with the other delegation members in Florence, Barkat had directed what seems like a veiled threat at Plessner: "We are not a police state; but you endanger your stature in the eyes of your students, who will not want to study with a teacher like you."[218] Responding to a supportive report about Plessner in the weekly *Ha'olam Haze*, published by Uri Avnery, one anonymous HUSOS student complained that the attempt to make the professor into a national hero was "grotesque."[219]

The tumult died down before long, and in late November Plessner wrote to Eliyahu Sasson—whose conduct in the face of the crisis had earned him Plessner's admiration—that "little by little, life is returning to normal. The frying pan (and the fire?) are cooling."[220] But in the face of his loud vilification, including comments on his status as an academic, the university's silence spoke loudly, especially that of the School of Oriental Studies and its director. Nobody from the university seems ever to have publicly addressed the Florence Affair, for better or worse.[221] News articles on the affair made no mention of Heyd's activities during those days in Florence, apart from one reporting that he had been the one to convince Plessner to confer with the delegation's other members.[222]

Despite this lack of public backing, and although Heyd had been sent to Florence as a statist counterweight to him in the first place, Plessner was full of praise for his director mere weeks later, writing in correspondence with Sasson that he was "a refreshing force," someone with "common sense" that the institute was very lucky to have at its head.[223] The meaning of this positivity is clarified in Plessner's own report on the events of Florence. The private conversation he had with Heyd at the hotel may not have caused him to agree to the latter's request that he reconsider his participation in the conference, but he described it as a heartfelt and comfortable discussion. After continuing to discuss unrelated subjects, personal and Oriental ("*Persönliches und Orientalia*"), the two parted in good spirits.[224] All of this indicates that the supposed confrontation between the generations was not a true confrontation. In the end, despite their different starting points, Plessner and Heyd had common factors as well: both were born and educated in

172 ::: A NEW ORIENT

Germany (Plessner in its east and Heyd in its west, admittedly), and were forced to leave after the Nazi rise to power. Thus, they could certainly find a shared language of habitus, to say nothing of an actual spoken language: for both, German was their mother tongue.

The gap between their political stances had to do in part with generational circumstances: Plessner came to Palestine at age thirty-four after years of activity in the vicinity of dovish German-Zionist circles, while Heyd arrived at age twenty-one in time for the brutal violence of the second half of the 1930s to shape much of his political consciousness. It is safe to assume that he participated in the funeral of his murdered teacher Levi Billig in 1936. Moreover, after completing his doctoral studies, Plessner continued an academic career in Germany that emphasized philological research of medieval Arabic texts. His career was only interrupted by the Nazi race laws, which led to his firing. Heyd's career, meanwhile, was delayed after completing his master's degree in Jerusalem, and he brought his expertise in Oriental Studies to the very heart of the Zionist diplomatic establishment, first working at the Political Department and later at the Israeli Foreign Ministry.

This gap left no lasting tension between the two scholars, as we noted, and was dwarfed by the intellectual and sociological common ground they shared—that is, their belonging to the same social group.[225] Plessner stood out among his generation of Orient scholars in Jerusalem for the advanced age at which he joined the faculty, his public opposition to the government, and certainly his defiant style. Still, his impact on the institute's agenda was limited, to say the least, certainly in comparison with his contemporary Goitein, or to Mayer.[226] For this precise reason, the discourse around the Florence episode illustrates a fundamental point regarding the institute's first fifteen years in the state—and statist—era: one should not see these as years of intergenerational struggle or attempts by the younger generation to bring about a revolution. On the contrary: they were years of collaboration between the two generations around the ideas and actions with which they attempted to establish and institutionalize HUSOS's relationship with the government, especially to the Foreign Ministry.

It might be said that the expansion of the institute and the incorporation of modern subjects was the first generation's response to ongoing pressure from their students. As the previous chapter illustrated, this pressure certainly had an impact on shaping the world of Oriental Studies. But those same students could also be the ones to delay the "modernization" of the curriculum—Ayalon's insistence on "Modern" rather than "Contemporary" in opposition to Goitein, Mayer, and Baneth, stood out, but Heyd spoke out similarly as well. It would be a mistake to see the School of Oriental Studies' pursuit of new directions in research and instruction, with hopes of securing government funding and the needs of the government in mind, as a product of the dominance of a generation of students distancing themselves from their teachers. Certainly, those teachers maintained the institute's philological research projects, and apart from Goitein none shifted drastically in their scholarly interests; but at the same time, they hardly objected to development and expansion initiatives, which overwhelmingly involved modern history; they encouraged these, and reaped the ensuing advantages.[227] Perhaps this is the heart of the matter, then: the German legacy of Orient scholarship was multifaceted. It was encapsulated not solely in the index cards of the concordance, but equally in the Israel Oriental Society.

# EPILOGUE

## "TRULY, JERUSALEM HAS ONE BENEFIT: LYING WITHIN THE ORIENT"

Conducting research within a hostage population to produce scientific knowledge, like the studies carried out at the POW camps near Berlin with the participation of Josef Horovitz and Gotthold Weil—from the School of Oriental Studies' founding generation—was exclusive neither to Germany nor to World War I. Years later, Israeli Oriental Studies would make use of this practice as well.

In a 1977 study on twentieth-century Egyptian society, Gabriel Baer addressed questions about family planning, among other topics. He noted that, while the Muslim tradition is ambivalent regarding the question of birth control, common belief among the popular classes holds that this practice is forbidden by the religion. Among the reasons given for this conclusion in his study was the personal impression gained "when the writer of these lines, after the 1956 War, was allowed to converse with many Egyptians of the lower classes."[1] The meaning of this hint is that Baer spoke with Egyptian POWs held by Israel. From early November 1956, when the war in the Sinai Peninsula ended, until the prisoner exchange process between Egypt and Israel began in January 1957, some 5,500 Egyptian soldiers were detained by Israel.[2] Baer was an intelligence officer in the IDF Reserves who remained mobilized at least two weeks after the war's conclusion, with no end to his turn of duty in sight;[3] the most reasonable assumption is that he gained access to these POWs within the framework of this role, whether as a scholar or under other circumstances.[4]

Baer's conversations with the Egyptian prisoners of war were hardly more than anecdotal, and were certainly not institutionalized actions grounded in collaboration by Oriental Studies scholars with the military or government, as the German study of POWs during the World War I had been. This situation changed fundamentally after 1967: the Institute of Asian and African Studies—headed by Baer, then a professor and David Ayalon's replacement—began to collaborate with the Coordinator of Government Activities in the Territories (COGAT) on a series of studies aim-

*Epilogue* ::: 175

ing to create systematic and organized knowledge on political, economic, social, cultural, and religious aspects of the lives of West Bank and Gaza Strip residents. The studies were funded by the Prime Minister's Office and formed part of a wider apparatus of university-based studies approved by a committee of academics (mostly from the Hebrew University) and government figures; appointed by Prime Minister Levi Eshkol, it was known as the "Professors Committee." Established a short time after the occupation of the territories, the committee's goal was to assist the government in collecting information about and shape its policy towards them.[5]

As of early 1971, the list of studies approved by the committee included eleven conducted by personnel of the Institute of Asian and African Studies.[6] In accordance with the goals of the entire research apparatus, they dealt with subjects like political parties, clubs and associations, the religious establishment, immigration, and the economic and social structures of various towns—all in the West Bank. Most of the studies were conducted by students at the institute; at the time the list was drawn up, most were still works in progress.

Among these, one completed study carried out by Gabriel Baer himself stood out: "Mukhtars and Village Councils in Judea and Samaria," which had also been sent to the Prime Minister's Office.[7] Like many of the other studies overseen by the institute as part of the project, Baer's study was based on Jordanian security services materials that had been seized by the Israeli military in 1967.[8] After the war and the occupation of the territories, such materials became the basis of studies by a number of young researchers at the Hebrew University, members of the third generation of Oriental Studies scholars: students of Baer, Heyd, Ayalon, and others. They enjoyed exclusive access to these materials—sometimes thanks to their employment, either alongside or preceding their academic research, in the framework of the bureau of the advisor on Arab affairs at the Prime Minister's Office, or the military.[9] Much like Gotthold Weil and his study on the Tatars, Baer's research on the *mukhtars* contributed to his scholarly development. A modified and expanded version of it was published about seven years later by the Hebrew University's Magnes Press.[10] Like Weil, Baer addressed the circumstances under which the study had been carried out in his introduction, in which he suggests that initiative for the "History of Judea and Samaria under Jordanian rule" study had come from the institute and was carried out with help from COGAT.[11]

A further study from this series approved by the Professors Committee

176 ::: A NEW ORIENT

trafficked in another aspect that characterized Horovitz and Weil's activities during World War I—the censorship of letters. One document written by a HUSOS student, published only as an internal booklet but carrying the names of the university and the institute on its cover, discussed the views and opinions of West Bank Palestinian Arabs on social issues.[12] The data, as stated in the introduction, were collected by means of "content analysis of a probability sample from written correspondence between West Bank residents and individuals abroad"; this practice of analysis was far from routine: using information pulled from the letters, the research team filled out surveys, each letter serving as an ostensible interviewee responding to its questions. Yet the letter-writers—slightly less than 3,600 were surveyed, in total—were not willing interviewees and were not even aware that their private letters were being used for research. The letters were filtered through the censorship system of the Israeli authorities in the West Bank, then handed to the research team for analysis before being sent along to their destinations.[13] Israeli Oriental Studies, like its ancestor, German Orientalism, transformed itself: no longer just research for its own sake, but now also research mobilized to serve the immediate political and security needs of the state.

From this point of view, 1967 was an important dividing line. Until that point, Orient experts' collaboration with the security apparatus had generally remained outside the university campus. It took two primary forms —individual activity, particularly by students; and through the Shiloah Institute, established at the Military Headquarters and government center (known as *Hakirya*) in central Tel Aviv under the auspices of the Israel Oriental Society.

Recruiting Oriental expertise for individual work along the dividing line between academia and the security apparatus had accompanied the institute's scholars since the founding of the state. Indeed, military personnel served on the council of the Israel Oriental Society, founded in 1949; but it was the Bureau of the Advisor on Arab Affairs that regularly asked the university directly for the details of institute students who could aid in tasks requiring the competencies of Oriental expertise.[14] Then, as now, even students earning scholarships and prizes had to find additional means of funding their student years, and projects in cooperation with governmental institutions were a possible source of income.

The archive of the Arab affairs advisor's bureau contains numerous examples. In 1956, its personnel wanted to process a detailed survey of "the minorities in the state," and sought external assistance in producing the historical chapters—on the Ottoman period, the Mandate period, and the war in 1948. They approached Uriel Heyd, then director of the institute, who agreed to propose names of institute students who, in exchange for payment from the bureau, would write the relevant chapters; Heyd would supervise the quality of their work.[15]

Some two years later, the bureau ordered additional surveys from institute students on a variety of topics—"the educated Arab youth," "the Arab refugees and Israel," "public advocacy [Hasbara] for minorities," "the problem of lands and the present absentees," and more.[16] In 1961, the advisor's bureau produced the "Census of Oriental experts in Israel" (mifkad hamizrahanim beyisra'el), for which Heyd provided the addresses of all the institute's students, bachelor's graduates, and master's alumni. The bureau kept a list with their names alongside various data points, including level of literary and colloquial Arabic and fields of specialization.[17] At times the advisor on Arab affairs also facilitated such contract work for other bodies: when the Shabak (Israel's internal security service known popularly by its Hebrew acronym, and in English as the Israel Security Agency) approached the advisor's bureau asking for a study on Arab conversion to Judaism since the founding of the state, the bureau reached out to the university and received the details of a master's student who was a graduate of HUSOS and the Department of Sociology.[18]

At the time, institutional collaboration with the military took place within the Reuven Shiloah Research Center of the Israel Oriental Society, typically known as the Shiloah Center for short. Its establishment in 1959 was initiated by Shiloah himself, an official at the Foreign Ministry and in the security apparatus who became its namesake after dying before the center's opening. It was to serve as a separate research arm of the Israel Oriental Society, which would also be a separate legal entity and deal with topics from current events, or in the words of Shiloah himself, "the studies necessary for diplomatic-security purposes";[19] as such, these were intentionally outside the purview of the School of Oriental Studies' research (in contrast with instruction on related topics), in the spirit of Heyd and Ayalon's approach discussed in detail in chapter 3.[20]

While the tone at the Israel Oriental Society was set by the Foreign Ministry, at the Shiloah Center this was the role of the Military Intelligence Directorate (Aman). Yitzhak Oron (1924–2014), a senior official in the research division of Aman, became the prime figure in the center's planning

178 ::: A NEW ORIENT

and its first director. In a letter to executive director of the Prime Minister's Office Teddy Kollek, another figure intimately involved in the founding of the center and especially in raising funds for it abroad, Oron declared that the Shiloah Center "must be established in the close vicinity of the Aman building, since the research center will receive libraries and archives that Aman will need to use in its day-to-day work."[21] Subsequently, a five-person administrative body was set: a representative of the Hebrew University and the Israel Oriental Society; a representative of the Prime Minister's Office; a representative of the Foreign Ministry; the director of Aman; and another representative from Aman.[22] The center's budget came partially from the Foreign Ministry and Aman (the Prime Minister's Office transferred an additional one-time sum), and further income came from the donations raised by Kollek, apart from donations for the Israel Oriental Society. The salaries of Aman officials who worked at the center preparing studies were paid by the military, and the center paid other researchers for studies they began or that were ordered by Aman and the Foreign Ministry—some for internal use and others for publication in the quarterly *The New East* and other fora.[23] The flagship of the Shiloah Center's publications was the yearly *Middle East Record*, published in English under Oron's editorship, surveying developments in politics and international relations in the Middle East on the basis of newspapers and other freely available sources, organized by topic. In effect, this was an English-language expansion of the press survey published in Hebrew in issues of *The New East*.[24]

Within a few years, the Shiloah Center's income stream became insufficient. It found itself in deficit, was forced to cut costs, and delay the publication of its yearly journal. In 1964, David Ayalon, now director of the Institute of Asian and African Studies and a member of the Shiloah Center's Scientific Council, approached Prime Minister Levi Eshkol requesting his assistance in funding the center. The Prime Minister's Office responded by noting that, while Eshkol viewed the subject positively, there were budgetary constraints.[25] In addition, relations between the Shiloah Center and the Israel Oriental Society had experienced ups and downs from the outset thanks to the two bodies' overlapping subject areas and competition, which also included the School of Oriental Studies/Institute of Asian and African Studies, over governmental and donor funds;[26] perhaps this situation contributed to Aman's decision in 1965 to stop supporting the center's activities as an extra-university body. The solution proposed by Shiloah Center personnel was to be transferred into the Hebrew University.[27]

*Epilogue* ::: 179

What followed was a formative moment in the development of the Israeli ethos of Oriental expertise—a line drawn in the sand: the proposal was rejected out of hand by David Ayalon, director of the institute, and Uriel Heyd, his predecessor and still a dominant figure there, since they objected to the incorporation of "current issues" into the institute's work and were apprehensive about the damage such a move might do to the scientific integrity and status of the institute's other research subjects. This proposal was quickly ruled out.[28] Instead, the Shiloah Center was brought under the auspices of Tel Aviv University; in effect, the association under which it operated was dissolved, and the center was reestablished in 1966, after negotiations between the young university and the IDF, as a research unit within the university that operated alongside the Department of Middle Eastern and African Studies founded there. The military made ongoing funding conditional on its publications' continued engagement with the modern Middle East.[29] The center (known today as the Dayan Center) and department were staffed primarily by doctoral students and young lecturers from the Institute of Asian and African Studies in Jerusalem, members of the third generation of Orient scholars who were yet to be fully integrated into the Hebrew University and were generally interested in late modern and contemporary subjects.[30]

For Ayalon at least, preventing the Hebrew University's annexation of the Shiloah Center was a source of pride. He referred to it in retrospect as "one of the most intelligent moves ever made by the institute," since in his eyes "it was this uncompromising stance that created the conditions for maintaining the high level of our Islamic studies [at the Hebrew University]."[31] His life path, beginning his studies at the university as an employee of the Foreign Ministry, suggests this was no categorical rejection of the idea that Oriental expertise could be mobilized for statist purposes. While he opposed this move, he simultaneously agreed to advise the director of the Mossad (Institute for Intelligence and Special Operations) regarding the possibility of reaching a peace settlement with Egypt.[32] Nevertheless, Jerusalemite Oriental Studies would for years continue to be associated, even in critical scholarship, with scientific and disinterested classical and philological research, but also closed off in its ivory tower, while its sister institution in Tel Aviv had a modern and up-to-date image but was also accused, whether implicitly or explicitly, of blurring the borders between academia and the political and security establishment.[33]

Over time, this relationship became less oppositional. Historians of the

Middle East at the Hebrew University, where Israeli Oriental Studies originated, actively engage with modern and contemporary issues. For quite some time, Arabists at the university have explored dialectology and modern literature. Nearly a century of research has witnessed the integration of new methodologies and trends in Jerusalem, facilitated by productive interactions with the global scholarly community and the recruitment of faculty with international training. Some of these academics initiated their academic pursuits in Tel Aviv and other Israeli universities under the guidance of the first and second generations of ex-Jerusalem scholars. The profound changes that have taken place over the last fifty years extend, of course, beyond the scope of this book. Nevertheless, even today, one may occasionally encounter whimsical references to the scholars in Jerusalem as "those *Germans*."

To what degree did these images reflect reality? When it came to Jerusalem, the reality was far more complex. In 1967, not long after the Shiloah Center was rejected and moved to Tel Aviv, Ayalon completed his term as director of the institute and was replaced by Gabriel Baer. The last of the second generation to lead HUSOS, Baer oversaw the institute's collaboration with military rule of the West Bank on the basis of his perspective that "the diplomatic, social, and geographic developments in the State of Israel's situation following the Six Day War—oblige state institutions, and especially its educational, scientific, and research institutions, to expand significantly their efforts to familiarize themselves with the Arabs of the Land of Israel and the Arab world around us."[34] He urged the establishment of a new research center at the Hebrew University—the Center for the Study of Palestinian Arabs and Israel-Arab Relations—which was finally established in 1972, as a collaboration between the Institute of Asian and African Studies and the Harry S. Truman Research Institute for the Advancement of Peace, which had been founded at the university several years earlier. The subjects studied at the new center overlapped in large part with those of the Shiloah Center, and while the work conducted there was based on Arabic newspapers, it also utilized surplus materials sent over by the IDF, the *Shai* (Information Services, Haganah intelligence arm) archive at the Ministry of Defense, the Foreign Ministry, and the bureau of the advisor for Arab affairs, and were located in Jerusalem rather than Tel Aviv.[35] A report on its establishment in the daily *Ma'ariv* based on a press release from the university said the center would "serve pure academic needs and the needs of the state and the IDF."[36]

*Epilogue* ::: 181

It is tempting to see 1967 and the dramatic war's consequences on Israeli history as a moment of break from the aspiration to keep science and politics separate, and from the German Orientalist heritage. Certainly, the collaboration between Oriental Studies scholars and the security apparatus in the wake of the conquest of the West Bank, East Jerusalem, and the Gaza Strip took place on a scale never seen within the Hebrew University and, since its establishment in 1926, its Orientalist institute. Most of the existing scholarship on Israeli Oriental Studies focuses on this point: the mobilization of Orient scholars to the cause of security beginning in the mid-1960s, and indeed primarily after the watershed of 1967. This book, on the other hand, has sought to examine the years that preceded this moment and therefore provide historical depth to the process that formed the discipline of Oriental Studies. The same news clipping, in clarifying that the university center in Jerusalem would serve both academic and statist-security needs, expressed the duality at the very heart of German-Jewish Oriental Studies in Mandatory Palestine and Israel: research and instruction that emerged from a stable and reputable academic legacy, but which were established and repeatedly developed in ways that were shaped by shifting political demands.

This was the path taken by the discipline of Oriental Studies in Jerusalem. The School of Oriental Studies was founded in the 1920s with the conscious and explicit goal of serving as a basis for intellectual affinity between Jews and Arabs and of exemplifying the universalist aspirations the Hebrew University, though a Zionist project, nonetheless harbored. On the institutional level, this was pursued by means of text-centered philological research endeavors that intentionally engaged with early Islam and classical Arabic. Matters were intertwined: the scholars who led these research initiatives relied upon methodologies and practices associated with a *fin-de-siècle* Berlin School and they owed their competencies to an academic chain of transmission reaching back to the founders of Oriental Studies—Goitein had studied in Frankfurt with Horovitz, himself a student of Eduard Sachau at the University of Berlin, who wrote his doctoral dissertation in Leipzig under the supervision of Heinrich Fleischer. In Jerusalem, at least in the eyes of decision-makers—Horovitz, Weil, Mayer, and Baneth—what was familiar from their days in Germany and what was necessary in Palestine were nearly one and the same.

The Orient scholars in Jerusalem, educated at German universities, were strangers neither to the necessity of mobilizing for extra-academic demands

182 ::: A NEW ORIENT

nor to the need to develop the discipline in relation with other people and institutions within the university and without. These feats were possible because they required no fundamental deviation from the scholarly tools with which their training equipped them. This continuity never damaged their academic progress and was even welcomed: on the one hand, they paid their cultural debt to the nation-building ideal by publishing some of their studies in Hebrew, giving lectures to the wider pubic, and mediating ongoing developments at the cutting edge of German science through book reviews and surveys that appeared in new Hebrew-language fora such as *Kiryat Sefer, Zion,* or *Tarbitz.*[37] On the other hand, they continued to publish work in German—in publications based in Germany, so long as political developments there allowed—in parallel to studies in the rising academic language of English, all while dutifully attending international conferences. In doing so, they maintained their status in the European academic community that birthed them and continued to serve as their point of reference.

The scientific work of the faculty remained as essentially textual as it had at the German universities. As they established their fields of specialization—Baneth in the philological study of Judaeo-Arabic, Mayer in the study of material and artistic aspects of Muslim culture, or Plessner in his work on the history of science in Islam—these resonated closely with the subjects they had been engaged with during their training in Europe. This is especially true of Gotthold Weil, who arrived in Jerusalem from Frankfurt—where he held a full professorship until the legislation of the Nazi race laws—already an established expert in Arabic and Turkish in the world of German Orientalism and beyond. Even Goitein—whose research interests probably shifted more fundamentally than all the others after leaving Frankfurt for Palestine—continued to rely upon an existing ethnographic-linguistic tradition only rather recently arrived in Germany itself, during World War I. He was, in any case, an outlier within his generation: whatever disciplinary shift he did experience took place primarily outside the institutional frame of the university. Within it, he continued his textual work.

In other words, Orient scholarship could maintain its fertile relationship with politics because politics did not require it to change. The transition from Berlin and Frankfurt to Jerusalem turned the textual encounter with the Orient into a tactile one, but did not divert the focus away from the text. The scholars on Mount Scopus studying the Orient had no difficulty cooperating with the use of their discipline for political purposes—encouraged during the British Mandate by both university president and chancellor Magnes and by the Jewish Agency—through the development of relationships with intellectuals in the Arab world and building the reputation of the Hebrew University and of the Zionist project. These political demands changed completely in the build-up to 1948, and especially after the establishment of the State of Israel, but those at the institute were accustomed to the discipline's mobilization towards goals other than scientific achievement, especially when budgetary questions were in the balance.

The institute's second generation of Orient scholars, those whose training in the discipline came in Palestine, acquired their classical knowledge at the institute and their modern historical knowledge elsewhere—as part of their employment by the Political Department of the Jewish Agency or the Foreign Ministry. Integrating them within the School of Oriental studies as scholars of modern history occurred as part of, not at the expense of the process of expanding its existing fields of research and instruction. In the new fields they developed, these scholars became influential international figures—Heyd in the study of Ottoman imperial history, for example, or Ayalon as a Mamluk expert, or Baer in the social and economic history of Egypt. Their teachers encouraged this (at times even pushing them to do so more than the students themselves), in part because it did not require that they change the direction of their own research or give up on the large institutional research initiatives that the institute continued to pursue in subsequent decades. Of course, there were also those among the second generation who insisted on continuing the classical philological mission, mostly within the Department of Arabic Language and Literature—M. J. Kister being an obvious example. Those of both the former and the latter types were memorialized in international scientific journals, and their studies are still mentioned in the contemporary scholarly literature.

In many ways, the intricate dynamic between reason of state and the nature of the discipline was only disturbed in 1967, even if only in part: in the face of the state's urgent political and security needs, Oriental Studies as a discipline was enlisted as an active player in the Jewish-Arab conflict. Even if topics associated with the German-Jewish scientific heritage continued to draw study at the institute, this occurred alongside the intensive, institutional production of knowledge to serve decision-makers on the Israeli side, designed to help them assert control over the recently conquered territories and develop policies accordingly.

Incorporating historical depth in our outlook shows that there was no

184 ::: A NEW ORIENT

contradiction between the Germanness, the Zionism, and the statism of German-Jewish study of the Orient in Mandatory Palestine and Israel. Indeed, the German legacy included its own statist element, relationships that may have reached their peak during World War I but were in no way limited to it. Perhaps, then, rather than discussing *the* German legacy one ought to discuss German *legacies*. The goals of the German Oriental Society, for example, did not differ significantly from those of its Israeli equivalent, though the two were founded nearly a century apart. Such continuity was apparent structurally, too: the centralized structure under which Horovitz administered the institute in its early years may have relaxed somewhat with his death in 1931, but was renewed under Goitein and Heyd, its undisputed leaders during the first decade and a half of the State of Israel.

In this sense, the case of knowledge transfer to Jerusalem, thus transposing a discipline out of its original context, pinpoints a fundamental realization regarding German Orientalism as a whole: although it did not develop as an applied field of knowledge against the background of colonial aspirations, it could nonetheless be used to fulfill political and national purposes. The very act of creating knowledge on the Orient, even if the knowledge itself was not directly used, could be redirected and mobilized time and again—whether to advance affinity between Jews and Arabs, or in order to provide support for diplomatic efforts.

"As a place for research on the Orient, truly, Jerusalem has one benefit: lying within the Orient," wrote D. H. Baneth in 1926, two years after arriving from Berlin. He was referring to the city's geographical proximity to "the modern and ancient centers of Near Eastern culture," but emphasized that "Jerusalem itself is not such a center."[38] Like Baneth, so, too, the other scholars—to say nothing of the books, research materials, and research practices of the School of Oriental Studies and later of the Institute of Asian and African Studies—arrived primarily from Europe. Transplanting the discipline to Jerusalem did not make it local, but it did grant it new local contexts within which to grow. Israeli Oriental Studies continued to draw upon its various eries of German roots years after parting ways with Germany itself.

# NOTES

## LIST OF ABBREVIATIONS

AJMIA     Archives of the Jerusalem Museum for Islamic Art
ANLI     Archives of the National Library of Israel
CAHU     Central Archives of the Hebrew University
CZA     Central Zionist Archives
ISA     Israel State Archive
LHAS     Library of the Hungarian Academy of Science
YCW     Yad Chaim Weizmann

## INTRODUCTION

1. S. D. Goitein, "Mada'ey hamizrah ba'universita ha'ivrit," *Davar*, April 10, 1935, 12.

2. Mitchell G. Ash, "Wissens- und Wissenschaftstransfer: Einführende Bemerkungen," *Berichte zur Wissenschaftsgeschichte* 29, no. 3 (2006): 182.

3. Ibid., 183. See also Veronika Lipphardt and David Ludwig, "Knowledge Transfer and Science Transfer," *European History Online (EGO)*, published by the Institute of European History (IEG), Mainz, December 12, 2011, http://www.ieg-ego.eu /lipphardtv-ludwigd-2011-en.

4. The first use of the term in Hebrew would seem to date to 1917, in the article "On Translations of the Holy Scriptures," published by the Jewish-American bibliographer and scholar of Semitic languages Israel Shapira (1882–1957), when referring to Orientalists, or those dealing in Orientalism. The article was published in the United States in the periodical *Hatoren* (Year 4, Issue 12, 11).

5. In the English-language scholarship, various tactics have been formulated in response to the possible challenges of using the term Orientalism. Suzanne Marchand, writing about German Orientalism, chose to use the German term for the discipline, *Orientalistik*. See Marchand, *German Orientalism in the Age of Empire: Religion, Race and Scholarship* (Cambridge: Cambridge University Press, 2009), xxiv.

6. In his socio-anthropological work on contemporary Israeli Orientalism, Eyal Clyne retains the Hebrew term *mizrahanut* in English transliteration in order to emphasize its continued use in the Orientalist discourse in Israel today, unlike the use of the term Orientalism to describe this field of expertise in English. See Clyne, *Orientalism, Zionism and Academic Practice: Middle East and Islam Studies in Israeli Universities* (London: Routledge, 2019), 15–16. Note that in recent decades, academics active in the field in Israel have preferred to describe themselves as historians of the Middle East, Islam scholars, and so on. See, for example, Simon Shamir, "Tshuva le'Eyal Clyne," *Forum for Regional Thinking*, August 7, 2019, http://www.regthink.org /articles/an-answer-to-eyal-klein.

186 ::: NOTES TO INTRODUCTION

7. Clyne, *Orientalism, Zionism and Academic Practice*, 16–17.

8. Edward Said, *Orientalism* (New York: Pantheon Books, 1978).

9. Ibid., 2–3.

10. Ibid., 18–19.

11. Bernard Lewis, *Islam and the West* (New York: Oxford University Press, 1993); Robert Irwin, *For Lust of Knowing: The Orientalists and Their Enemies* (London: Allen Lane, 2006).

12. Preceding these works was the study by the Orientalist Johann Fück in 1955 surveying the leading figures in the development of Arabic studies in Europe until the beginning of the twentieth century and their contribution to scholarship. See Fück, *Die arabischen Studien in Europa bis in den Anfang des 20. Jahrhunderts* (Leipzig: O. Harrassowitz, 1955).

13. Baber Johansen, "Politics and Scholarship: The Development of Islamic Studies in the Federal Republic of Germany," in *Middle East Studies: International Perspectives on the State of the Art*, ed. Tareq Y. Ismael (New York: Praeger, 1990), 71–130.

14. Sabine Mangold, *Eine "weltbürgerliche Wissenschaft"—Die deutsche Orientalistik im 19. Jahrhundert* (Stuttgart: Franz Steiner Verlag, 2004).

15. Susannah Heschel, "German Jewish Scholarship on Islam as a Tool for De-Orientalizing Judaism," *New German Critique* 39, no. 3 (2012): 91–107.

16. John Efron, "Orientalism and the Jewish Historical Gaze," in *Orientalism and the Jews*, ed. Ivan D. Kalmar and Derek J. Penslar (Waltham: Brandeis University Press, 2005), 80–93. Also, see Sabine Schmidtke's recent contributions to the study of German Orientalism in the twentieth century in general, and the role of German Jews within it specifically: Schmidtke, *German Orientalism in Times of Turmoil: The Kahle-Strothmann Correspondence (1933 through 1938, 1945 through 1950)* (Budapest: Eötvös Loránd University Chair for Arabic Studies & Csoma de Kőrös Society Section of Islamic Studies, 2022); Schmidtke, "From *Wissenschaft des Judentums* to *Wissenschaft des Islams*: Eugen Mittwoch between Jewish and Islamic Studies," *Historical Interactions of Religious Cultures* 1, no. 1 (2024): 103–45.

17. Lena Salaymeh, "The 'Good Orientalists,'" in *Westernness: Critical Reflections on the Spatio-temporal Construction of the West*, ed. Christopher GoGwilt, Holt Meyer, and Sergey Sistiaga (Berlin: De Gruyter Oldenbourg, 2022), 105–36.

18. Christian Wiese, *Challenging Colonial Discourse: Jewish Studies and Protestant Theology in Wilhelmine Germany* (Leiden: Brill, 2005).

19. David N. Myers, *Re-inventing the Jewish Past: European Jewish Intellectuals and the Zionist Return to History* (New York: Oxford University Press, 1995).

20. Ismar Schorsch, "Converging Cognates: The Intersection of Jewish and Islamic Studies in Nineteenth Century Germany," *Leo Baeck Institute Year Book* 55 (2010): 3–36; Amnon Raz-Krakotzkin, "Orientalism, Jewish Studies and Israeli Society: A Few Comments," *Philological Encounters* 2, no. 3–4 (2017): 237–69.

21. Raz-Krakotzkin, "Orientalism, Jewish Studies and Israeli Society," 253.

22. Ursula Wokoeck, *German Orientalism: The Study of the Middle East and Islam from 1800 to 1945* (London: Routledge, 2009). On the rise, origins, and influence of the philological method—that is, the historical and comparative approach to

# NOTES TO INTRODUCTION ::: 187

analyzing texts—see James Turner, *Philology: The Forgotten Origins of the Modern Humanities* (Princeton: Princeton University Press, 2014).

23. Wokoeck, *German Orientalism*, 211.

24. Gottfried Hagen, "German Heralds of Holy War: Orientalists and Applied Oriental Studies," *Comparative Studies of South Asia, Africa and the Middle East* 24, no. 2 (2004): 145–62; Maren Bragulla, *Die Nachrichtenstelle für den Orient: Fallstudie einer Propagandainstitution im Ersten Weltkrieg* (Saarbrücken: VDM Verlag Dr. Müller, 2007).

25. Marchand, *German Orientalism in the Age of Empire*.

26. Ibid., xx.

27. Ibid., xxi.

28. Ibid., xxvi.

29. Yoav Gelber, "The Historical Role of the Central European Immigration to Israel," *The Leo Baeck Institute Year Book* 38, no. 1 (1993): 329, 338. The English article cited here is based on his more comprehensive book in Hebrew: Gelber, *Moledet hadasha: 'Aliyat yehudey merkaz eropa uklitatam, 1933–1948* (Jerusalem: Yad Ben Zvi, 1990).

30. Doron Niederland, "Deutsche Ärzte-Emigration und gesundheitspolitische Entwicklungen in 'Eretz Israel' (1933–1948)," *Medizinhistorisches Journal* 20, no. 1–2 (1985): 149–84; Alona Nitzan-Shiftan, "Contested Zionism—Alternative Modernism: Erich Mendelsohn and the Tel Aviv Chug in Mandate Palestine," *Architectural History* 39 (1996): 147–80; Fania Oz-Salzberger and Eli Salzberger, "The Secret German Sources of the Israeli Supreme Court," *Israel Studies* 3, no. 2 (1998): 159–92; Yfaat Weiss, "The Golem and Its Creator, or How the Jewish Nation-State Became Multiethnic," in *Challenging Ethnic Citizenship: German and Israeli Perspectives on Immigration*, ed. Daniel Levy and Yfaat Weiss (New York: Berghahn Books, 2002), 82–104; Rakefet Zalashik, *'Ad nafesh: Mehagrim, 'olim vehamimsad hapsikhiyatri beyisra'el* (Tel Aviv: Hakibbutz Hameuchad, 2008); Dani Schrire, *Isuf shivrey hagola: Heker hafolklor hatziyoni lenokhah hasho'a* (Jerusalem: The Hebrew University Magnes Press, 2018); Miriam Szamet, "Contested Pedagogy: Modern Hebrew Education and the Segregation of National Communities in Pre-state Palestine," in *Israel-Palestine: Lands and Peoples*, ed. Omer Bartov (New York: Berghahn Books, 2021), 181–97; Shira Wilkof, "An 'Ordinary Modernist'? Empire and Nation in Ariel Kahane's Large-Scale Planning," *Planning Perspectives* 35, no. 5 (2020): 805–26.

31. Dan Diner and Moshe Zimmerman, "Israel's German Academic Legacy: An Introduction," in *Disseminating German Tradition*, ed. Dan Diner and Moshe Zimmerman (Leipzig: Leipziger Universitätsverlag, 2009), 10.

32. See, for example, Tania Forte, "Sifting People, Sorting Papers: Academic Practice and the Notion of State Security in Israel," *Comparative Studies of South Asia, Africa and the Middle East* 23, no. 1–2 (2003): 215–23; Doron Matza, *He'asor shebo noldu 'arveiyey yisra'el': Yisra'el ve'ezrahea ha'aravim-falastinim 1966-1976* (Tel Aviv: Resling, 2022), 41–78; Wael B. Hallaq, *Restating Orientalism: A Critique of Modern Knowledge* (New York: Columbia University Press, 2018), 217–26; Clyne, *Orientalism, Zionism and Academic Practice*.

188 ::: NOTES TO INTRODUCTION

33. See, for example, Muhammad Jala Idris, *Al-'Istishraq al-isra'ili fil-dirasat al-'ibriyya al-mu'asira* (Cairo: Al-'arabi lil-nashr wal-tawzi', 1995); Said Musatafa Motahhari, *Al-mustashriq al-mu'asir Etan Kohlberg wahadith al-'imamiyya* (Karbala: Al-'ataba al-'abbasiyya al-muqaddasa, 2014).

34. Liora R. Halperin, *Babel in Zion: Jews, Nationalism, and Language Diversity in Palestine, 1920–1948* (New Haven: Yale University Press, 2015), 142–80; Amos Noy, *'Edim 'o mumhim: Yehudim maskilim bney yerushalayim vehamizrah bithilat hame'a ha'esrim* (Tel Aviv: Resling, 2017); Abigail Jacobson and Moshe Naor, *Oriental Neighbors: Middle Eastern Jews and Arabs in Mandatory Palestine* (Waltham, MA: Brandeis University Press, 2016), especially 54–120, 150–95.

35. Gil Eyal, *The Disenchantment of the Orient: Expertise in Arab Affairs and the Israeli State* (Stanford: Stanford University Press, 2006). See also the response of Ehud Toledano of the Department of Middle Eastern and African History at Tel Aviv University to Eyal's book: Toledano, "Review of *The Disenchantment of the Orient*, by Gil Eyal," *Ruah mizrahit* 5 (2007): 36–42. While Toledano agrees that a discussion of the history of Israeli Oriental Studies is necessary, he rejects Eyal's sociological approach and critiques the book for its insufficiently rich archival corpus.

36. Eyal, *Disenchantment of the Orient*, 62–68.

37. Ibid., 70.

38. Yonatan Mendel, "From German Philology to Local Usability: The Emergence of 'Practical' Arabic in the Hebrew Reali School in Haifa—1913–48," *Middle Eastern Studies* 52, no. 1 (2016): 1–26. See also idem, *Safa mihutz limkoma: Orientalism, modi'in veha'aravit beyisra'el* (Tel Aviv: Van Leer Institute and Hakibbutz Hameuchad, 2020), 29–37.

39. Baruch Kimmerling, *Zionism and Territory: The Socio-Territorial Dimensions of Zionist Politics* (Berkeley: Institute of International Studies, University of California Press, 1983); Gershon Shafir, *Land, Labour and Origins of the Israeli-Palestinian Conflict 1882–1914* (Cambridge: Cambridge University Press, 1989). For a discussion of the various historiographical approaches with regards to this topic, see Ran Aharonson, "Settlement in Eretz Israel—A Colonialist Enterprise? 'Critical' Scholarship and Historical Geography," *Israel Studies* 1, no. 2 (1996): 214–29. Another analytical paradigm sees Zionism as a clear case of settler colonialism, that is, one that seeks to disengage from its metropole and establish a new sovereignty that implements a different set of relations with the indigenous population than the colonial conquering power had practiced. On how this category might be applied to the Zionist case, see Arnon Degani, "Zionism's Flipside: A Reconsideration of Settler-Colonialism in Israel/Palestine," *Academia.edu*. 2023, www.academia.edu/108390348 /Zionisms_Flipside_A_Reconsideration_of_Settler_Colonialism_in_Israel_Palestine.

40. Derek J. Penslar, *Zionism and Technocracy: The Engineering of the Jewish Settlement in Palestine, 1870–1918* (Bloomington: Indiana University Press, 1991); Shalom Reichman and Shlomo Hasson, "A Cross-Cultural Diffusion of Colonization: From Posen to Palestine," *Annals of the Association of American Geographers* 74, no. 1 (1984): 57–70.

NOTES TO INTRODUCTION ::: 189

41. Yfaat Weiss, "Central European Ethnonationalism and Zionist Binationalism," *Jewish Social Studies* 11, no. 1 (2004): 93–117.

42. Menahem Milson, "The Beginnings of Arabic and Islamic Studies at the Hebrew University of Jerusalem," *Judaism* 45, no. 2 (Spring 1996): 168–83.

43. Ibid., 181.

44. Hava Lazarus-Yafeh, "The Transplantation of Islamic Studies from Europe to the Yishuv and Israel," in *The Jewish Discovery of Islam: Studies in Honor of Bernard Lewis*, ed. Martin Kramer (Tel Aviv: The Moshe Dayan Center for Middle Eastern and African Studies, Tel Aviv University, 1999), 249–60.

45. Shaul Katz, "The Scion and Its Tree: The Hebrew University of Jerusalem and Its German Epistemological and Organizational Origins," in *The Institution of Science and the Science of Institutions: The Legacy of Joseph Ben-David*, ed. Marcel Herbst (Dordrecht: Springer, 2014), 103–44.

46. Zachary Lockman, *Contending Visions of the Middle East: The History and Politics of Orientalism* (Cambridge: Cambridge University Press, 2004).

47. Ruchama Johnston-Bloom, "Symbiosis Relocated: The German-Jewish Orientalist Ilse Lichtenstadter in America," *Leo Baeck Institute Year Book* 58, no. 1 (2013): 95–110.

48. Ruchama Johnston-Bloom, "'Dieses wirklich westöstlichen Mannes': The German-Jewish Orientalist Josef Horovitz in Germany, India, and Palestine," in *The Muslim Reception of European Orientalism: Reversing the Gaze*, ed. Susannah Heschel and Umar Ryad (London: Routledge, 2018), 168–83; Hanan Harif, "The Orient between Arab and Jewish National Revivals: Josef Horovitz, Shelomo Dov Goitein and Oriental Studies in Jerusalem," in *Modern Jewish Scholarship on Islam in Context: Rationality, European Borders, and the Search for Belonging*, ed. Ottfried Fraisse (Berlin: De Gruyter, 2018), 319–36; Sabine Mangold-Will, "Josef Horovitz und die Gründung des Instituts für Arabische und Islamische Studien an der Hebräischen Universität in Jerusalem: ein Orientalisches Seminar für Palästina," *Naharaim* 10, no. 1 (2016): 7–37.

49. Noteworthy in this context is the article by Razak Khan on the connections between German Jews and Muslim intellectuals from India as reflected in British colonial and other archives: Khan, "Entanglements in the Colony: Jewish–Muslim Connected Histories in Colonial India," *Modern Asian Studies* 56, no. 6 (2022): 1845–71.

50. Sabine Mangold-Will, "Gotthold Weil, die Orientalische Philologie und die deutsche Wissenschaft an der Hebräischen Universität," *Naharaim* 8, no. 1 (2014): 74–90.

51. A number of these studies were written by other *Geniza* scholars who studied with Goitein directly or were influenced by his larger body of work, and were based on analyses of the tendencies emerging from his studies, for example, Joel L. Kraemer, "Goitein vehahevra hayam tikhonit shelo," *Zmanim* 34/35 (1990): 4–17; Gideon Libson, "Hidden Worlds and Open Shutters: S. D. Goitein, between Judaism and Islam," in *The Jewish Past Revisited: Reflections on Modern Jewish Historians*, ed. David N. Myers and David B. Ruderman (New Haven, CT: Yale University Press, 1998), 183–98;

190 ::: NOTES TO INTRODUCTION

Miriam Frenkel, "Ktivat hahistoria shel yehudey artzot ha'islam bimey habeinayim: Tziuney derekh vesikuyim," *Pe'amim* 92 (2002): 23–61; Norman (Noam) A. Stillman, "Islamici nil a me alienum puto: The Mindset of Jewish Scholars of Islamic Studies," in *Modern Jewish Scholarship on Islam in Context*, ed. Ottfried Fraisse (Berlin: De Gruyter, 2018), 181–98. For a comprehensive list of such works see Hanan Harif, "A Bridge or a Fortress? S. D. Goitein and the Role of Jewish Arabists in the American Academy," *Jewish Social Studies* 26, no. 2 (2021): 87–88, n7. In recent years, a number of new studies have appeared, based on the rich archival sources left behind by Goitein during his years in Germany, Israel, and the United States: Harif, "The Orient between Arab and Jewish National Revivals"; Tom Fogel, "Hamehkar hateimani shel S. D. Goitein" (PhD diss., Hebrew University of Jerusalem, 2019). Generally, these studies do not examine Goitein's involvement in the development of the discipline of Oriental Studies at the Hebrew University or his important institutional impact on the field during his tenure as head of HUSOS between 1949 and 1956.

52. Hanan Harif, "Islam in Zion? Yosef Yo'el Rivlin's Translation of the Qur'an and Its Place Within the New Hebrew Culture," *Naharaim* 10, no. 1 (2016): 39–55; Amit Levy, "A Man of Contention: Martin Plessner (1900–1973) and His Encounters with the Orient," *Naharaim* 10, no. 1 (2016): 79–100; Yonatan Mendel, "German Orientalism, Arabic Grammar and the Jewish Education System: The Origins and Effect of Martin Plessner's 'Theory of Arabic Grammar,'" *Naharaim* 10, no. 1 (2016): 57–77; Mostafa Hussein, "Scholarship on Islamic Archaeology between Zionism and Arab Nationalist Movements," in *The Muslim Reception of European Orientalism: Reversing the Gaze*, ed. Susannah Heschel and Umar Ryad (Oxon: Routledge, 2019), 184–208; Sarah Irving, "Stephan Hanna Stephan and Evliya Çelebi's Book of Travels: Tracing Cooperation and Conflict in Mandate Palestinian Translations," in *Cultural Entanglement in the Pre-Independence Arab World: Arts, Thought and Literature*, ed. Anthony Gorman and Sarah Irving (London: Bloomsbury Academic, 2020), 217–37.

53. Marchand, *German Orientalism in the Age of Empire*, p. xxiii.

54. Eyal, *Disenchantment of the Orient*, 34.

55. Pierre Bourdieu, *Homo Academicus*, trans. Peter Collier (Stanford: Stanford University Press, 1988), 152.

56. Wokoeck, *German Orientalism*, 22–23.

57. Bruno Latour, *Reassembling the Social: An Introduction to Actor-Network Theory* (Oxford: Oxford University Press, 2007), especially 63–86. For the characteristics of the theory and its development as part of the thinking of the French philosopher and anthropologist Bruno Latour, see Sal Restivo, "Bruno Latour: The Once and Future Philosopher," in *The Wiley-Blackwell Companion to Major Social Theorists*, ed. George Ritzer and Jeffrey Stepnisky (Malden: Wiley-Blackwell, 2011), 520–40.

58. Outstanding examples are the study by Thomas Irish on networks in the Anglo-Saxon academic world during and after World War I. See Tomás Irish, *The University at War, 1914–25: Britain, France, and the United States* (Basingstoke: Palgrave Macmillan, 2015), as well as the aforementioned work of Dani Schrire. Schrire proposes a detailed discussion of the ways Latour's thinking can contribute

to the writing of the history of folklore studies, and his proposals can also be adopted for the study of other disciplines (*Isuf shivrey hagola*, 28–51).

59. Recent years have brought an intra-disciplinary discourse among Oriental Studies scholars concerning the need to record the field's history. See, for example, Toledano, "Limudey hamizrah hatikhon beyisrael beyameinu," MEISAI, last modified July 10, 2007, www.meisai.org.il; Shamir, "Tshuva le'Eyal Clyne."

## 1. THE SCIENCE OF THE ORIENT

1. A. B. Yehoshua, "Hakdama," in *Yerushalayim hayeshana ba'ayn uvalev: Mivhar ktavim*, by Ya'akov Yehoshua (Jerusalem: Keter, 1988), 8.

2. Yoav Alon and Ido Shahar, "Re'ayon 'im Prof. Jacob Landau," *Hamizrah hehadash* 58 (2019): 16.

3. A comprehensive analysis of the state of research on the term "Germanness" can be found in Alexander Maxwell and Sacha E. Davis, "Germanness beyond Germany: Collective Identity in German Diaspora Communities," *German Studies Review* 39, no. 1 (2016): 1–15.

4. Yfaat Weiss, "Central European Ethnonationalism and Zionist Binationalism," *Jewish Social Studies* 11, no. 1 (2004): 113.

5. Shaul Katz, "The Scion and Its Tree: The Hebrew University of Jerusalem and Its German Epistemological and Organizational Origins," in *The Institution of Science and the Science of Institutions: The Legacy of Joseph Ben-David*, ed. Marcel Herbst (Dordrecht: Springer, 2014), 109–10.

6. Ibid., 120.

7. Menahem Milson, "The Beginnings of Arabic and Islamic Studies at the Hebrew University of Jerusalem," *Judaism* 45, no. 2 (Spring 1996): 177–78.

8. Suzanne L. Marchand, *German Orientalism in the Age of Empire: Religion, Race and Scholarship* (Cambridge: Cambridge University Press, 2009), 28–29.

9. Ursula Wokoeck, *German Orientalism: The Study of the Middle East and Islam from 1800 to 1945* (London: Routledge, 2009), 86.

10. Stephen G. Burnett, *Christian Hebraism in the Reformation Era (1500–1660): Authors, Books, and the Transmission of Jewish Learning* (Leiden: Brill, 2012), 271.

11. Marchand, *German Orientalism in the Age of Empire*, 15. See also James Pasto, "Islam's 'Strange Secret Sharer': Orientalism, Judaism, and the Jewish Question," *Comparative Studies in Society and History* 40, no. 3 (1998): 437–74; Amnon Raz-Krakotzkin, "Orientalism, Jewish Studies and Israeli Society: A Few Comments," *Philological Encounters* 2, no. 3–4 (2017): 237–69.

12. Wokoeck, *German Orientalism*, 95–96. On Schlegel's work see Todd Kontje, *German Orientalisms* (Ann Arbor: The University of Michigan Press, 2004), 105–10; Marchand, *German Orientalism in the Age of Empire*, 58–65. Much has been written about the roots of Indological research in Germany, its development, and its influence on scientific and political discourses in Germany and Europe more broadly. See, for example, Sheldon Pollock, "Deep Orientalism? Notes on Sanskrit and Power Beyond the Raj," in *Orientalism and the Postcolonial Predicament*, ed. Carol A. Breckenridge and Peter van der Veer (Philadelphia: University of Pennsylvania

192 ::: NOTES TO CHAPTER 1

Press, 1993), 76–133; Tuska Benes, "Comparative Linguistics as Ethnology: In Search of Indo-Germans in Central Asia, 1770–1830," *Comparative Studies of South Asia, Africa and the Middle East* 24, no. 2 (2004): 117–32; and the volume edited by Douglas T. McGetchin, Peter K. J. Park, and Damodar SarDesai, *Sanskrit and "Orientalism": Indology and Comparative Linguistics in Germany, 1750–1958* (New Delhi: Manohar Publishers & Distributors, 2004).

13. Wokoeck, *German Orientalism*, 86.

14. Sabine Mangold, *Eine "weltbürgerliche Wissenschaft"—Die deutsche Orientalistik im 19. Jahrhundert* (Stuttgart: Franz Steiner Verlag, 2004), 42. She describes the period between 1810 and 1840 as the definitive point in the development of the modern discipline; in 1810 the University of Berlin was founded.

15. Robert Irwin, *For Lust of Knowing: The Orientalists and Their Enemies* (London: Allen Lane, 2006), 141–42.

16. Wokoeck, *German Orientalism*, 88. For a detailed list of positions and their titles, collected by Wokoeck and arranged by town and by field, see ibid., 235–87.

17. For a historiographical discussion of the topic, see ibid., 89–95. Wokoeck relies upon a series of previous studies following German Orientalism and connections between Germany and the Middle East to show that the development of the discipline was not driven by colonial interests.

18. Mangold, *Eine "weltbürgerliche Wissenschaft"*, 52–59. For critical discussion of the idea of the Humboldtian university and its influence, see Mitchell G. Ash, "Bachelor of What, Master of Whom? The Humboldt Myth and Historical Transformations of Higher Education in German-Speaking Europe and the US," *European Journal of Education* 41, no. 2 (2006): 245–67.

19. Wokoeck, *German Orientalism*, 95, 107, 113–16.

20. Ibid., 87.

21. Conrad, "Editor's Introduction," in *The Earliest Biographies of the Prophet and Their Authors*, by Josef Horovitz, ed. Lawrence I. Conrad (Princeton: The Darwin Press, 2002), xi–xii.

22. Ibid., xi; Marchand, *German Orientalism in the Age of Empire*, 120–21.

23. Ismar Schorsch, "Converging Cognates: The Intersection of Jewish and Islamic Studies in Nineteenth Century Germany," *Leo Baeck Institute Year Book* 55 (2010): 22–33.

24. Wokoeck, *German Orientalism*, 120. Compare with Mangold, *Eine "weltbürgerliche Wissenschaft"*, 176–225.

25. Wokoeck, *German Orientalism*, 132–33.

26. Marchand, *German Orientalism in the Age of Empire*, 158.

27. Ibid., 162.

28. Wokoeck, *German Orientalism*, 142–45.

29. Compare Mangold, *Eine "weltbürgerliche Wissenschaft"*, 266–78, and Wokoeck, *German Orientalism*, 164–84. *Islamkunde* should be contrasted with *Islamwissenschaft*, scholarship involving study of the Islamic religion through historicist and scientific methods, specifically in the field of religious studies.

30. Wokoeck, *German Orientalism*, 182.

# NOTES TO CHAPTER 1 ::: 193

31. Ibid., 184.

32. Wilhelm Doegen, ed., *Unter Fremden Völkern: Eine neue Völkerkunde* (Berlin: Otto Stollberg Verlag für Politik und Wirtschaft, 1925).

33. Andrew E. Evans, *Anthropology at War: World War I and the Science of Race in Germany* (Chicago: The University of Chicago Press, 2010), 131, 136–37; Doegen, *Unter Fremden Völkern*, 12–13. The recordings have been preserved and became the primary basis of the audio archive (*Lautarchiv*), initially housed at the Prussian State Library and later at the University of Berlin (today: Humboldt Universität), where they underwent digitization in the late 1990s.

34. Ibid., 9.

35. Heike Liebau, "Networks of Knowledge Production: South Asian Muslims and German Scholars in Berlin (1915–30)," *Comparative Studies of South Asia, Africa and the Middle East* 40, no. 2 (2020): 312. On the German strategy of sowing rebellion among the Muslim populations of Asia and Africa, see Tilman Lüdke, *Jihad Made in Germany: Ottoman and German Propaganda and Intelligence Operations in World War I* (Münster: Lit Verlag, 2005).

36. Martin Gussone, "Architectural Jihad: The 'Halbmondlager' Mosque of Wünsdorf as an Instrument of Propaganda," in *Jihad and Islam in World War I: Studies on the Ottoman Jihad at the Centenary of Snouck Hurgronje's "Holy War Made in Germany"*, ed. Erik-Jan Zürcher (Leiden: Leiden University Press, 2015), 181. German historian Gerhard Höpp dedicated much of his work to the presence of Muslims in Germany during the first half of the twentieth century, especially the POWs. For a detailed and systematic study of the camps in Wünsdorf and Zossen, see Gerhard Höpp, *Muslime in der Mark: Als Kriegsgefangene und Internierte in Wünsdorf und Zossen* (Berlin: Das Arabische Buch, 1997).

37. Some of the propaganda materials from the Halbmondlager ended up in the Archive of the National Library in Jerusalem. One folder in the repository (ANLI, Ms. Ar. 514) contains 172 loose pages printed at the camp between June 1915 and January 1916. Among them are orders issued by the camp's commanders and news from the front, including items describing German victories and updates on the Muslim population. Most of the material is in Arabic, but some has been translated into Hindi and Urdu. Nor was the folder's journey a matter of chance: markings on the folder suggest that it was stored at the Prussian State Library after the war but later removed from its holdings. It seems reasonable that Gotthold Weil, director of the library's Oriental department, was responsible for removing the folder, and that it reached the Archive of the National Library along with his estate. On the origins of the folder and the documents themselves, see Ephraim Wust, "Tik mahane hasahar: 'Mu'askar al-hilal / Halbmondlager', yuli 1915–yanuar 1916," in *Sefer Rafael Weiser: 'Iyunim bekhitvey yad, be'arkhionim uvitzirat S. Y. Agnon*, ed. Gil Weissblei (Jerusalem: Mineged, 2020), 91–100.

38. Marchand dedicates a short sub-chapter to the German Orientalists' mobilization to the war effort outside the universities, between 1914 and 1918: Marchand, *German Orientalism in the Age of Empire*, 446–54. However, she does not address Doegen's recording enterprise there.

194 ::: NOTES TO CHAPTER 1

39. Ibid., xix. See also Nina Berman, *German Literature on the Middle East: Discourses and Practices, 1000–1989* (Ann Arbor: University of Michigan Press, 2011).

40. See, for example, Lisa Lowe, *Critical Terrains: French and British Orientalisms* (Ithaca: Cornell University Press, 1991).

41. Orientalist studies in other fields often took shape outside of universities in the nineteenth century among independent scholars not in frequent contact with European scholars. One clear example comes from Arabic dialectology, the study of spoken dialects and their analysis via transcription and agreed-upon rules: foundational studies were carried out by diplomats and others on site in the Orient. University-based scholars only entered the field in the early twentieth century, and it enjoyed neither the venerability nor the firm position of philological studies of classical Arabic: Alexander Borg, *Rewriting Dialectal Arabic Prehistory: The Ancient Egyptian Lexical Evidence* (Leiden: Brill, 2021), 18–19. I would like to thank Amos Noy for bringing this topic to my attention.

42. Schorsch, "Converging Cognates," 7; John Efron, "Orientalism and the Jewish Historical Gaze," in *Orientalism and the Jews*, ed. Ivan D. Kalmar and Derek J. Penslar (Waltham: Brandeis University Press, 2005), 93. See also Achim Rhode, "Der Innere Orient: Orientalismus, Antisemitismus und Geschlecht im Deutschland des 18. bis 20. Jahrhunderts," *Die Welt des Islams*, New Series 45, no. 3 (2005): 370–411, and the excellent recent analysis by Sabine Schmidtke, "From *Wissenschaft des Judentums* to *Wissenschaft des Islams*: Eugen Mittwoch between Jewish and Islamic Studies," *Historical Interactions of Religious Cultures* 1, no. 1 (2024): 103–45.

43. Schorsch, "Converging Cognates," 32–33. A quantitative analysis of the doctoral theses evaluated by Fleischer between 1866 and 1886 reveals that 52 of 131 were written by Jewish authors: Holger Preißler, "Heinrich Leberecht Fleischer: Ein Leipziger Orientalist, seine jüdischen Studenten, Promovenden und Kollegen," in *Bausteine einer jüdischen Geschichte der Universität Leipzig*, ed. Stephan Wendehorst (Leipzig: Leipziger Universitätsverlag, 2006), 266n81.

44. Susannah Heschel, "Abraham Geiger and the Emergence of Jewish Philoislamism," in *"Im vollen Licht der Geschichte": Die Wissenshaft des Judentums und die Anfänge der kritischen Koranforschung*, ed. Dirk Hartwig et. al (Würzburg: Ergon, 2008), 69–70.

45. Mangold, *Eine "weltbürgerliche Wissenschaft"*, 104–5.

46. Susannah Heschel, "German Jewish Scholarship on Islam as a Tool for De-Orientalizing Judaism," *New German Critique* 39, no. 3 (2012): 96–97.

47. Wokoeck, *German Orientalism*, 177–78; Heschel, "German Jewish Scholarship," 99–101. For a detailed discussion of the coalescence of *Islamwissenschaft*, and of Goldziher's scholarly and religious views regarding Islam, see David Moshfegh, "Ignaz Goldziher and the Rise of Islamwissenschaft as a 'Science of Religion'" (PhD diss., University of California at Berkeley, 2012). Goldziher's legacy for the development of Oriental Studies in Jerusalem is discussed at length later in this chapter.

48. Goldziher's extensive scholarly network is attested to by the archive of his correspondence at the Library of the Hungarian Academy of Sciences, of which he

NOTES TO CHAPTER 1 ::: 195

was a member: it includes over thirteen thousand letters from around 1,650 different correspondents, in ten languages. For a list of materials in this archive that have already been published in various studies, see Kinga Dévényi and Sabine Schmidtke, "The Published Correspondences of Ignaz Goldziher: A Bibliographical Guide," in *Building Bridges: Ignaz Goldziher and His Correspondents. Islamic and Jewish Studies around the Turn of the Twentieth Century*, ed. Hans-Jürgen Becker et. al (Leiden: Brill, 2024), 413–28.

49. Marchand, *German Orientalism in the Age of Empire*, 220–27; Wokoeck, *German Orientalism*, 179.

50. Though the circumstances under which Mayer turned to Oriental Studies were similar to those of Jews from elsewhere in the German-speaking world, as I show later in this chapter, his Viennese education led him down a somewhat different path, one that—though notably still based primarily on work with textual sources—emphasized the study of Islamic archaeology and art.

51. Max Weber, "Science as a Vocation," in *The Vocation Lectures*, trans. Rodney Livingstone (Indianapolis: Hackett Publishing, 2004), 20.

52. On the characteristics of the principle of separation between science and politics at German universities and the motivations behind it, see Charles E. McClelland, *State, Society, and University in Germany, 1700–1914* (Cambridge: Cambridge University Press, 1980), 314–21. Additionally, see William Clark, *Academic Charisma and the Origins of the Research University* (Chicago: University of Chicago Press, 2006), for context on the development of the German university model in the eighteenth and nineteenth centuries and its comparison with alternative European models, focusing on both material and cultural dimensions.

53. David N. Myers, *Re-Inventing the Jewish Past: European Jewish Intellectuals and the Zionist Return to History* (New York: Oxford University Press, 1995), 18.

54. Fritz K. Ringer, *The Decline of the German Mandarins: The German Academic Community, 1890–1933* (Cambridge, MA: Harvard University Press, 1969), 143.

55. McClelland, *State, Society, and University*, 320.

56. Diana Dolev, *The Planning and Building of the Hebrew University, 1919–1948: Facing the Temple Mount* (Lanham, MD: Lexington Books, 2016), 13–16.

57. Jehuda Reinharz, *Chaim Weizmann: The Making of a Statesman* (New York: Oxford University Press, 1993), 259; Arthur A. Goren, "The View from Scopus: Judah L. Magnes and the Early Years of the Hebrew University," *Judaism* 45 (1996): 204.

58. David G. Myers, "Hebräische Universität," in *Enzyklopädie jüdischer Geschichte und Kultur*, vol. 3, ed. Dan Diner (Stuttgart and Weimar: Metzler, 2012), 14. On the origins and evolution of the Hebrew University idea, see Israel Bartal, "The Emergence of Modern Jewish Academe: From Religious Academies in Eastern Europe to a Secular University," in *Konstellationen: Über Geschichte, Erfahrung und Erkenntnis; Festschrift für Dan Diner zum 65. Geburtstag*, ed. Nicolas Berg et al. (Göttingen: Vandenhoeck & Ruprecht, 2011), 15–43. On the Zionist image of the university in Jerusalem as a modern-era Temple, see Dolev, *Planning and Building*, 16–21.

59. Judah M. Bernstein, "A Preacher in Exile: Shemaryahu Levin and the Making

196 ::: NOTES TO CHAPTER 1

of American Zionism, 1914–1919," *American Jewish History* 102, no. 3 (2018): 323–24. For Levin's biography see Shimon Shur, *Kivrosh basa'ar: 'Al hayav ufo'alo shel Dr. Shmaryahu Levin* (Haifa: The Herzl Institute for Study of Zionism–University of Haifa, 2007); and Levin's autobiographical writings, translated and edited in Shmarya Levin, *Forward from Exile: The Autobiography of Shmarya Levin*, trans. and ed. Maurice Samuel (Philadelphia: Jewish Publication Society of America, 1967).

60. Hagit Lavsky, "Bein hanahat 'even hapina laptiha: Yesud ha'universita ha'ivrit, 1918–1925," in *Toldot ha'universita ha'ivrit birushalayim*, ed. Shaul Katz and Michael Heyd, vol. 1: *Shorashim vehathalot* (Jerusalem: The Hebrew University Magnes Press, 1997), 127.

61. Shmaryahu Levin to Ignác Goldziher, October 30, 1919, LHAS Oriental Collection, GIL/25/18/03. Levin sent an identically-worded letter to the prominent German-Jewish Orientalist Eugen Mittwoch on the same day: CZA, L12/102/1.

62. Copy of letter from Goldziher to Levin, [November 6, 1919]. Attached to a letter from Levin to Zwi Perez Hajes, January 7, 1920, CZA, A30/142. Goldziher was accustomed to corresponding in Hebrew, as attested by dozens of letters written to him in Hebrew that survive in his estate at the Library of the Hungarian Academy of Sciences.

63. On the striking similarity between these suggestions, and an 1880 memorandum that the young Goldziher prepared with proposals for the curriculum of the Rabbinical Seminary in Budapest, see Tamás Turán, *Ignaz Goldziher as a Jewish Orientalist: Traditional Learning, Critical Scholarship, and Personal Piety* (Berlin: De Gruyter, 2023), 114–16. According to Turán, Goldziher's 1880 proposals "encountered strong opposition."

64. Goldziher to Levin, [November 6, 1919].

65. Stefan Arvidsson, *Aryan Idols: Indo-European Mythology as Ideology and Science*, trans. Sonia Wichmann (Chicago: University of Chicago Press, 2006), esp. 91–96. See also Céline Trautmann-Waller, "Semites and Semitism: From Philology to the Language of Myth," *Philological Encounters* 2, no. 3–4 (2017): 346–67, which provides a wider historical-intellectual context for Semitism as a modern category that combined linguistics, psychology, and cultural history.

66. Arvidsson, *Aryan Idols*, 95.

67. Lawrence I. Conrad, "Ignaz Goldziher on Ernest Renan: From Orientalist Philology to the Study of Islam," in *The Jewish discovery of Islam: Studies in Honor of Bernard Lewis*, ed. Martin Kramer (Tel Aviv: The Moshe Dayan Center for Middle Eastern and African Studies, Tel Aviv University, 1999, 137–80), 145; Moshfegh, "Ignaz Goldziher," 198–99. See also Sabine Mangold, "Ignác Goldziher et Ernest Renan—Vision du monde et innovation scientifique," in *Ignác Goldziher: Un autre orientalisme?*, ed. Céline Trautmann-Waller (Paris: Librairie Orientaliste Paul Geuthner, 2011), 73–88.

68. Tamás Turán, "Academic Religion: Goldziher as a Scholar and a Jew," in *Modern Jewish Scholarship in Hungary: The "Science of Judaism" between East and West*, ed. Tamás Turán and Carsten Wilke (Berlin: De Gruyter, 2016), 251; Moshfegh, "Ignaz Goldziher," 306. Goldziher himself had attested to the general disapproval

## NOTES TO CHAPTER 1 ::: 197

his work met in the scholarly community: Ignác Goldziher, *Tagebuch*, ed. Alexander Scheiber (Leiden: Brill, 1978), 86–87.

69. Moshfegh, "Ignaz Goldziher," 189. Compare with Lena Salaymeh, "The 'Good Orientalists,'" in *Westernness: Critical Reflections on the Spatio-temporal Construction of the West*, ed. Christopher GoGwilt, Holt Meyer, and Sergey Sistiaga (Berlin: De Gruyter Oldenbourg, 2022), 105–36, where Goldziher's attitude toward Islam in his scholarship is analyzed as reproductive of imperialist and colonialist thought.

70. Goldziher to Levin, [November 6, 1919].

71. On Goldziher's attitude towards Zionism, see Turán, *Ignaz Goldziher as a Jewish Orientalist*, 159–65.

72. Donald Malcom Reid, "Cairo University and the Orientalists," *International Journal of Middle East Studies* 19, no. 1 (1987): 56.

73. In 1921, Nahum Sokolov attempted to recruit Goldziher, a short time before his death, on a trip aimed at improving relations between the Zionist movement and the Arabs of Palestine and the region. Goldziher refused, first and foremost thanks to his age, but also hinted between the lines that his refusal was related to his opposition to Zionism in principle: Goitein, *Goldziher lefi mikhtavav (mikhtavey Goldziher 'el S. A. Poznanski bashanim 1901–1921): Tadpis misefer hazikaron likhvod Yitzhaq Yehuda Goldziher* (Budapest: 1948), 21, 25.

74. The subject is discussed at length in Ariel Rein, "Historia klalit vehistoria yehudit: Bimshutaf 'o benifrad? Leshe'elat hagdarat limudey hahistoria ba'universita ha'ivrit be'asor harishon lekiyuma," in *Toldot ha'universita ha'ivrit birushalayim*, ed. Shaul Katz and Michael Heyd, vol. 1: *Shorashim vehathalot* (Jerusalem: The Hebrew University Magnes Press, 1997), 516–37.

75. Schorsch, "Converging Cognates," 6–7. See Alfred Jospe, "The Study of Judaism in German Universities before 1933," *Leo Baeck Institute Year Book* 27, no. 1 (1982): 295–319; Ottfried Fraisse, "From Geiger to Goldziher: Historical Method and Its Impact on the Conception of Islam," in *Modern Jewish Scholarship in Hungary: The "Science of Judaism" between East and West*, ed. Tamás Turán and Carsten Wilke (Berlin: De Gruyter, 2016), 203–22.

76. Rein, "Historia klalit vehistoria yehudit," 525–28. Rein notes that Baer later modified his view somewhat, moving closer to the camp that advocated separation between the subjects.

77. Ibid., 531–32, 536. On the emergence of the Institute for Jewish Studies and the "Jerusalem School" of Jewish history against the background of the question of continuity or change with respect to the field's European roots, see Myers, *Re-Inventing the Jewish Past*.

78. At most Israeli universities, this separation continues to this day: each has a department for Jewish history, which is separate from that for general or European history.

79. In a letter to Chaim Weizmann dated January 2, 1922, Hugo Bergmann suggested "to begin immediate work on the creation of an Oriental Department the plans for which have been made by Chayes [*sic*] and Goldziher and are in the archives of the London office": YCW, Chaim Weizmann Archive, 5-688. These plans,

198 ::: NOTES TO CHAPTER 1

"a detailed memorandum in Hebrew," were also mentioned in a newspaper article published in the Israeli daily *Ha'aretz* on the 25th anniversary of Goldziher's passing: Aharon Fuerst, "Lezekher Prof. Yitzhaq Goldziher: 25 shana liftirato," *Ha'aretz*, December 13, 1946, 9. That article did not mention Chajes's involvement. It is likely that the said plan is, in fact, the letter of suggestions Goldziher sent to Levin. Another possibility is that Chajes, to whom Levin had sent Goldziher's suggestions, reworked them into a more detailed memorandum. In any case, if such a plan ever existed, no archival traces of it have been found to date.

80. This despite the fact that Levin wrote in response to the proposals letter —employing the flowery language exclusive to this kind of thank you letter—that "every single article in his important missive is the product of the thought of a Hebrew heart great in our nation, birthed by a higher insight . . . and it is our strong hope that we may make effective use of them shortly." Levin to Goldziher, December 30, 1919, LHAS Oriental Collection, GIL/25/18/01.

81. Abraham Shalom Yahuda, "Die Bedeutung der Goldziherschen Bibliothek für die zukünftige hebräische Universität," *Der Jude* 8 (1924): 576. An earlier, shorter version of this text was published in English: A. S. Yahuda, "The Goldziher Library," *The Jewish Chronicle Supplement*, April 25, 1924, iv–v. See also Heinrich Loewe, *Ignaz Goldziher (Ein Wort des Gedenkens von Heinrich Loewe)* (Berlin: Soncino, 1929).

82. Wokoeck, *German Orientalism*, 211.

83. Goldziher had already received a letter from L. A. Mayer in Jerusalem in 1921, on the eve of his death, requesting permission to translate the book to Hebrew (Mayer to Goldziher, November 19, 1921, LHAS Oriental Collection, GIL/29/06/01). Its translation, and particularly its publication, encountered numerous difficulties and delays, and was published only in 1951. A year later, HUSOS graduate and future professor Pessah Shinar translated a textbook written by Goldziher in Bosnian on the history of Arabic literature. See Katalin Franciska Rac, "Arabic Literature for the Colonizer and the Colonized: Ignaz Goldziher and Hungary's Eastern Politics (1878–1918)," in *The Muslim Reception of European Orientalism: Reversing the Gaze*, ed. Susannah Heschel and Umar Ryad (London: Routledge, 2018), 97n7.

84. Hugo Bergmann, "Have'ida ha'universitait," *Ha'olam*, December 26, 1919, 5.

85. From the twelfth meeting on the seventh meeting day of the Zionist General Council, February 18, 1920, quoted in Gedalia Yogev and Yehoshua Freundlich, eds., *Haprotokolim shel hava'ad hapo'el hatziyoni 1919–1929*, vol II: *February 1920–August 1921* (Jerusalem: Hasifriya hatziyonit, 1985), 105.

86. The spelling of Mayer's first name shifted over the years. At times, in the Latin alphabet he used both Leo and Leon, Ary and Aryeh, but usually simply signed L. A. Mayer, which I use as well.

87. H. Z. Hirschberg, "Leon Aryeh Mayer: Hamesh shanim liftirato," *Eretz Israel: Mehkarim biydi'at ha'aretz va'atikoteha* 7 (1964): 12–13.

88. Robert Lemon, *Imperial Messages: Orientalism as Self-Critique in the Habsburg Fin De Siècle* (Rochester: Camden House, 2011), 2; Mostafa Hussein, "Scholarship on Islamic Archaeology between Zionism and Arab Nationalist Movements," in *The*

*Muslim Reception of European Orientalism: Reversing the Gaze*, ed. Susannah Heschel and Umar Ryad (Oxon: Routledge, 2019), 187.

89. Sarah Irving, "Stephan Hanna Stephan and Evliya Çelebi's Book of Travels: Tracing Cooperation and Conflict in Mandate Palestinian Translations," in *Cultural Entanglement in the Pre-Independence Arab World: Arts, Thought and Literature*, ed. Anthony Gorman and Sarah Irving (London: Bloomsbury Academic, 2020), 225.

90. Zwi Perez Chajes to Herbert Samuel, April 1 [no year], AJMIA, LAM/3/7.

91. Lavsky, "Bein hanahat 'even hapina laptiha," 142–44.

92. Protocol of meeting for the establishment of a Faculty of Oriental Studies at the Hebrew University in Palestine, April 10, 1922, CZA, S2/390. Participating in the meeting were: Menachem Ussishkin, Ahad Ha'am, Norman Bentwich, Eliezer Ben-Yehuda, Heinrich Loewe, L. A. Mayer, Hayyim Hermann Pick, Josef Klausner, David Yellin, Saul (Shlomo) Rosenblum and Salman Schocken. The following quotes, originally in Hebrew, are taken from this document.

93. On the relationship between Jewish Studies—*Wissenschaft des Judentums*—and the study of Judaism within Protestant theology, see Christian Wiese, *Challenging Colonial Discourse: Jewish Studies and Protestant Theology in Wilhelmine Germany* (Leiden: Brill, 2005).

94. Protocol of meeting of the Temporary Committee for the Opening of a Department of Humanities at the Hebrew University of Jerusalem, January 28, 1923, 1, CZA, S81/3.

95. The life and unique worldview of the charismatic and active figure of Magnes, who left a significant public imprint despite his marginal ideological position in the Zionist discourse, has been the subject of a broad literature. See, for example, Norman Bentwich, *For Zion's Sake: A Biography of Judah L. Magnes* (Philadelphia: Jewish Publication Society of America, 1954); Hedva Ben-Israel, "Bi-Nationalism versus Nationalism: The Case of Judah Magnes," *Israel Studies* 23, no. 1 (2018): 86–105; David Barak-Gorodetsky, *Judah Magnes: The Prophetic Politics of a Religious Binationalist*, trans. Merav Datan (Lincoln: University of Nebraska Press and the Jewish Publication Society of America, 2021).

96. Temporary Committee for the Opening of a Department of Humanities, January 28, 1923, 5.

97. Lavsky, "Bein hanahat 'even hapina laptiha," 146–47. Lavsky notes that the London committee's discussions also mentioned Arabic language studies.

98. Ibid., 148–49.

99. The protocol of the assembly noted that, were Mittwoch not immediately available, Gotthold Weil of the State Library in Berlin would be invited for a year. Protocol of the assembly of committees for the foundation of an Institute for Jewish Studies in Jerusalem, July 21, 1924, CZA, S25/737/1.

100. During World War I, Mittwoch headed the Bureau of Information for the Orient (*Nachrichtenstelle für den Orient*, NfO) at the German Foreign Ministry, the mission of which was to foment unrest and rebellions among nations in the Orient under the control of Germany's wartime enemies and to broadcast pro-German

200 ::: NOTES TO CHAPTER 1

propaganda in their languages. His successful tenure at the head of the bureau was, apparently, a significant factor in his appointment as professor at the University of Berlin after the war. See Maja Šcrbacic, "Eugen Mittwoch gegen das Land Preußen: Die Entlassungsmaßnahmen in der Berliner Orientalistik, 1933–1938," in *Ein Paradigma der Moderne: Jüdische Geschichte in Schlüsselbegriffen; Festschrift für Dan Diner zum 70. Geburtstag*, ed. Arndt Engelhardt et al. (Göttingen: Vandenhoeck & Ruprecht, 2016), 40–41. Šcrbacic's article contains further biographical details on Mittwoch, including following the Nazi rise to power, which forced him to flee to England on the eve of World War II. See also Schmidtke, "From *Wissenschaft des Judentums* to *Wissenschaft des Islams*," 119–39. On the role of the Intelligence Bureau, see Marchand, *German Orientalism in the Age of Empire*, 452–54.

101. Lavsky, "Bein hanahat 'even hapina laptiha," 129, 140; Schmidtke, "From *Wissenschaft des Judentums* to *Wissenschaft des Islams*," 131.

102. Mittwoch's name was later circulated as a potential member of the steering committee of the School of Oriental Studies (memorandum of a conversation on the establishment of the School of Oriental Studies, London, July 24, 1925, CZA, L12/27), but no evidence of his direct involvement in the institute's affairs is contained in the HUSOS archive.

103. L. A. Mayer to J. L. Magnes, Memorandum regarding the establishment of an institute for the study of Islam of the Hebrew University in Jerusalem, n.d. Appended to a letter from Mayer to D. Z. Baneth, September 9, 1924, ANLI, Arc. 4° 1559/03/17. In the letter to Baneth, Mayer notes that he sent the memorandum to Magnes "some time ago"—so that it was perhaps composed for the London assembly that began on July 21 of that year. It could also have been written afterwards, however. Magnes, the letter informs us, had asked Mayer to send the memorandum to Baneth as well.

104. Shelomo Dov Goitein, "Igeret brakha lahevra hamizrahit hayisra'elit bimlot la shloshim shana," *Hamizrah hehadash* 28, no. 3–4 (1979): 173.

105. Gideon Libson, "Hidden Worlds and Open Shutters: S. D. Goitein, between Judaism and Islam," in *The Jewish Past Revisited: Reflections on Modern Jewish Historians*, ed. David N. Myers and David B. Ruderman (New Haven: Yale University Press, 1998), 164–65.

106. Shelomo Dov Goitein, "The School of Oriental Studies: A Memoir," in *Like All the Nations? The Life and Legacy of Judah L. Magnes*, ed. William M. Brinner and Moses Rischin (Albany: State University of New York Press, 1987), 170.

107. Baneth and Goitein were, effectively, relatives: Goitein's paternal grandmother was Baneth's aunt (on his father's side). The two scholars tended to refer to each other as cousins: Hava Lazarus-Yafeh, "The Transplantation of Islamic Studies from Europe to the Yishuv and Israel," in *The Jewish Discovery of Islam: Studies in Honor of Bernard Lewis*, ed. Martin Kramer (Tel Aviv: The Moshe Dayan Center for Middle Eastern and African Studies, Tel Aviv University, 1999), 256.

108. Ibid., 257.

109. D. H. Baneth to the Hebrew University Secretariat, May 15, 1931, CAHU, Personnel File—D. H. Baneth, until 1960; Secretariat of the Jewish Agency to the Permits Section of the Mandate Government, 6 October 1924, CZA, S25/737/2.

The kabbalah scholar Gershom Scholem (1897–1982) of the Institute for Jewish Studies, also employed at the National Library at the time, later recounted how he had suggested Baneth, his old friend from Berlin, to Bergmann, the director of the library. Baneth had also been offered a librarianship in Cincinnati, but since he was interested in immigrating to Palestine in any case, he accepted the offer to come to Jerusalem: Gershom Scholem, *From Berlin to Jerusalem: Memories of My Youth* (New York: Schocken Books, 1980), 164.

110. Milson, "The Beginnings of Arabic and Islamic Studies," 181n13; David Tidhar, "Avinoam Yellin," in *Encyclopedia leheker hayeshuv uvonav: Dmuyot utmunot*, vol. II, 894–95, www.tidhar.tourolib.org/tidhar/view/2/894. Yellin was murdered in 1937 outside his office on Mount Zion during one of the waves of violence of the Arab Revolt of the second half of the 1930s.

111. McClelland, *State, Society and University*, 280–87.

112. Katz, "Scion and Its Tree," 111. The dominance of the single-executive model is apparent in the list of appointments at German universities in the Orientalist professions compiled by Ursula Wokoeck: Wokoeck, *German Orientalism*, 235–87.

113. Mayer uses the English term "Fellow" (within the otherwise Hebrew letter); he is referring to the "Fellows" he was busy recruiting—Goitein, Baneth, and Yellin.

114. Judah L. Magnes, *Addresses by the Chancellor of the Hebrew University* (Jerusalem: Hebrew University, 1936), 15, 70–71.

115. Hayah Katz, *The Changing Landscape of Israeli Archaeology: Between Hegemony and Marginalization* (London: Routledge, 2023), 10–13, 35–37.

116. Ehud R. Toledano, "The Arabic-Speaking World in The Ottoman Period: A Socio-Political Analysis," in *The Ottoman World*, ed. Christine Woodhead (London: Routledge, 2012), 457–59.

117. Roger Owen, "Studying Islamic History (Review of the Cambridge History of Islam)," *The Journal of Interdisciplinary History* 4, no. 2 (1973): 294.

118. Hussein, "Scholarship of Islamic Archaeology," 190–92.

119. Leonard Greenspoon, *Max Leopold Margolis: A Scholar's Scholar* (Atlanta: Scholars Press, 1987), 44. On the American School of Oriental Research in Jerusalem, which was led by the American biblical archaeologist William F. Albright (1891–1971), see Philip J. King, *American Archaeology in the Mideast: A History of the American Schools of Oriental Research* (Philadelphia: The American Schools of Oriental Research, 1983).

120. *Yedi'ot hamakhon lemada'ey hayahadut*, no. 1 (April 1925), 53.

121. Speech marking the inauguration of the Institute for Jewish Studies, December 22, 1924, in Magnes, *Addresses by the Chancellor*, 1–8. In his speech, Magnes noted that Margolis would head the Department of Philology at the Institute for Jewish Studies, but no such department was ever opened. He began his remarks with a word of condolence for Margolis, one of whose sons had fallen victim to disease during his family's time in the country. On this tragic event see Greenspoon, *Max Leopold Margolis*, 46.

122. Max Leopold Margolis, "Tokhnit zmanit shel hamahlaka latarbut ha'aravit," 1925, CAHU, 91:1925–27.

202 ::: NOTES TO CHAPTER 1

123. The document appears in the Archive of the Hebrew University in Mayer's handwriting and may well be a summary of Margolis's comments during a conversation between the two.

124. The Alexandria-born philologist Ahmed Zaki Pasha (1867–1934) was professor of Arabic Literature at the French Institute for Oriental Archaeology in Cairo and served for many years as Secretary of the Egyptian Government. Zaki was associated with the idea of Arabness and the revival of the Arab tradition, and travelled to Jerusalem in 1929 to testify on behalf of the Muslim side before the commission of inquiry founded to investigate the events of 1929. On Zaki, see Umar Ryad, "'An Oriental Orientalist': Aḥmad Zakī Pasha (1868–1934), Egyptian Statesman and Philologist in the Colonial Age," *Philological Encounters* 3, no. 1–2 (2018): 129–66. Sa'ud al-'Uri was the *qadi* of Jerusalem and later taught *hadith* at al-Aqsa Mosque. In the early period at least, it seems he was on good terms with the founders of the School of Oriental Studies—S. D. Goitein noted off-hand in an article that he studied *hadith* with al-'Uri: Goitein, *Studies in Islamic History and Institutions* (Leiden: Brill, 2010), 78n6.

125. An extensive discussion of this issue appears in the following chapter.

126. Judah L. Magnes, *Dissenter in Zion: From the Writings of Judah L. Magnes*, ed. Arthur A. Goren (Cambridge, MA: Harvard University Press, 1982), 8–9; Sabine Mangold-Will, "Josef Horovitz und die Gründung des Instituts für Arabische und Islamische Studien an der Hebräischen Universität in Jerusalem: ein Orientalisches Seminar für Palästina," *Naharaim* 10, no. 1 (2016): 14. Horovitz, whose doctoral thesis was written under the supervision of Eduard Sachau (1845–1930), completed his Habilitation in 1902: Shelomo Dov Goitein, "Josef Horovitz," *Der Islam* 22, no. 2 (1934): 124. This was the year Magnes—then earning his doctoral degree at the University of Heidelberg—completed his studies.

127. Magnes recalled this in a eulogy he delivered in memory of Horovitz: "I had known him while a student in Berlin. [Arthur] Biram, Horovitz, [Eugen] Mittwoch, [Eugen] Täubler, [Max] Schlössinger, [Gotthold] Weil and I used often to lunch together." Magnes, *Addresses by the Chancellor*, 296.

128. Goitein, "Josef Horovitz," 124.

129. Ibid., 126.

130. On the influence of this period on Horovitz, see Hanan Harif, "The Orient between Arab and Jewish National Revivals: Josef Horovitz, Shelomo Dov Goitein and Oriental Studies in Jerusalem," in *Modern Jewish Scholarship on Islam in Context: Rationality, European Borders, and the Search for Belonging*, ed. Ottfried Fraisse (Berlin: De Gruyter, 2018), 319–36; Johnston-Bloom, "'Dieses wirklich westöstlichen Mannes': The German-Jewish Orientalist Josef Horovitz in Germany, India, and Palestine," in *The Muslim Reception of European Orientalism: Reversing the Gaze*, ed. Susannah Heschel and Umar Ryad (London: Routledge, 2018), 168–83.

131. In 1932, the university's name became the Goethe-Universität Frankfurt in tribute to the author, poet, and native son of the city, Johann Wolfgang von Goethe.

132. Mangold-Will, "Josef Horovitz und die Gründung," 19–20.

133. S. D. Goitein, "Josef Horovitz," *Davar*, March 13, 1931, 10.

NOTES TO CHAPTER 1 ::: 203

134. Magnes, *Addresses by the Chancellor*, 295–96.

135. Ibid.; Mangold-Will, "Josef Horovitz und die Gründung," 25.

136. Horovitz's lecture, of a rather philological nature, discussed the formation of the collection of stories *A Thousand and One Nights*. Initially published in Hebrew, Menahem Milson notes that an English version was later published in the journal *Islamic Culture*: Milson, "Beginnings of Arabic and Islamic Studies," 181n9. This journal was published in the largely Muslim southern Indian town of Hyderabad, where Horovitz maintained close ties with the intellectual community.

137. A publication overseen by the Institute for Jewish Studies noted that one of the reasons for his arrival in April 1925 was "to consult with the institute regarding the Arabic department": *Yedi'ot hamakhon (April)*, 77.

138. Milson, "Beginnings of Arabic and Islamic Studies," 171.

139. "Hamakhlaka ha'aravit," excerpt from protocol of meeting XI [apparently of the faculty of the Institute for Jewish Studies], March 21, 1925, CAHU, 91:1925–27.

140. Mayer to M. L. Margolis [Max Leopold Margolis], 1925, CAHU, 91:1925–27. Baneth and Yellin were also asked to submit similar proposals by the faculty of the Institute for Jewish Studies. Mayer proposed to work on one of his research interests, Muslim heraldry during the Mamluk period, a field in which he indeed later published a pioneering study.

141. *Yedi'ot hamakhon lemada'ey hayahadut*, no. 2 (August 1925), 102–3.

142. Josef Horovitz, "Vorschläge für die Errichtung eines Institute of Arabic and Islamic Studies in Jerusalem," May 14, 1925, CAHU, 91:1925–27.

143. Especially notable is Sabine Mangold-Will's 2016 article, which centers on the memorandum (Mangold-Will, "Josef Horovitz und die Gründung"), as well as Milson, "Beginnings of Arabic and Islamic Studies," 172–73, and Johnston-Bloom, "'Dieses wirklich westöstlichen Mannes,'" 177.

144. Though this idea, as we saw, had already appeared in Margolis's plan. This aspect of Horovitz's proposal, the efforts to realize it, and their failure are discussed at length in the following chapter.

145. Horovitz mentioned the Creswell collection of photographs of traditional Muslim architectural structures in Syria, Palestine, Egypt, and Constantinople that was indeed eventually purchased by the institute at Mayer's behest (Mayer to Magnes, June 13, 1926, CAHU, 91:1925–27), as well as the collection of photographs of Arabic inscriptions collected by the Swiss historian Max van Berchem (1863–1921), which might have assisted Mayer in his epigraphic research. Apart from these, he mentioned the names of rare book shops in England, France, and Germany that might provide the books required to complement the existing Orientalist library in Jerusalem.

146. The names he proposed were: Marcel Cohen from Paris; Richard Gottheil from New York; Josef Horovitz from Frankfurt; Levi Della Vida from Rome; Herbert Loewe from Cambridge; Eugen Mittwoch from Berlin; William Popper from San Francisco; Oskar Rescher from Breslau; Gotthold Weil from Berlin; and Juda Lion Palache from Amsterdam.

147. On Popper and his work in the field of Islamic studies, see Walter J. Fischel, "William Popper (1874–1963) and His Contribution to Islamic Scholarship: In

204 ::: NOTES TO CHAPTER 1

Memoriam," *Journal of the American Oriental Society* 84, no. 3 (1964): 213–20. Horovitz also wrote that if Popper should refuse, Rescher from Breslau might be approached, though Horovitz did not know him well and was unsure of his opinion on Jewish matters ("jüdischen Dingen"). He was referring to the German-Jewish Orientalist Oskar Rescher (1883–1972), a historian of classical Arabic literature born in Stuttgart who had been an irregular (*extraordinarius*) professor at the University of Breslau. The question posed by Horovitz was a reasonable one: in 1927, for unknown reasons, Rescher left Germany angrily and moved to Istanbul, where he converted to Islam and changed his name to Osman Reşer, leading to a break from Jewish organizations: Bertold Spuler, "Oskar Rescher/Osman Reşer: Zum 100. Geburtstag 1. Okt. 1883/1983," *Der Islam* 61, no. 1 (1984): 12.

148. Memorandum of an informal conversation on the establishment of an Institute of Oriental Studies, London, June 24, 1925, CZA, L12/27.

149. Sabine Mangold-Will, "Gotthold Weil, die Orientalische Philologie und die deutsche Wissenschaft an der Hebräischen Universität," *Naharaim* 8, no. 1 (2014): 81.

150. In the margins of the meeting, the four also discussed the proposal to found a "School of Comparative Religion" and to recruit Martin Buber in the matter.

151. Leo Kohn to the Committees for the Support of the Hebrew University in Jerusalem, January 15, 1926, CZA, S25/738, 4–5.

152. Untitled document [from Mayer, around January 1926], CAHU, 91:1925–27.

153. "Ba'universita ha'ivrit," *Davar*, February 18, 1926, 4.

154. Josef Horovitz, "Report on a Course of Lectures and Seminar held in March April 1926," n.d., CAHU, 91/1:1926.

155. Esther Agnon to the Hebrew University administration, February 22, 1926, CAHU, 91/1:1926. Golda Reiss, who held a PhD from the University of Vienna, also appeared on the initial list of participants, but Horovitz's reports suggest that she never ended up attending the meetings. She later became a teacher in Tel Aviv: "Va'ad hadash lisnif hamorim beTel Aviv," *Hatzofe*, June 4, 1945, 3.

156. The full list of auditors approved by Horovitz included: Yehoshua Radler-Feldman (Rabbi Binyamin), Shalom Pushinsky, Asher Rand, Victor Shaer, Issachar Joel, David Shalem Mahboub, Yehoshua Hoter Hacohen, Avraham Shalom Shaki, Edmund Reich, Yosef Yekutieli, Golda Reiss, Shmuel Rosenblatt, Shelomo Dov Goitein, Noah Braun, L. A. Mayer, Esther Agnon, and Avinoam Yellin. Yosef Chai Panigel also signed up for the course, and though Horovitz approved his inclusion, his name does not appear on the final list of participants (Shlomo Ginzberg to Panigel et al., March 7, 1926, CAHU, 91/1:1926). The fact that students from the Mizrahi Teacher Training College were likely in their final year and had not yet graduated constituted another factor contributing to their ineligibility to serve as active participants: Meeting of HUSOS faculty, April 25, 1926, CAHU, 91/2:1926–30.

157. Josef Horovitz, "Report on a Course of Lectures."

158. Shelomo Dov Goitein, "Mada'ey hamizrah ba'universita ha'ivrit," *Davar*, April 10, 1935, 12.

159. "Tna'ey kabalat talmidim lamakhon lemada'ey hamizrah," [the document was presented at a meeting held on March 24, 1926], CAHU, 91/2:1926–30.

160. "Yeshiva 'a[l]'d[var] beit midrash lemada'ey hamizrah," March 24, 1926, CAHU, 91/2: 1926–30.

161. At this stage, except for the definition of who could be a regular or an irregular auditor, the formal status of the students had not been discussed in any case, since formal instruction at the entire university had only been conducted university-wide since 1928/29: Katz, "Scion and its Tree," 113n18.

162. Ibid., 117.

163. Lazarus-Yafeh, "Transplantation of Islamic Studies," 252. At the same time, Sabine Mangold-Will notes that Horovitz typically accepted the suggestions of the institute's Jerusalem faculty: Mangold-Will, "Josef Horovitz und die Gründung," 27.

164. Lazarus-Yafeh, "Transplantation of Islamic Studies," 252.

165. Goitein, "Josef Horovitz," *Der Islam*, 125; idem, "The Concordance of Pre-Islamic and Umayyad Arabic Poetry," appended to a letter from Goitein to Yosef Tekoah, July 16, 1955, CAHU, 226:1955.

166. Goitein, "Concordance of Pre-Islamic and Umayyad Arabic Poetry."

167. David Leon Higdon, "Concordance: Mere Index or Needful Census?," *Text: An Interdisciplinary Annual of Textual Studies* 15 (2002): 52–53.

168. Ibid., 57.

169. Ibid., 55–56.

170. Johann Fück, *Die arabischen Studien in Europa bis in den Anfang des 20. Jahrhunderts* (Leipzig: O. Harrassowitz, 1955), 314.

171. Mangold-Will, "Josef Horovitz und die Gründung," 36. The concordance room in Jerusalem still exists, nowadays back on Mount Scopus.

172. Little is known about the life of al-Baladhuri, who lived most of his life in Baghdad and its environs. He was also the author of *Futuh al-Buldan* (conquest of the countries), which recounts the history of the Muslim conquests after the rise of Muhammad: C. H. Becker and F. Rosenthal, "Al-Balādhurī," in *Encyclopaedia of Islam*, ed. P. Bearman et al., 2nd ed., http://dx.doi.org/10.1163/1573-3912_islam_COM _0094.

173. Paul Kahle, "Review of *Ansāb al-Ashrāf of al-Balādhurī*, volume V, by S. D. F. Goitein," *ZDMG* 90, no. 3–4 (1936): 716.

174. Fück, *Die arabischen Studien*, 313–17.

175. Ibid., 234–36.

176. Shelomo Dov Goitein, "Hakdama," in *Sefer Ansāb al-Ashrāf shel al-Balādhurī*, published by Shelomo Dov Goitein, vol. V (Jerusalem: Hebrew University, 1935), 7. On the process by which Becker copied the manuscript and its implications, see Sabine Mangold-Will, "Photo-Kopieren als wissenschaftliche Praxis? Technische Innovation und gelehrte Distinktion in der Orientalischen Philologie des frühen 20. Jahrhunderts," in *Kolossale Miniaturen: Festschrift für Gerrit Walther*, ed. Matei Chihaia and Georg Eckert (Münster: Aschendorff, 2019), 59–68.

177. Ibid., 60.

178. Goitein, "The School of Oriental Studies," 171; idem, "Hakdama," 7.

179. See, for example, the correspondence appended to the letter from Shlomo Ginzberg to Leo Kohn, June 12, 1927, CZA, L12/27.

206 ::: NOTES TO CHAPTER 1

180. "Gebetsruf der Mohammedaner, Arabisch von e. Tataren gespr." December 11, 1946, Lautarchiv der Humboldt-Universität zu Berlin, KP 626. The full catalog of recordings can be found at the website of the audio archive: https://www.lautarchiv.hu-berlin.de.

181. German ethnographic interest in the Jews of Eastern Europe as an expression of the spirit of the Jewish people preceded the Great War. Already in the late nineteenth century, the Society for Jewish Folklore (*Gesellschaft für jüdische Volkskunde*) was founded in Hamburg. See Dani Schrire, "Max Grunwald and the Formation of Jewish Folkloristics: Another Perspective on Race in German-Speaking *Volkskunde*," in *Ideas of 'Race' in the History of the Humanities*, ed. Amos Morris-Reich and Dirk Rupnow (Cham: Palgrave Macmillan, 2017), 116–19.

182. Mangold-Will, "Josef Horovitz und die Gründung," 19.

183. Marchand, *German Orientalism in the Age of Empire*, 452–54; see also Maren Bragulla, *Die Nachrichtenstelle für den Orient: Fallstudie einer Propagandainstitution im Ersten Weltkrieg* (Saarbrücken: VDM Verlag Dr. Müller, 2007).

184. Liebau, "Networks of Knowledge Production," 312.

185. Josef Horovitz, *Indien unter britischer Herrschaft* (Leipzig: B. G. Teubner, 1928). On Horovitz's experiences in India that led to the writing of this book, see Johnston-Bloom, "'Dieses wirklich westöstlichen Mannes,'" 171–76; Razak Khan, "Entanglements in the Colony: Jewish–Muslim Connected Histories in Colonial India," *Modern Asian Studies* 56, no. 6 (2022): 1848–55.

186. Suzanne Wertheim, "Reclamation, Revalorization, and Re-Tatarization via Changing Tatar Orthographies," in *Orthography as Social Action*, ed. Alexandra Jaffe et al. (Berlin: De Gruyter, 2012), 69. In accordance with Soviet policy, the language was recorded in adapted Latin letters beginning in 1927, and in 1938, as part of Stalin's Russification effort, the writing system was changed once more to Cyrillic letters, which remains the norm in most areas where Tatars live to this day.

187. Sabine Mangold, "Gotthold Weil et les Tatars," in *Passeurs d'Orient : Les Juifs dans l'orientalisme*, ed. Michel Espagne (Paris: Éditions de l'Éclat, 2013), 211.

188. In 1917, with the war still on, Weil published a book on Ottoman-Turkish grammar: Mangold-Will, "Gotthold Weil," 80.

189. Gotthold Eljakim Weil, "Bericht über meine Arbeiten im Weinbergslager (Wünsdorf) vom 10. November 1917 bis 5. März 1918," in *Sitzungsberichte der Preussischen Akademie der Wissenschaften*, Jahrgang 1918, Zweiter Halbband: Juli bis Dezembem (Berlin: Verlag der Akademie der Wissenschaften, 1918), 795.

190. Gotthold Eljakim Weil, *Tatarische Texte: Nach den in der Lautabteilung der Staatsbibliothek befindlichen Originalplatten* (Berlin: Walter de Gruyter, 1930).

191. Jacob M. Landau, "Gotthold Eljakim Weil (Berlin, 1882–Jerusalem, 1960)," *Die Welt des Islams*, New Series 38, no. 3 (1998): 283; Mangold, "Gotthold Weil et les Tatars," 212.

192. The photo appears in Doegen's unpublished autobiography, written in the mid-1960s. The sound archive at Humboldt University holds a copy of this document.

193. Evans, *Anthropology at War*, 144.

194. Ibid., 166.

NOTES TO CHAPTER 1 ::: 207

195. For a survey demonstrating the abundance of such ethnographic and anthropological studies during World War I—not only in Germany—see Heather Jones, "A Missing Paradigm? Military Captivity and the Prisoner of War, 1914–18," *Immigrants & Minorities* 26, no. 1–2 (2008): 38.

196. Jacob M. Landau, who studied with Weil in the 1940s, mentioned the latter's work at the Weinberg camp in a biographical article written in Weil's memory. The article relied on archival material and an analysis of Weil's publications, seemingly, rather than on past conversations with Weil himself: Landau, "Gotthold Eljakim Weil." In Weil's curriculum vitae and list of publications that he submitted to Jerusalem upon his recruitment to the Hebrew University faculty (in 1934 at the latest, following his dismissal from the University of Frankfurt due to Nazi racial laws, at which point he was offered the position of director of the National and University Library in Jerusalem), he mentioned *Tatarische Texte* but made no reference to his role as a censor or his involvement in the recording project in the POW camps: CAHU, Personnel File—Gotthold Eljakim Weil, until 1951.

197. Magnes was concerned that the complexity of manuscript preparation and concordance compilation would render it impossible for the institute to undertake both projects simultaneously. However, Horovitz reassured him that this would be feasible: Horovitz to Magnes, November 29, 1926, CAHU, 91:1925–27.

198. Goitein, "Hakdama," 8. Among the numerous challenges that arose in the publication process was the ironic revelation that, specifically at the printing press in Jerusalem, there were no suitable Arabic letters, necessitating their procurement from abroad.

199. The final section published under the auspices of the institute is the second part of the sixth volume, which was edited by the institute's student, Khalil Athaminah (1939–2023), as part of his doctoral work in the Department of Arabic Language and Literature. It was published in 1993. In the meantime, additional institutions in Egypt and Lebanon took on the task of publishing the manuscript, and in practice, the work at the institute came to a halt: Goitein, "The School of Oriental Studies," 172.

200. Retrospectively, work on the concordance was also justified by its potential utility as a tool for working on *Ansab al-Ashraf*: a significant portion of this composition consists of poetic segments, and HUSOS anticipated that the existence of a concordance would facilitate the identification of parallels outside the text and elucidate the meanings of words: Mayer, "Hamakhon lemada'ey hamizrah," *Niv hastudent* 3 (1937): 9.

201. After publication of the first volume of *Ansab al-Ashraf*, the newspaper *Davar* wrote: "to judge by the impression, already made upon the world of international and Arab scholars, the researchers were successful in their choice in a cultural-political sense." Michael Assaf, "Mif'al 'aravi shel ha'universita ha'ivrit," *Davar*, March 12, 1937, 13.

202. See, for example, a memorandum about the institute that was in use at the Political Department of the Jewish Agency: L. A. Mayer, "Makhon lemada'ey hamizrah shel ha'universita ha'ivrit birushalayim," [around 1935], CZA, S25/6724.

208 ::: NOTES TO CHAPTER 1

203. Goitein, "David Hartwig (Zvi) Baneth, 1893–1973," in *Studia Orientalia: Memoriae D. H. Baneth Dedicata* (Jerusalem: The Hebrew University Magnes Press, 1979), 1.

204. Though Baneth was a member of the institute's faculty from its inception until his retirement, in some years he taught only one course and in other he did not teach at all; in the meanwhile, he held small and informal meetings with his students. In 1936, after the death of Levi Billig, he began to teach regularly on a full schedule: Baneth to Edward Poznansky, January 30, 1958, CAHU, Personal File—D. H. Baneth, until 1960.

205. In a preliminary division of responsibilities formulated by Horovitz, Yellin was proposed as an appointee for a year to teach beginner courses: Untitled document in Horovitz's hand, around September 1925, CAHU, 91:1925-27.

206. Goitein to Norman Bentwich, June 10, 1963, ANLI, Arc. 4° 1911/01/37.

207. For further biographical details on Billig, see Roy Vilozny, "Levi Billig vehelko he'alum beheker hitpathut hashi'a," *Hamizrah hehadash* 60 (2021): 77–80.

208. Leo Kohn to Levi Billig, February 5, 1926, and Billig to Kohn, February 8, 1926, CZA, L12/27.

209. Kohn to Magnes, April 13, 1926, CZA, L12/27.

210. Meeting of the School of Oriental Studies, April 22, 1926, CAHU, 91/2:1926–30.

211. Shelomo Dov Goitein, "Oriental Studies in Israel (Hebrew and the Ancient East excluded)," in *Hebrew University Garland: A Silver Jubilee Symposium*, ed. Norman Bentwich (London: Constellation Books, 1952), 101.

212. On the relationship between the university and the British authorities in this period, within the British imperial context, see chapter 2 of Adi Livny, "The Hebrew University in Mandatory Palestine: A Relational History (1918–1948)" (PhD diss., Hebrew University of Jerusalem, 2021).

213. In the year between the inauguration of the university and the opening of HUSOS in Jerusalem, and for several months more, the terms Institute and School were both used at times, but in newspaper copy the university already used the latter by 1925, and it became the standard. Inspiration for the name may also have come from the name of the American School for Oriental Research.

214. Ian Brown, *The School of Oriental and African Studies: Imperial Training and the Expansion of Learning* (Cambridge: Cambridge University Press, 2016), 14, 41–42. In 1938, the decision by administrators of the British institute to incorporate the term "African" into its name was implemented. This decision was reflective of the de facto developments within the institute and did not indicate a shift in its objectives (ibid., 75).

215. David Yeroushalmi, "Fischel, Walter Joseph," in *Encyclopædia Iranica* IX/6 (1999): 654–55. Fischel never seems to have taught at the institute, focusing only on the research enterprises, although he did aspire to teach (Fischel to the Administration of the Hebrew University, February 12, 1935, CAHU, Personnel File —Walter Yosef Fischel). In addition to his work as a research assistant at HUSOS, the university also sent Fischel on propaganda and fundraising missions abroad. During the 1940s, while in the United States, he was offered a position as professor

NOTES TO CHAPTER 1 ::: 209

of Semitic languages at the University of California Berkeley and left the Hebrew University.

216. Hanoch Bar-On, "Toldotav," in *Sefer Adam-Noah: Divrey tora, hagut, mehkar veha'arakha, zikaron leR. Adam-Noah Dr. Braun*, ed. S. Y. Cohen, Hayim Lifshitz, and Zvi Kaplan (Jerusalem: Hava'ada lehantzahat zikhro shel Dr. Adam-Noah Braun, 'al-yad mekhon Harry Fischel, 1969), 9–11; Adam Noah Braun (at times also written "Bar-On") worked for years preparing the concordance at HUSOS before being transferred at Goitein's request to the Institute for Jewish Studies: Goitein to the Administration of the Hebrew University, February 28, 1951, CAHU, 226:1951.

217. It was Horovitz who suggested inviting Joel to attend the institute's opening lectures in 1926 (Ginzberg to Mayer, February 9, 1926, CAHU, 91:1925–27), creating the connection that led to the university hiring him. In 1927, Joel moved to the National and University Library, where he became director of the Jewish Division: Issachar Joel, "Mahalakh hayim," November 19, 1933, CAHU, Personnel File—Issachar Joel.

218. Bravmann came to Jerusalem in 1934 following the Nazi rise to power in Germany. Unlike most of the institute's other research assistants, he did receive a teaching position there, but it was not a permanent one. He eventually immigrated to the United States in 1951, where he taught part-time at Columbia University and Dropsie College, though not as a tenure-track professor: Edward L. Greenstein, "M. M. Bravmann: A Sketch," *Journal of the Ancient Near Eastern Society* 11, no. 1 (1979): 1.

219. Hanan Harif, "Islam in Zion? Yosef Yo'el Rivlin's Translation of the Qur'an and Its Place Within the New Hebrew Culture," *Naharaim* 10, no. 1 (2016): 39–41; Ruth Roded, "A Voice in the Wilderness? Rivlin's 1932 Hebrew *Life of Muhammad*," *Middle East Critique* 18, no. 1 (2009): 40–44.

220. Billig to Ginzberg, December 21, 1927, CAHU, 91:1925–27.

221. Billig to Magnes, November 8, 1926, CAHU, 91:1925–27; Baneth to the Hebrew University administration, [n.d.—in response to a letter of November 16, 1926], ANLI, Arc. 4° 1559/03/17.

222. Magnes expressed great appreciation for Goitein, referring to him as a "rare soul," and was pleased to have the opportunity to include him in the university faculty. This move was met with disappointment from Arthur Biram, the director of the Haifa Reali School and a longstanding acquaintance of Magnes from their student days in Berlin. Biram hoped that Goitein would choose to remain in Haifa and teach at his school: Magnes to Billig, July 25, 1927, CAHU, 91:1925–27.

223. Note from Levi Billig, CAHU, 98alef:1928; Goitein to the university administration, [1928], CAHU, 98alef:1928.

224. Announcement to HUSOS students, February 10, 1931, CAHU, 202:1931.

225. Levi Billig, "Report to the Board of Governors," May 1931, CAHU, 202:1931.

226. Chief secretariat to Billig, July 24, 1931, CAHU, 202:1931.

227. Weil to Magnes, September 14, 1931, CAHU, 202:1931. Before Weil was declared the institute's new director, staff approached Carl Heinrich Becker entreating him to take on the Chief Editor role for *Ansab al-Ashraf* volumes, which Horovitz had

210 ::: NOTES TO CHAPTER 1

once held. Becker acceded: Max Schloessinger to Becker, March 15, 1931, and a note from Moshe ben-David, July 15, 1931, CAHU, 202:1931. Still, when Weil was given the position, the new director was also given the role of editor of the volumes.

228. Mayer to Magnes, August 24, 1932, CAHU, Personnel File—L. A. Mayer, 1926–1945. The chair was named after David's father, Sassoon David.

229. In the margins of his report to Weil on the celebration of the establishment of the chair in February, the vice chancellor of the university Max Schloessinger wrote: "It was with deepest regret that I heard of the political developments in Germany. Do they impact your position in any way?" Schloessinger to Weil, February 9, 1933, CAHU, 2261:1933.

230. Yfaat Weiss, "Ad Acta: Nachgelassenes in Jerusalem," *Naharaim* 13, no. 1–2 (2019): 104. See also Norman Bentwich, *The Rescue and Achievement of Refugee Scholars: The Story of Displaced Scholars and Scientists 1933–1952* (The Hague: Martinus Nijhoff, 1953), 56–61.

231. Reich Ministry of Science, Education and Culture to Weil, December 13, 1934, Universitätsarchiv Frankfurt, Abt. 134, Nr. 621, Bl. 22.

232. Magnes to Weil, June 6, 1935, and Ginzberg to Weil, October 14, 1935, CAHU, Personnel File—Gotthold Weil, until 1951.

233. Ben-David to Mayer, January 27, 1936, CAHU, Personnel File—Leo Aryeh Mayer, 1926–1945. The message sent to Mayer regarding his appointment noted that the Executive Committee was cancelling the position of visiting director. Numerous documents from the archive of the School of Oriental Studies give the impression that—Weil being preoccupied with the political developments in Germany— Mayer directed much of the institute's activity in practice even before his official appointment.

234. Edward Ullendorff, "H. J. Polotsky (1905–1991): Linguistic Genius," *Journal of the Royal Asiatic Society* 4, no. 1 (1994): 5–6. Polotsky would become the secretary and even interim director of HUSOS but grew increasingly identified with the Department of Linguistics at the Hebrew University, of which he was among the founders.

235. See, for example, the detailed proposal on the subject delivered to Magnes by the archaeologist Samuel Yeivin in 1928: Yeivin to Magnes, May 7, 1928, CAHU, 91/5:1928. Egyptology studies were eventually founded, it seems, on the basis of aid money for refugees from Germany, as Magnes suggested: Moshe Ben-David to the Committee for the creation of an Egyptology program, December 28, 1933, CAHU, 226:1933. This lack of personnel and budget also touched another field concerned with the study of the ancient Near East, Assyriology; a proposal for the opening of a Department of Assyriology was approved by the university administration as early as 1924, but never materialized due to a lack of funding sources. Josef Horovitz, "Suggestions for the Budget of the Institute of Oriental Studies," [1925], CZA, L12/27. In 1939, the Vienna-born Eli Strauss joined the institute (later Eliyahu Ashtor, 1914–1984). His recruitment to HUSOS is discussed in the third chapter.

236. In contrast with these two stands the exceptional story of another scholar of German training, the Prague-born Orientalist Paul Kraus (1904–1944). Kraus

NOTES TO CHAPTER 1 ::: 211

immigrated to Palestine in 1925 and studied at HUSOS (official permit signed by Shlomo Ginzberg, April 8, 1927, CAHU, 91:1925–1927), but later, Kraus returned to Europe, and completed his doctoral studies in Berlin. Following the passing of the Nazi race laws, he received a position at the Egyptian University in Cairo but was fired a few years later due to political developments in Egypt. With no prospects of employment in Cairo or Jerusalem, he ended his life. In January 1945, HUSOS held a memorial event for him; D. H. Baneth, with whom Kraus was close, was the first speaker: Invitation to the Memorial for Dr. Paul Kraus, to be held on January 17, 1945, sent on January 10, 1945, CZA, S25/6842. On various aspects of Kraus's personal and professional path, and his tragic end, see Joel L. Kraemer, "The Death of an Orientalist: Paul Kraus from Prague to Cairo," in *The Jewish discovery of Islam: Studies in Honor of Bernard Lewis*, ed. Martin Kramer (Tel Aviv: The Moshe Dayan Center for Middle Eastern and African Studies, Tel Aviv University, 1999), 181–205; Maja Šcrbacic, "Von der Semitistik zur Islamwissenschaft und zurück—Paul Kraus (1904–1944)," *Dubnow Institute Yearbook* 12 (2013): 389–416.

237. With the arrival of Weil and Polotsky, the division into five departments under the aegis of HUSOS was set, and remained in place until the end of the 1940s: primary departments—Arabic Language and Literature, and Islamic Culture; and secondary departments—Art and Archaeology of the Near East, Semitic Linguistics, and Egyptology.

238. On the background for the formation of the Hartog Commission and the results of the report it produced, see Uri Cohen and Adi Sapir, "Models of Academic Governance during a Period of Nation-Building: The Hebrew University in the 1920s–1960s," *History of Education* 45, no. 5 (2016): 610–13; Livny, "The Hebrew University in Mandatory Palestine," 91–92. Formation of the commission was urged by Albert Einstein, who resigned from the Board of Governors in 1928 and harshly criticized Magnes's centralized control.

239. "Obituary: Sir Philip Hartog," *Bulletin of the School of Oriental and African Studies, University of London* 12, no. 2 (1948): 491; Sanjay Seth, *Subject Lessons: The Western Education of Colonial India* (New York: Duke University Press, 2007), 230.

240. "Obituary: Sir Philip Hartog," 491–92. Hartog was offered the position of SOAS's first director, but refused; later, he filled numerous administrative roles there.

241. Letter to the Editor by Philip Hartog, *The Times*, April 15, 1930, 12.

242. Philip Hartog, Louis Ginzberg, and Redcliffe Salaman, *Report of the Survey Committee of the Hebrew University of Jerusalem* (Jerusalem: The Hebrew University, 1934), 20.

243. Ibid., 21. The report links the development of research and instruction at HUSOS to the political goals of Horovitz and his desire to foster affinity between Jews and Arabs. This discussion in the report, and the response of HUSOS faculty, appear in the following chapter of this book, which focusses on political issues in the operations of the institute.

244. Marchand, *German Orientalism in the Age of Empire*, 350–56; Wokoeck, *German Orientalism*, 148–49. For insights into the significance of the SOS in the German military efforts within the territories of the Ottoman Empire during World

212 ::: NOTES TO CHAPTER 1

War I, see Gottfried Hagen, "German Heralds of Holy War: Orientalists and Applied Oriental Studies," *Comparative Studies of South Asia, Africa and the Middle East* 24, no. 2 (2004): 145–62.

245. Richard Koebner, Fritz Baer, L.A. Mayer, and S. D. Goitein, "Hatza'ot lesidur kursim 'al hayesodot shel hayey hamedina vehahevra beyameinu," submitted to the Senate of the Hebrew University in meeting no. 14, June 17, 1936, CAHU, Senate Meetings.

246. "Divrey Gabriel Baer," in *'Al Prof. Alfred Bonne z"l* (Jerusalem: The Hebrew University Magnes Press, 1960), 19.

247. Shamosh was appointed following the murder of Levi Billig in 1936. I delve into his arrival at HUSOS and his integration into the institute in the subsequent chapter.

248. Pierre Bourdieu, *Homo Academicus*, trans. Peter Collier (Stanford: Stanford University Press, 1988), 152.

249. Lavsky, "Bein hanahat 'even hapina laptiha," 154.

250. Livny, "The Hebrew University in Mandatory Palestine," chap. 2.

251. Yuval Evri, *Translating the Arab-Jewish Tradition: From Al-Andalus to Palestine/Land of Israel* (Berlin: Forum Transregionale Studien, 2016), 14–16.

252. According to the testimony of Heinrich Loewe: Loewe, *Ignaz Goldziher*, [5].

253. Allyson Gonzalez, "Abraham S. Yahuda (1877–1951) and the Politics of Modern Jewish Scholarship," *Jewish Quarterly Review* 109, no. 3 (2019): 430. Even earlier, Yahuda was invited to a large committee of Jewish scholars that was to convene in Basel in early 1920 to discuss the planning of the university: Shmaryahu Levin to Yahuda, November 26, 1919, ANLI, Arc. Ms. Var. Yah 38/01/1265. As a result of organizational failures and low turnout, the committee never met in the end: Lavsky, "Bein hanahat 'even hapina laptiha," 129.

254. Gonzalez, "Abraham S. Yahuda," 430.

255. See, for example, Abigail Jacobson and Moshe Naor, *Oriental Neighbors: Middle Eastern Jews and Arabs in Mandatory Palestine* (Waltham, MA: Brandeis University Press, 2016), 42–43. The topic was discussed extensively in the study by Yuval Evri on Sephardicness in the Jewish intellectual world in the early twentieth century: Yuval Evri, *Hashiva le'Andalus: Mahalokot 'al tarbut vezehut yehudit-sfaradit bein 'araviyut le'ivriyut* (Jerusalem: The Hebrew University Magnes Press, 2020), 129–49. For a shorter English version, see Yuval Evri, "Return to al-Andalus beyond German-Jewish Orientalism: Abraham Shalom Yahuda's Critique of Modern Jewish Discourse," in *Modern Jewish Scholarship on Islam in Context: Rationality, European Borders, and the Search for Belonging*, ed. Ottfried Fraisse (Berlin: De Gruyter, 2018), 337–54.

256. Ibid., 342. In a letter from Weizmann to Yahuda, after the latter had already left Jerusalem, Weizmann remarked: "I am fully aware that you have offered your services and I have been trying my best to come to an arrangement with you. Unfortunately, for reasons over which I had no control, this arrangement was not completed . . . owing to your engagement and subsequent marriage you had gone away and the pour parlers were interrupted": July 19, 1922, YCW, Chaim Weizmann Archive, 18-741.

NOTES TO CHAPTER 1 ::: 213

257. A. S. Yahuda, "Maduʿa nimna haprofessor Yahuda lehartzot bamikhlala haʿivrit," *Doʾar hayom*, May 21, 1929, 4.

258. Walid Abd El Gawad, "Dreifache Vermittlung: Israel Wolfensohn als Pionier der israelischen Orientwissenschaft," in *Ein Paradigma der Moderne: Jüdische Geschichte in Schlüsselbegriffen; Festschrift für Dan Diner zum 70. Geburtstag*, ed. Arndt Engelhardt et al. (Göttingen: Vandenhoeck & Ruprecht, 2016), 288.

259. Ben-Zeʾev to Yosef Rivlin, August 7, 1931. The letter is located in the uncatalogued archive of Yosef Yoʾel Rivlin at the Municipality of Jerusalem.

260. Aviv Derri, "The Construction of 'Native' Jews in Late Mandate Palestine: An Ongoing Nahda as a Political Project," *International Journal of Middle East Studies* 53, no. 2 (2021): 258–59. In her research on Ben-Zeʾev, Aviv Derri notes the limited archival sources on this topic, but according to the testimony of Ben-Zeʾevʾs daughter, he repeatedly expressed his desire to teach at HUSOS.

261. For instance, he reported to the university about the chances that Egyptian scholars will attend the celebrations marking the tenth anniversary of its opening: Ernst Simon to Eliyahu Epstein, March 26, 1935, Central Zionist Archives, S25/6721. In 1938, Ben-Zeʾev visited Jerusalem and delivered a lecture in Arabic on the topic of his German doctoral dissertation: Hebrew University School of Oriental Studies to an undisclosed recipient, February 11, 1938, The Hebrew University Archives, 226:1938. Ben-Zeʾev also served as the secretary of the Jewish community in Cairo and was active in various Zionist organizations in the city.

262. Derri, "Construction of 'Native' Jews," 256, 261–62. Note that alongside his job as supervisor, Ben-Zeʾev taught for several years at Bar Ilan University, but not in a permanent position.

263. Yahuda to Ben-Zeʾev, December 7, 1946, quoted in Hebrew in Aviv Derri, "Mizrahanut alternativit vehishtalvut bamerhav haʿaravi hamekomi: Dr. Israel Ben-Zeʾev, hasifriya haʿaravit beyafo vehamaʾavak ʿal sfarim falastiniyim 'netushim', 1948–1952" (master's thesis, Ben-Gurion University of the Negev, 2013), 81.

264. Even before Ben-Zeʾev completed his second doctorate in Frankfurt, S. D. Goitein published a negative review of his book *Hayehudim beʿarav* (Jews in Arabia) noting that the book contained "serious mistakes," and that parts of it suggested a lack of "familiarity or willingness to use the scientific literature": Goitein, "Review of *Hayehudim beʿarav*, by Israel Ben-Zeʾev," *Kiryat sefer* 8, no. 3 (1932): 304. When, in 1942, Ben-Zeʾevʾs joining the teacher training program at the university was discussed, Rector Haim Yehuda Roth wrote in a letter to L. A. Mayer that he had spoken with the director of the education department for the Jewish National Council, who promised him "that nobody will be forced on you," and that this director's opinion on Ben-Zeʾev "is the same as ours," suggesting the rector's —and apparently also Mayer's—reservation: Roth to David Werner Senator and to L. A. Mayer, May 17, 1942, CAHU, 226-2260:1942.

265. Letter from Ben-Zeʾev to Yahuda from 1947, quoted in Hebrew in Derri, "Mizrahanut alternativit," 82.

266. Derri, "Construction of 'Native' Jews," 259.

267. For Plessner's biography see Amit Levy, "A Man of Contention: Martin

214 ::: NOTES TO CHAPTER 2

Plessner (1900–1973) and His Encounters with the Orient," *Naharaim* 10, no. 1 (2016): 82–84.

268. The matter resurfaced in informal conversations I had in recent years with students and colleagues of Plessner.

269. Meir Jacob Kister, "MiGalicia letarbut 'arav," *Igeret ha'akademia hale'umit hayisra'elit lemada'im* 26 (2004): 20.

270. List of classes for 1948/49 in the Faculty of Humanities, CAHU, 2120:1949.

271. Libson, "Hidden Worlds and Open Shutters," 165–66.

272. Gil Eyal, *The Disenchantment of the Orient: Expertise in Arab Affairs and the Israeli State* (Stanford: Stanford University Press, 2006), 62.

## 2. "WITH ITS BACK TO THE ORIENT"?

1. Cited in Shalom Schwartz, *Ussishkin be'igrotav* (Jerusalem: Reuven Mass, 1949–1950), 151.

2. *Stenographisches Protokoll der Verhandlungen des XI. Zionisten-Kongresses in Wien vom 2. bis 9. September 1913* (Berlin: Juedischen Verlag, 1914), 305.

3. "Ha'universita ha'ivrit birushalayim," *Hatzfira*, October 3, 1918, 9.

4. William Ormsby-Gore to Chaim Weizmann, April 11, 1918, CZA, L3/87.

5. "Opening of the Hebrew University: Historic Speeches," *Palestine Bulletin*, April 2, 1925, 1.

6. Lutfi al-Sayyid was also the director of the Egyptian National Library, and was appointed the Egyptian Minister of Education three years after the ceremony. See Israel Gershoni, "Luṭfi al-Sayyid, Aḥmad," in *Encyclopaedia of Islam*, ed. Kate Fleet et al., 3rd ed., http://dx.doi.org/10.1163/1573-3912_ei3_COM_35916.

7. "'Iftitah al-jami'a al-yahudiyya," *Filastin*, March 31, 1925, 2.

8. Mahmud 'Awad, *Wa'alaykum al-salam..* (Cairo: Dar al-mustaqbal al-'arabi, 1984), 82. Quoted in Shimon Shamir, "Kishrey hinukh vetarbut," *Cathedra* 67 (1993): 97. Israel Gershoni's forthcoming study on Lutfi al-Sayyid will be the first English work to exhaustively deal with this episode.

9. Protocol of meeting for the establishment of a Faculty of Oriental Studies at the Hebrew University in Palestine, April 10, 1922, CZA, S2/390, 4.

10. The British initiative, led by Jerusalem Governor Ronald Storrs, never came to fruition, in part due to opposition from Jewish candidates to teach at the institution —Eliezer Ben-Yehuda, David Yellin, and Josef Klausner—to cooperate with the initiative, fearing that this would constitute "a threat to Hebrew culture in Palestine and that it meant competition to the projected Hebrew University" (quoted in Adi Livny, "Hebrew University in Mandatory Palestine: A Relational History (1918-1948)" [PhD diss., Hebrew University of Jerusalem, 2021], 62–63). Evidence regarding the Arab response to the initiative has apparently not been preserved. See Abdul Latif Tibawi, *Arab Education in Mandatory Palestine: A Study of Three Decades of British Administration* (London: Luzac, 1956), 102. For a full account of the Hebrew University's preemptive measures against the establishment of British or Arab universities in Palestine, see chapter 2 in Livny's work.

NOTES TO CHAPTER 2 ::: 215

11. Hugo Bergmann to Weizmann, January 2, 1922, YCH, Chaim Weizmann Archive, 5-688.

12. "As Jews we have a mission to be interpreters between East and West. We want to establish a great institute of Oriental and Islamic studies, and we are expecting to invite both as teachers and as students not only Jews but our Moslem cousins as well." (Speech delivered by Judah Magnes in New York at a 1925 event of the World Zionist Organization: Magnes, *Addresses by the Chancellor of the Hebrew University* [Jerusalem: Hebrew University, 1936], 15); "The Hebrew University has from the very beginning planned its school of Oriental Studies in order that it might contribute to international friendship and understanding in Palestine and other parts of the Near East, and it is not too much to say that this school has already served in a modest way to bring about some degree of mutual intellectual and spiritual appreciation as between Jews and Arabs." (Speech marking the opening of the academic year 1928–29: Ibid., 70). On Magnes's worldview and the various initiatives for Jewish-Arab rapprochement with which he was directly and indirectly involved during the Mandate, as well as the connection between his political activities and his role at the Hebrew University, see Hedva Ben-Israel, "Bi-Nationalism versus Nationalism: The Case of Judah Magnes," *Israel Studies* 23, no. 1 (2018): 86–105.

13. Moshe Yegar, *Toldot hamahlaka hamedinit shel hasokhnut hayehudit* (Jerusalem: Hasifriya hatziyonit, 2010), 137. This proposal—an idea suggested by Colonel Frederick Kisch during his term as director of the Political Department (1929–1931)—was quickly abandoned, and Horovitz was apparently never approached on the matter.

14. Speech in memory of Horovitz given to mark the hanging of his portrait in the work-room of the School of Oriental Studies, November 24, 1931, Magnes, *Addresses by the Chancellor*, 295.

15. Sabine Mangold-Will, "Josef Horovitz und die Gründung des Instituts für Arabische und Islamische Studien an der Hebräischen Universität in Jerusalem: ein Orientalisches Seminar für Palästina," *Naharaim* 10, no. 1 (2016): 7–37; Hanan Harif, "The Orient between Arab and Jewish National Revivals: Josef Horovitz, Shelomo Dov Goitein and Oriental Studies in Jerusalem," in *Modern Jewish Scholarship on Islam in Context: Rationality, European Borders, and the Search for Belonging*, ed. Ottfried Fraisse (Berlin: De Gruyter, 2018), 319–36; Ruchama Johnston-Bloom, "'Dieses wirklich westöstlichen Mannes': The German-Jewish Orientalist Josef Horovitz in Germany, India, and Palestine," in *The Muslim Reception of European Orientalism: Reversing the Gaze*, ed. Susannah Heschel and Umar Ryad (London: Routledge, 2018), 168–83.

16. Josef Horovitz, "Die Universität Jerusalem," *Frankfurter Zeitung*, August 16, 1925.

17. Unaddressed letter from Horovitz, March 28, 1928, CAHU, 91/I:1928.

18. L. A. Mayer to Magnes, in a letter attached to a letter from Mayer to D. H. Baneth, September 9, 1924, ANLI, Arc. 4°1559/03/17.

19. Baneth to the Hebrew University Administration, in response to a letter of November 16, 1926, ANLI, Arc. 4°1559/03/17.

216 ::: NOTES TO CHAPTER 2

20. Levi Billig, "Memorandum on Research," undated [late 1926], CAHU, 91:1925–27.

21. "Notes for a memorandum on the School of Oriental Studies," n.d. [apparently late 1926], CAHU, 91:1925–27.

22. Louis Massignon to Dr. Jacobson, July 19, 1926, CAHU, 91:1925–27.

23. On Massignon and his activities in this realm, see Jacques Waardenburg, "Louis Massignon (1883–1962) as a Student of Islam," *Die Welt des Islams*, New Series, 45, no. 3 (2005): 312–42.

24. Baneth and Billig to the Hebrew University Administration, October 11, 1926, CAHU, 91:1925–27.

25. For a critical discussion of the idea of negation of the Diaspora in Zionist thought and its part in the formation of the Zionist point of view on the Palestinian past, see Amnon Raz-Krakotzkin, "Exile within Sovereignty: Critique of 'The Negation of Exile' in Israeli Culture," in *The Scaffolding of Sovereignty: Global and Aesthetic Perspectives on the History of a Concept*, ed. Zvi Benite, Stefanos Geroulanos, and Nicole Jerr (New York: Columbia University Press, 2017), 393–420. In recent years, historical research has also subverted the homogeneous image of the new Jew in the time of the *Yishuv*—see, for example, the work of Liora R. Halperin, which discusses the effective presence not only of Hebrew but of numerous languages within the spatial boundaries of the *Yishuv* across all the layers of the social fabric: Halperin, *Babel in Zion: Jews, Nationalism, and Language Diversity in Palestine, 1920–1948* (New Haven: Yale University Press, 2015).

26. Based on lists created by Aharon Kedar on the basis of archival evidence: Kedar, "Letoldoteha shel 'Brit Shalom' bashanim 1925–1928," in *Pirkey mehkar betoldot hatziyonut: Mugashim leIsrael Goldstein bahagi'o ligvurot*, ed. Yehuda Bauer, Moshe Davis, and Israel Kolatt (Jerusalem: Hasifriya hatziyonit, 1976), 281–85. Kedar included in the list of friends and supporters only those who paid membership fees and/or expressed public support for the association's activities.

27. From the regulations of the Brit Shalom association, translated from the original Hebrew in Noam Zadoff, *Gershom Scholem: From Berlin to Jerusalem and Back*, trans. Jeffrey Green (Waltham, MA: Brandeis University Press, 2017), 39. On the complexity and diversity of German influence on the political thought of Brit Shalom, see Shalom Ratsabi, *Between Zionism and Judaism: The Radical Circle in Brith Shalom, 1925–1933* (Leiden: Brill, 2002); Yfaat Weiss, "Central European Ethnonationalism and Zionist Binationalism," *Jewish Social Studies* 11, no. 1 (2004): 93–117; Zohar Maor, "Moderation from Right to Left: The Hidden Roots of Brit Shalom," *Jewish Social Studies* 19, no. 2 (2013): 79–108.

28. This description, which distills the essence of Horovitz's lecture, is taken from Kedar, "Letoldoteha shel 'Brit Shalom,'" 230.

29. Ibid. According to Kedar, Rabbi Binyamin and Yosef Rivlin exaggerated Horovitz's importance in the founding of the association, thus influencing the manner in which the entry Brit Shalom in the Hebrew Encyclopedia was formulated; whereas Ruppin, Hugo Bergmann, and Gershom Scholem gave a more precise impression.

NOTES TO CHAPTER 2 ::: 217

30. Hebrew University faculty were present mainly in the radical faction of Brit Shalom: Livny, "The Hebrew University in Mandatory Palestine," 10–11.

31. Menahem Milson, "Beginnings of Arabic and Islamic Studies at the Hebrew University of Jerusalem," *Judaism* 45, no. 2 (Spring 1996): 181.

32. Magnes, *Addresses by the Chancellor*, 71.

33. Jane Burbank and Frederick Cooper, *Empires in World History: Power and the Politics of Difference* (Princeton: Princeton University Press, 2010), 2.

34. For an extended discussion of the connections and meetings between Zionists and Arabs in the late Ottoman period, see Jonathan Gribetz, *Defining Neighbors: Religion, Race, and the Early Zionist-Arab Encounter* (Princeton: Princeton University Press, 2014).

35. An analysis of British involvement in the events taking place in Palestine as a result of British imperial strategy can be found, for example, in Naomi Shepherd, *Ploughing Sand: British Rule in Palestine 1917–1948* (New Brunswick, NJ: Rutgers University Press, 2000). For a particular focus on British involvement in Hebrew University affairs, see Livny, "The Hebrew University in Mandatory Palestine."

36. Naturally, connections were also made in other contexts within the British imperial realm between scholars from different non-British groups pursuing interests other than those of the regime. Kris Manjapra discusses connections between German and Indian scholars under the British regime, showing that, in contrast to the assumption that the influence was unidirectional, from West to East, these connections formed intellectual cooperation that had a mutual influence: Manjapra, *Age of Entanglement: German and Indian Intellectuals across Empire* (Cambridge, MA: Harvard University Press, 2014).

37. On the term "Invisible College," its history, and the possibilities of its use as a sociological category of analysis, see Alesia Zuccala, "Modeling the Invisible College," *Journal of the American Society for Information Science and Technology* 57, no. 2 (2006): 152–68. The term has its roots in the seventeenth-century British academy, and the general definition used above is a variation based on preceding widespread definitions: ibid., 155.

38. For a recent English biography of Hussein, who was politically active and for a short period even served as Egyptian Minister of Education, see Hussam R. Ahmed, *The Last Nahdawi: Taha Hussein and Institution Building in Egypt* (Stanford: Stanford University Press, 2021).

39. Norman Bentwich, *For Zion's Sake: A Biography of Judah L. Magnes* (Philadelphia: Jewish Publication Society of America, 1954), 187n.

40. Shelomo Dov Goitein, "Goldziher abu al-dirasat al-'islamiyya: Bimunasabat murur khams wa'ishrin sana 'ala wafatihi," *al-Katib al-misri* 5, no. 14 (1947): 85–95.

41. Ibid., 85n11.

42. Mohamed El-Bendary, *The Egyptian Press and Coverage of Local and International Events* (Lanham, MD: Lexington Books, 2010), 3; Reuven Snir, "Arabic in the Service of Regeneration of Jews: The Participation of Jews in Arabic Press and Journalism in the 19th and 20th Centuries," *Acta Orientalia* 59, no. 3 (2006): 301–2; Yoav Di-Capua, "Changing the Arab Intellectual Guard: On the Fall of the Udaba',

218 ::: NOTES TO CHAPTER 2

1940–1960," in *Arabic Thought against the Authoritarian Age: Towards an Intellectual History of the Present*, ed. Jens Hanssen and Max Weiss (Cambridge: Cambridge University Press, 2018), 45.

43. Suzanne L. Marchand, *German Orientalism in the Age of Empire: Religion, Race and Scholarship* (Cambridge: Cambridge University Press, 2009), 325–26; Lawrence I. Conrad, "The Dervish's Disciple: On the Personality and Intellectual Milieu of the Young Ignaz Goldziher," *The Journal of the Royal Asiatic Society of Great Britain and Ireland* 122, no. 2 (1990): 240–43.

44. On the Arab College (in Arabic: *Al-Kuliyya al-'arabiyya*, formerly known as *Dar al-mu'alimin*), see Yoni Furas, *Educating Palestine: Teaching and Learning History under the Mandate* (Oxford: Oxford University Press, 2020), especially 110–23. The Arab College was run under the aegis of the British Mandate government.

45. Meir Abulafiya, "Sofer falastini rodef shalom betokh ha'intifada: 'al hasofer hafalastini Ishaq Musa al-Husseini vesifro zikhronot tarnegolet," *Moznaim* 62, no. 9–10 (1988–1989): 21. On the book "Memoirs of a Hen" and interpretations of it since its publication, see George J. Kanazi, "Ishaq Musa al-Husayni and His Memoirs of a Hen," introduction to *Memoirs of a Hen*, by Ishaq Musa al-Husayni, trans. George J. Kanazi (Toronto: York Press, 1999), 5–15.

46. Soheir Al-Qalamawi, *Dhikra Taha Hussein* (Cairo: Dar al-ma'arif, 1974), 25.

47. The first lecture in the series was given by Hussein on September 28 on "Egypt and Arabic literature": *Al-Difa'*, September 29, 1942, 2. On the station, founded in 1941, which was secretly funded by the British Foreign Office and articulated an Arab national viewpoint, see Douglas A. Boyd, "Sharq al-Adna/The Voice of Britain: The UK's 'Secret' Arabic Radio Station and Suez War Propaganda Disaster," *Gazette: The International Journal for Communication Studies* 65, no. 6 (2003): 443–55; Sahar Mor Bostock, "Radio Listenership in Palestinian Society: Reshaping Cultural Practices and Political Debate under the British Mandate, 1930–1948," *Contemporary Levant* 8, no. 1 (2023): 75.

48. A. S. [Eliyahu Sasson] to M. S. [Moshe Shertok], September 24, 1942, CZA, S25/3102. Several days later, Shamosh informed Yosef Rivlin that a party scheduled in Hussein's honor had been cancelled at Hussein's own request. He did not specify who had initiated the party or why Hussein asked to cancel it (Shamosh to Rivlin, October 1, 1942. The short letter is located in the Yosef Yo'el Rivlin Archive at the uncatalogued Jerusalem Municipal Archive).

49. "D. Hussein Fawzi.. yuhadir fi isra'il!!" *Uktober* 157, October 28, 1979, 3.

50. Abigail Jacobson and Moshe Naor, *Oriental Neighbors: Middle Eastern Jews and Arabs in Mandatory Palestine* (Waltham, MA: Brandeis University Press, 2016), 60–66. For a comprehensive biography of Sasson, including a detailed treatment of the years when he formed his outlook in Damascus, see Yaron Ran, *Ha'aravist: Eliyahu Sasson vehama'avak hatziyoni bamered ha'aravi* (Modi'in: Hotza'at Effie Meltzer, 2018).

51. Ibid., 281.

52. Ibid., 642.

53. Yegar, *Toldot hamahlaka hamedinit*, 306–307.

NOTES TO CHAPTER 2 ::: 219

54. "Kalimat Dr. Taha Hussein," in *Al-Buhuth wal-muhadarat: mu'tamar al-dawra al-hadiya wal-thalathin, 1964-1965*, by Majma' al-lugha al-'arabiyya bil-qahira (Cairo, n.d.), 6, cited in Shlomit Shraybom-Shivtiel, "Mehayey halashon ha'aravit mul thiyat halashon ha'ivrit," in *Mehkarim be'aravit uvtarbut ha'Islam*, ed. Binyamin Abrahamov, vol. 1 (Ramat Gan: Bar Ilan University, 2000), 192.

55. Additional evidence of the visit was revealed years later by Yitzhak Navon, President of the State of Israel, in the wake of his presidential visit to Egypt after the signing of the Peace Accord between Egypt and Israel. In the 1940s, alongside his activities in the Haganah and his work as a teacher, Navon was a student at HUSOS. He recounted that, during Hussein's visit to Palestine, L. A. Mayer tapped him to accompany Hussein on his visit (after the proposal from Sasson was passed on through Shamosh). At Hussein's request, Navon took him to visit Kibbutz Kiryat Anavim near Jerusalem, which left a striking impression on the Egyptian scholar. The details were given in Navon's speech before the Egyptian president during his 1980 visit to Cairo (ISA, PRES-349/5), and in a recorded meeting held a year later with kibbutz members (TS-164/93, 24:35). Note that the archive at Kibbutz Kiryat Anavim preserves no evidence of the visit.

56. See, for example, Magnes to Mahmoud Fawzi, August 17, 1941, CAHU 226:1941; "Conversation with Mr. Cattaoui of Egypt," September 4, 1941, CAHU, 226:1941. Before Magnes set off for Cairo in 1928, Mayer and Billig equipped him with letters to present to a number of scholars and directors of libraries and collections there, meant to facilitate Magnes's access to manuscripts, libraries, and archaeological sites during his stay: Mayer and Billig to Magnes, December 3, 1928, CAHU, 91alef:1928. The question of access to manuscripts and libraries in neighboring countries was a matter of great interest to the institute's scholars, who hoped to rely on the plentiful materials there for their studies. See, for example, the Egyptian Library in Cairo's response to Baneth in 1932 agreeing to send him facsimiles of manuscripts he required for one of his studies. The entire correspondence, located at the ANLI, Arc. 4° 1559/03/17, was conducted in Arabic.

57. Billig to Magnes, December 3, 1928, CAHU, 91alef:1928.

58. On Gad al-Mawla and his role in the Egyptian education system, see Ahmad al-Sa'id Gad al-Mawla, "al-'Alim al-'islami al-marhum al-'ustadh / Muhammad Ahmad Gad al-Mawla (Bek)," in *Dustur al-'afrad wal-'umam fi sunan sayd al-'arab wal-'ajam Muhammad*, by Muhammad Ahmad Gad al-Mawla (Bek) (Cairo: Al-dar al-misriyya al-lubnaniyya, 2000), 611–13.

59. On August 17, 1941, Magnes wrote on this to the Egyptian Consul in Jerusalem, Mahmoud Fawzi: "This project did not materialize for reasons that we have not been able to fathom" (CAHU, 226:1941).

60. Rainer Hermann, *Kulturkrise und konservative Erneuerung: Muḥammad Kurd 'Alī (1876–1953) und das geistige Leben in Damaskus zu Beginn des 20. Jahrhunderts* (Frankfurt am Main: Peter Lang, 1990), 65.

61. On the formation of the various academies of Arabic language and competition between them as questions of nationalism and pan-Arabism swirled in the background, see Chaoqun Lian, *Language, Ideology and Sociopolitical Change in*

220 ::: NOTES TO CHAPTER 2

*the Arabic-speaking World: A Study of the Discourse of Arabic Language Academies* (Edinburgh: Edinburgh University Press, 2020).

62. On Kurd Ali's life and political thought, see Hermann, *Kulturkrise und konservative Erneuerung*. Like Hussein, Kurd Ali too served as Minister of Education (he served in this role twice during the period of French rule in Syria).

63. On a visit by Kurd Ali to Hebron in the late Ottoman period and an ideological argument he had with an Old *Yishuv* Zionist, see Hillel Cohen, *Year Zero of the Arab-Israeli Conflict 1929*, trans. Haim Watzman (Waltham, MA: Brandeis University Press, 2015), 145.

64. Frederick Kisch to the Head Secretary of the Hebrew University, August 27, 1930, CZA, S25/6727. The Bessarabia-born Tuvia Ashkenazi (1904–1970) was a writer for *Ha'aretz* and *Davar*, and prepared reports on the Palestinian population for the Jewish Agency and the Jewish National Fund. Even though he was awarded a doctoral degree in Oriental Studies from the Sorbonne, he was never integrated into the academic establishment either in Palestine or elsewhere, and in parallel to conducting research, he continued his work with the Jewish National Fund, the American State Department, and the World Zionist Organization. See Moshe Sharon, "Petah davar," in *Habeduim be'Eretz Israel*, by Tuvia Ashkenazi (Jerusalem: Ariel, 2000). For examples of his intelligence and diplomatic activities see Yoav Gelber, "Antecedents of the Jewish-Druze Alliance in Palestine," *Middle Eastern Studies* 28, no. 2 (1992): 352; Muhammad Suwaed, "Cooperation between the Galilee Bedouins and the Yishuv during the 1948 War," *Israel Affairs* 26, no. 2 (2020): 214.

65. Moshe Ben-David to Kisch, September 4, 1930, CZA, S25/6727. As noted, during a 1905–1906 visit to the Middle East, Horovitz was in Egypt and Syria for the purposes of scientific research in the service of the Italian Orientalist and politician Leone Caetani: Shelomo Dov Goitein, "Josef Horovitz," *Der Islam* 22, no. 2 (1934): 124. It could be that the relationship began at this time; some years later, Kurd Ali visited Caetani's library in Rome for a month of research: Muhammad Kurd Ali, *al-Mudhakkarat* (Riyadh: Dar adwa al-salaf, 2010), 188.

66. Within the list of academy members on its website, Horovitz's name appears under the category "irregular members" (*al-a'ida al-murasilun*)—that is, scholars from various countries who were members of the academy without taking part regularly in its activities. Additional German members on this list include, for example, Eduard Sachau, Eugen Mittwoch, Carl Brockelmann, and Hellmut Ritter: www.arabacademy.gov.sy/ar/page16278/.

67. Joseph H. Escovitz, "Orientalists and Orientalism in the Writings of Muhammad Kurd Ali," *International Journal of Middle East Studies* 15, no. 1 (1983): 95–96.

68. S. Hareli, "Bikur bilvanon uvesuria," [1936 or 1937], CZA, S25/5570, 15.

69. Muhammad Kurd Ali, *al-Mu'asirun* (Beirut: Dar sadir, 1993), 134.

70. S. Hareli, "Bikur bilvanon uvesuria." Hareli joined the Political Department in 1935. He was an expert on Turkish affairs and edited the Arab Bureau's Hebrew newsletter, *Yalkut hamizrah hatikhon*: Ran, *Ha'aravist*, 696.

NOTES TO CHAPTER 2 ::: 221

71. S. Hareli, "Bikur bilvanon uvesuria," 14.

72. Ibid.

73. Ibid., 16.

74. "Al-Hadith al-thalith lil-'ustadh Muhammad Kurd Ali," *al-Difa'*, September 30, 1941, 1. Kurd Ali also came to Jerusalem in 1943 to broadcast lectures for Ramadan (Kurd Ali, *al-Mudhakkarat*, 474). The broadcasts of the *Jerusalem Calling* station were intended for Jews, Arabs, and Britons; content was either broadcast in English, Arabic, and Hebrew in parallel or only one of those languages. From the outset, its operators saw the Jewish and Arab target audiences as separate crowds in need of separate content. For a comprehensive study on this station, see Andrea L. Stanton, *This Is Jerusalem Calling: State Radio in Mandate Palestine* (Austin: University of Texas Press, 2013).

75. Entry in S. D. Goitein's diary, September 27, 1941, ANLI, Arc. 4° 1911/02/9.

76. Kurd Ali to Goitein, March 23, 1941, ANLI, Arc. 4° 1911/03/332.

77. Goitein to Billig, October 26, 1932, ANLI, Arc. 4° 1911/03/14.

78. Goitein to Kurd Ali, [n.d.], ANLI, Arc. 4° 1911/03/332.

79. "Melumad suri birushalayim," *Haboker*, September 25, 1941, 3.

80. For a biography of Nashashibi, see Jihad Ahmed Salih, *Muhammad Issaf Nashashibi (1882–1948), 'alamat filastin wa'adib al-'arabiyya* (Ramallah: Al-'Ittihad al-'am lil-kuttab wal-'udaba al-filastiniyin, 2010). In 1947, as hostilities escalated in Jerusalem, Nashashibi left for Cairo, where he died a year later. According to the testimony of his nephew, Nashashibi's vast library was plundered by both Jews and Arabs in 1948, and books from its shelves entered the possession of the National Library: Gish Amit, "Salvage or Plunder? Israel's 'Collection' of Private Palestinian Libraries in West Jerusalem," *Journal of Palestine Studies* 40, no. 4 (2011): 16–17. I return to this issue in the next chapter.

81. "Met Issaf Nashashibi," *Davar*, January 23, 1948, 10.

82. Muhammad Issaf Nashashibi, *al-Batal al-khalid Salah al-Din wal-sha'ir al-khalid Ahmed Shawqi* (Jerusalem: Bayt al-maqdis, 1932).

83. Nashashibi's essay (Ibid., 50–51) cites claims from Nordau's writing on the psychophysiology of genius and talent, using a French translation of Max Nordau, *Paradoxe* (Chicago: F. Gindele, 1885).

84. [Baneth] to Issaf Nashashibi, [first half of the 1930s], ANLI, Arc. 4° 1559/03/17.

85. Nashashibi's essay was sent to Baneth by a neighbor of his from the Sheikh Jarrah neighborhood of Jerusalem, Ahmed al-Kinani, whose activities are sparsely documented but who seems to have been involved with a milieu of Jewish and Arab intellectuals in the mid-1930s and participated in some events under its aegis ("No'em 'aravi ba'emek," *Davar*, September 24, 1935, 8). On this group, established by the authors and translators Immanuel Olsvanger and Asher Beilin, see subsequently in this chapter. In 1938, Goitein (ANLI, Arc. 4° 1911/03/301) and Hugo Bergmann (ANLI, Arc. 4° 1502/01/495) received Sukkot greetings in Arabic from the same al-Kinani. On Baneth's tendency towards self-criticism and hesitancy, see Hava Lazarus-Yafeh, "The Transplantation of Islamic Studies from Europe to the Yishuv and Israel," in

222 ::: NOTES TO CHAPTER 2

*The Jewish Discovery of Islam: Studies in Honor of Bernard Lewis*, ed. Martin Kramer (Tel Aviv: The Moshe Dayan Center for Middle Eastern and African Studies, Tel Aviv University, 1999), 256–59.

86. Baneth and Billig to the Hebrew University Administration, October 11, 1926, CAHU, 91:1925–27.

87. Israel Gershoni, "Egyptian Liberalism in an Age of 'Crisis of Orientation': Al-Risala's Reaction to Fascism and Nazism, 1933–39," *International Journal of Middle East Studies* 31, no. 4 (1999): 555. Issaf Nashashibi is not mentioned among the weekly's writers in Gershoni's article, but a perusal of its tables of contents indicates that it published almost 160 of Nashashibi's texts between 1937 and 1948. On the liberal movement in Arab countries over the course of the nineteenth and twentieth centuries, see Albert Hourani's treatment of, among others, Kurd Ali, Hussein, and the liberal circles within which they operated: Hourani, *Arabic Thought in the Liberal Age: 1798–1939* (Cambridge: Cambridge University Press, 1983), 222–44, 324–40.

88. On Goldziher's reformist approach to Islam in the context of the establishment of the field of Islamic studies, see David Moshfegh, "Ignaz Goldziher and the Rise of Islamwissenschaft as a 'Science of Religion'" (PhD diss., University of California at Berkeley, 2012). On the historical method for the study of Islam that he developed and improved, see also Ottfried Fraisse, "From Geiger to Goldziher: Historical Method and Its Impact on the Conception of Islam," in *Modern Jewish Scholarship in Hungary: The "Science of Judaism" between East and West*, ed. Tamás Turán and Carsten Wilke (Berlin: De Gruyter, 2016), 203–22.

89. Ismar Schorsch finds "the process by which Judaism and Islam were historicized" in Germany during the nineteenth century "strikingly similar": Ismar Schorsch, "Converging Cognates: The Intersection of Jewish and Islamic Studies in Nineteenth Century Germany," *Leo Baeck Institute Year Book* 55 (2010): 4.

90. On Mayer's uniqueness and the reception of his studies among scholars from Arab countries, see Mostafa Hussein, "Scholarship on Islamic Archaeology between Zionism and Arab Nationalist Movements," in *The Muslim Reception of European Orientalism: Reversing the Gaze*, ed. Susannah Heschel and Umar Ryad (Oxon: Routledge, 2019,) 184–208.

91. On the history of the British Mandate's Department of Antiquities, see Shimon Gibson, "British Archaeological Institutions in Mandatory Palestine, 1917–1948," *Palestine Exploration Quarterly* 131, no. 2 (1999): 129–31; Sarah Irving, "Palestinian Christians in the Mandate Department of Antiquities: History and Archaeology in a Colonial Space," in *European Cultural Diplomacy and Arab Christians in Palestine, 1918–1948: Between Contention and Connection*, ed. Karène Sanchez Summerer and Sary Zananiri (London: Palgrave Macmillan, 2021), 164–69.

92. Gabriel Stern, "Beleil haseder—saviv lahoma," *'Al hamishmar*, April 22, 1959, 12. Eliahu Elath claimed in a 1984 interview that Mayer had "outstanding relations . . . with the Arab intelligentsia. He really knew them." (Transcription of interview with Eliahu Elath, October 10, 1984, interviewer: Geoffrey Wigoder, 18. The transcription is held at the Oral History Division of the Hebrew University).

93. Hussein, "Scholarship on Islamic Archaeology," 197–98. Mayer gave two

lectures on Arab architecture at the Arab College, in 1928 and 1935. After the first was published in its periodical, Mayer passed it along to the university administration. In internal correspondence, Magnes, recognizing the distinctiveness of the publication, added in his own hand: "This must be used vis-à-vis America" (comment on letter from Mayer to the Head Secretary of the Hebrew University, March 1, 1928, CAHU, Personnel File—Leo Aryeh Mayer, 1926-1948).

94. On Canaan's life, see Khaled Nashef, "Tawfik Canaan: His Life and Works," *Jerusalem Quarterly* 16 (2002): 12-26. After leaving his home in Musrara in May 1948 together with his family, Canaan's large library was apparently looted: Amit, "Salvage or Plunder," 16. Canaan, who was a staunch opponent of the Zionist Movement and of British rule (and was even imprisoned by the authorities), lived thereafter in East Jerusalem.

95. Most of the information about the Palestine Oriental Society is drawn from Mathilde Sigalas, "Between Diplomacy and Science: British Mandate Palestine and Its International Network of Archaeological Organisations, 1918-1938," in *European Cultural Diplomacy and Arab Christians in Palestine, 1918-1948: Between Contention and Connection*, ed. Karène Sanchez Summerer and Sary Zananiri (London: Palgrave Macmillan, 2021), 199-202.

96. Albert Glock, "Archaeology as Cultural Survival: The Future of the Palestinian Past," *Journal of Palestine Studies* 23, no. 3 (1994): 75-76. Mayer and Levi Billig were even involved in organizational activities within the society, and Mayer served as president for one year.

97. On this circle of Palestinian ethnographers connected to the JPOS and led by Canaan, see Salim Tamari, *Mountain against the Sea: Essays on Palestinian Society and Culture* (Berkeley: University of California Press, 2009), 93-112. Mayer worked in the Mandate's Department of Antiquities alongside another member of the circle, Stephan Hanna Stephan (1894-1949), hailing from a Syrian Christian family from Beit Jala. Between the years 1935 and 1942, Stephan published translations (from Ottoman Turkish to English) of selections from the travel diary of the well-known fifteenth-century Ottoman traveler Evliya Çelebi describing his journey in Palestine. The excerpts were published in a series of articles in the periodical of the Antiquities Department, *Quarterly of the Department of Antiquities of Palestine* (QDAP). Within some of these articles, Mayer added comments on the text, while Stefan himself did so in others. On the series of translations and the varying emphases of Mayer's and Stefan's comments, see Sarah Irving, "Stephan Hanna Stephan and Evliya Çelebi's Book of Travels: Tracing Cooperation and Conflict in Mandate Palestinian Translations," in *Cultural Entanglement in the Pre-Independence Arab World: Arts, Thought and Literature*, ed. Anthony Gorman and Sarah Irving (London: Bloomsbury Academic, 2020), 217-37.

98. Glock, "Archaeology as Cultural Survival," 76.

99. Ben Hamidbar, "Plea for Museum of Palestine Costumes," *Palestine Bulletin*, July 26, 1931, 3. A newspaper clipping giving notification of this lecture by Mayer was kept in his personnel file at the Hebrew University's archive, evidence of the importance attributed to it and the interest it generated.

224 ::: NOTES TO CHAPTER 2

100. H. Z. Hirschberg, "Leon Aryeh Mayer: Hamesh shanim liftirato," *Eretz Israel: Mehkarim biydi'at ha'aretz va'atikoteha* 7 (1964): 15.

101. Inbal Ben-Asher Gitler and Bar Leshem, "Creating Museum Culture in Mandate Palestine," *Israel Studies* 26, no. 3 (2021): 143. On the museum and the process of its establishment, see ibid., 142–44; Nisa Ari, "Cultural Mandates, Artistic Missions, and 'The Welfare of Palestine,' 1876–1948" (PhD diss., Massachusetts Institute of Technology, 2019), 203–15.

102. Salim Tamari, *Year of the Locust: A Soldier's Diary and the Erasure of Palestine's Ottoman Past* (Berkeley: University of California Press, 2011), 10.

103. Tamari, *Mountain against the Sea*, 97–98.

104. "A Folk Museum for Palestine," *Palestine Post*, December 22, 1935, 10. The museum's file within the ISA suggests that the makeup of the committee was the subject of much deliberation and indicates the involvement of the high commissioner in the planning: ISA, M-31/11.

105. Ben-Asher Gitler and Leshem, "Creating Museum Culture," 143; Ari, "Cultural Mandates, Artistic Missions," 215.

106. Only several decades later was the Palestinian Heritage Museum, incorporating elements from the Mandate-era Folk Museum, established in a new location in East Jerusalem's Sheikh Jarrah neighborhood.

107. A number of biographical articles and sketches have been published on Aref al-Aref; he also kept a diary, which has been preserved. A synthesis of these materials, as well as an account of what Zionist figures thought of him, can be found in Bernard Wasserstein, "'Clipping the Claws of the Colonisers': Arab Officials in the Government of Palestine, 1917–48," *Middle Eastern Studies* 13, no. 2 (1977): 180–82. On al-Aref's early years and how the experience of World War I shaped his political consciousness, see Tamari, *Year of the Locust*, 63–85. Tamari mentions that al-Aref, like Issaf Nashashibi, was a member of the nationalist political organization named "The Arab Club" that sought to unify Syria (including its southern portion, Palestine) and fight Zionism: ibid., 77–78.

108. A. H. Elhanani, "Nose dvaram vehelekh ruham shel ehav," *Bama'arakha* 81 (1968): 10. The Arabic teacher in this group was the leading Palestinian educator Khalil Sakakini.

109. Wasserstein argues, on the basis of contemporary Arab, British, and Jewish sources, as well as an interview conducted with al-Aref himself, that the latter was working in collaboration with the British Police when he faced the crowd on his horse and that he was seeking to mollify rather than aggravate the situation. Nevertheless, the British government and Zionist figures in the *Yishuv* later presented him as one of the primary inciters of the events.

110. These secret relations were eventually discovered, and al-Aref was reprimanded. See Wasserstein, "'Clipping the Claws of the Colonisers,'" 181–82.

111. Elyakim Rubinstein, "Hatipul bashe'ela ha'aravit bishnot ha'esrim vehashloshim: Hebetim mosdiyim," *Hatziyonut* 12 (1987): 222n51.

112. Menahem Kapeliuk, "'Im ishiut dgula beRamallah: Aref al-Aref ba'al 'avar 'ashir," *Davar*, June 30, 1967, 9–10.

NOTES TO CHAPTER 2 ::: 225

113. "Pgishat 'itona'im 'ivrim ve'aravim," *Hatzofe*, February 23, 1941, 1.

114. The books were translated by the journalist and HUSOS student Menahem Kapeliuk (1900–1988). Kapeliuk had previously translated Taha Hussein's autobiographical book *Days* (1929) into Hebrew.

115. David Werner Senator to Shertok, December 8, 1940, CZA, S25/6724.

116. "Aref al-Aref ore'ah ha'universita ha'ivrit," *Haboker*, May 9, 1941, 8.

117. "Minhagim bamidbar (hartza'at hamelumad ha'aravi mar Aref al-Aref mita'am hamakhon lemdad'ey hamizrah shel ha'universita ha'ivrit)," *Ha'olam*, August 21, 1941, 4–6. His lecture appeared in full within this weekly, which was the official newspaper of the World Zionist Organization.

118. An off-the-cuff remark about meeting the former mayor of Jerusalem, Raghib Nashashibi, for example, February 8, 1944 (ANLI, Arc. 4° 1911/02/12). Menachem Klein cites the testimony of the researcher and publicist Rada Carmi that Goitein invited her father Hassan Carmi, his coworker at the Department of Education, to participate in a Brit Shalom meeting, but that he came home unimpressed with the event: Klein, *Lives in Common: Arabs and Jews in Jerusalem, Jaffa, and Hebron*, trans. Haim Watzman (New York: Oxford University Press, 2014), 78–79.

119. An example of this is the close intellectual friendship between Martin Plessner—who joined HUSOS only in the late 1940s but was tied to the institution years earlier—and the lawyer and literary scholar Iskandar al-Khoury al-Beitjali, who leased Plessner and his family the apartment in which they lived in the Qatamon neighborhood: Amit Levy, "A Man of Contention: Martin Plessner (1900–1973) and His Encounters with the Orient," *Naharaim* 10, no. 1 (2016): 95–96. Friendly terms, of course, could precede an interest in Oriental Studies as well, for example in the case of the Jerusalem-born Yosef Rivlin, who maintained good relations with acquaintances from his childhood and adolescence after joining the institute: Hanan Harif, "Islam in Zion? Yosef Yo'el Rivlin's Translation of the Qur'an and Its Place Within the New Hebrew Culture," *Naharaim* 10, no. 1 (2016): 40–41. Menahem Klein explains that, though changing living situations after expansion beyond the Old City walls—from a compound with a joint courtyard to modern, spacious family homes —also changed the type of contact between Jews and Arabs in Jerusalem, meetings between the two in business, work, and leisure areas were typically "warm and friendly." Klein, *Lives in Common*, 80.

120. Ran, *Ha'aravist*, 334–36.

121. Hareli and Sasson to Shertok, January 5, 1936, CZA, S25/3106.

122. Yehuda Koren, "55 shana shimarti et tza'ar moto," *Ha'aretz*, August 30, 1991, 25–26; "Birkat student 'aravi shel ha'universita," *Ha'aretz*, February 20, 1940, 6.

123. After 1967 and the Israeli occupation of East Jerusalem, al-Nubani renewed his contacts with a number of former fellow students and found work as a translator in the courts. His poetic Hebrew and interest in Jewish texts made him a somewhat popular subject in the Israeli press during these years. See, for example, Ehud Ya'ari, "Metargem hamishna le'aravit—mehusar 'avoda," *Davar*, July 31, 1967, 3; Ya'akov Edelstein, "Hamdi Nubani: Metargem hamishna le'aravit," *Hatzofe*, February 16, 1968, 4. In the late 1940s, on the other hand, al-Nubani's attempts to make inroads within

226 ::: NOTES TO CHAPTER 2

Jewish society in Jerusalem were met with a cold shoulder; the Haganah forbade him entry to Jewish neighborhoods: "Ma'ase be'aravi shenitpas meshotet balayla birushalayim ha'ivrit," *Hatzofe*, December 26, 1947, 1.

124. The only Palestinian Arab who studied at HUSOS except for al-Nubani was a student by the name of Muhammad Yunis al-Husseini (during the 1930–31 academic year, before al-Nubani). He seems to have been a native of Jerusalem, born in 1910, and also never completed his degree at HUSOS; he studied at the Arab College, completed his Economics course of study at the American University of Beirut in 1929 and worked as an economist and banker in Jerusalem and Cairo: Mu'asasat al-Quds lil-thaqafa wal-turath, "Muhammad Yunis al-Husseini," https://alqudslana .com/index.php?action=individual_details&id=1987. Al-Nubani and al-Husseini's names appear on the aforementioned alphabetical list of non-Jewish students at the Hebrew University drawn up in 1938: CAHU, 21/I:1938. No later list is known. The only other Arab name on this list is that of Sami Wafa al-Dajani, a student of Inorganic Chemistry. Not on this list is Jamal al-Muzaffar: Yosef Rivlin recalled that Sheikh 'Abd al-Qadir al-Muzaffar—who had been among the leaders of the Arab national movement in Jerusalem in the late Ottoman period—had urged his nephew Jamal to study Quran interpretations with Rivlin as a student at the Hebrew University: Y. Y. Rivlin, "Beit Hashem bama'arbolet," *Hed hamizrah*, March 17, 1950, 4. On the elder al-Muzaffar, who sought to mollify the rage at the beginning of the 1929 Palestine Riots in Jaffa, and met Rivlin when both were staying in Damascus at the end of World War I, see Cohen, *Year Zero*, 24–25.

125. Shamir, "Kishrey hinukh vetarbut," 99. According to Shamir, attempts to encourage student exchanges in other fields of study had only limited success, for example the arrival of two Egyptians to study mathematics on Mount Scopus.

126. *Who's Who in the Arab World 2007–2008*, 18th ed. (Beirut: Publitec and K. G. Saur München, 2007), 848. In 1966, during his time in Beirut, Zaza made contact with his teacher S. D. Goitein, who had already immigrated to the United States. The two corresponded in Hebrew and invited each other to return visits in Philadelphia and Beirut, though Goitein recognized the obstacles that might be involved. See the correspondence at ANLI, Arc. 4° 1911/01/49, Arc. 4° 1911/01/56.

127. Muhammad 'Atiyat, "Muhammad Salim al-Rashdan.. Hams al-dhikrayat," *al-Rai*, December 5, 2008, http://alrai.com/article/309682/.

128. "De'otav shel student 'aravi ba'universita ha'ivrit," *Hamashkif*, April 4, 1946, 4.

129. This according to an interview conducted with al-Rashdan in 1995 and quoted in Hisham Fawzi Abd al-Aziz, "Ma'had al-'ulum al-sharqiyya fil-jami'a al-'ibriyya fil-quds 1926–1948," *'Alam al-fikr* 1 (1997): 257.

130. "De'otav shel student." No echoes of this episode were uncovered at the archive of the Hebrew University.

131. Caroline Kahlenberg, "The Star of David in a Cedar Tree: Jewish Students and Zionism at the American University of Beirut (1908–1948)," *Middle Eastern Studies* 55, no. 4 (2019): 573.

132. On Jewish and Zionist activities at the American University of Beirut, see ibid.

NOTES TO CHAPTER 2 ::: 227

133. David Neustadt (Ayalon) to Goitein, March 29, 1934, ANLI, Arc. 4° 1911/03/121; Ayalon, "Mistudent legimlai 1932–1994," *Igeret ha'akademia hale'umit hayisra'elit lemada'im* 24 (2003): 39. In this short autobiographical article, Ayalon names the students, in chronological order: Aviva Tourovsky-Landman, Ayalon himself who was in Beirut during the spring and summer of 1935, Eliyahu Barak (Burak), Uriel Heyd, and Gabriel Baer. Another student of the institute, Eliahu Epstein (Elath), left HUSOS in 1931 and began a course of study at the AUB, which he completed in 1934. According to Ayalon, Meir Jacob Kister also made his way to Beirut, but unrelated to the Hebrew University.

134. Ibid., 40.

135. Kahlenberg, "Star of David," 578.

136. Yegar, *Toldot hamahlaka hamedinit*, 160, 214. On Epstein and his connections with various figures in the Jewish Agency during his time in Lebanon, see Rubinstein, "Hatipul bashe'ela ha'aravit," 221. As for Aviva Tourovsky, in Beirut she met Amos Landman, a student and math teacher at the American University who also passed reports along to the Jewish Agency. The two later married (Mahmoud Muhareb, "Zionist Disinformation Campaign in Syria and Lebanon during the Palestinian Revolt, 1936–1939," *Journal of Palestine Studies* 42, no. 2 [2013]: 9). David Ayalon and Uriel Heyd also joined the Political Department during the 1930s after returning from Beirut and completing their studies.

137. Taha Hussein served as dean of the Humanities Faculty at the University of Cairo, which Lutfi al-Sayyid headed at the time of his participation in the 1925 ceremony. Hussein idolized Lutfi and the two corresponded for many years: Abdelrashid Mahmoudi, *Taha Husain's Education: From Al Azhar to the Sorbonne* (Surrey: Curzon, 1998), 225.

138. "D. Hussein Fawzi.. yuhadir fi isra'il!!"

139. For a discussion of the accusations leveled at Taha Hussein, see Shalash, "Taha Hussein wal-as'ila al-muriba," *Shu'un 'adabiyya* 24 (1993): 16–39. Shalash focuses primarily on Hussein's involvement in the journal *al-Katib al-Misri*, published by the Jewish Harari family, and concluded that Hussein did not support the Zionist project. The debate over Hussein's connection with Zionism is ongoing, and his most vitriolic critics point, for one, to his visit to Mount Scopus. For an example from 2016, see Yasir Bakr, "Taha Hussein wal-Sahyuniyya," Masr al-'arabiyya, May 8, 2016, https://masralarabia.net/.

140. Eliahu Epstein to Bernard [Dov] Yosef, December 13, 1942, CZA, S25/7516.

141. Ernst Simon to Dr. [Yitzhak] Levi, March 8, Ernst Simon to Epstein, March 26, 1935, CZA, S25/6721. Yitzhak (Isacco) Giuseppe Levi (1878–1961), born in Istanbul before moving to Egypt in the early twentieth century, was a statistician and economic researcher, a member of the Steering Committee for the Cairo Friends of the Hebrew University and other organizations active in Egypt's Jewish community. Levi had connections with various forces in the Egyptian government, including Prince (later King) Fuad. See Uri M. Kupferschmidt, "Memory and History: 'Uncle Isaac' and/or Dr. Isacco Giuseppe Levi," Lecture given on the occasion of the inauguration of the Barda Chair for the Study of the History of Egyptian Jewry,

228 ::: NOTES TO CHAPTER 2

University of Haifa, October 14, 2013, http://srjhechair.haifa.ac.il/images/pdf/lecture
_English.pdf.

142. In November 1931, Hussein bin Faydullah al-Hamdani (1901–1962)—born
in the Indian town of Surat to a Yemenite family belonging to the Shi'a-Ismailite
sect—reached Jerusalem. He spent a month visiting Palestine on his way back to
India after completing his doctorate at the University of London in 1931 (his studies
also took him to Heidelberg and Berlin) under the supervision of the Orientalist
Hamilton A. R. Gibb (1895–1971) on the subject of Ismaili writings from fifteenth-
century Yemen. Gibb was in contact with scholars at HUSOS in Jerusalem, and
may have assisted in arranging a lecture for al-Hamdani at the Hebrew University,
which dealt with unknown Arab Ismaili essays and were based on manuscripts in
the possession of his family, which had also been central sources for his doctorate:
Farhad Daftary, "Al Hamdani, Husayn F. (1901–1962)," in *Historical Dictionary of
the Ismailis* (Lanham: The Scarecrow Press, 2012), 64–65. Several months after the
lecture, Magnes asked Baneth to draft a short message about the Muslim scholar's
visit; Baneth, skeptical, agreed to write something "about Dr. Hamdani and his
lecture for publication abroad, but not within the country [of Palestine], because this
might provoke unwanted attacks on the man in the Arabic press": Baneth to Magnes,
January 29, 1933, CAHU, 226:1933. Nonetheless, the lecture was published in full as
an article in the *Journal of the Royal Asiatic Society* (Al-Hamdani, "Some Unknown
Isma'ili Authors") a year and a half later, where a note described it as the proceedings
of a lecture given at the Hebrew University of Jerusalem. He and Baneth remained in
contact after the visit, and exchanged drafts of articles they had written: Al-Hamdani
to Baneth, September 4, 1932, ANLI, Arc. 4° 1559/03/17.

143. When L. A. Mayer was invited by the government of Persia to participate
in the celebrations of a millennium since the birth of the Persian national poet
Ferdowsi, he, too, asked the university administration explicitly not to announce
the fact: "The significance of the invitation of a Shi'a Islamic government (and
certainly official in this case) is quite clear and as such I ask, Sir, that you be sure not
to mention *anything* until the celebrations have concluded" (Mayer to the Hebrew
University Administration, March 29, 1934, CAHU, Personnel File—Leo Aryeh
Mayer, Years 1926–1945).

144. Josef Horovitz, "Vorschläge für die Errichtung eines Institute of Arabic and
Islamic Studies in Jerusalem," May 14, 1925, CAHU, 91:1925–27.

145. Mangold-Will, "Josef Horovitz und die Gründung," 30n62.

146. Ibid., 29.

147. Marchand, *German Orientalism in the Age of Empire*, 224. According to
Marchand, these Lektors were "ill-compensated." To the best of Mangold-Will's
knowledge, "this was the first time in the global history of western-influenced
universities that a European professor seriously asked that 'an Oriental' [*Orientalen*]
be appointed a professor, and thus a colleague": Mangold-Will, "Josef Horovitz und
die Gründung," 29. While this conclusion is not strictly accurate—Arab and European
professors both taught at the AUB, for example, where the administrators were
American—it was nevertheless a precedent for universities in the German tradition.

NOTES TO CHAPTER 2 ::: 229

148. Horovitz to Magnes, July 8, 1925, CAHU, 91:1925-27.

149. Summary of HUSOS meeting, March 17, 1926, CAHU, 91:1925–27.

150. Summary of HUSOS meeting, April 22, 1926, CAHU, 91:1925–27.

151. Horovitz to Weizmann, October 23, 1926, CAHU, 91:1925–27.

152. Billig to Magnes, November 8, 1926, CAHU, 91:1925–27.

153. Baneth to Hebrew University administration, n.d. (in response to a letter of November 16, 1926), ANLI, Arc. 4° 1559/03/17.

154. Levi Billig, "Memorandum on Research," late 1926, CAHU, 91:1925–27.

155. Billig to Magnes, May 23, 1927, CAHU, 91:1925–27. On the weaknesses identified by German-Jewish Orientalists in the study of Arabic in Hebrew-language schools (and especially at the Reali School in Haifa) and the efforts made over the course of the 1930s to bring them up to Western academic standards, see Yonatan Mendel, "From German Philology to Local Usability: The Emergence of 'Practical' Arabic in the Hebrew Reali School in Haifa—1913–48," *Middle Eastern Studies* 52, no. 1 (2016): 1–26, especially 2–12.

156. Shlomo Ginzberg to Billig, May 17, 1927; and Billig to Magnes, June 1, 1927, CAHU, 91:1925–27.

157. Billig to Magnes, May 23, 1927; and Billig to Ginzberg, May 23, 1927, CAHU, 91:1925–27.

158. Billig to Ginzberg, January 29, 1928, CAHU, 91alef:1928.

159. Magnes to Horovitz, August 14, 1927, CAHU, 91:1925–1927.

160. On the establishment and goals of the foundation see Michael Rosenthal, *Nicholas Miraculous: The Amazing Career of the Redoubtable Dr. Nicholas Murray Butler* (New York: Columbia University Press, 2005), 156–71.

161. Nicholas Murray Butler to Magnes, November 3, 1927, CAHU, 91alef:1928.

162. Ginzberg to the instructors of HUSOS, March 16, 1928, CAHU, 91alef:1928.

163. "List of proposals considered by the university regarding the expansion of the operations of the School of Oriental Studies," July 1, 1928, CAHU, 91alef:1928.

164. Magnes to Cyrus Adler, November 12, 1928, CAHU, 91alef:1928.

165. Billig to Magnes, January 28, 1929, CAHU, 91alef:1928.

166. Ben-Israel, "Bi-Nationalism versus Nationalism," 93.

167. On these trends, see Avraham Sela, "The 'Wailing Wall' Riots (1929) as a Watershed in the Palestine Conflict," *The Muslim World* 84, no. 1–2 (1994): 60–94. The title of Hillel Cohen's book on the subject describes 1929 as "Year Zero of the Arab-Israeli Conflict."

168. Abraham Shalom Yahuda, "Madu'a nimna haprofessor Yahuda lehartzot ba'universita ha'ivrit," *Do'ar hayom*, May 21, 1929, 4.

169. M. A. [Michael Assaf], "Hamakhon lemada'ey hamizrah," *Davar*, March 30, 1933, 3.

170. Philip Hartog, Louis Ginzberg, and Redcliffe Salaman, *Report of the Survey Committee of the Hebrew University of Jerusalem* (Jerusalem: The Hebrew University, 1934), 21–22.

171. Herein lay the gap between the Hebrew name of the institute, literally "The Institute for Oriental Studies," and its English moniker, "School of Oriental Studies,"

230 ::: NOTES TO CHAPTER 2

which in the eyes of the committee members—Philip Hartog himself was among the founders of the School of Oriental and African Studies in London (SOAS)—had more to do with training than research.

172. Ibid., 21.

173. Ben-David to Gotthold Weil, July 27, 1934, CAHU, 226: 1934.

174. Max Weber, "Science as a Vocation," in *The Vocation Lectures*, trans. Rodney Livingstone (Indianapolis: Hackett Publishing, 2004), 1–31.

175. HUSOS students to the Hebrew University Executive Board, February 9, 1936, CAHU, 226: 1936.

176. On the militarization of the *Yishuv* beginning in 1936, see Uri Ben-Eliezer, *The Making of Israeli Militarism* (Bloomington: Indiana University Press, 1998), especially the first portion of the book dealing with the years 1936–1942.

177. S. D. Goitein, "Mada'ey hamizrah ba'universita ha'ivrit," *Davar*, April 10, 1935, 12.

178. The changes demanded included cancelling the required course on Islamic archeology. At least judging by the biting response he sent to Magnes, this was a clear blow to Mayer, who was in charge of instruction on the subject: July 15, 1936, CAHU, 2261:1936.

179. Meeting 24 of the Standing Committee of the Academic Senate, April 27, 1936, CAHU, Protocol of the Standing Committee Folder.

180. M. Schneersohn to Mayer, January 6, 1937, CAHU, 2262:1937.

181. "Levayato shel Dr. Levi Billig z"l," *Ha'aretz*, August 23, 1936, 1–2. On the fate of Billig's unfinished studies, see Roy Vilozny, "Levi Billig vehelko he'alum beheker hitpathut hashi'a," *Hamizrah hehadash* 60 (2021): 71–98.

182. An editorial in the newspaper *Filastin* said after the murder: "We are filled with sorrow at the killing of the lecturer Billig, who was known for the breadth of his knowledge and his expertise in Arabic literature, but this sorrow does not prevent us from repeating what we have said, that the Jews and the [British] government are the ones who embarked upon a policy of attacking the innocent": *Filastin*, August 23, 1936, 3; see also Yehuda Litani, "Mi ratzah et Levi Billig," *Ha'aretz*, September 11, 1992. The archive of the Political Department of the Jewish Agency contains transcriptions of intercepted conversations that took place in the home of Jerusalem's mayor at the time, Hussein al-Khalidi; in one, his conversation partner, the ethnographer and political activist Omar al-Salih al-Barghouti, expressed sorrow at the killing of Billig, "among the best friends of mine and your brother Ahmed [Ahmed Samih al-Khalidi, director of the Arab College]." Al-Barghouti is also overheard saying that "the death of such people is a loss to humanity": conversation from August 21, 1936, 1:00 PM, CZA, S25/3769.

183. Shimon Garidi, "'Al limud mada'ey hamizrah ba'universita ha'ivrit (divrey student)," *Davar*, April 2, 1936, 4. The writer, Shimon Garidi (1912–2003), became a teacher, scholar of Yemenite Jewry, and a member of the Israeli Knesset.

184. Excerpt of discussion of the Standing Committee of the Academic Senate, January 18, 1937, CAHU, Personnel File—Isaac Shamosh, until 1967.

185. Esther Moyal to Goitein, March 31, 1937, ANLI, Arc. 4° 1911/03/52. On the

NOTES TO CHAPTER 2 ::: 231

intellectual circles in which Moyal operated and her movements between Lebanon, Egypt, Palestine, and France, see Lital Levy, "Partitioned Pasts: Arab Jewish Intellectuals and the Case of Esther Azhari Moyal (1873-1948)," in *The Making of the Arab Intellectual (1880-1960): Empire, Public Sphere, and the Colonial Coordinates of Selfhood*, ed. Dyalah Hamzah (London: Routledge, 2012), 128–63.

186. Michael Assaf to Magnes, May 2, 1943, CAHU, Personnel File—Isaac Shamosh, until 1967. The biographical details on Shamosh that follow were collected from various documents in his personnel file at CAHU.

187. Ginzberg to Shamosh, January 29, 1937, CAHU, Personnel File—Isaac Shamosh, until 1967.

188. Goitein to Shamosh, March 2, Goitein to the rector, July 4, Mayer to the rector, June 22, 1937, CAHU, Personnel File—Isaac Shamosh, until 1967.

189. When the question of Shamosh's salary was raised in 1943, the university administrator D. W. Senator explained: "The problem is that other institutions that were supposed to give him additional work are not giving him that work": Senator to Michael Assaf, May 10, 1943, CAHU, Personnel File—Isaac Shamosh, until 1967; he had corresponded with Moshe Shertok in 1940 to ask if the Political Department would be able to employ Shamosh for propaganda work and drafting articles in Arabic: Senator to Shertok, [probably June] 1940, CZA, S25/3114. The question of Shamosh's status and the pay he deserved continued to come up even after he had completed his doctoral studies at the Hebrew University, eventually leading to the early retirement of Baneth, at least partially in protest against the conditions of Shamosh's employment: Baneth to Poznansky, May 11, 1959, CAHU, Personnel File—David Zvi Baneth, until 1960.

190. Goitein to the Hebrew University Administration, June 28, 1938, CAHU, Personnel File—Isaac Shamosh, until 1967.

191. Mayer to Senator, September 10, 1942, CAHU, Personnel File—Isaac Shamosh, until 1967.

192. Regarding precision, Shamosh himself claimed in the early 1940s that most of the teachers of Arabic in Palestine were not sufficiently qualified to carry out their jobs. See Jacobson and Naor, *Oriental Neighbors*, 111.

193. Ibid., 9.

194. Yehouda Shenhav, *The Arab Jews: A Postcolonial Reading of Nationalism, Religion, and Ethnicity* (Stanford: Stanford University Press, 2006); Gil Eyal, *The Disenchantment of the Orient: Expertise in Arab Affairs and the Israeli State* (Stanford: Stanford University Press, 2006).

195. Eyal, *Disenchantment of the Orient*, 7–8, 10.

196. Due to Shamosh's partial appointment, he continued to hold other positions —at the Political Department, in the Arabic News Division of the Israeli "Kol Yerushalyim" radio (which he headed for a short time), and eventually in Israel's Ministry of Justice, where he was in charge of the editing and improvement of Arabic records.

197. One of his students in the 1950s, Yohanan Friedmann, notes that "the literature classes were characterized by an exaggerated emphasis on the biography

232 ::: NOTES TO CHAPTER 3

of the writers, almost completely ignoring the content of their books . . . however, I saw great value in Shamosh's wonderful ability to give eloquent lectures in flawless literary Arabic . . . we were all enthused by this rare ability, and in translation exercises we tried to inherit some of the marvelous talents with which Shamosh was blessed." Yohanan Friedmann, *MiZákamenné lirushalayim: Pirkey zikaron* (Jerusalem: self-pub., 2019), 67.

198. Al-Habash was authorized to serve as a *qadi* and worked as the secretary of the Shari'a court in Haifa and Tiberias. In 1948, he fled from Haifa to Nazareth and was appointed the *qadi* of Nazareth by the State of Israel: Alisa Rubin Peled, *Debating Islam in the Jewish State: The Development of Policy Toward Islamic Institutions in Israel* (Albany: State University of New York Press, 2001), 160.

199. Hassan [Amin] al-Habash to the rector of the Hebrew University, January 22, 1938, CAHU, 165:1938.

200. Ben-David to al-Habash, February 15, 1938, CAHU, 165:1938.

201. Al-Habash to Ben-David, March 2; Senator to al-Habash, March 9; al-Habash to Ben-David, March 20; al-Habash to Ben-David, April 3; al-Habash to Ben-David, May 6, 1938, CAHU, 165:1938.

202. On al-Khalidi's relations with Magnes see Furas, *Educating Palestine*, 66.

203. Conversation with Ahmed Samih al-Khalidi, Director of the Arab College, Jerusalem, December 5, 1946, from the Private Archive of Alexander Lutzky-Dotan. My thanks to Hillel Cohen for providing me with this document.

204. Derek J. Penslar, *Zionism and Technocracy: The Engineering of the Jewish Settlement in Palestine, 1870–1918* (Bloomington: Indiana University Press, 1991), 14.

205. Moshe Brill, Pessah Schusser, and David Neustadt to Moshe Shertok, October 22, 1940, CZA, S25/22165.

206. Ibid. The publication of this edition was part of a developing trend in the late 1930s and throughout the 1940s, when a series of textbooks and "collated" booklets based on excerpts from the Arabic press were published. See Mendel, "German Orientalism, Arabic Grammar," 70.

207. For portrayals of connections of this type in recent scholarship, see Halperin, *Babel in Zion*, 142–80; Jacobson and Naor, *Oriental Neighbors*, 86–120. An outstanding figure in this regard was the Oriental expert Israel Ben-Ze'ev. As noted in the previous chapter, he was also occasionally at odds with HUSOS personnel, especially after his appointment as Inspector of Arabic Instruction. Nevertheless, at various points during the Mandate period, he was involved in crafting relations between the university and Arab scholars, for example around celebrations of the ten-year anniversary of the establishment of the university: Ernst Simon to Eliahu Epstein, March 26, 1935, CZA, S25/6721.

208. Halperin, *Babel in Zion*, 157–58.

209. Baneth to Assaf, April 27, 1946, CZA, S25/9069.

3. ORIENT RENEWED

1. "Prof. L. A. Mayer mesaye'a lamemshala," December 27, 1948, CAHU, Personnel File—L. A. Mayer, 1946–1954.

# NOTES TO CHAPTER 3 ::: 233

2. On the study of Islam and the Middle East in Germany between 1933 and 1945, see Ursula Wokoeck, *German Orientalism: The Study of the Middle East and Islam from 1800 to 1945* (London: Routledge, 2009), 185–209; for a detailed discussion of the fate of the Orientalist chair at the University of Frankfurt after the departure of Josef Horovitz's successor, Gotthold Weil, see Gudrun Jäger, "Der jüdische Islamwissenschaftler Josef Horovitz und der Lehrstuhl für semitische Philologie an der Universität Frankfurt am Main 1915-1949," in *Frankfurter Wissenschaftler zwischen 1933 und 1945*, ed. Jörn Kobes and Jan-Otmar Hesse (Göttingen: Wallstein, 2008), 71–75.

3. This is evident from the 1948/49 catalog, in which most of the courses—not only in the Department of Arabic Language and Literature, but also in the Department of Islamic Culture—involved the reading of classical sources (List of courses in the Faculty of Humanities for 1948/49, CAHU, 2120:1949). Among the courses added were Lessons in Practical Arabic with Isaac Shamosh and Arabic Newspaper Reading Practicum taught by Yosef Rivlin.

4. On the formation of the demilitarized exclave on Mount Scopus and the political, legal, and spatial issues resulting from its unique status, see Theodor Meron, "The Demilitarization of Mount Scopus: A Regime That Was," *Israel Law Review* 3, no. 4 (1968): 501–25; Yfaat Weiss, *Niemandsland: Hader am Berg Scopus* (Göttingen: Vandenhoeck & Ruprecht, 2021).

5. Regarding the temporary relocation to the Terra Sancta Compound and the difficulties this entailed, see Marik Shtern, "Ben shney harim: Hakampus ha'ironi shel ha'universita ha'ivrit," in *Toldot ha'universita ha'ivrit birushalayim*, ed. Yfaat Weiss and Uzi Rebhun, vol. 5: *Medinat hale'om vehahaskala hagvoha* (Jerusalem: The Hebrew University Magnes Press, 2024), 175–205.

6. The term "budgetary formula" was coined by Adi Livny to emphasize the functional rather than the ideological elements of the relationship between the university and the state. Livny, "Ha'universita, hamedina umishva'at hatiktzuv," in *Toldot ha'universita ha'ivrit birushalayim*, ed. Yfaat Weiss and Uzi Rebhun, vol. 5: *Medinat hale'om vehahaskala hagvoha* (Jerusalem: The Hebrew University Magnes Press, 2024), 71–114.

7. Prominent examples of this include: Gil Eyal, *The Disenchantment of the Orient: Expertise in Arab Affairs and the Israeli State* (Stanford: Stanford University Press, 2006); Yonatan Mendel, *The Creation of Israeli Arabic: Political and Security Considerations in the Making of Arabic Language Studies in Israel* (London: Palgrave Macmillan, 2014); Doron Matza, *He'asor shebo noldu 'arveiyey yisra'el': Yisra'el ve'ezrahea ha'aravim-falastinim 1966–1976* (Tel Aviv: Resling, 2022); Eyal Clyne, *Orientalism, Zionism and Academic Practice: Middle East and Islam Studies in Israeli Universities* (London: Routledge, 2019).

8. Matza, *He'asor shebo noldu 'arveiyey yisra'el'*, 53. See also Omri Shafer Raviv, "Studying an Occupied Society: Social Research, Modernization Theory and the Early Israeli Occupation, 1967-8," *Journal of Contemporary History* 55, no. 1 (2020): 161–81.

9. Menaham Milson, "The Beginnings of Arabic and Islamic Studies at the Hebrew University of Jerusalem," *Judaism* 45, no. 2 (Spring 1996): 178.

234 ::: NOTES TO CHAPTER 3

10. The journal's official English title was initially *The Modern East* and later *The New East*, as the Hebrew *hadash* could potentially translate to both.

11. When Mayer set off in March 1949, the rector asked Goitein to serve as head of the institute in his place (Ernst Simon to Goitein, March 6, 1949, CAHU, 226:1949). As he was preparing to return, Mayer gave notice that he did not intend to return to the role of institute director, at which point the Executive Committee decided to officially appoint Goitein to the position (Goitein to the university administration, October 15, 1949, CAHU, 226:1949).

12. Uri Cohen and Adi Sapir, "Models of Academic Governance during a Period of Nation-Building: The Hebrew University in the 1920s–1960s," *History of Education* 45, no. 5 (2016): 608, 611.

13. Livny, "Ha'universita," 74.

14. Cohen and Sapir, "Models of Academic Governance," 615.

15. Livny, "Ha'universita," 89–91.

16. Cohen and Sapir, "Models of Academic Governance," 616.

17. I am using the term "Statism" as a translation of the Hebrew term *mamlakhtiyut*, a concept closely associated with David Ben-Gurion but with broader contextual implications. For an in-depth exploration of the term and its political and theoretical origins, see Kedar, "Ben-Gurion's *Mamlakhtiyut*." Acknowledging the potential limitations of any English translation in capturing the full essence of the Hebrew term, Kedar opts for its transliterated form. According to him, Ben-Gurion's *mamlakhtiyut* drew upon European, and particularly Russian, democratic-republican ideals of the late nineteenth and early twentieth centuries: ibid., 122–25.

18. Goitein to university administration, [October 15, 1949].

19. This was the case, for example, with the books provided by David Ayalon, although in effect he borrowed them from the Foreign Ministry library (Ayalon to the university curriculum committee, January 1, 1950, CAHU, 2262:1950). The last of the books were returned to the Foreign Ministry library only nine years later (Helena Flaum to the School of Oriental Studies, August 6, 1958, CAHU, 222:1957–1958; Nissim Tokatly to the Financial Department of the Foreign Ministry, January 9, 1959, CAHU, 222:1959).

20. In a 2011 article, later integrated into a 2014 Hebrew book, Gish Amit explores the library's collection practices, providing a critical analysis. He proposes a bifurcated interpretation of the book collection process: on the one hand, it saved the books from an even more bitter fate, and in effect also preserved evidence of the Arab presence in Palestine; on the other hand, Amit claims, it confiscated and appropriated the books from their original owners under the pretext of bringing the Enlightenment to a failed region, removing cultural treasures from their rightful owners who were considered incapable of providing them with the proper care. See Amit, "Salvage or Plunder? Israel's 'Collection' of Private Palestinian Libraries in West Jerusalem," *Journal of Palestine Studies* 40, no. 4 (2011): 6–23. Among other criticisms, critics argued that the book's claims were overly general and rested on a limited and unrepresentative base of archival evidence: Zeev Gries, "Adding Insult to Injury: Zionist Cultural Colonialism," *Judaica Librarianship* 19 (2016): 82–86.

NOTES TO CHAPTER 3 ::: 235

A recent study on the history of the library after 1948 and the severance of Mount Scopus emphasizes the contemporaneous evidence located in the institution's archive: it suggests that the book collection endeavor, undertaken in the midst of the war, was seen by those involved primarily as a project of rescue from ongoing acts of looting, and also provided the opportunity to strengthen the relationship between the university and the state: Anna Holzer-Kawalko and Enrico Lucca, "Sifriyat hagola: Tkumat beit hasfarim hale'umi birushalayim vekibutz ha'osafim," in *Toldot ha'universita ha'ivrit birushalayim*, ed. Yfaat Weiss and Uzi Rebhun, vol. 5: *Medinat hale'om vehahaskala hagvoha* (Jerusalem: The Hebrew University Magnes Press, 2024), 719–66. See also Amit Levy, "A Man of Contention: Martin Plessner (1900–1973) and His Encounters with the Orient," *Naharaim* 10, no. 1 (2016): 93–97.

21. Shlomo Shunami, a representative of the library, recounted the visit he made together with D. H. Baneth to the abandoned home of Tawfiq Canaan in the Musrara neighborhood. The dry description describes how, in spite of the danger, they reached the house in order to find books related to the study of "Palestinian folklore" (*hafolklor ha'e[retz]-y[isra'eli]*), which had apparently already been looted, since Shunami says "we found no trace of the folkloristic library." The pair recommended no more chances be taken in order to remove the books that were left in this library—German classical literature alongside medical books and manuscripts. The archival record does not preserve any documentation kept by Baneth himself on the visit to the abandoned home of Canaan—who was, as the previous chapter illustrated, friendly with L. A. Mayer (Shunami to Senator, August 10, 1948, CAHU, 042:1948–1949).

22. HUSOS meeting protocols, January 26 and February 16, 1950, CAHU, 2260:1950.

23. Curt Wormann to L. Briskman, October 19, 1949, CAHU, Personnel File—Meir Plessner, until 1958. HUSOS doctoral student Yehoshua Blau worked alongside Plessner.

24. Shlomo Shunami's report for the administration of the National and University Library surveying the collection of books from abandoned neighborhoods in Jerusalem by the library between May 1948 and March 1949, March 13, 1949, CAHU, 042:1948–1949, 5.

25. Ian Black and Benny Morris, *Israel's Secret Wars: A History of Israel's Intelligence Services* (New York: Grove Weidenfeld, 1991), 42–3.

26. Levy, "A Man of Contention," 83.

27. Among other tactics seeking to advance the process, which was complicated by the large amount of material, Goitein sought to mobilize support from various international sources who had shown an interest in them. He tried to leverage a 1952 visit by the Swedish theologian Helmer Ringgren (1917–2012) to the Mount Scopus exclave, where he was slated to work on the concordance materials with the permission of the military, into an operation to remove the materials from the mount under the auspices of the Swedish Consulate. This effort does not seem to have borne fruit: Goitein to Schwabe, May 12, and to military officials, June 7, 1952, CAHU, 226:1952.

28. S. D. Goitein, "Matzav hamakhon lemada'ey hamizrah behar hatzofim,"

236 ::: NOTES TO CHAPTER 3

following his visit on March 7, 1957, CAHU, 226:1956. An agreement between Israel and Jordan was reached in early 1958 arranging for Israeli convoys to Mount Scopus to gradually remove books and research materials, including the index cards of the concordance, to the western portion of the city: Weiss, *Niemandsland*, 108–10, 126–31.

29. Quoted in Amit, "Salvage or Plunder," 11.

30. Aviv Derri, "Mizrahanut alternativit vehishtalvut bamerhav ha'aravi hamekomi: Dr. Israel Ben-Ze'ev, hasifriya ha'aravit beyafo vehama'avak 'al sfarim falastiniyim 'netushim', 1948–1952" (master's thesis, Ben-Gurion University of the Negev, 2013), 56–57. In 1952, Ben-Ze'ev's Arabic Library was closed by the state and the books in it were scattered, many of them reaching the National and University Library with the assistance of the Ministry of Education and the Bureau of the Advisor on Arab Affairs at the Prime Minister's Office.

31. "While an 'Orientalist' education is one thing, an education to do work in the Orient is another." S. D. Goitein, "Mada'ey hamizrah ba'universita ha'ivrit," *Davar*, April 10, 1935, 12.

32. On Goitein's public activities surrounding subjects connected to his Orientalist training, see, for example, Marco Di Giulio, "Protecting the Jewish Throat: Hebrew Accent and Hygiene in the Yishuv," *Journal of Israeli History* 35, no. 2 (2016): 163–66; Hanan Harif, "Infanticide, Orientalism and British Law in Mandate Palestine," *Jewish Quarterly Review* 114, no. 2 (2024): 263–92.

33. Excerpt from Humanities Faculty meeting protocol, Meeting IV, May 11, 1949, CAHU, 2262:1949.

34. Goitein to Heyd, March 1, 1949, CAHU, Personnel File—Uriel Heyd, 1949–1959. Of the numerous bureaucratic stages necessary to gain approval for the plan, Goitein wrote ruefully: "The proposal has already passed the 'Plenum' of the institute and I hope it shall successfully adorn the curriculum committee, the faculty, the Executive Committee, as well as the rest of the institutions with which our university is so well-endowed."

35. Biographical details have been taken from Ayalon's letter to Goitein, February 22, 1949, CAHU, Personnel File—David Ayalon, until 1955.

36. Aharon Layish, "Uriel Heyd's Contribution to the Study of the Legal, Religious, Cultural, and Political History of the Ottoman Empire and Modern Turkey," *British Journal of Middle Eastern Studies* 9, no. 1 (1982): 35. Kurt Levy, the brother of Heyd's mother, studied Oriental and Romance languages and, after completing his doctorate on Hebrew phonology, became a scientific assistant to the professor of Semitic languages Paul Kahle in Bonn. Levy met a tragic end: he lost his position following the Nazi racial laws but continued secretly assisting his non-Jewish replacement, with whom he was romantically involved. In practice, he took over the tasks delegated to her from Kahle, apparently as part of a private arrangement between Levy and him. At a certain point, this arrangement seems to have been exposed, and Levy took his own life in 1935, a year after his nephew arrived in Palestine: Ludmila Hanisch, *Die Nachfolger der Exegeten: Deutschsprachige Erforschung des Vorderen Orients in der ersten Hälfte des 20. Jahrhunderts* (Wiesbaden: Harrassowitz, 2003), 115–17. Levy's associate in Bonn, the Jewish writer Leah Goldberg, believed that the replacement

was a member of the Nazi party, and it is possible that she played a role in exposing the covert arrangement: Yfaat Weiss, "'A Man with His Life at Both Ends of Time': Lea Goldberg, Paul Ernst Kahle, and Appreciating the Mundane," *Yad Vashem Studies* 37, no. 1 (2009): 11–12.

37. Layish, "Uriel Heyd's Contribution," 35–36; Heyd's Curriculum Vitae, CAHU, Personnel File—Uriel Heyd, 1949–1959.

38. Moshe Yegar, "Moshe Sharett and the Origins of Israel's Diplomacy," *Israel Studies* 15, no. 3 (2010): 5–6, 8.

39. Shmuel Cohen-Shani, "Hamahlaka hamedinit shel hasokhnut hayehudit ve-'beit hasefer lediplomatim'—binuy mosdoteha shel medina hadasha," *Hatziyonut* 19 (1995): 334–41.

40. Yegar, "Moshe Sharett," 6; idem, "Moshe Shertok (Sharett) and the Jewish Agency's Political Department—Precursor to Israel's Ministry of Foreign Affairs (Part II)," *Israel Journal of Foreign Affairs* 11, no. 2 (2017): 232.

41. Goitein to Eytan, March 20, 1949, CAHU, Personnel File—David Ayalon, until 1955. We saw how HUSOS personnel were greatly concerned with the separation of science from politics as early as the institute's first decade, after the delivery of the Hartog Report. This subject, and its connection to the professional ethos of the German scientific world, is discussed in the previous chapters.

42. Compare with the cooperation between the university and the Israel Defense Forces during the first years of the state era, when an academic officer training program known as 'Atuda and an IDF medical school were established: Elad Neemani, "Ha'universita ha'ivrit vetzahal bereshit hamdina: Bein shituf pe'ula lishmira 'al otonomia mosdit," in *Toldot ha'universita ha'ivrit birushalayim*, ed. Yfaat Weiss and Uzi Rebhun, vol. 5: *Medinat hale'om vehahaskala hagvoha* (Jerusalem: The Hebrew University Magnes Press, 2024), 586–614.

43. Ayalon to Goitein, February 22, 1949.

44. Eytan to Goitein, two letters of April 1, 1949, CAHU, Personnel File—David Ayalon, until 1955. Eytan agreed on the condition that "whenever the Foreign Ministry finds itself in need of the labor of Mr. Ayalon, the latter will be made available for this"; Goitein discussed this condition with Senator, who did not think it would cause any difficulties (note from Senator to Goitein, April 26, 1949, CAHU, Personnel File—David Ayalon, until 1955).

45. Excerpts from April–June 1949 protocols, CAHU, 2262: 1949. The legist Avraham Granovsky (Granot), a member of the Provisional State Council representing the Progressive Party, noted during the Executive Committee meeting that the Foreign Ministry's opinion on the curriculum should be solicited. The Foreign Ministry, he was told, "had expressed its satisfaction with the proposed curriculum," but that it would receive final approval only after the rector confirmed that it was satisfactory to the ministry: excerpt from protocol of the Executive Committee, Meeting XIV, June 9, 1949, CAHU, 2262:1949.

46. "Tokhnit limudim lehug mishni: Hamizrah hatikhon bahove," May 15, 1949, CAHU, 226:1949. The curriculum noted that another instructor might teach the course rather than Goitein.

238 ::: NOTES TO CHAPTER 3

47. Goitein to Ayalon, July 22, 1949, CAHU, 2262:1949.

48. Transcription of interview with David Ayalon, January 22, 1990, interviewer: Margalit Bejarano, 60. The transcription is held at the Oral History Division of the Hebrew University. In the interview, conducted some forty years after the events in question, Ayalon notes of his insistence: "I think that, in doing so, I saved Islamic Studies in Israel."

49. Ibid.

50. This stands out from the list of Ayalon's publications before joining the institute as a lecturer in 1949: four articles on the Mamluk military; three articles relating to the Jews in medieval Egypt; and one study, published by the Political Department of the Jewish Agency, on "Oil and Oil Policy in the Middle East": Curriculum Vitae of David Ayalon (Neustadt), CAHU, Personnel File—David Ayalon, until 1955.

51. List of courses for 1949/50, CAHU, 2120:1949; Interview with Ayalon, January 22, 1990, 62. According to Ayalon, the lectures dealt primarily with Egypt; he decided to teach the course on Jordan in the middle of the academic year, after recognizing student interest. Since the course did not appear in the catalog, he was obliged to have it specially approved by the Curriculum Committee.

52. Statements to this effect can be found in Eyal, *Disenchantment of the Orient*, 70; Matza, *He'asor shebo noldu 'arveiyey yisra'el'*, 45; Clyne, *Orientalism, Zionism and Academic Practice*, 40.

53. Eyal, *Disenchantment of the Orient*, 71.

54. Gil Eyal believes that, with the appointments in the 1930s of Bonne and Isaac Shamosh, instructor of "Practical Arabic," senior HUSOS members already saw themselves absolved of the need to touch on these matters themselves and "did not change their teaching or research one iota" (ibid.)

55. Interview with Ayalon, January 22, 1990, 60; Goitein also clarified in the letter to Ayalon rejecting his initial request to change the name of the department, that the institute faculty were of one mind in refusing and in their justifications for doing so: Goitein to Ayalon, July 22, 1949.

56. Goitein to Eytan, July 20, 1950, CAHU, Personnel File—David Ayalon, until 1955.

57. Emphasis in original. Goitein to Heyd, April 26, 1949, CAHU, Personnel File—Uriel Heyd, 1949–1959. Unlike modern Persian, Heyd knew contemporary Turkish because of his time pursuing research in the country during his studies. See also Mayer to Poznansky, May 4, 1949, CAHU, Personnel File—David Ayalon, until 1955.

58. Correspondence between Goitein and Heyd, March 1 to April 25, 1949, CAHU, Personnel File—Uriel Heyd, 1949–1959.

59. Mayer was sorry to hear this, as he believed it more urgent for Heyd to go to Iran (Mayer to Poznansky, May 4, 1949, CAHU, Personnel File—David Ayalon, until 1955).

60. George E. Gruen, "Dynamic Progress in Turkish-Israeli Relations," *Israel Affairs* 1, no. 4 (1995): 44–45. See also Jean-Loup Samaan, *Israel's Foreign Policy beyond the Arab World: Engaging the Periphery* (London: Routledge, 2018), 47–49, as

## NOTES TO CHAPTER 3 ::: 239

well as a broader discussion on the Israeli effort to establish closer ties with non-Arab countries subsequently in this chapter.

61. Curriculum Vitae, Dr. Uriel Heyd, and letter from Goitein to the Standing Committee, November 18, 1950, CAHU, Personnel File—Uriel Heyd, 1949–1959. At this point, Heyd found himself at a crossroads: he was already wavering between a career in diplomacy or academia. In both, his superiors—Eytan and Goitein, respectively—foresaw a promising future (summary of conversation between Senator and Eytan, November 29, 1950, CAHU, Personnel File—Uriel Heyd, 1949–1959); when the mission to Iran was tabled, there was trepidation at the institute that, if he was not offered an academic position soon, his next role would be in another part of the world, distancing him from his connection with HUSOS: Goitein to the Standing Committee of the Senate, November 18, 1950.

62. Yaacov Shimoni to Goitein, August 30, 1950, CAHU, 2262:1950.

63. Sagi Barmak, "Hakamat misrad hahutz hayisra'eli, 1946–1953" (master's thesis, Hebrew University of Jerusalem, 2015), 47–51.

64. Goitein to Haim Raday, September 7, 1950, CAHU, 2262:1950.

65. Excerpt from the protocol of the Standing Committee of the Senate, April 28, 1950, and excerpt from the protocol of the Academic Senate, Meeting I, May 31, 1950, CAHU, 226:1950.

66. See, for example, Goitein to Senator, May 1, 1950, Personnel File—Uriel Heyd, 1949–1959. Among other things, they agreed that Heyd would also teach Turkish once Weil retired.

67. As early as the 1950–51 academic year, even before Heyd joined the teaching faculty, a "random census" of all those present in classes was conducted, which found fifty-eight students in the courses of the new department, the highest number of any HUSOS department; there were fifty in the courses of the Department of Arabic Language and Literature, and thirty-five in the Department of Islamic Culture: "Homer lafakulta lemada'ey haruah: Liv'ayat hitma'atut hatalmidim bemada'ey hayahadut," January 7, 1951, CAHU, 225:1951.

68. Ayalon and Heyd to the Budget Committee, May 21, 1953, CAHU, Personnel File—Gabriel Baer, until 1968.

69. Information on Baer's life has been taken from Thomas Philipp, "In Memoriam: Gabriel Baer 1919–1982," *Middle Eastern Studies* 19, no. 3 (1983): 275–76, as well as from documents in his personnel file at the Hebrew University archives. One significant aspect of his life is missing from these sources, however: while studying at the university, Baer encountered the Trotskyist circle led by his fellow student Yigael Glückstein, later Tony Cliff (1917–2000). Along with Cliff, Baer was a central member of the small "Revolutionary Communists League" (*Brit Hakommunistim Hamahapkhaniyim*), and published articles in Socialist fora under the Arab underground pen name "Munir" or "S. Munir." Little is known about his involvement in the group, but it seems that Baer, like Cliff, left Palestine for England. Baer later returned to Palestine, and while he continued to publish occasional articles under the pen name Munir, he gradually grew apart from the circle around Cliff, who became an outspoken anti-Zionist voice. By the mid-1960s Cliff had already

240 ::: NOTES TO CHAPTER 3

denounced Baer as someone who had given in to the Zionist pressures in Israel: Ian Birchall, *Tony Cliff: A Marxist for His Time* (London: Bookmarks, 2011), 56–58. The academic tributes written about Baer after his death make no mention of the Trotskyite episode in his life. On the Trotskyite circle to which Baer belonged and its place in history, see also Lutz Fiedler, *Matzpen: A History of Israeli Dissidence*, trans. Jake Schneider (Edinburgh: Edinburgh University Press, 2020), 86–102. In any case, the influence of this period is evident in Baer's selection of research questions having to do with land, economy, and agriculture.

70. Goitein to the rector, June 25, 1959, CAHU, 226:1950. Preliminary attempts to teach the spoken language seem to have been made as early as the 1940s: during the 1948–49 academic year, Shamosh taught a short practicum of one hour weekly under the title "Practicum in Colloquial Arabic Language," and even earlier in the decade, Goitein occasionally taught courses on Arabic Dialectology, on the basis of his experience studying the dialects of Yemenite Jews (Goitein to the secretariat of instruction, September 5, 1945, CAHU, 226:1945). There does not seem to have been any systematic instruction of colloquial Arabic in any case.

71. Protocol of the School of Oriental Studies faculty meeting, June 19, 1950, CAHU, 2260:1950. The "Basic Studies" program was downsized in 1953 and subsequently cancelled, as the university preferred bachelor's degree studies under the British model of specializing in two central subjects: Livny, "Ha'universita," 91–2.

72. While this was never stated explicitly, it can be surmised based on subsequent discussions that they preferred a candidate having proven prior familiarity with dialectological work according to Western research methods, of which there were none among the potential Arab candidates whose names had been given to Goitein by the Municipal Education Department of Jerusalem (the delivery of the names is mentioned in Goitein's letter to the rector, June 25, 1950).

73. The biographical details on Piamenta, whose personnel file at the Hebrew University has yet to be made available for scholarly research, are taken from Yehoshua Halamish, "Hamore le'aravit huval lamikhla'a," *Yediot aharonot*, August 11, 1964, 14; Uri Dromi, "'Aravi, daber 'aravit: Prof. Moshe Piamenta, hatan pras Israel, 1921–2012," *Ha'aretz*, August 17, 2012, 21. Another candidate, recommended by Rivlin and Ayalon, was Jacob M. Landau (1924–2020), who had also studied at HUSOS in the 1940s. Landau was an Arabic teacher and, according to Rivlin, "had a system" (Protocol of School of Oriental Studies meeting, June 19, 1950). Goitein preferred Piamenta because he spoke Arabic as a mother tongue, as detailed below, but expressed hope that Landau could also be employed at the institute in the future. This never materialized and Landau eventually found a home in the Political Science Department at the Hebrew University. On his biography see Yoav Alon and Ido Shahar, "Re'ayon 'im Prof. Jacob Landau," *Hamizrah hehadash* 58 (2019): 15–24.

74. At the meeting where he presented Piamenta as a candidate, Goitein emphasized the need for a speaker of Arabic "with an excellent accent" (Protocol from meeting of School of Oriental Studies, June 19, 1950). The pronunciation issue continued to concern Goitein in subsequent years, and in 1954 he recommended that HUSOS students sign up for an Arabic accent course, since "as a result of the complete

neglect of the mother-tongue spoken culture in our schools, our students, and not only the beginners, also pronounce the Arabic language such that one can hardly understood what they are saying or reading" (Goitein to HUSOS instructors, April 17, 1953, CAHU, 2264:1953). The course was taught by Moscow-born Irene Garbell (1901–1966), who had studied Arabic at the University of Berlin in the 1920s, where she first met Goitein, who was impressed by her powers of pronunciation ("she spoke Arabic with an accent and linguistic usage so accurate, that I thought the young Jewess from Moscow was a Syrian Arab," Goitein to Polotsky, June 9, 1964, ANLI, Arc. 4° 1911/01/32). Garbell immigrated to Palestine in 1929 and taught Hebrew and Arabic at schools and teaching seminaries, meanwhile specializing in the phonetics and phonology of Jewish dialects. Despite her extensive academic activities, for example as the first woman member of the Academy of the Hebrew Language, she was made Professor of Semitic Linguistics at the Hebrew University only in 1964: Arye Olman, "Irene Garbell—Hahavera harishona ba'akademia," *Academy of the Hebrew Language*, March 14, 2021, https://hebrew-academy.org.il/; "Ha'ala'ot ledargot professor ba'universita birushalayim," *'Al hamishmar*, July 9, 1964. 5. On Goitein's involvement in discussing the question of proper pronunciation of Hebrew, see Di Giulio, "Protecting the Jewish Throat," 163–67.

75. Alongside his work at the institute, Piamenta served as a translator between Arabic and Hebrew at the Knesset, the Israeli parliament. His fluency in colloquial Arabic was also useful when, in 1948, he served as assistant director of the Arab Department in Jerusalem for the Haganah's intelligence unit.

76. Charles A. Ferguson, "Diglossia," *Word* 15, no. 2 (1959): 325–40; Allon J. Uhlmann, *Arabic Instruction in Israel: Lessons in Conflict, Cognition and Failure* (Leiden: Brill, 2017), 24–25. The question of diglossia and its influence on the study of Arabic continues to engage both those interested in the study of Arabic and its instruction in Israel. As evidence of the continuing debate on the matter, Arabic Language and Literature Department member and former director of the Institute of Asian and African Studies, Menahem Milson, said in 2017: "Schools cannot teach everything, and therefore the decision must be one or the other: either the basics of the classical tongue, used in literature and in media throughout the Arab world, or the colloquial language—which, since there is no universal form, comes down to the particular dialect spoken in the region of the Arab world where one happens to live. To me, and I say this as a comfortable speaker of colloquial Arabic, it's obvious that the correct answer is to build a foundation in classical Arabic before moving on to the spoken dialect": Menahem Milson, "My Early Life with Arabic," *Mosaic*, March 8, 2018. https://mosaicmagazine.com/observation/israel-zionism/2018/03/my-early-life -with-arabic/. Milson was a student in the department during the early 1950s.

77. Memorandum of conversation between Joshua Prawer and Moshe Piamenta, September 6, 1953, CAHU, 2264:1953. The increasing number of students speaking Arabic as a mother tongue—Arab citizens of Israel and Jews born in Arab countries —exacerbated the challenge that had faced the Department of Arabic Language and Literature since its establishment. At various points over the course of the 1950s head of department D. H. Baneth raised the issue of the gap between the language ability

242 ::: NOTES TO CHAPTER 3

these students brought with them from home, and the department's grammatical demands, with no fundamental solution to the issue ever being found. See, for example, "Mekomot haturpa betokhnit halimudim hakayemet lesafa vesifrut 'aravit," January 24, 1954, CAHU, 2264:1954. On the instruction of Arabic at the Hebrew University in light of this gap, see also Levy, "Man of Contention," 97–98.

78. For example, Walter Eytan was invited to the institute to give a guest lecture on the Foreign Ministry's policy, not open to the wider public (invitation formulated by Goitein, May 20, 1951, CAHU, 226:1951); at least until the mid-1950s, the Foreign Ministry contributed a yearly prize awarded by HUSOS to one of its students (Goitein to Eytan, August 19, 1955, CAHU, 226:1955); and in 1951, institute personnel were in contact with the ministry regarding their participation in the 22nd International Congress of Orientalists held in Istanbul. Representing HUSOS at the conference were Mayer, Goitein, and Weil, who were then away from Israel on academic business. Heyd, who was staying in Turkey at the time, joined them. On the preparations for the congress and a summary of the Israeli delegation's uneventful participation in it, see various sets of Foreign Ministry correspondence between August 28 and October 14, ISA, MFA-1964/11. There had been trepidation at the ministry, in part, about the recurrence of an incident a short time earlier, when Goitein had been ejected from a conference on Muslim law held in Paris after a "Syrian outcry" against his participation: "Sha'aruriya bekhinus mada'i beParis," Ha'aretz, August 13, 1951, 2.

79. On European-Jewish scholarly interest in Yemenite Jews, see Yosef Tobi, "Trends in the Study of Yemenite Jewry," in *The Jews of Yemen*, by Yosef Tobi (Leiden: Brill, 1999), 267–78.

80. Quoted in Norman (Noam) A. Stillman, "Jews of the Islamic World," *Modern Judaism* 10, no. 3 (1990): 368. On Goitein's scholarly research on the topic between the 1930s and the 1950s, see Tom Fogel, "Hamehkar hateimani shel S. D. Goitein" (PhD diss., Hebrew University of Jerusalem, 2019), especially the second and third chapters of this work.

81. Goitein to the university administration, October 31, 1949, CAHU, 226:1949. Goitein's belief that this was a historical opportunity not to be missed was only strengthened after he travelled to visit Hashed Camp near the Yemenite city of Aden, where Jews gathered prior to immigrating to Israel: Fogel, "Hamehkar hateimani," 57.

82. Yitzhak Hoffman to Goitein, January 5, 1950, CAHU, 2261:1950.

83. Goitein to Ben-Zion Dinaburg, February 29, 1952, CAHU, 226:1952. Yosef Rivlin was one of those involved in the study of the Kurdistani Jewish language.

84. On the Cairo *Geniza*, the vast repository of documents found in the attic of the "Ben Ezra" synagogue in Fustat (Old Cairo), the story of its discovery, and how it was revealed to scholars piecemeal, see Peter Cole and Adina Hoffman, *Sacred Trash: The Lost and Found World of the Cairo Geniza* (New York: Nextbook and Schocken, 2011).

85. See Goitein's introduction to the bibliography of his own writings: Shelomo Dov Goitein, "The Life Story of a Scholar," in *A Bibliography of the Writings of Prof. Shelomo Dov Goitein*, ed. Robert Attal (Jerusalem: Israel Oriental Society and the Institute of Asian and African Studies, The Hebrew University of Jerusalem, 1975), xiii–xxviii.

NOTES TO CHAPTER 3 ::: 243

86. Fitzroy Morrissey, "Jewish-Muslim Symbiosis, Islamic Hellenism, and the Purpose of Islamic Studies: The Humanistic Legacy of Samuel Stern's Teachers," *Journal of Modern Jewish Studies* 20, no. 4 (2021): 428–29.

87. Goitein to Itzhak Baer and Dinaburg, June 20, 1949, CAHU, 226:1949.

88. On this initiative of Goitein's, its reception at the university, and the stances of various scholars on the topic of Jewish history, as well as skepticism of the figure of Ashtor, see Hanan Harif and Amit Levy, "Disciplina shlema rabat panim: Hapulmus 'al limudey hahistoria shel yehudey artzot ha'islam bamekhonim lemada'ey hayahadut ulmada'ey hamizrah," in *Toldot ha'universita ha'ivrit birushalayim*, ed. Yfaat Weiss and Uzi Rebhun, vol. 5: *Medinat hale'om vehahaskala hagvoha* (Jerusalem: The Hebrew University Magnes Press, 2024), 687–718. On Ashtor, see also Miriam Frenkel, "Eliyahu Ashtor—A Forgotten Pioneer Researcher of Jewish History under the Mamluks," in *Muslim-Jewish Relations in the Middle Islamic Period: Jews in the Ayyubid and Mamluk Sultanates (1171–1517)*, ed. Stephan Conermann (Göttingen: Vandenhoeck & Ruprecht, 2017), 63–74.

89. "Hatza'at tokhnit lehug mishni: Hayahadut be'artzot ha'Islam," February 3, 1952, CAHU, 226:1952.

90. Uri Ram, "Mizrahim or Mizrahiyut? Equality and Identity in Israeli Critical Social Thought," *Israel Studies Forum* 17, no. 2 (2002): 121.

91. Yehouda Shenhav, *The Arab Jews: A Postcolonial Reading of Nationalism, Religion, and Ethnicity* (Stanford: Stanford University Press, 2006), 15.

92. In a letter sent in 1963 to the newly-elected President of Israel, Zalman Shazar, Goitein explicitly noted the need "[to cleanse] our mouths and hearts of this phrase, Oriental communities": Goitein to Shazar, June 2, 1963, ANLI, Arc. 4° 1911/01/32.

93. In 1896, Max Grunwald founded the *Society for Jewish Folklore* (*Gesellschaft für jüdische Volkskunde*) in Hamburg with the intention of establishing Jewish folklore as an independent scientific field; while in Eastern Europe, S. An-Ski (Shlomo Zeinbil Rapoport) launched an ethnographic expedition to the Pale of Settlement on the eve of World War I. See Dani Schrire, "Max Grunwald and the Formation of Jewish Folkloristics: Another Perspective on Race in German-Speaking *Volkskunde*," in *Ideas of 'Race' in the History of the Humanities*, ed. Amos Morris-Reich and Dirk Rupnow (Cham: Palgrave Macmillan, 2017), 116–19; Itzik Nakhmen Gottesman, *Defining the Yiddish Nation: The Jewish Folklorists of Poland* (Detroit: Wayne State University Press, 2003).

94. Dani Schrire, *Isuf shivrey hagola: Heker hafolklor hatziyoni lenokhah hasho'a* (Jerusalem: The Hebrew University Magnes Press, 2018), 16.

95. On Brauer and his studies, see Vered Madar and Dani Schrire, "From Leipzig to Jerusalem: Erich Brauer, a Jewish Ethnographer in Search of a Field," *Naharaim* 8, no. 1 (2014): 91–119. Most of the decision-makers at the Hebrew University had little appreciation for Brauer's work, and the university stopped funding his activities in the 1940s: Orit Abuhav, *In the Company of Others: The Development of Anthropology in Israel* (Detroit: Wayne State University Press, 2015), 24–25.

96. David N. Myers, *Re-Inventing the Jewish Past: European Jewish Intellectuals and the Zionist Return to History* (New York: Oxford University Press, 1995), 89–93.

## 244 ::: NOTES TO CHAPTER 3

On the tensions inherent to the studies of European ethnographers among the
Jews of Palestine in the early years of the twentieth century, see Amos Noy, *'Edim 'o
mumhim: Yehudim maskilim bney yerushalayim vehamizrah bithilat hame'a ha'esrim*
(Tel Aviv: Resling, 2017).

97. Schrire, *Isuf shivrey hagola*, 15–20.

98. "Hatza'a limgamat limud hayahadut be'artzot ha'Islam," December 5, 1952,
CAHU, 226:1952. Ashtor had already been invited to join the December 1952 HUSOS
faculty meeting. Still, resistance from the Institute for Jewish Studies faculty
continued to hang over his appointment process, which dragged on for another
two years; only in March 1955 was final approval received for the creation of a "half-
appointment of a lecturer in Muslim history with a special emphasis on the history
of the Jews in Islamic lands": Excerpt from protocol of the Academic Senate, Meeting
IV, March 23, 1955, CAHU, 2263:1955.

99. Uri Ram, "Israeli Sociology: Social Thought Amidst Struggles and Conflicts,"
*Irish Journal of Sociology* 23, no. 1 (2015): 101.

100. Uri Ram, *The Changing Agenda of Israeli Sociology: Theory, Ideology, and
Identity* (Albany: State University of New York Press, 1995), 25.

101. On how the study of Jews from the Islamic world was handed from historians
to sociologists, see Yaron Tsur, "Israeli Historiography and the Ethnic Problem," in
*Making Israel*, ed. Benny Morris (Ann Arbor: University of Michigan Press, 2007),
233–38.

102. Partial government funding to study the history of the Jews from the Islamic
world was granted to the Institute for the Study of Oriental Jewish Communities
(later the Ben-Zvi Institute), which was founded in 1947 at the initiative of Yitzhak
Ben-Zvi. While HUSOS and the Institute for Jewish Studies were involved in its
establishment and administration, the Institute for the Study of Oriental Jewish
Communities remained of marginal stature over the years. The research and
publications it oversaw—based primarily on textual sources from communities
that emigrated from the Islamic world dating from the sixteenth century onwards
—earned it little scientific prestige, particularly during its early years. On the early
days of the Ben-Zvi Institute and difficulties involved in founding and funding it,
see Shimon Rubinstein, "'Al yesudo vereshito shel hamakhon leheker kehilot yisra'el
bamizrah," *Pe'amim* 23 (1985): 127–49.

103. Heydt [Heyd] to Shertok [Sharett], July 1945, CZA, S25/8961. In his letter
to Moshe Sharett, director of the Political Department, Heyd proposed a name:
"The Palestine Association for the New East" (*Ha'aguda Ha'e[retz-Yisra'el]it
Lamizrah Hehadash*). In 1935, the Political Department was already publishing a
Hebrew-language periodical named "Middle East Compilation" (*Yalkut Hamizrah
Hatikhon*) with surveys of the Arabic-language press and analyses regarding
diplomatic, economic, and social questions in the Middle East by various writers,
including personnel of the Political Department. The periodical was distributed to
subscribers only.

104. Alon and Shahar, "Re'ayon," 16. According to Landau, "The entire
organization was actually in his hands [Goitein's]" (ibid., 17).

NOTES TO CHAPTER 3 ::: 245

105. James Hopkins, "The Role of Learned Societies in Knowledge Exchange and Dissemination: The Case of the Regional Studies Association, 1965–2005," *History of Education* 40, no. 2 (2011): 259–60. Hopkins's article offers a discussion of various definitions proposed over the course of the years for learned societies. On the development of these frameworks, see John Heilbron, "Academies and Learned Societies," in *The Oxford Companion to the History of Modern Science*, ed. John Heilbron (Oxford: Oxford University Press, 2003,) 1–5.

106. Mathilde Sigalas, "Between Diplomacy and Science: British Mandate Palestine and Its International Network of Archaeological Organisations, 1918–1938," in *European Cultural Diplomacy and Arab Christians in Palestine, 1918–1948: Between Contention and Connection*, ed. Karène Sanchez Summerer and Sary Zananiri (London: Palgrave Macmillan, 2021), 201.

107. "Yedi'ot hahevra: Hahevra hamizrahit hayisra'elit," *Hamizrah hehadash* 1, no. 1 (1949). The assembly was preceded by discussions held at branches that had been established in Jerusalem, Tel Aviv, and Haifa before the society's official foundation. The first meeting at the Tel Aviv branch ("of the Israeli Society for Middle Eastern Affairs," as the invitation put it) was held in early January 1949. The discussions held there were preceded by lectures by Mayer (on the teaching of Islam at European and American universities) and Goitein (on the International Congress of Orientalists held in Paris), and the Government's Cabinet Secretary Ze'ev Sherf was among the attendees (Initiatory Committee to Sherf, December 24, 1948, ISA, G-5575/30).

108. Sigalas, "Between Diplomacy and Science," 207.

109. After the establishment of the Israel Oriental Society, another association that had been established several years previously was incorporated into it: the Kedem association, which had the goal of developing relations of friendship and exchange with the peoples of Asia. The association was founded in the wake of a Zionist delegation's participation in the Asian Relations Conference held in New Delhi in 1947. At the head of both the delegation and the association stood Hugo Bergmann of the Hebrew University: Shimon Lev, "'I read Sri Aurobindo to find some light in our difficult days': Hugo Bergmann's Encounter with India, Aurobindo, and the Mother," in *The Cosmic Movement: Sources, Contexts, Impact*, ed. Julie Chajes and Boaz Huss (Beersheba: Ben-Gurion University of the Negev Press, 2020), 528. In 1950, the press received notification that the Kedem association had become part of the Israel Oriental Society (*Hatzofe*, December 27, 1950, 3).

110. List of institutions created and individuals elected to them at the founding assembly of the Israel Oriental Society on May 17, 1949, ISA, G-5575/30.

111. Clyne, *Orientalism, Zionism and Academic Practice*, 42.

112. Alon and Shahar, "Re'ayon," 16.

113. Suzanne L. Marchand, *German Orientalism in the Age of Empire: Religion, Race and Scholarship* (Cambridge: Cambridge University Press, 2009), 95.

114. Wokoeck, *German Orientalism*, 135. For a comprehensive discussion of the DMG and its establishment and activities in the nineteenth century, see Sabine Mangold, *Eine "weltbürgerliche Wissenschaft"—Die deutsche Orientalistik im 19. Jahrhundert* (Stuttgart: Franz Steiner Verlag, 2004), 176–225.

246 ::: NOTES TO CHAPTER 3

115. Wokoeck, *German Orientalism*, 133.

116. "Hahevra hamizrahit hayisra'elit: Pirtei-kol meha'asefa hameyasedet," May 17, 1949, ISA, G-5575/30.

117. Subsequently the number of council members shrunk but the variety of professions represented was maintained. For example, in 1950 the list of members included outgoing mayor of Jerusalem Daniel Auster, the minister Bechor-Shalom Sheetrit, and member of Knesset Zalman Shazar; while H. Z. Hirschberg and Yaakov Yehoshua of the Ministry of Religions as well as Mordechai Gichon, one of the founders of the Research Wing (later, the Research Division) at the Intelligence Department (Aman) of the IDF's Central Command also joined: list of members of Israel Oriental Society institutions, December 3, 1952, ISA, MFA-1964/11.

118. "Hahevra hamizrahit hayisra'elit: Takanon," May 17, 1949, ISA, G-5575/30.

119. For example, between 1949 and 1954, governmental allocations made up between 35 percent and 50 percent of the society's income (Financial Report and Budgets, December 6, 1949, CAHU, 226:1949; proceedings of Israel Oriental Society committee meeting, July 7, 1954, ISA, MFA-1964/11). No regular budget seems to have arrived from the military.

120. Meeting I of the Israel Oriental Society council, December 6, 1949, CAHU, 226:1949.

121. The yearly lecture schedule appearing in the first issue of *The New East* included talks by Michael Assaf, Alfred Bonne, Uriel Heyd, Yehuda Leib Benor, H. Z. Hirschberg, Gotthold Weil, Yigael Yadin, L. A. Mayer, Yaacov Shimoni, and Meir Plessner: "Yedi'ot hahevra (1949)."

122. Pessah Shinar (Schusser, 1914–2013), Ayalon's colleague in preparing the Arabic-Hebrew Dictionary, completed his doctoral degree at the institute during the 1950s, and became a lecturer there in 1960.

123. The proportion of pieces written by academics began to grow gradually over the years, especially after the role of editor was passed on to Gabriel Baer, and some were given an academic apparatus as well. It became a yearly rather than a quarterly journal, but began essentially to change its character only in the 1960s: in 1963, the long-standing newspaper survey section was cancelled and editing duties were handed down to Baer's student, Yehoshua Porath (1938–2019), who sought to strengthen its academic elements still more. At the same time, surveys and current events articles continued to be published throughout the 1970s. For more, see Clyne, *Orientalism, Zionism and Academic Practice*, 42–46. In subsequent years, the journal took on a fully academic character, including the implementation of peer review process for articles. Its publication is ongoing.

124. At one point, Goitein hoped to utilize the money coming from the Society to publish writing by HUSOS students: Goitein to the rector, February 25, 1950, CAHU, 226:1950.

125. Eyal, *Disenchantment of the Orient*, 65. In this way the Society could offer, for example, a lecture by Goitein on internal developments within the Arab world, Weil on the future of the Muslim culture, and Polotsky on the Oriental languages spoken in the Soviet Union: "Yedi'ot hahevra (1949)."

NOTES TO CHAPTER 3 ::: 247

126. Goitein to Schwabe, December 8, 1952, 226:1952.

127. Livny, "Ha'universita," 83.

128. Goitein to Hoffmann, December 26, 1952, CAHU, 226:1952.

129. See note 31 above on the distinction. Shelomo Dov Goitein, "Mada'ey hamizrah ba'universita ha'ivrit," *Davar*, April 10, 1935, 12.

130. For a survey of Goitein's scholarly activity in the years following his departure from Israel, see Cole and Hoffman, *Sacred Trash*, 192–224. For a discussion on the circumstances around his departure and his public activities in the American academy, see Hanan Harif, "A Bridge or a Fortress? S. D. Goitein and the Role of Jewish Arabists in the American Academy," *Jewish Social Studies* 26, no. 2 (2021): 68–92.

131. After departing in 1957, Goitein extended his stay in the United States time and again. In 1960, he hoped to delay once more but encountered bitter refusal from the university administration. Since he eventually decided not to return to the country, the Standing Committee eventually took action to effectively end his employment by the university: Excerpt from protocol of the Standing Committee, meeting XVII, July 3, 1960, CAHU, 222:1960.

132. Goitein to Polotsky, July 4, 1956, and excerpt from protocol of the Standing Committee of the Academic Senate, meeting III, November 23, 1956, CAHU, 225:1956. Heyd was already running the institute the year before Goitein's departure, beginning in the 1956–57 academic year.

133. Yohanan Friedmann, *MiZákamenné lirushalayim: Pirkey zikaron* (Jerusalem: self-pub., 2019), 70.

134. Heyd to Senator, November 18, 1948, CAHU, 2262:1948.

135. On Senator and his role at the university after Magnes's death, see Adi Livny, "Fighting Partition, Saving Mount Scopus: The Pragmatic Binationalism of D. W. Senator (1930–1949)," *Studies in Cotemporary Jewry* 31 (2020): 225–46.

136. R. Bayly Winder, "Four Decades of Middle Eastern Study," *Middle East Journal* 41, no. 1 (1987): 40–42; Zachary Lockman, *Contending Visions of the Middle East: The History and Politics of Orientalism* (Cambridge: Cambridge University Press, 2004), 121. In general, the study of Arabic and Islam in the United States before World War II was underdeveloped: only in 1927 was the Department for Oriental Languages and Literatures founded at Princeton, which was also the first to host an Arabic and Islamic Studies program: Timothy Mitchell, "The Middle East in the Past and Future of Social Science," in *The Politics of Knowledge: Area Studies and the Disciplines*, ed. David Szanton (Berkeley: University of California Press, 2004), 78.

137. Lockman, *Contending Visions of the Middle East*, 123–25; Martin Kramer, *Ivory Towers on Sand: The Failure of Middle Eastern Studies in America* (Washington, DC: The Washington Institute for Near East Policy, 2001), 6–7. The state only began funding instruction and research in these areas in the late 1950s. For a survey of the development of Middle Eastern Studies in the United States see Winder, "Four Decades"; on the historical and methodological aspects of incorporating social sciences into the area studies framework for studying the Middle East, see Mitchell, "The Middle East in the Past and Future."

248 ::: NOTES TO CHAPTER 3

138. Heyd to Senator, November 18, 1948, CAHU, 2262:1948.

139. For a discussion of this approach in the context of Zionist thought in Europe and Palestine, see Hanan Harif, *Anashim ahim anahnu: Hapniya mizraha bahagut hatziyonit* (Jerusalem: Zalman Shazar Center for Jewish History, 2019), especially 81–86.

140. Institute students to the Executive Committee of the Hebrew University, February 9, 1936, CAHU, 226:1936.

141. Heyd to Goitein, March 31, 1949, Personnel File—Uriel Heyd, 1949–1959; Mayer to Poznansky, May 4, 1949, CAHU, 226:1949.

142. Uriel Heyd, *Hamizrah hatikhon bazman hehadash kenose lemehkar ulhoraa* (Jerusalem: The Hebrew University Magnes Press, 1952). The lecture was read on May 14, 1952, at Terra Sancta as part of an evening in honor of Weil that included, in addition to Heyd's lecture, greetings from Goitein and "Words of Appreciation" from Martin Plessner: "Batzibur," *Davar*, May 14, 1952, 3.

143. L. A. Mayer, *Reshita vaaliyata shel haarkheologia hamuslemit: Neum ptiha meet L. A. Mayer, professor bakatedra laomanot velaarkheologia shel hamizrah hakarov 'al-shem Sir Sassoon David bauniversita haivrit* (Jerusalem: Hebrew University Press, 1935).

144. Heyd, *Hamizrah hatikhon bazman hehadash*, 6.

145. Ibid., 7.

146. Ibid., 8.

147. Ibid., 8–9. Heyd added that, while it was true that modern literature in the Orient was no longer as original as it had once been, being influenced by the language, style, and form of Western literature, he did not believe this reduced its value.

148. Ibid., 9–10. In this context Heyd specifically named the controversial English historian Arnold Toynbee, mockingly quoting his claim that the peoples of the Orient would never contribute more to the culture of humanity than, at best, simply achieving "the negative achievement of material survival": Toynbee, *Civilization on Trial* (New York: Oxford University Press, 1948), 199.

149. For additional examples of intra-disciplinary critique that preceded Said, see Daniel Schroeter, "From Sephardi to Oriental: The 'Decline' Theory of Jewish Civilizations in the Middle East and North Africa," in *The Jewish Contribution to Civilization: Reassessing an Idea*, ed. Jeremy Cohen and Richard I. Cohen (Oxford: Littman Library, 2008), 129n17.

150. Still under the influence of the consequences of the Nazi regime's intervention in university research and instruction, Oriental Studies scholars in West Germany avoided engaging with subjects that might be suspected of political or ideological influence. For this reason, study of the modern Middle East remained firmly in the margins for the first two decades after World War II: Baber Johansen, "Politics and Scholarship: The Development of Islamic Studies in the Federal Republic of Germany," in *Middle East Studies: International Perspectives on the State of the Art*, ed. Tareq Y. Ismael (New York: Praeger, 1990), 92–93.

151. Heyd, *Hamizrah hatikhon bazman hehadash*, 11. Heyd's recollections accord

NOTES TO CHAPTER 3 ::: 249

with the findings of contemporary scholarship: that unlike the United States, study of the modern Middle East in Britain was characterized until the 1970s by work that was neither integrative nor "regional"; see Timothy C. Niblock, "The State of the Art in British Middle Eastern Studies," in *Middle East Studies: International Perspectives on the State of the Art*, ed. Tareq Y. Ismael (New York: Praeger, 1990), 41–42. On the development of Anglo Orientalism on the eve of World War II as reflected in the history of various Orientalist academic institutions, see studies from recent years by Ian Brown, *The School of Oriental and African Studies: Imperial Training and the Expansion of Learning* (Cambridge: Cambridge University Press, 2016), 115–56; Edward Andrew Preece, "Building an Academic Tradition: Durham University and the Development of British Oriental Studies in the Post-War Era" (master's thesis, Durham University, 2017), 25–41.

152. Heyd, *Hamizrah hatikhon bazman hehadash*, 12.

153. In his response, Heyd mentioned the Berlin SOS, a separate institute for practical training, as an example of the separation of the two types of training into two facilities, but did not explain why an institute of this kind would not be possible to establish in Israel, and the two models would have to cohabitate.

154. Heyd, *Hamizrah hatikhon bazman hehadash*, 13.

155. Ibid., 16–17. In contrast with what was implied by Heyd's words, in the first years following the establishment of the state, the study of Arabic in high schools was gradually reduced from the rate at which it had been implemented under the British Mandate. This seems to have been founded, among other things, in a perception that with the diminishing of contact between the Jewish and Arab populations, the study of Arabic had little civil or integrational purpose. The status of the language as a high school subject of study continued to deteriorate until 1967, when, seeing the students as potential candidates for military service in need of knowledge in Arabic, the IDF began to participate in the Arabic study budget on the basis of security interests. See Mendel, *Creation of Israeli Arabic*, 45–66.

156. Heyd, *Hamizrah hatikhon bazman hehadash*, 17–18.

157. See, for example, the list of names surrounding this discourse in Alexander Lyon Macfie, *Orientalism* (London: Pearson Education, 2002), 225–29. Heyd is not included. It should be noted that he died in 1968, before the public zenith of the critical discourse on the field.

158. Edward W. Said, *Orientalism* (New York: Pantheon Books, 1978), 18–19.

159. Heyd to Poznansky, December 20, 1956, CAHU, 226:1956.

160. Excerpt from protocol of the curriculum committee in Humanities and Social Sciences, meeting VIII, March 20, 1959, CAHU, 222:1959.

161. Excerpt from protocol of the curriculum committee in Humanities and Social Sciences, meeting VI, June 18, 1959, CAHU, 2221:1959.

162. Friedmann, *MiZákamenné lirushalayim*, 71. Many of these graduates, who would make up the third generation of Oriental Studies scholars (at the institute and at the other universities that were now being established), were sent to study at universities in England, the United States, and Canada.

163. Milson, "Beginnings of Arabic and Islamic Studies," 180; on Kister's influence

250 ::: NOTES TO CHAPTER 3

as a teacher, see Friedmann, *MiZákamenné lirushalayim*, 50–55. Before joining the university, Kister was a supervisor on behalf of the Education Ministry over the "Oriental Classes" program in high schools. This program was the joint initiative of the Prime Minister's Office, the Foreign and Education Ministries, Military Intelligence, and the Military Government, and outlined the study of Arabic that emphasized training for high school students to serve in the Intelligence Corps: Mendel, *Creation of Israeli Arabic*, 66–97.

164. Goitein to Poznansky, June 29, and Poznansky to Goitein, July 2, 1956, CAHU, 226:1956.

165. Uriel Heydt [Heyd], "Pakistan: Habe'aya hamuslemit—hindu'it behodu," March 1944, CZA, S25/3538.

166. On the Erfurt-born Zander, who emigrated from Germany to England after the Nazi rise to power and became secretary of the Friends of organization between 1944 and 1970, see Michael Zander, "Dr. Walter Zander: 8 June 1898–7 April 1993. An Address by Michael Zander. Delivered at the Annual Dinner of the Friends of the Hebrew University, Glasgow Branch, May 8, 1994," www.walterzander.info /in_memoriam.html.

167. Poznansky to Zander, June 22, 1958, 222:1957-1958.

168. "Oriental Studies: Meeting held at 237 Baker Street, N.W.1. on Tuesday, June 24th, 1958," CAHU, 222:1957–1958.

169. On Israeli diplomacy and its emergence during the state's first years, see Uri Bialer, *Israeli Foreign Policy: A People Shall Not Dwell Alone* (Bloomington: Indiana University Press, 2020), 77–108. On the strategy of approaching the non-Arab countries and the roots of this idea, see Samaan, *Israel's Foreign Policy*, especially 15–28.

170. On the origins of Israeli diplomacy in Asia, see Jacob Abadi, *Israel's Quest for Recognition and Acceptance in Asia: Garrison State Diplomacy* (London: Frank Cass, 2004). The Israeli turn to Asia in general and to India in particular actually preceded the establishment of the state. On the meeting between the Jewish-Zionist world and India, see Shimon Lev, "Gandhi and the Jews, the Jews and Gandhi: An Overall Perspective," *Hindu Studies* 27, no. 3 (2023): 393–409; for a discussion of the Zionist attempts to draw parallels between the Zionist movement and non-Arab national movements, see Rephael G. Stern and Arie M. Dubnov, "A Part of Asia or Apart from Asia? Zionist Perceptions of Asia, 1947–1956," in *Unacknowledged Kinships: Postcolonial Studies and the Historiography of Zionism*, ed. Stefan Vogt, Derek J. Penslar, and Arieh Bruce Saposnik (Waltham, MA: Brandeis University Press, 2023), 233–71.

171. Benyamin Neuberger, *Israel's Relations with the Third World* (Tel Aviv: The S. Daniel Abraham Center for International and Regional Studies, Tel Aviv University, 2009), 16–18. Interestingly, one of this move's motives was to prevent the spread of the Israeli-Arab conflict to the entire Muslim world, through the establishment of relationships with Muslim countries in both continents (ibid., 15). See also Bialer, *Israeli Foreign Policy*, 224–53. In parallel to public declarations, Israel reached secret diplomatic agreements with Turkey, Iran, and Ethiopia in 1958 as part of what was called the "Alliance of the Periphery" with nearby non-Arab countries.

NOTES TO CHAPTER 3 ::: 251

See on this Ofra Bengio, *The Turkish-Israeli Relationship: Changing Ties of Middle Eastern Outsiders* (New York: Palgrave Macmillan, 2004), 33–69; Samaan, *Israel's Foreign Policy*, 41–101.

172. Neuberger, *Israel's Relations with the Third World*, 10–11.

173. "Oriental Studies: Meeting," 2.

174. Brown, *School of Oriental and African Studies*, 52–55.

175. On this period in the life of Lewis, before his move to the United States and his establishment as a public intellectual, see Carole Hillenbrand, "Bernard Lewis: 31 May 1916–19 May 2018," *Biographical Memoirs of Fellows of the British Academy* XIX (2020): 234–37. Zander contacted Lewis on the subject several months before their meeting and asked for his opinion: copy of a letter from Lewis to Zander, May 1, 1958, CAHU, 2228:1958.

176. Wokoeck, *German Orientalism*, 120; Marchand, *German Orientalism in the Age of Empire*, 344–45.

177. On the HKI, which lost the colonial justification for its existence in the wake of World War I but served as one of the bases for the establishment of the University of Hamburg, see Jens Ruppenthal, *Kolonialismus als "Wissenschaft und Technik": Das Hamburgische Kolonialinstitut 1908 bis 1919* (Stuttgart: Franz Steiner Verlag, 2007).

178. Marchand, *German Orientalism in the Age of Empire*, 351, 354.

179. On Mittwoch's specialization in Ethiopian languages and his familiarity with the Ethiopian scholar Tayyä Gäbrä Maryam (1860–1924), see Edward Ullendorff, "Eugen Mittwoch and the Berlin Seminar for Oriental Studies," in *Studies in Honour of Clifford Edmund Bosworth*, ed. Ian Richard Netton, vol. I: *Hunter of the East: Arabic and Semitic Studies* (Leiden: Brill, 1999), 145–58. According to Ullendorff, this scholar held regular meetings with Mittwoch as well as with two future directors of HUSOS in Jerusalem, Josef Horovitz and Gotthold Weil (ibid., 150). Various research materials of Mittwoch's on the subject of Ethiopian languages have been preserved in the holdings of the National Library in Jerusalem, which were delivered by his widow (ANLI, Arc. 4° 1559/02/3).

180. See, for example, Zander's letter to Mazar, September 22, 1958, CAHU, 2228:1958. Elath became president of the university himself in 1962.

181. Zander to Ben-Gurion, March 10, 1959, CAHU, 2228:1959.

182. Ben-Gurion to Zander, January 12, 1959, CAHU, 2228:1959. His family would later attest that Zander took pride in the expansion of the institute and Ben-Gurion's praise for the initiative: Zander, "Dr. Walter Zander," 7.

183. Zander to Mazar, January 21, 1959, CAHU, 2228:1959.

184. Heyd approached, among others, the Sinologist Zvi Harold Schiffrin (b. 1922), who was born in the United States but moved to Israel in 1948 and completed his doctorate at the Hebrew University; and Tuvia Gelblum (1928–2007), who had set off to study in Delhi and, while there, served as an unofficial Israeli representative in India and as contact person between Nehru, the Prime Minister of India, and Ben-Gurion. He subsequently trained in Sanskrit in London: J. C. Wright, "Obituary: Dr Tuvia Gelblum, 1928–2007," *Bulletin of the School of Oriental and African Studies* 71, no. 3 (2008): 555.

252 ::: NOTES TO CHAPTER 3

185. The School of Oriental Studies, Program for Asian Studies, [1961], CAHU, 2228:1961; Proposal for African Studies, December 30, 1960, CAHU, 2228:1961.

186. See, for example, the letter from Zvi Loker to Shmuel Noah Eisenstadt, August 16, 1961, CAHU, 2228:1961.

187. Eisenstadt to Chaim Yahil, December 27, 1961, CAHU, 2228:1961; Yahil to Eisenstadt, January 22, 1962, CAHU, 2228:1962. The foundation's funds were used in part to financially support current faculty to train in topics relevant to the African Studies curriculum. For example, Hedva Ben-Israel (1925–2023) of the Department of History travelled to Cambridge for supplementary training in preparation for teaching a course on colonial history: Chaim Birnbaum to Ben-Israel, July 4, 1962, CAHU, 2228:1962.

188. The Foreign Ministry passed along a report, for example, about relevant professors located in Congo (Lea Sidis to Eisenstadt, February 14, 1962, CAHU, 2228:1962), and on reports in a Ghanaian newspaper regarding a forthcoming conference (Lorch to Eisenstadt, April 1, 1962, CAHU, 2228:1962).

189. Layish, "Uriel Heyd's Contribution"; Friedmann, *MiZákamenné lirushalayim*, 67–68.

190. For example, in a letter to the Ministry of Education written in preparation for an educational tour he was about to lead in Turkey, Heyd emphasized: "We see this tour as an important complement to the students' studies in the field of Turkish history and language. We also attribute great importance to this tour in terms of strengthening the political and cultural links between the two countries." (Heyd to Carmella Doron, June 2, 1952, CAHU, 226:1954).

191. Heyd to Joshua Prawer, February 26, 1962, CAHU, 222:1962.

192. Heyd to Prawer, February 26, 1962.

193. Excerpt from protocol of the Standing Committee, meeting XXI, May 25, 1962, CAHU, 222:1962.

194. "Maskanot hava'ada lamakhon lelimudey asia ve'afrika, mugashot lava'ada hamatmedet," June 21, 1962, CAHU, 2228:1962.

195. Excerpt from protocol of the Humanities and Social Sciences Faculty Council, Meeting I, January 2, 1963, CAHU 222:1963.

196. Invitation to press conference on the foundation of the Institute of Asian and African Studies at the Hebrew University to be held on January 6, sent on January 3, 1963, CAHU, 222:1963. The name change put an end to the confusing incongruence of its English translation—it was now an institute not only in Hebrew but in English as well, rather than a school. The word "Studies" was kept, now finally congruent with the Hebrew "*limudey*," unlike the previous "*mada'ey*" (lit. Sciences).

197. "Press Release," January 6, 1963, CAHU, 222:1963.

198. Poznansky to Yoel Racah, March 13, and Eliahu Elath to Ayalon, June 25, 1963, CAHU, 222:1963.

199. David Ayalon, "Mistudent legimlai, 1932–1994," *Igeret ha'akademia hale'umit hayisra'elit lemada'im* 24 (2003): 40.

200. Scholars writing about the institute's history agree on this distinction. According to Menahem Milson, the members of the first generation are Josef

NOTES TO CHAPTER 3 ::: 253

Horovitz, Gotthold Weil, Yosef Yoel Rivlin, D. H. Baneth, L. A. Mayer, Levi
Billig, S. D. Goitein, Hans Jakob Polotsky, and Martin Plessner (Milson did not
explicitly note whether Isaac Shamosh and Alfred Bonne also belonged to the
founding generation in his eyes); among the second generation he counted Uriel
Heyd, David Ayalon, Meir Kister, Eliyahu Ashtor, Pessah Shinar, Yehoshua Blau,
Gabriel Baer, Moshe Piamenta, and Haim Blank: Milson, "Beginnings of Arabic
and Islamic Studies," 178–80. Following Milson, Eyal Clyne also mapped out the
following generations—the third (Milson's own generation), fourth, and fifth: Clyne,
*Orientalism, Zionism and Academic Practice*, chapters 1 and 2.

201. Karl Mannheim, "Das Problem der Generationen," *Kölner Vierteljahrshefte
für Soziologie 7* (1928): 157–85, 309–30. Following Mannheim came scholars who
noted that the more precise term to describe the sociological category he was seeking
to characterize was "cohort": Jane Pilcher, "Mannheim's Sociology of Generations:
An Undervalued Legacy," *The British Journal of Sociology* 45, no. 3 (1994): 483.

202. According to his student, Yohanan Friedmann, Kister knowingly adopted
the image of being protective of classical Arabic, but had a certain interest in modern
and colloquial Arabic as well: Friedmann, *MiZákamenné lirushalayim*, 51–52.

203. Gabriel Baer, "Hamizrahanut beyisra'el bishloshim hashanim ha'aharonot,"
*Hamizrah hehadash* 28, no. 3–4 (1979): 176.

204. The Florence Conference is mentioned with great brevity in the scholarship
dealing with initiatives for solutions to the conflict in the Middle East; for
example, see Aharon Cohen, "Israel and Jewish-Arab Peace: Governmental and
Nongovernmental Approaches," in *Elusive Peace in the Middle East*, ed. Malcolm
H. Kerr (Albany: State University of New York Press, 1975), 136. Next to no
scholarship in English exists on the background of the conference, and existing
information on the event is found primarily in reports and impressions published
in the press in the year following the conference.

205. Shmuel Segev, "Have'ida shel Joe Golan me'avihayil: Giluyim hadashim
'al parashat florentz," *Ma'ariv*, October 15, 1958, 2. According to the account of
Uri Avnery (who was a close associate of Golan's), the wJC's President, Nahum
Goldmann, recommended that the government agree to the participation of persons
not serving an official governmental role, like Moshe Sharett or Martin Buber: Uri
Avnery, "Retzah biflorentz: Nituah le'ahar hamavet—hasipur hamale harishon 'al
'asher hitrahesh bave'ida," *Ha'olam haze*, October 22, 1958, 3.

206. This claim was made by Golan himself, who felt personally persecuted
by Meir. The enmity between the two reached a peak several years later, when he
was stripped of his Israeli passport. The story of Golan's relations with Meir winds
through the portions of his diaries that have been published, and also include his
impressions of the Florence Conference: Joe Golan, *Dapim meyoman* (Jerusalem:
Carmel, 2005), 320–23. Considering that a newspaper report displaying little
sympathy for Golan and his activities hinted at this cause as well (Segev, "Have'ida
shel Joe Golan"), the argument that his involvement led to the refusal of the
invitation is not far-fetched.

207. Bialer, *Israeli Foreign Policy*, 79–86.

254 ::: NOTES TO CHAPTER 3

208. Uri Bialer, *Between East and West: Israel's Foreign Policy Orientation 1948-1956* (Cambridge: Cambridge University Press, 1990), 276.

209. The title of the lecture was "Cultural Values of the Monotheistic Civilizations." It was subsequently published in English in the magazine *New Outlook*: Martin Plessner, "Cultural Values of the Monotheistic Civilizations," *New Outlook: Middle East Monthly* II, no. 3 (November–December 1958): 40–43.

210. Segev, "Have'ida shel Joe Golan."

211. Sasson recommended Michael Assaf be invited as well, but this never happened (encoded message from Sasson to the Jerusalem office, September 18, 1958, ISA, MFA-2358/4).

212. "'En 'adayin tokhnit lifgisha yisra'elit 'aravit befirentze," *Davar*, September 26, 1958; Avnery, "Retzah biflorentz," 4.

213. Note in Plessner's handwriting, Florence, October 4, 1958, CZA, A530/15.

214. Segev, "Have'ida shel Joe Golan"; "Mishlahat yisra'el 'azva 'et firentze," *Davar*, October 5, 1958. According to Uri Avnery's account, Fischer and Shiloah were only asked to move from the participant benches to the diplomatic benches.

215. Shmuel Segev, "Parashat florentz garma bizayon leyisra'el," *Ma'ariv*, October 5, 1958, 1; Yosef Shofman, "Bizyonot firentze," *Herut*, October 24, 1958, 2.

216. "Haprofessor hatimhoni," *Ma'ariv*, October 5, 1958, 2; Shalom Rosenfeld, "Kabluhu bevuz, 'et haprofessor haze!" *Ma'ariv*, October 10, 1958, 3. The *Ahdut Ha'avoda* representative at the conference, Shlomo Derekh, said in an interview to the movement's newspaper, *Lamerhav*: "The objection, the enmity, and the disregard towards most of the other Israeli representatives, as well as the words of slander directed at every opportunity towards the government and its institutions, indubitably have their origins in the same well-known psychological roots that the circles around Ihud foster towards the state, its institutions, and its emissaries": "Ha'italkim lo iymu 'al mishlahat yisra'el sheyevutal bikuro shel Fanfani," *Lamerhav*, October 22, 1958.

217. Protocol of the Third Knesset, session DXX, October 22, 1958, ISA, K-113/4, 18. Ben-Gurion explicitly attacked Plessner during a Government meeting, though he varied the name: "On Professor Plossner I have no desire to speak, this is a free country and everyone can do as they please. I was told at the time that, when he sees me from time to time leaving the house, he raises his hand and says: Heil Ben-Gurion. Well, let him do that, there are all kinds of people here": Protocol of session 2/1958–1959 of the government of Israel, October 12, 1958, 23.

218. Plessner quoted from memory in German in a letter sent soon after the events to his life partner: "Wir sind ja kein Polizeistaat, aber Du gefährdest Deine Stellung den Studenten gegenüber, die bei einem solchen Lehrer nicht werden lernen wollen": Plessner to Thea Buki, October 4, 1958, CZA, A530/15.

219. Letter to the editor from an "Oriental Studies student," *Ha'olam haze*, October 29, 1958, 2. On the public atmosphere and attitude towards Plessner in the wake of the Florence episode, see also Levy, "A Man of Contention," 89–90.

220. Plessner to Sasson, November 29, 1958, CZA, A530/15.

221. Privately, Plessner met with university president Mazar after his return from Florence, gave his version of events, and explained certain misunderstandings, such

NOTES TO EPILOGUE ::: 255

as the mistaken report in the Italian press that he had introduced himself as the university rector. Plessner attested that the meeting with Mazar ended "on the best of terms." (Ibid.)

222. "Ha'italkim lo iymu."

223. Plessner to Sasson, December 7, 1958, CZA, A530/15. Heyd seems to have held Plessner in some esteem as well, at least professionally—towards the end of his stint as director of the institute, he recommended Plessner's appointment as head of the Department of Muslim Culture, although to that point his teaching had focused on Arabic language and literature: Heyd to Prawer, March 6, 1963, CAHU, 2221:1963.

224. Plessner to Buki, October 4, 1958. No archival record of the unfolding of events from Heyd's perspective has been preserved.

225. Pierre Bourdieu, *Homo Academicus*, trans. Peter Collier (Stanford: Stanford University Press, 1988), 152.

226. In 1958, for example, Plessner submitted a proposal that all the institute's departments be folded into one Department of Islamic Culture, which would incorporate all relevant subjects (Plessner to Sasson, December 7, 1958, CZA, A530/15). The archival documentation appearing in the institutional folders of HUSOS suggest that, like some of the other proposals made by Plessner, this one was not given serious consideration.

227. In 1956, during the short window between the conquest of the Sinai Peninsula by Israel and its evacuation under international pressure, the university was able to send scientific expeditions to the area in coordination with military and government forces. One of them was headed by Benjamin Mazar and included L. A. Mayer and Hans Jakob Polotsky (along with a research assistant, the HUSOS student Uri Ben-Horin). They visited Saint Catherine's Monastery and studied both the building itself and the manuscripts in its library: Hebrew University of Jerusalem, *Sinai Survey*, n.d. [1956 or 1957]. This pamphlet is accessible through the National Library of Israel's website, system number 990028143920205171. The expedition was also documented in photographs found in the Hebrew University's Archive and in a short English-language film entitled "Sinai: Ancient Caravan Trails."

EPILOGUE

1. Gabriel Baer, "Gormey yesod utmurot bahevra hamitzrit bat zmanenu," in *Hevra umishtar ba'olam ha'aravi*, ed. Menahem Milson (Jerusalem: Van Leer Institute, 1977), 9. Eyal Clyne references this quotation in *Orientalism, Zionism and Academic Practice: Middle East and Islam Studies in Israeli Universities* (London: Routledge, 2019), 56.

2. A. Avner, "Hasber panekha lashavuy," *Mabat malam* 61 (2011): 45.

3. Uriel Heyd to Asher Reshef, November 18, 1956, CAHU, 226:1956. As the newly-appointed director of HUSOS, Heyd wrote to Reshef, secretary of the university administration, asking that it contact the military regarding the release from service of four instructors at the institute, which included Baer.

4. The POWs went on organized tours of the country during their time in Israel, and the officers among them even met with civilians: Avner, "Hasber panekha

lashavuy." Conceivably, Baer could also have had the opportunity to speak with them in such an instance.

5. Omri Shafer Raviv, "Studying an Occupied Society: Social Research, Modernization Theory and the Early Israeli Occupation, 1967–8," *Journal of Contemporary History* 55, no. 1 (2020): 164.

6. List of studies conducted using the budget for studies on the territories held by Israel (*hashtahim hamuhzakim*), that the Professors Committee recommended conducting, ISA, G-6495/26.

7. Aharon Zar to the Prime Minister's office, June 29, 1971, ISA, G-6495/8.

8. Aharon Layish to Paul Abraham Alsberg, August 10, 1971, ISA, G-7110/21. Layish (born Liskovski, 1933–2022) served as deputy advisor on Arab affairs during the mid-1960s. He wrote a dissertation under Baer's supervision and in the early 1970s became, as he put it in the letter, "coordinator of projects about Judea and Samaria" for the Institute of Asian and African Studies.

9. Tania Forte, "Sifting People, Sorting Papers: Academic Practice and the Notion of State Security in Israel," *Comparative Studies of South Asia, Africa and the Middle East* 23 (2003): 215–23. See also Clyne, *Orientalism, Zionism and Academic Practice*, 46–59.

10. Gabriel Baer, *Hamukhtar hakafri be'Eretz Israel: Toldot ma'amado vetafkidav* (Jerusalem: The Hebrew University Magnes Press, 1978).

11. Ibid., 7.

12. Rivka Yadlin, *'Amadot vede'ot bekerev 'arviyey hagada* (Jerusalem: The Hebrew University of Jerusalem, Institute of Asian and African Studies, Center for Research on Palestinian Arabs, 1973). The National Library in Jerusalem preserves an iteration of the booklet.

13. Ibid., 1.

14. On the role of the bureau of Arab affairs in the formation of the body of security knowledge on the Orient, see Doron Matza, *He'asor shebo noldu "arveiyey yisra'el': Yisra'el ve'ezrahea ha'aravim-falastinim 1966-1976* (Tel Aviv: Resling, 2022), 19–78. See also Yonatan Mendel, *The Creation of Israeli Arabic: Political and Security Considerations in the Making of Arabic Language Studies in Israel* (London: Palgrave Macmillan, 2014), 66–97.

15. Aharon Natan to Emanuel Marx, April 10, 1956, ISA, GL-17041/14. The students were asked to prepare the surveys within six months and were paid 200 Israeli pounds: Shmuel Divon to Aharon Liskovski [Layish] and to Eliezer Zilberman, August 9, 1956, ISA, GL-17041/14.

16. Emanuel Marx to Uri Lubrani, Yaacov Sapir, and Liskovski, December 8, 1958, ISA, GL-17041/14. Meetings regarding the Arab youth survey were arranged for one HUSOS student with school principals from Umm al-Fahm and Taybeh by representatives of the Military Government: Y. Berkovitz, Administrative Officer in the Military Government, Central Division, to the Advisor on Arab Affairs, March 26, 1959, ISA, GL-17041/14.

17. For details on the census as well as the preliminary lists prepared in 1961 and 1962, see folder GL-17028/3 in the Israel State Archives.

NOTES TO EPILOGUE ::: 257

18. The student was granted police permission to examine the conversion files at the Rabbinate's offices. See the correspondence of various officials between July 3, 1961, and March 12, 1963, ISA, GL-7451/14.

19. Reuven Shiloah to Benjamin Mazar, April 28, 1959, ISA, MFA-4488/14. On the Shiloah Center, primarily after 1965, see Gil Eyal, *The Disenchantment of the Orient: Expertise in Arab Affairs and the Israeli State* (Stanford: Stanford University Press, 2006), 197–206; Forte, "Sifting People, Sorting Papers," 220–22; Clyne, *Orientalism, Zionism and Academic Practice*, 47–52.

20. In a memorandum sent by the center's founders to the director general of the Prime Minister's Office for fundraising purposes, the Hebrew University and the Israel Oriental Society were said to "see the new institution as a welcome complement to their activities": Yitzhak Oron, a memorandum on the research center for overseas fundraising, May 26, 1959, ISA, G-5545/23. Some present at the society's general assembly balked at the collaboration lest it came at the expense of its own activities, but Heyd explained that this was necessary in order to "join forces, to prevent redundancies": "Yedi'ot hahevra," *Hamizrah hehadash* 10, no. 3 (1960): 277–78, quoted in Clyne, *Orientalism, Zionism and Academic Practice*, 50.

21. Yitzhak Oron to Teddy Kollek, March 24, 1959, ISA, G-5545/23. Hoping to receive an appropriate plot near Military Headquarters in Tel Aviv, Oron approached Yosef Weitz of the Jewish National Fund, which owned the land, noting that the center must be established "in the near vicinity of *Aman*, which was to be not just an important client of the center but also its primary patron . . . The Prime Minister is personally very interested in the establishment of this center in the location most appropriate to the aforementioned requirements": Oron to Weitz, April 15, 1959, ISA, G-5545/23.

22. Protocol of the administration of the Reuven Shiloah Research Center, December 15, 1959, ISA, G-5545/16.

23. Analysis of income and expenditure of the Reuven Shiloah Research Center from the date of its establishment in September 1959 until June 1961, ISA, G-6367/20. The studies mentioned in the document had to do with various current affairs such as the Syrian Ba'ath Party, the United Arab Republic's foreign policy in Africa, and the political history of Iraq. Among the studies listed, one commissioned by the Foreign Ministry to Rony Gabbay stands out: "On the Departure of the Arabs from the Land of Israel in 1948." Shai Hazkani's research indicates that Ben-Gurion himself commissioned the study; in order to carry it out, Gabbay was granted permission to browse the plundered documents collected by the Intelligence Corps and relevant Shabak materials, which were subsequently destroyed: Shay Hazkani, "Catastrophic Thinking: Did Ben-Gurion Try to Rewrite History?" *Ha'aretz*, May 16, 2013, https://www.haaretz.com/2013-05-16/ty-article/.premium/ben-gurion-grasped-the-nakbas-importance/0000017f-e12d-d38f-a57f-e77fcfdd0000?lts=1706518165576; see also Shay Hazkani, "Israel's Vanishing Files, Archival Deception and Paper Trails," *Middle East Report* 49 (2019): 10–15.

24. Nissim Rejwan, "1960—Bir'i hamizrah hatikhon," *Haboker*, July 20, 1962, 7; Clyne, *Orientalism, Zionism and Academic Practice*, 44. According to Clyne, the

## 258 ::: NOTES TO EPILOGUE

publication of the catalogue made redundant *The New East*'s press survey, which was made significantly briefer as a result.

25. Ayalon to Levi Eshkol, March 15, and Uri Lubrani to Ayalon, March 20, 1964, ISA, G-6367/20.

26. See, for example, Walter Zander to Benjamin Mazar, November 20, 1959, CAHU, 2229:1959; Eliahu Elath to Yitzhak Oron, January 13, 1963, CAHU, 2229:1963.

27. Clyne, *Orientalism, Zionism and Academic Practice*, 47.

28. Transcription of interview with David Ayalon, January 22, 1990, interviewer: Margalit Bejarano, 68. The transcription is preserved at the Oral History Division of the Hebrew University; David Ayalon to Menahem Milson, June 16, 1997, CAHU, Personnel File—David Ayalon, from 1967.

29. Yehoshafat Harkabi and Yitzhak Oron to members of the Reuven Shiloah Research Center, December 28, 1965, CAHU, 2229:1965.

30. Eyal, *Disenchantment of the Orient*, 200–201. Historian of the modern Middle East Shimon Shamir (b. 1933), then a young lecturer in the Department of History of the Islamic Lands in Jerusalem, headed the new center and department and took the initiative in transferring the Shiloah Center to Tel Aviv University.

31. Ayalon to Milson, June 16, 1997.

32. Ayalon was invited to a meeting at the home of Mossad director Meir Amit, along with a group of members of Knesset, past and current directors of Aman, senior Foreign Ministry officials, and Mossad personnel. The meeting sought to assess the chances of reaching a peace agreement with Egypt, and Ayalon was invited as an expert in the country's modern history: Ronen Bergman, "Shalom? Tenase aharey hamilhama," *Yedi'ot aharonot*, June 3, 2005, 7 yamim, 20–26.

33. Eyal, *Disenchantment of the Orient*, 201. See also, for example, Forte, "Sifting People, Sorting Papers."

34. Press release, December 24, 1967, CAHU, 225:1967. Several members of the second generation at the Institute of Asian and African Studies, including David Ayalon, Meir Kister, Eliyahu Ashtor, and Pessah Shinar opposed the changes spearheaded by Baer, in the Department of Arabic Language and Literature for example. In fact, they approached the dean asking to have his appointment cancelled for professional and procedural reasons: Ayalon, Shlomo Pines, Kister, Blau, Ashtor, and Shinar to Zvi Adar, July 8, 1970, CAHU, 225:1970–1971. On their relationship with Baer, see Yohanan Friedmann, *MiZákamenné lirushalayim: Pirkey zikaron* (Jerusalem: self-pub., 2019), 97–98.

35. Gabriel Baer to Avraham Harman, July 16, 1971, CAHU, 225:1970–1971; Moshe Ma'oz to Avraham Harman, n.d. [1973], CAHU, 225:1972–1973.

36. Zvi Lavi, "Merkaz mada'i leheker toldot ha'aravim ba'artez yukam behar hatzofim," *Ma'ariv*, January 31, 1972. Details in the article were based on press releases distributed by the publishing division of the university on January 26, 1972, CAHU, 225:1972–1973.

37. For example, between 1925 and 1936, D. H. Baneth published thirteen book reviews in the *Kiryat Sefer* journal of the National and University Library, where he

NOTES TO EPILOGUE ::: 259

worked. Most discussed German-language books. See Avraham Attal, "Bibliografia shel kitvey Prof. David Zvi Baneth," in *Studia Orientalia: Memoriae D. H. Baneth Dedicata* (Jerusalem: The Hebrew University Magnes Press, 1979), 175–79.

38. D. H. Baneth to the Hebrew University administration, [n.d. The letter notes that it was written in response to a letter of November 16, 1926], ANLI, Arc. 4° 1559/03/17.

# BIBLIOGRAPHY

Abadi, Jacob. *Israel's Quest for Recognition and Acceptance in Asia: Garrison State Diplomacy*. London: Frank Cass, 2004.

Abd al-Aziz, Hisham Fawzi. "Ma'had al-'ulum al-sharqiyya fil-jami'a al-'ibriyya fil-quds 1926–1948." *'Alam al-fikr* 1 (1997): 251–82.

Abd El Gawad, Walid. "Dreifache Vermittlung: Israel Wolfensohn als Pionier der israelischen Orientwissenschaft." In *Ein Paradigma der Moderne: Jüdische Geschichte in Schlüsselbegriffen; Festschrift für Dan Diner zum 70. Geburtstag*, edited by Arndt Engelhardt, Lutz Fiedler, Elisabeth Gallas, Natasha Gordinsky, and Philipp Graf, 287–308. Göttingen: Vandenhoeck & Ruprecht, 2016.

Abuhav, Orit. *In the Company of Others: The Development of Anthropology in Israel*. Detroit: Wayne State University Press, 2015.

Abulafiya, Meir. "Sofer falastini rodef shalom betokh ha'intifada: 'al hasofer hafalastini Ishaq Musa al-Husseini vesifro zikhronot tarnegolet." *Moznaim* 62, no. 9–10 (1988–1989): 20–25.

Aharonson, Ran. "Settlement in Eretz Israel—A Colonialist Enterprise? 'Critical' Scholarship and Historical Geography." *Israel Studies* 1, no. 2 (1996): 214–29.

Ahmed, Hussam R. *The Last Nahdawi: Taha Hussein and Institution Building in Egypt*. Stanford: Stanford University Press, 2021.

Al-Hamdānī, Ḥusain F. "Some Unknown Ismā'īlī Authors and Their Works." *Journal of the Royal Asiatic Society of Great Britain & Ireland* 65, no. 2 (1933): 359–78.

Alon, Yoav, and Ido Shahar. "Re'ayon 'im Prof. Jacob Landau." *Hamizrah hehadash* 58 (2019): 15–24.

Al-Qalamawi, Soheir. *Dhikra Taha Hussein*. Cairo: Dar al-ma'arif, 1974.

Amit, Gish. "Salvage or Plunder? Israel's 'Collection' of Private Palestinian Libraries in West Jerusalem." *Journal of Palestine Studies* 40, no. 4 (2011): 6–23.

Ari, Nisa. "Cultural Mandates, Artistic Missions, and 'The Welfare of Palestine,' 1876–1948." PhD diss., Massachusetts Institute of Technology, 2019.

Arvidsson, Stefan. *Aryan Idols: Indo-European Mythology as Ideology and Science*. Translated by Sonia Wichmann. Chicago: University of Chicago Press, 2006.

Ash, Mitchell G. "Bachelor of What, Master of Whom? The Humboldt Myth and Historical Transformations of Higher Education in German-Speaking Europe and the US." *European Journal of Education* 41, no. 2 (2006): 245–67.

———. "Wissens- und Wissenschaftstransfer—Einführende Bemerkungen." *Berichte zur Wissenschaftsgeschichte* 29, no. 3 (2006): 181–89.

Attal, Avraham. "Bibliografia shel kitvey Prof. David Zvi Baneth." In *Studia Orientalia: Memoriae D. H. Baneth Dedicata*, 175–79. Jerusalem: The Hebrew University Magnes Press, 1979.

## 262 ::: BIBLIOGRAPHY

Avner, A. "Hasber panekha lashavuy." *Mabat malam* 61 (2011): 45.

'Awad, Mahmud. *Wa'alaykum al-salam.*. Cairo: Dar al-mustaqbal al-'arabi, 1984.

Ayalon, David. "Mistudent legimlai, 1932–1994." *Igeret ha'akademia hale'umit hayisra'elit lemada'im* 24 (2003): 39–42.

Baer, Gabriel. "Gormey yesod utmurot bahevra hamitzrit bat zmanenu." In *Hevra umishtar ba'olam ha'aravi*, edited by Menahem Milson, 1–23. Jerusalem: Van Leer Institute, 1977.

———. "Hamizrahanut beyisra'el bishloshim hashanim ha'aharonot." *Hamizrah hehadash* 28, no. 3–4 (1979): 175–81.

———. *Hamukhtar hakafri be'eretz Israel: Toldot ma'amado vetafkidav*. Jerusalem: The Hebrew University Magnes Press, 1978.

Bakr, Yasir. "Taha Hussein wal-sahyuniyya!" Masr al-'arabiyya, May 8, 2016. https://masralarabia.net/.

Barak-Gorodetsky, David. *Judah Magnes: The Prophetic Politics of a Religious Binationalist*. Translated by Merav Datan. Lincoln: University of Nebraska Press and the Jewish Publication Society of America, 2021.

Barmak, Sagi. "Hakamat misrad hahutz hayisra'eli, 1946–1953." Master's thesis, Hebrew University of Jerusalem, 2015.

Bar-On, Hanoch. "Toldotav." In *Sefer Adam-Noah: Divrey tora, hagut, mehkar veha'arakha, zikaron leR. Adam-Noah Dr. Braun*, edited by S. Y. Cohen, Hayim Lifshitz, and Zvi Kaplan, 9–11. Jerusalem: Hava'ada lehantzahat zikhro shel Dr. Adam-Noah Braun, 'al-yad mekhon Harry Fischel, 1969.

Bartal, Israel. "The Emergence of Modern Jewish Academe: From Religious Academies in Eastern Europe to a Secular University." In *Konstellationen: Über Geschichte, Erfahrung und Erkenntnis; Festschrift für Dan Diner zum 65. Geburtstag*, edited by Nicolas Berg, Omar Kamil, Markus Kirchhoff, and Susanne Zepp, 15–43. Göttingen: Vandenhoeck & Ruprecht, 2011.

Becker, C. H., and F. Rosenthal. "Al-Balādhurī." In *Encyclopaedia of Islam*, edited by P. Bearman, T. Bianquis, C. E. Bosworth, E. van Donzel, and W. P. Heinrichs. 2nd ed. http://dx.doi.org/10.1163/1573-3912_islam_COM_0094.

Ben-Eliezer, Uri. *The Making of Israeli Militarism*. Bloomington: Indiana University Press, 1998.

Benes, Tuska. "Comparative Linguistics as Ethnology: In Search of Indo-Germans in Central Asia, 1770–1830." *Comparative Studies of South Asia, Africa and the Middle East* 24, no. 2 (2004): 117–32.

Bengio, Ofra. *The Turkish-Israeli Relationship: Changing Ties of Middle Eastern Outsiders*. New York: Palgrave Macmillan, 2004.

Ben-Israel, Hedva. "Bi-Nationalism versus Nationalism: The Case of Judah Magnes." *Israel Studies* 23, no. 1 (2018): 86–105.

Bentwich, Norman. *For Zion's Sake: A Biography of Judah L. Magnes*. Philadelphia: Jewish Publication Society of America, 1954.

———. *The Rescue and Achievement of Refugee Scholars: The Story of Displaced Scholars and Scientists 1933–1952*. The Hague: Martinus Nijhoff, 1953.

BIBLIOGRAPHY ::: 263

Berman, Nina. *German Literature on the Middle East: Discourses and Practices, 1000–1989*. Ann Arbor: The University of Michigan Press, 2011.

Bernstein, Judah M. "A Preacher in Exile: Shemaryahu Levin and the Making of American Zionism, 1914–1919." *American Jewish History* 102, no. 3 (2018): 323–50.

Bialer, Uri. *Between East and West: Israel's Foreign Policy Orientation 1948-1956*. Cambridge: Cambridge University Press, 1990.

———. *Israeli Foreign Policy: A People Shall Not Dwell Alone*. Bloomington: Indiana University Press, 2020.

Birchall, Ian. *Tony Cliff: A Marxist for His Time*. London: Bookmarks, 2011.

Black, Ian, and Benny Morris. *Israel's Secret Wars: A History of Israel's Intelligence Services*. New York: Grove Weidenfeld, 1991.

Borg, Alexander. *Rewriting Dialectal Arabic Prehistory: The Ancient Egyptian Lexical Evidence*. Leiden: Brill, 2021.

Bostock, Sahar Mor. "Radio Listenership in Palestinian Society: Reshaping Cultural Practices and Political Debate under the British Mandate, 1930–1948." *Contemporary Levant* 8, no. 1 (2023): 70–86.

Bourdieu, Pierre. *Homo Academicus*. Translated by Peter Collier. Stanford: Stanford University Press, 1988.

Boyd, Douglas A. "Sharq al-Adna/The Voice of Britain: The UK's 'Secret' Arabic Radio Station and Suez War Propaganda Disaster." *Gazette: The International Journal for Communication Studies* 65, no. 6 (2003): 443–55.

Bragulla, Maren. *Die Nachrichtenstelle für den Orient: Fallstudie einer Propaganda-institution im Ersten Weltkrieg*. Saarbrücken: VDM Verlag Dr. Müller, 2007.

Brown, Ian. *The School of Oriental and African Studies: Imperial Training and the Expansion of Learning*. Cambridge: Cambridge University Press, 2016.

Burbank, Jane, and Frederick Cooper. *Empires in World History: Power and the Politics of Difference*. Princeton: Princeton University Press, 2010.

Burnett, Stephen G. *Christian Hebraism in the Reformation Era (1500–1660): Authors, Books, and the Transmission of Jewish Learning*. Leiden: Brill, 2012.

Clark, William. *Academic Charisma and the Origins of the Research University*. Chicago: University of Chicago Press, 2006.

Clyne, Eyal. *Orientalism, Zionism and Academic Practice: Middle East and Islam Studies in Israeli Universities*. London: Routledge, 2019.

Cohen, Aharon. "Israel and Jewish-Arab Peace: Governmental and Non-governmental Approaches." In *Elusive Peace in the Middle East*, edited by Malcolm H. Kerr, 102–65. Albany: State University of New York Press, 1975.

Cohen, Hillel. *Year Zero of the Arab-Israeli Conflict 1929*. Translated by Haim Watzman. Waltham, MA: Brandeis University Press, 2015.

Cohen-Shani, Shmuel. "Hamahlaka hamedinit shel hasokhnut hayehudit ve-'beit hasefer lediplomatim'—binuy mosdoteha shel medina hadasha." *Hatziyonut* 19 (1995): 325–44.

Cohen, Uri, and Adi Sapir. "Models of Academic Governance during a Period of

Nation-Building: The Hebrew University in the 1920s–1960s." *History of Education* 45, no. 5 (2016): 602–20.

Cole, Peter, and Adina Hoffman. *Sacred Trash: The Lost and Found World of the Cairo Geniza*. New York: Nextbook and Schocken, 2011.

Conrad, Lawrence I. "The Dervish's Disciple: On the Personality and Intellectual Milieu of the Young Ignaz Goldziher." *The Journal of the Royal Asiatic Society of Great Britain and Ireland* 122, no. 2 (1990): 225–66.

———. "Editor's Introduction." In *The Earliest Biographies of the Prophet and Their Authors*, by Josef Horovitz, ix–xxxviii. Edited by Lawrence I. Conrad. Princeton: The Darwin Press, 2002.

———. "Ignaz Goldziher on Ernest Renan: From Orientalist Philology to the Study of Islam." In *The Jewish discovery of Islam: Studies in Honor of Bernard Lewis*, edited by Martin Kramer, 137–80. Tel Aviv: The Moshe Dayan Center for Middle Eastern and African Studies, Tel Aviv University, 1999.

Daftary, Farhad. "Al Hamdani, Husayn F. (1901–1962)." In *Historical Dictionary of the Ismailis*, 64–65. Lanham: The Scarecrow Press, 2012.

Degani, Arnon. "Zionism's Flipside: A Reconsideration of Settler-Colonialism in Israel/Palestine." *Academia.edu*. 2023. www.academia.edu/108390348/Zionisms _Flipside_A_Reconsideration_of_Settler_Colonialism_in_Israel_Palestine.

Derri, Aviv. "The Construction of 'Native' Jews in Late Mandate Palestine: An Ongoing Nahda as a Political Project." *International Journal of Middle East Studies* 53, no. 2 (2021): 253–71.

———. "Mizrahanut alternativit vehishtalvut bamerhav ha'aravi hamekomi: Dr. Israel Ben-Ze'ev, hasifriya ha'aravit beyafo vehama'avak 'al sfarim falastiniyim 'netushim', 1948–1952." Master's thesis, Ben-Gurion University of the Negev, 2013.

Dévényi, Kinga, and Sabine Schmidtke. "The Published Correspondences of Ignaz Goldziher: A Bibliographical Guide." In *Building Bridges: Ignaz Goldziher and His Correspondents. Islamic and Jewish Studies around the Turn of the Twentieth Century*, edited by Hans-Jürgen Becker, Kinga Dévényi, Sebastian Günther, and Sabine Schmidtke, 413–28. Leiden: Brill, 2024.

Di-Capua, Yoav. "Changing the Arab Intellectual Guard: On the Fall of the Udaba', 1940–1960." In *Arabic Thought against the Authoritarian Age: Towards an Intellectual History of the Present*, edited by Jens Hanssen and Max Weiss, 41–61. Cambridge: Cambridge University Press, 2018.

Di Giulio, Marco. "Protecting the Jewish Throat: Hebrew Accent and Hygiene in the Yishuv." *Journal of Israeli History* 35, no. 2 (2016): 153–75.

Diner, Dan, and Moshe Zimmerman. "Israel's German Academic Legacy: An Introduction." In *Disseminating German Tradition*, edited by Dan Diner and Moshe Zimmerman, 7–14. Leipzig: Leipziger Universitätsverlag, 2009.

"Divrey Gabriel Baer." In *'Al Prof. Alfred Bonne z"l*, 19–21. Jerusalem: The Hebrew University Magnes Press, 1960.

Doegen, Wilhelm, ed. *Unter Fremden Völkern: Eine neue Völkerkunde*. Berlin: Otto Stollberg Verlag für Politik und Wirtschaft, 1925.

BIBLIOGRAPHY ::: 265

Dolev, Diana. *The Planning and Building of the Hebrew University, 1919–1948: Facing the Temple Mount*. Lanham, MD: Lexington Books, 2016.

Efron, John. "Orientalism and the Jewish Historical Gaze." In *Orientalism and the Jews*, edited by Ivan D. Kalmar and Derek J. Penslar, 80–93. Waltham: Brandeis University Press, 2005.

El-Bendary, Mohamed. *The Egyptian Press and Coverage of Local and International Events*. Lanham, MD: Lexington Books, 2010.

Elhanani, A. H. "Nose dvaram vehelekh ruham shel ehav." *Bama'arakha* 81 (1968): 10–11.

Escovitz, Joseph H. "Orientalists and Orientalism in the Writings of Muhammad Kurd Ali." *International Journal of Middle East Studies* 15, no. 1 (1983): 95–109.

Evans, Andrew E. *Anthropology at War: World War I and the Science of Race in Germany*. Chicago: University of Chicago Press, 2010.

Evri, Yuval. *Hashiva le'Andalus: Mahalokot 'al tarbut vezehut yehudit-sfaradit bein 'araviyut le'ivriyut*. Jerusalem: The Hebrew University Magnes Press, 2020.

———. "Return to al-Andalus beyond German-Jewish Orientalism: Abraham Shalom Yahuda's Critique of Modern Jewish Discourse." In *Modern Jewish Scholarship on Islam in Context: Rationality, European Borders, and the Search for Belonging*, edited by Ottfried Fraisse, 337–54. Berlin: De Gruyter, 2018.

———. *Translating the Arab-Jewish Tradition: From Al-Andalus to Palestine/Land of Israel*. Berlin: Forum Transregionale Studien, 2016.

Eyal, Gil. *The Disenchantment of the Orient: Expertise in Arab Affairs and the Israeli State*. Stanford: Stanford University Press, 2006.

Ferguson, Charles A. "Diglossia." *Word* 15, no. 2 (1959): 325–40.

Fiedler, Lutz. *Matzpen: A History of Israeli Dissidence*. Translated by Jake Schneider. Edinburgh: Edinburgh University Press, 2020.

Fischel, Walter J. "William Popper (1874–1963) and His Contribution to Islamic Scholarship: In Memoriam." *Journal of the American Oriental Society* 84, no. 3 (1964): 213–20.

Fogel, Tom. "Hamehkar hateimani shel S. D. Goitein." PhD diss., Hebrew University of Jerusalem, 2019.

Forte, Tania. "Sifting People, Sorting Papers: Academic Practice and the Notion of State Security in Israel." *Comparative Studies of South Asia, Africa and the Middle East* 23, no. 1–2 (2003): 215–23.

Fraisse, Ottfried. "From Geiger to Goldziher: Historical Method and Its Impact on the Conception of Islam." In *Modern Jewish Scholarship in Hungary: The "Science of Judaism" between East and West*, edited by Tamás Turán and Carsten Wilke, 203–22. Berlin: De Gruyter, 2016.

Frenkel, Miriam. "Eliyahu Ashtor—A Forgotten Pioneer Researcher of Jewish History under the Mamluks." In *Muslim-Jewish Relations in the Middle Islamic Period: Jews in the Ayyubid and Mamluk Sultanates (1171–1517)*, edited by Stephan Conermann, 63–74. Göttingen: Vandenhoeck & Ruprecht, 2017.

———. "Ktivat hahistoria shel yehudey artzot ha'islam bimey habeinayim: Tziuney derekh vesikuyim." *Pe'amim* 92 (2002): 23–61.

266 ::: BIBLIOGRAPHY

Friedmann, Yohanan. *MiZákamenné lirushalayim: Pirkey zikaron.* Jerusalem: Self-published, 2019.

Fück, Johann. *Die arabischen Studien in Europa bis in den Anfang des 20. Jahrhunderts.* Leipzig: O. Harrassowitz, 1955.

Furas, Yoni. *Educating Palestine: Teaching and Learning History under the Mandate.* Oxford: Oxford University Press, 2020.

Gad al-Mawla, Ahmad al-Sa'id. "Al-'Alim al-'islami al-marhum al-'ustadh / Muhammad Ahmad Gad al-Mawla (Bek)." In *Dustur al-'afrad wal-'umam fi sunan sayd al-'arab wal-'ajam Muhammad,* by Muhammad Ahmad Gad al-Mawla (Bek), 611–13. Cairo: Al-dar al-misriyya al-lubnaniyya, 2000.

Gelber, Yoav. "Antecedents of the Jewish-Druze Alliance in Palestine." *Middle Eastern Studies* 28, no. 2 (1992): 352–73.

———. "The Historical Role of the Central European Immigration to Israel." *The Leo Baeck Institute Year Book* 38, no. 1 (1993): 323–39.

———. *Moledet hadasha: 'Aliyat yehudey merkaz eropa uklitatam, 1933–1948.* Jerusalem: Yad Ben Zvi, 1990.

Gershoni, Israel. "Egyptian Liberalism in an Age of 'Crisis of Orientation': Al-Risala's Reaction to Fascism and Nazism, 1933–39." *International Journal of Middle East Studies* 31, no. 4 (1999): 551–76.

———. "Luṭfi Al-Sayyid, Aḥmad." In *Encyclopaedia of Islam,* edited by Kate Fleet, Gudrun Krämer, Denis Matringe, John Nawas, and Everett Rowson. 3rd edition. http://dx.doi.org/10.1163/1573-3912_ei3_COM_35916.

Gibson, Shimon. "British Archaeological Institutions in Mandatory Palestine, 1917–1948." *Palestine Exploration Quarterly* 131, no. 2 (1999): 115–43.

Gitler, Inbal Ben-Asher, and Bar Leshem. "Creating Museum Culture in Mandate Palestine." *Israel Studies* 26, no. 3 (2021): 138–57.

Glock, Albert. "Archaeology as Cultural Survival: The Future of the Palestinian Past." *Journal of Palestine Studies* 23, no. 3 (1994): 70–84.

Goitein, Shelomo Dov. "David Hartwig (Zvi) Baneth, 1893–1973." In *Studia Orientalia: Memoriae D. H. Baneth Dedicata,* 1–5. Jerusalem: The Hebrew University Magnes Press, 1979.

———. "Goldziher abu al-dirasat al-'islamiyya: Bimunasabat murur khams wa'ishrin sana 'ala wafatihi." *Al-Katib al-misri* 5, no. 14 (1947): 85–95.

———. *Goldziher lefi mikhtavav (mikhtavey Goldziher 'el S. A. Poznanski bashanim 1901–1921): Tadpis misefer hazikaron likhvod Yitzhaq Yehuda Goldziher.* Budapest: 1948.

———. "Hakdama." In *Sefer Ansāb al-Ashrāf shel al-Balādhurī,* published by Shelomo Dov Goitein, 7–8. Vol. 5. Jerusalem: Hebrew University, 1935.

———. "Igeret brakha lahevra hamizrahit hayisra'elit bimlot la shloshim shana." *Hamizrah hehadash* 28, no. 3–4 (1979): 173–74.

———. "Josef Horovitz." *Der Islam* 22, no. 2 (1934): 122–27.

———. "The Life Story of a Scholar." In *A Bibliography of the Writings of Prof. Shelomo Dov Goitein,* edited by Robert Attal, xiii–xxviii. Jerusalem: Israel Oriental

Society and the Institute of Asian and African Studies, The Hebrew University of Jerusalem, 1975.

———. "Oriental Studies in Israel (Hebrew and the Ancient East excluded)." In *Hebrew University Garland: A Silver Jubilee Symposium*, edited by Norman Bentwich, 96–110. London: Constellation Books, 1952.

———. "Review of *Hayehudim be'arav*, by Israel Ben-Ze'ev." *Kiryat sefer* 8, no. 3 (1932): 304.

———. "The School of Oriental Studies: A Memoir." In *Like All the Nations? The Life and Legacy of Judah L. Magnes*, edited by William M. Brinner and Moses Rischin, 167–73. Albany: State University of New York Press, 1987.

———. *Studies in Islamic History and Institutions*. Leiden: Brill, 2010.

Golan, Joe. *Dapim meyoman*. Jerusalem: Carmel, 2005.

Goldziher, Ignác. *Tagebuch*. Edited by Alexander Scheiber. Leiden: Brill, 1978.

Gonzalez, Allyson. "Abraham S. Yahuda (1877–1951) and the Politics of Modern Jewish Scholarship." *Jewish Quarterly Review* 109, no. 3 (2019): 406–33.

Goren, Arthur A. "The View from Scopus: Judah L. Magnes and the Early Years of the Hebrew University." *Judaism* 45, no. 2 (1996): 203–24.

Gottesman, Itzik Nakhmen. *Defining the Yiddish Nation: The Jewish Folklorists of Poland*. Detroit: Wayne State University Press, 2003.

Greenspoon, Leonard. *Max Leopold Margolis: A Scholar's Scholar*. Atlanta: Scholars Press, 1987.

Greenstein, Edward L. "M. M. Bravmann: A Sketch." *Journal of the Ancient Near Eastern Society* 11, no. 1 (1979): 1–2.

Gribetz, Jonathan. *Defining Neighbors: Religion, Race, and the Early Zionist-Arab Encounter*. Princeton: Princeton University Press, 2014.

Gries, Zeev. "Adding Insult to Injury: Zionist Cultural Colonialism." *Judaica Librarianship* 19 (2016): 73–92.

Gruen, George E. "Dynamic Progress in Turkish-Israeli Relations." *Israel Affairs* 1, no. 4 (1995): 40–70.

Gussone, Martin. "Architectural Jihad: The 'Halbmondlager' Mosque of Wünsdorf as an Instrument of Propaganda." In *Jihad and Islam in World War I: Studies on the Ottoman Jihad at the Centenary of Snouck Hurgronje's "Holy War Made in Germany,"* edited by Erik-Jan Zürcher, 179–222. Leiden: Leiden University Press, 2015.

Hagen, Gottfried. "German Heralds of Holy War: Orientalists and Applied Oriental Studies." *Comparative Studies of South Asia, Africa and the Middle East* 24, no. 2 (2004): 145–62.

Hallaq, Wael B. *Restating Orientalism: A Critique of Modern Knowledge*. New York: Columbia University Press, 2018.

Halperin, Liora R. *Babel in Zion: Jews, Nationalism, and Language Diversity in Palestine, 1920–1948*. New Haven: Yale University Press, 2015.

Hanisch, Ludmila. *Die Nachfolger der Exegeten: Deutschsprachige Erforschung des Vorderen Orients in der ersten Hälfte des 20. Jahrhunderts*. Wiesbaden: Harrassowitz, 2003.

## 268 ::: BIBLIOGRAPHY

Harif, Hanan. *Anashim ahim anahnu: Hapniya mizraha bahagut hatziyonit.* Jerusalem: Zalman Shazar Center for Jewish History, 2019.

———. "A Bridge or a Fortress? S. D. Goitein and the Role of Jewish Arabists in the American Academy." *Jewish Social Studies* 26, no. 2 (2021): 68–92.

———. "Infanticide, Orientalism and British Law in Mandate Palestine." *Jewish Quarterly Review* 114, no. 2 (2024): 263–92.

———. "Islam in Zion? Yosef Yo'el Rivlin's Translation of the Qur'an and Its Place within the New Hebrew Culture." *Naharaim* 10, no. 1 (2016): 39–55.

———. "The Orient between Arab and Jewish National Revivals: Josef Horovitz, Shelomo Dov Goitein and Oriental Studies in Jerusalem." In *Modern Jewish Scholarship on Islam in Context: Rationality, European Borders, and the Search for Belonging*, edited by Ottfried Fraisse, 319–36. Berlin: De Gruyter, 2018.

Harif, Hanan, and Amit Levy. "Disciplina shlema rabat panim: Hapulmus 'al limudey hahistoria shel yehudey artzot ha'islam bamekhonim lemada'ey hayahadut ulmada'ey hamizrah." In *Toldot ha'universita ha'ivrit birushalayim*, edited by Yfaat Weiss and Uzi Rebhun, 687–718. Vol. 5: *Medinat hale'om vehahaskala hagvoha.* Jerusalem: The Hebrew University Magnes Press, 2024.

Hartog, Philip, Louis Ginzberg, and Redcliffe Salaman. *Report of the Survey Committee of the Hebrew University of Jerusalem.* Jerusalem: The Hebrew University, 1934.

Hazkani, Shay. "Israel's Vanishing Files, Archival Deception and Paper Trails." *Middle East Report* 49 (2019): 10–15.

Heilbron, John. "Academies and Learned Societies." In *The Oxford Companion to the History of Modern Science*, edited by John Heilbron, 1–5. Oxford: Oxford University Press, 2003.

Hermann, Rainer. *Kulturkrise und konservative Erneuerung: Muḥammad Kurd ʿAlī (1876–1953) und das geistige Leben in Damaskus zu Beginn des 20. Jahrhunderts.* Frankfurt am Main: Peter Lang, 1990.

Heschel, Susannah. "Abraham Geiger and the Emergence of Jewish Philoislamism." In *"Im vollen Licht der Geschichte": Die Wissenshaft des Judentums und die Anfänge der kritischen Koranforschung*, edited by Dirk Hartwig, Walter Homolka, Michael J. Marx, and Angelika Neuwirth, 65–86. Würzburg: Ergon, 2008.

———. "German Jewish Scholarship on Islam as a Tool for De-Orientalizing Judaism." *New German Critique* 39, no. 3 (2012): 91–107.

Heyd, Uriel. *Hamizrah hatikhon bazman hehadash kenose lemehkar ulhora'a.* Jerusalem: The Hebrew University Magnes Press, 1952.

Higdon, David Leon. "The Concordance: Mere Index or Needful Census?" *Text: An Interdisciplinary Annual of Textual Studies* 15 (2002): 51–68.

Hillenbrand, Carole. "Bernard Lewis: 31 May 1916–19 May 2018." *Biographical Memoirs of Fellows of the British Academy* XIX (2020): 231–54.

Hirschberg, H. Z. "Leon Aryeh Mayer: Hamesh shanim liftirato." *Eretz Israel: Mehkarim biydi'at ha'aretz va'atikoteha* 7 (1964): 11–16.

Holzer-Kawalko, Anna, and Enrico Lucca. "Sifriyat hagola: Tkumat beit hasfarim hale'umi birushalayim vekibutz ha'osafim." In *Toldot ha'universita ha'ivrit birushalayim*, edited by Yfaat Weiss and Uzi Rebhun, 719–66. Vol. 5: *Medinat hale'om vehahaskala hagvoha*. Jerusalem: The Hebrew University Magnes Press, 2024.

Hopkins, James. "The Role of Learned Societies in Knowledge Exchange and Dissemination: The Case of the Regional Studies Association, 1965–2005." *History of Education* 40, no. 2 (2011): 255–71.

Höpp, Gerhard. *Muslime in der Mark: Als Kriegsgefangene und Internierte in Wünsdorf und Zossen*. Berlin: Das Arabische Buch, 1997.

Horovitz, Josef. *Indien unter britischer Herrschaft*. Leipzig: B. G. Teubner, 1928.

Hourani, Albert. *Arabic Thought in the Liberal Age: 1798–1939*. Cambridge: Cambridge University Press, 1983.

Hussein, Mostafa. "Scholarship on Islamic Archaeology between Zionism and Arab Nationalist Movements." In *The Muslim Reception of European Orientalism: Reversing the Gaze*, edited by Susannah Heschel and Umar Ryad, 184–208. Oxon: Routledge, 2019.

Idris, Muhammad Jala. *Al-'Istishraq al-isra'ili fil-dirasat al-'ibriyya al-mu'asira*. Cairo: Al-'arabi lil-nashr wal-tawzi', 1995.

Irish, Tomás. *The University at War, 1914–25: Britain, France, and the United States*. Basingstoke: Palgrave Macmillan, 2015.

Irving, Sarah. "Palestinian Christians in the Mandate Department of Antiquities: History and Archaeology in a Colonial Space." In *European Cultural Diplomacy and Arab Christians in Palestine, 1918–1948: Between Contention and Connection*, edited by Karène Sanchez Summerer and Sary Zananiri, 161–85. London: Palgrave Macmillan, 2021.

———. "Stephan Hanna Stephan and Evliya Çelebi's Book of Travels: Tracing Cooperation and Conflict in Mandate Palestinian Translations." In *Cultural Entanglement in the Pre-Independence Arab World: Arts, Thought and Literature*, edited by Anthony Gorman and Sarah Irving, 217–37. London: Bloomsbury Academic, 2020.

Irwin, Robert. *For Lust of Knowing: The Orientalists and Their Enemies*. London: Allen Lane, 2006.

Jacobson, Abigail, and Moshe Naor. *Oriental Neighbors: Middle Eastern Jews and Arabs in Mandatory Palestine*. Waltham, MA: Brandeis University Press, 2016.

Jäger, Gudrun. "Der jüdische Islamwissenschaftler Josef Horovitz und der Lehrstuhl für semitische Philologie an der Universität Frankfurt am Main 1915–1949." In *Frankfurter Wissenschaftler zwischen 1933 und 1945*, edited by Jörn Kobes and Jan-Otmar Hesse, 61–79. Göttingen: Wallstein, 2008.

Johansen, Baber. "Politics and Scholarship: The Development of Islamic Studies in the Federal Republic of Germany." In *Middle East Studies: International Perspectives on the State of the Art*, edited by Tareq Y. Ismael, 71–130. New York: Praeger, 1990.

Johnston-Bloom, Ruchama. "'Dieses wirklich westöstlichen Mannes': The German-

270 ::: BIBLIOGRAPHY

Jewish Orientalist Josef Horovitz in Germany, India, and Palestine." In *The Muslim Reception of European Orientalism: Reversing the Gaze,* edited by Susannah Heschel and Umar Ryad, 168–83. London: Routledge, 2018.

———. "Symbiosis Relocated: The German-Jewish Orientalist Ilse Lichtenstadter in America." *Leo Baeck Institute Year Book* 58, no. 1 (2013): 95–110.

Jones, Heather. "A Missing Paradigm? Military Captivity and the Prisoner of War, 1914–18." *Immigrants & Minorities* 26, no. 1–2 (2008): 19–48.

Jospe, Alfred. "The Study of Judaism in German Universities before 1933." *Leo Baeck Institute Year Book* 27, no. 1 (1982): 295–319.

Kahlenberg, Caroline. "The Star of David in a Cedar Tree: Jewish Students and Zionism at the American University of Beirut (1908–1948)." *Middle Eastern Studies* 55, no. 4 (2019): 570–89.

Kahle, Paul. "Review of *Ansāb al-Ashrāf of al-Balādhurī,* Volume V, by S. D. F. Goitein." *ZDMG* 90, no. 3–4 (1936): 716–18.

"Kalimat Dr. Taha Hussein." In *Al-Buhuth wal-muhadarat: mu'tamar al-dawra al-hadiya wal-thalathin, 1964-1965,* by Majma' al-lugha al-'arabiyya bil-qahira, 6–7. Cairo, n.d.

Kanazi, George J. "Ishaq Musa al-Husayni and His Memoirs of a Hen." Introduction to *Memoirs of a Hen,* by Ishaq Musa al-Husayni, 5–15. Translated by George J. Kanazi. Toronto: York Press, 1999.

Katz, Hayah. *The Changing Landscape of Israeli Archaeology: Between Hegemony and Marginalization.* London: Routledge, 2023.

Katz, Shaul. "The Scion and Its Tree: The Hebrew University of Jerusalem and Its German Epistemological and Organizational Origins." In *The Institution of Science and the Science of Institutions: The Legacy of Joseph Ben-David,* edited by Marcel Herbst, 103–44. Dordrecht: Springer, 2014.

Kedar, Aharon. "Letoldoteha shel 'Brit Shalom' bashanim 1925–1928." In *Pirkey mehkar betoldot hatziyonut: Mugashim leIsrael Goldstein bahagi'o ligvurot,* edited by Yehuda Bauer, Moshe Davis, and Israel Kolatt, 224–85. Jerusalem: Hasifriya hatziyonit, 1976.

Kedar, Nir. "Ben-Gurion's *Mamlakhtiyut*: Etymological and Theoretical Roots." *Israel Studies* 7, no. 3 (2002): 117–33.

Khan, Razak. "Entanglements in the Colony: Jewish–Muslim Connected Histories in Colonial India." *Modern Asian Studies* 56, no. 6 (2022): 1845–71.

Kimmerling, Baruch. *Zionism and Territory: The Socio-Territorial Dimensions of Zionist Politics.* Berkeley: Institute of International Studies, University of California Press, 1983.

King, Philip J. *American Archaeology in the Mideast: A History of the American Schools of Oriental Research.* Philadelphia: The American Schools of Oriental Research, 1983.

Kister, Meir Jacob. "MiGalicia letarbut 'arav." *Igeret ha'akademia hale'umit hayisra'elit lemada'im* 26 (2004): 19–24.

Klein, Menachem. *Lives in Common: Arabs and Jews in Jerusalem, Jaffa, and Hebron.* Translated by Haim Watzman. New York: Oxford University Press, 2014.

BIBLIOGRAPHY ::: 271

Kontje, Todd. *German Orientalisms*. Ann Arbor: The University of Michigan Press, 2004.

Kraemer, Joel L. "The Death of an Orientalist: Paul Kraus from Prague to Cairo." In *The Jewish discovery of Islam: Studies in Honor of Bernard Lewis*, edited by Martin Kramer, 181–205. Tel Aviv: The Moshe Dayan Center for Middle Eastern and African Studies, Tel Aviv University, 1999.

———. "Goitein vehahevra hayam-tikhonit shelo." *Zmanim* 34/35 (1990): 4–17.

Kramer, Martin. *Ivory Towers on Sand: The Failure of Middle Eastern Studies in America*. Washington, DC: The Washington Institute for Near East Policy, 2001.

Kupferschmidt, Uri M. "Memory and History: 'Uncle Isaac' and/or Dr. Isacco Giuseppe Levi." Lecture given on the occasion of the inauguration of the Barda Chair for the Study of the History of Egyptian Jewry, University of Haifa, October 14, 2013. http://srjhechair.haifa.ac.il/images/pdf/lecture_English.pdf

Kurd Ali, Muhammad. *Al-Mu'asirun*. Beirut: Dar sadir, 1993.

———. *Al-Mudhakkarat*. Riyadh: Dar 'adwa al-salaf, 2010.

Landau, Jacob M. "Gotthold Eljakim Weil (Berlin, 1882–Jerusalem, 1960)." *Die Welt des Islams*, New Series, 38, no. 3 (1998): 280–85.

Latour, Bruno. *Reassembling the Social: An Introduction to Actor-Network Theory*. Oxford: Oxford University Press, 2007.

Lavsky, Hagit. "Bein hanahat 'even hapina laptiha: Yesud ha'universita ha'ivrit, 1918–1925." In *Toldot ha'universita ha'ivrit birushalayim*, edited by Shaul Katz and Michael Heyd, 120–59. Vol. 1: *Shorashim vehathalot*. Jerusalem: The Hebrew University Magnes Press, 1997.

Layish, Aharon. "Uriel Heyd's Contribution to the Study of the Legal, Religious, Cultural, and Political History of the Ottoman Empire and Modern Turkey." *British Journal of Middle Eastern Studies* 9, no. 1 (1982): 35–54.

Lazarus-Yafeh, Hava. "The Transplantation of Islamic Studies from Europe to the Yishuv and Israel." In *The Jewish Discovery of Islam: Studies in Honor of Bernard Lewis*, edited by Martin Kramer, 249–60. Tel Aviv: The Moshe Dayan Center for Middle Eastern and African Studies, Tel Aviv University, 1999.

Lemon, Robert. *Imperial Messages: Orientalism as Self-Critique in the Habsburg Fin De Siècle*. Rochester: Camden House, 2011.

Lev, Shimon. "Gandhi and the Jews, the Jews and Gandhi: An Overall Perspective." *Hindu Studies* 27, no. 3 (2023): 393–409.

———. "'I read Sri Aurobindo to find some light in our difficult days': Hugo Bergman's Encounter with India, Aurobindo, and the Mother." In *The Cosmic Movement: Sources, Contexts, Impact*, edited by Julie Chajes and Boaz Huss, 519–45. Beer Sheva: Ben-Gurion University of the Negev Press, 2020.

Levin, Shmarya. *Forward from Exile: The Autobiography of Shmarya Levin*. Translated and edited by Maurice Samuel. Philadelphia: Jewish Publication Society of America, 1967.

Levy, Amit. "A Man of Contention: Martin Plessner (1900–1973) and His Encounters with the Orient." *Naharaim* 10, no. 1 (2016): 79–100.

Levy, Lital. "Partitioned Pasts: Arab Jewish Intellectuals and the Case of Esther

## 272 ::: BIBLIOGRAPHY

Azhari Moyal (1873–1948)." In *The Making of the Arab Intellectual (1880–1960): Empire, Public Sphere, and the Colonial Coordinates of Selfhood*, edited by Dyalah Hamzah, 128–63. London: Routledge, 2012.

Lewis, Bernard. *Islam and the West*. New York: Oxford University Press, 1993.

Lian, Chaoqun. *Language, Ideology and Sociopolitical Change in the Arabic-speaking World: A Study of the Discourse of Arabic Language Academies*. Edinburgh: Edinburgh University Press, 2020.

Libson, Gideon. "Hidden Worlds and Open Shutters: S. D. Goitein, between Judaism and Islam." In *The Jewish Past Revisited: Reflections on Modern Jewish Historians*, edited by David N. Myers and David B. Ruderman, 163–98. New Haven: Yale University Press, 1998.

Liebau, Heike. "Networks of Knowledge Production: South Asian Muslims and German Scholars in Berlin (1915–30)." *Comparative Studies of South Asia, Africa and the Middle East* 40, no. 2 (2020): 309–21.

Lipphardt, Veronika, and David Ludwig. "Knowledge Transfer and Science Transfer." *European History Online (EGO)*, published by the Institute of European History (IEG), Mainz, December 12, 2011. www.ieg-ego.eu/lipphardtv-ludwigd-2011-en.

Livny, Adi. "Fighting Partition, Saving Mount Scopus: The Pragmatic Binationalism of D. W. Senator (1930–1949)." *Studies in Cotemporary Jewry* 31 (2020): 225–46.

———. "Ha'universita, hamedina umishva'at hatiktzuv." In *Toldot ha'universita ha'ivrit birushalayim*, edited by Yfaat Weiss and Uzi Rebhun, 71–114. Vol. 5: *Medinat hale'om vehahaskala hagvoha*. Jerusalem: The Hebrew University Magnes Press, 2024.

———. "The Hebrew University in Mandatory Palestine: A Relational History (1918–1948)." PhD diss., Hebrew University of Jerusalem, 2021.

Lockman, Zachary. *Contending Visions of the Middle East: The History and Politics of Orientalism*. Cambridge: Cambridge University Press, 2004.

Loewe, Heinrich. *Ignaz Goldziher (Ein Wort des Gedenkens von Heinrich Loewe)*. Berlin: Soncino, 1929.

Lowe, Lisa. *Critical Terrains: French and British Orientalisms*. Ithaca: Cornell University Press, 1991.

Lüdke, Tilman. *Jihad Made in Germany: Ottoman and German Propaganda and Intelligence Operations in the First World War*. Münster: Lit Verlag, 2005.

Macfie, Alexander Lyon. *Orientalism*. London: Pearson Education, 2002.

Madar, Vered, and Dani Schrire. "From Leipzig to Jerusalem: Erich Brauer, a Jewish Ethnographer in Search of a Field." *Naharaim* 8, no. 1 (2014): 91–119.

Magnes, Judah L. *Addresses by the Chancellor of the Hebrew University*. Jerusalem: Hebrew University, 1936.

———. *Dissenter in Zion: From the Writings of Judah L. Magnes*, edited by Arthur A. Goren. Cambridge, MA: Harvard University Press, 1982.

Mahmoudi, Abdelrashid. *Taha Husain's Education: From Al Azhar to the Sorbonne*. Surrey: Curzon, 1998.

Mangold, Sabine. *Eine "weltbürgerliche Wissenschaft"—Die deutsche Orientalistik im 19. Jahrhundert*. Stuttgart: Franz Steiner Verlag, 2004.

## BIBLIOGRAPHY ::: 273

———. "Gotthold Weil et les Tatars." In *Passeurs d'Orient: Les Juifs dans l'orientalisme*, edited by Michel Espagne, 207–18. Paris: Éditions de l'Éclat, 2013.

———. "Ignác Goldziher et Ernest Renan—Vision du monde et innovation scientifique." In *Ignác Goldziher: Un autre orientalisme?*, edited by Céline Trautmann-Waller, 73–88. Paris: Librairie Orientaliste Paul Geuthner, 2011.

Mangold-Will, Sabine. "Gotthold Weil, die Orientalische Philologie und die deutsche Wissenschaft an der Hebräischen Universität." *Naharaim* 8, no. 1 (2014): 74–90.

———. "Josef Horovitz und die Gründung des Instituts für Arabische und Islamische Studien an der Hebräischen Universität in Jerusalem: ein Orientalisches Seminar für Palästina." *Naharaim* 10, no. 1 (2016): 7–37.

———. "Photo-Kopieren als wissenschaftliche Praxis? Technische Innovation und gelehrte Distinktion in der Orientalischen Philologie des frühen 20. Jahrhunderts." In *Kolossale Miniaturen: Festschrift für Gerrit Walther*, edited by Matei Chihaia and Georg Eckert, 59–68. Münster: Aschendorff, 2019.

Manjapra, Kris. *Age of Entanglement: German and Indian Intellectuals across Empire*. Cambridge, MA: Harvard University Press, 2014.

Mannheim, Karl. "Das Problem der Generationen." *Kölner Vierteljahrshefte für Soziologie* 7 (1928): 157–85, 309–30.

Maor, Zohar. "Moderation from Right to Left: The Hidden Roots of Brit Shalom." *Jewish Social Studies* 19, no. 2 (2013): 79–108.

Marchand, Suzanne L. *German Orientalism in the Age of Empire: Religion, Race and Scholarship*. Cambridge: Cambridge University Press, 2009.

Matza, Doron. *He'asor shebo noldu 'arveiyey yisra'el': Yisra'el ve'ezrahea ha'aravim-falastinim 1966–1976*. Tel Aviv: Resling, 2022.

Maxwell, Alexander, and Sacha E. Davis. "Germanness beyond Germany: Collective Identity in German Diaspora Communities." *German Studies Review* 39, no. 1 (2016): 1–15.

Mayer, L. A. "Hamakhon lemada'ey hamizrah." *Niv hastudent* 3 (1937): 9–11.

———. *Reshita va'aliyata shel ha'arkheologia hamuslemit: Ne'um ptiha me'et L. A. Mayer, professor bakatedra la'omanot vela'arkheologia shel hamizrah hakarov 'al-shem Sir Sassoon David ba'universita ha'ivrit*. Jerusalem: Hebrew University Press, 1935.

McClelland, Charles E. *State, Society, and University in Germany, 1700–1914*. Cambridge: Cambridge University Press, 1980.

McGetchin, Douglas T., Peter K. J. Park, and Damodar SarDesai, eds. *Sanskrit and "Orientalism": Indology and Comparative Linguistics in Germany, 1750–1958*. New Delhi: Manohar Publishers & Distributors, 2004.

Mendel, Yonatan. *The Creation of Israeli Arabic: Political and Security Considerations in the Making of Arabic Language Studies in Israel*. London: Palgrave Macmillan, 2014.

———. "From German Philology to Local Usability: The Emergence of 'Practical' Arabic in the Hebrew Reali School in Haifa—1913–48." *Middle Eastern Studies* 52, no. 1 (2016): 1–26.

———. "German Orientalism, Arabic Grammar and the Jewish Education System:

The Origins and Effect of Martin Plessner's 'Theory of Arabic Grammar.'" *Naharaim* 10, no. 1 (2016): 57–77.

———. *Safa mihutz limkoma: Orientalism, modiʿin vehaʿaravit beyisraʾel.* Tel Aviv: Van Leer Institute and Hakibbutz Hameuchad, 2020.

Meron, Theodor. "The Demilitarization of Mount Scopus: A Regime That Was." *Israel Law Review* 3, no. 4 (1968): 501–25.

Milson, Menahem. "The Beginnings of Arabic and Islamic Studies at the Hebrew University of Jerusalem." *Judaism* 45, no. 2 (Spring 1996): 168–83.

Mitchell, Timothy. "The Middle East in the Past and Future of Social Science." In *The Politics of Knowledge: Area Studies and the Disciplines*, edited by David Szanton, 74–118. Berkeley: University of California Press, 2004.

Morrissey, Fitzroy. "Jewish-Muslim Symbiosis, Islamic Hellenism, and the Purpose of Islamic Studies: The Humanistic Legacy of Samuel Stern's Teachers." *Journal of Modern Jewish Studies* 20, no. 4 (2021): 421–53.

Moshfegh, David. "Ignaz Goldziher and the Rise of Islamwissenschaft as a 'Science of Religion.'" PhD diss., University of California at Berkeley, 2012.

Motahhari, Said Musatafa. *Al-mustashriq al-muʿasir Etan Kohlberg wahadith al-ʾimamiyya.* Karbala: Al-ʿataba al-ʿabbasiyya al-muqaddasa, 2014.

Muʾasasat al-Quds lil-thaqafa wal-turath. "Muhammad Yunis al-Husseini." https://alqudslana.com/index.php?action=individual_details&id=1987.

Muhareb, Mahmoud. "The Zionist Disinformation Campaign in Syria and Lebanon during the Palestinian Revolt, 1936–1939." *Journal of Palestine Studies* 42, no. 2 (2013): 6–25.

Myers, David G. "Hebräische Universität." In *Enzyklopädie jüdischer Geschichte und Kultur*, edited by Dan Diner, 14–18. Vol. 3. Stuttgart and Weimar: Metzler, 2012.

Myers, David N. *Re-Inventing the Jewish Past: European Jewish Intellectuals and the Zionist Return to History.* New York: Oxford University Press, 1995.

Nashashibi, Muhammad Issaf. *Al-Batal al-khalid Salah al-Din wal-shaʿir al-khalid Ahmed Shawqi.* Jerusalem: Bayt al-maqdis, 1932.

Nashef, Khaled. "Tawfik Canaan: His Life and Works." *Jerusalem Quarterly* 16 (2002): 12–26.

Neemani, Elad. "Haʾuniversita haʿivrit vetzahal bereshit hamdina: Bein shituf peʿula lishmira ʿal otonomia mosdit." In *Toldot haʾuniversita haʿivrit birushalayim*, edited by Yfaat Weiss and Uzi Rebhun, 586–614. Vol. 5: *Medinat haleʾom vehahaskala hagvoha.* Jerusalem: The Hebrew University Magnes Press, 2024.

Neuberger, Benyamin. *Israel's Relations with the Third World.* Tel Aviv: The S. Daniel Abraham Center for International and Regional Studies, Tel Aviv University, 2009.

Niblock, Timothy C. "The State of the Art in British Middle Eastern Studies." In *Middle East Studies: International Perspectives on the State of the Art*, edited by Tareq Y. Ismael, 39–57. New York: Praeger, 1990.

Niederland, Doron. "Deutsche Ärzte-Emigration und gesundheitspolitische Entwicklungen in 'Eretz Israel' (1933–1948)." *Medizinhistorisches Journal* 20, no. 1–2 (1985): 149–84.

Nitzan-Shiftan, Alona. "Contested Zionism—Alternative Modernism: Erich

BIBLIOGRAPHY ::: 275

Mendelsohn and the Tel Aviv Chug in Mandate Palestine." *Architectural History* 39 (1996): 147–80.

Nordau, Max. *Paradoxe*. Chicago: F. Gindele, 1885.

Noy, Amos. *'Edim 'o mumhim: Yehudim maskilim bney yerushalayim vehamizrah bithilat hame'a ha'esrim*. Tel Aviv: Resling, 2017.

"Obituary: Sir Philip Hartog." *Bulletin of the School of Oriental and African Studies, University of London* 12, no. 2 (1948): 491–93.

Olman, Arye. "Irene Garbell—Hahavera harishona ba'akademia." *Academy of the Hebrew Language*, March 14, 2021. https://hebrew-academy.org.il/2021/03/14/.

Owen, Roger. "Studying Islamic History (Review of the Cambridge History of Islam)." *The Journal of Interdisciplinary History* 4, no. 2 (1973): 287–98.

Oz-Salzberger, Fania, and Eli Salzberger. "The Secret German Sources of the Israeli Supreme Court." *Israel Studies* 3, no. 2 (1998): 159–92.

Pasto, James. "Islam's 'Strange Secret Sharer': Orientalism, Judaism, and the Jewish Question." *Comparative Studies in Society and History* 40, no. 3 (1998): 437–74.

Penslar, Derek J. *Zionism and Technocracy: The Engineering of the Jewish Settlement in Palestine, 1870–1918*. Bloomington: Indiana University Press, 1991.

Philipp, Thomas. "In Memoriam: Gabriel Baer 1919–1982." *Middle Eastern Studies* 19, no. 3 (1983): 275–76.

Pilcher, Jane. "Mannheim's Sociology of Generations: An Undervalued Legacy." *The British Journal of Sociology* 45, no. 3 (1994): 481–95.

Plessner, Meir. "Cultural Values of the Monotheistic Civilizations." *New Outlook: Middle East Monthly* II, no. 3 (November–December 1958): 40–43.

Pollock, Sheldon. "Deep Orientalism? Notes on Sanskrit and Power Beyond the Raj." In *Orientalism and the Postcolonial Predicament*, edited by Carol A. Breckenridge and Peter van der Veer, 76–133. Philadelphia: University of Pennsylvania Press, 1993.

Preece, Edward Andrew. "Building an Academic Tradition: Durham University and the Development of British Oriental Studies in the Post-War Era." Master's thesis, Durham University, 2017.

Preißler, Holger. "Heinrich Leberecht Fleischer. Ein Leipziger Orientalist, seine jüdischen Studenten, Promovenden und Kollegen." In *Bausteine einer jüdischen Geschichte der Universität Leipzig*, edited by Stephan Wendehorst, 245–68. Leipzig: Leipziger Universitätsverlag, 2006.

Rac, Katalin Franciska. "Arabic Literature for the Colonizer and the Colonized: Ignaz Goldziher and Hungary's Eastern Politics (1878–1918)." In *The Muslim Reception of European Orientalism: Reversing the Gaze*, edited by Susannah Heschel and Umar Ryad, 80–102. London: Routledge, 2018.

Ram, Uri. *The Changing Agenda of Israeli Sociology: Theory, Ideology, and Identity*. Albany: State University of New York Press, 1995.

——. "Israeli Sociology: Social Thought Amidst Struggles and Conflicts." *Irish Journal of Sociology* 23, no. 1 (2015): 98–117.

——. "Mizrahim or Mizrahiyut? Equality and Identity in Israeli Critical Social Thought." *Israel Studies Forum* 17, no. 2 (2002): 114–30.

276 ::: BIBLIOGRAPHY

Ran, Yaron. *Haʻaravist: Eliyahu Sasson vehamaʻavak hatziyoni bamered haʻaravi.* Modiʻin: Hotzaʻat Effie Meltzer, 2018.

Ratsabi, Shalom. *Between Zionism and Judaism: The Radical Circle in Brith Shalom, 1925–1933.* Leiden: Brill, 2002.

Raz-Krakotzkin, Amnon. "Exile within Sovereignty: Critique of 'The Negation of Exile' in Israeli Culture." In *The Scaffolding of Sovereignty: Global and Aesthetic Perspectives on the History of a Concept,* edited by Zvi Benite, Stefanos Geroulanos, and Nicole Jerr, 393–420. New York: Columbia University Press, 2017.

———. "Orientalism, Jewish Studies and Israeli Society: A Few Comments." *Philological Encounters* 2, no. 3–4 (2017): 237–69.

Reichman, Shalom, and Shlomo Hasson. "A Cross-Cultural Diffusion of Colonization: From Posen to Palestine." *Annals of the Association of American Geographers* 74, no. 1 (1984): 57–70.

Reid, Donald Malcolm. "Cairo University and the Orientalists." *International Journal of Middle East Studies* 19, no. 1 (1987): 51–75.

Rein, Ariel. "Historia klalit vehistoria yehudit: Bimshutaf ʻo benifrad? Lesheʻelat hagdarat limudey hahistoria baʻuniversita haʻivrit beʻasor harishon lekiyuma." In *Toldot haʻuniversita haʻivrit birushalayim,* edited by Shaul Katz and Michael Heyd, 516–37. Vol. 1: *Shorashim vehathalot.* Jerusalem: The Hebrew University Magnes Press, 1997.

Reinharz, Jehuda. *Chaim Weizmann: The Making of a Statesman.* New York: Oxford University Press, 1993.

Restivo, Sal. "Bruno Latour: The Once and Future Philosopher." In *The Wiley-Blackwell Companion to Major Social Theorists,* edited by George Ritzer and Jeffrey Stepnisky, 520–540. Malden: Wiley-Blackwell, 2011.

Rhode, Achim. "Der Innere Orient: Orientalismus, Antisemitismus und Geschlecht im Deutschland des 18. bis 20. Jahrhunderts." *Die Welt des Islams,* New Series, 45, no. 3 (2005): 370–411.

Ringer, Fritz K. *The Decline of the German Mandarins: The German Academic Community, 1890–1933.* Cambridge, MA: Harvard University Press, 1969.

Roded, Ruth. "A Voice in the Wilderness? Rivlin's 1932 Hebrew *Life of Muhammad.*" *Middle East Critique* 18, no. 1 (2009): 39–59.

Rosenthal, Michael. *Nicholas Miraculous: The Amazing Career of the Redoubtable Dr. Nicholas Murray Butler.* New York: Columbia University Press, 2005.

Rubin Peled, Alisa. *Debating Islam in the Jewish State: The Development of Policy Toward Islamic Institutions in Israel.* Albany: State University of New York Press, 2001.

Rubinstein, Elyakim. "Hatipul besheʻela haʻaravit bishnot haʻesrim vehashloshim: Hebetim mosdiyim." *Hatziyonut* 12 (1987): 209–41.

Rubinstein, Shimon. "ʻAl yesudo vereshito shel hamakhon leheker kehilot yisraʻel bamizrah." *Peʻamim* 23 (1985): 127–49.

Ruppenthal, Jens. *Kolonialismus als "Wissenschaft und Technik": Das Hamburgische Kolonialinstitut 1908 bis 1919.* Stuttgart: Franz Steiner Verlag, 2007.

Ryad, Umar. "'An Oriental Orientalist': Aḥmad Zakī Pasha (1868–1934), Egyptian

Statesman and Philologist in the Colonial Age." *Philological Encounters* 3, no. 1–2 (2018): 129–66.

Said, Edward W. *Orientalism*. New York: Pantheon Books, 1978.

Salaymeh, Lena. "The 'Good Orientalists.'" In *Westernness: Critical Reflections on the Spatio-temporal Construction of the West*, edited by Christopher GoGwilt, Holt Meyer, and Sergey Sistiaga, 105–36. Berlin: De Gruyter Oldenbourg, 2022.

Salih, Jihad Ahmed. *Muhammad Issaf Nashashibi (1882–1948), 'alamat filastin wa'adib al-'arabiyya*. Ramallah: Al-'Ittihad al-'am lil-kuttab wal-'udaba al-filastiniyin, 2010.

Samaan, Jean-Loup. *Israel's Foreign Policy beyond the Arab World: Engaging the Periphery*. London: Routledge, 2018.

Schmidtke, Sabine. "From *Wissenschaft des Judentums* to *Wissenschaft des Islams*: Eugen Mittwoch between Jewish and Islamic Studies." *Historical Interactions of Religious Cultures* 1, no. 1 (2024): 103–45.

———. *German Orientalism in Times of Turmoil: The Kahle-Strothmann Correspondence (1933 through 1938, 1945 through 1950)*. Budapest: Eötvös Loránd University Chair for Arabic Studies & Csoma de Körös Society Section of Islamic Studies, 2022.

Scholem, Gershom. *From Berlin to Jerusalem: Memories of My Youth*. New York: Schocken Books, 1980.

Schorsch, Ismar. "Converging Cognates: The Intersection of Jewish and Islamic Studies in Nineteenth Century Germany." *Leo Baeck Institute Year Book* 55 (2010): 3–36.

Schrire, Dani. *Isuf shivrey hagola: Heker hafolklor hatziyoni lenokhah hasho'a*. Jerusalem: The Hebrew University Magnes Press, 2018.

———. "Max Grunwald and the Formation of Jewish Folkloristics: Another Perspective on Race in German-Speaking *Volkskunde*." In *Ideas of 'Race' in the History of the Humanities*, edited by Amos Morris-Reich and Dirk Rupnow, 113–38. Cham: Palgrave Macmillan, 2017.

Schroeter, Daniel. "From Sephardi to Oriental: The 'Decline' Theory of Jewish Civilizations in the Middle East and North Africa." In *The Jewish Contribution to Civilization: Reassessing an Idea*, edited by Jeremy Cohen and Richard I. Cohen, 125–50. Oxford: Littman Library, 2008.

Schwartz, Shalom. *Ussishkin be'igrotav*. Jerusalem: Reuven Mass, 1949–1950.

Šcrbacic, Maja. "Eugen Mittwoch gegen das Land Preußen: Die Entlassungsmaßnahmen in der Berliner Orientalistik, 1933–1938." In *Ein Paradigma der Moderne: Jüdische Geschichte in Schlüsselbegriffen; Festschrift für Dan Diner zum 70. Geburtstag*, edited by Arndt Engelhardt, Lutz Fiedler, Elisabeth Gallas, Natasha Gordinsky, and Philipp Graf, 39–55. Göttingen: Vandenhoeck & Ruprecht, 2016.

———. "Von der Semitistik zur Islamwissenschaft und zurück—Paul Kraus (1904–1944)." *Dubnow Institute Yearbook* 12 (2013): 389–416.

Sela, Avraham. "The 'Wailing Wall' Riots (1929) as a Watershed in the Palestine Conflict." *The Muslim World* 84, no. 1–2 (1994): 60–94.

278 ::: BIBLIOGRAPHY

Seth, Sanjay. *Subject Lessons: The Western Education of Colonial India*. New York: Duke University Press, 2007.

Shafer Raviv, Omri. "Studying an Occupied Society: Social Research, Modernization Theory and the Early Israeli Occupation, 1967–8." *Journal of Contemporary History* 55, no. 1 (2020): 161–81.

Shafir, Gershon. *Land, Labour and Origins of the Israeli-Palestinian Conflict 1882–1914*. Cambridge: Cambridge University Press, 1989.

Shalash, Ali. "Taha Hussein wal-as'ila al-muriba." *Shu'un 'adabiyya* 24 (1993): 16–39.

Shamir, Shimon. "Kishrey hinukh vetarbut." *Cathedra* 67 (1993): 93–104.

———. "Tshuva le'Eyal Clyne." *Forum for Regional Thinking*, August 7, 2019. www.regthink.org/articles/an-answer-to-eyal-klein.

Sharon, Moshe. "Petah davar." In *Habeduim be'Eretz Israel*, by Tuvia Ashkenazi. Jerusalem: Ariel, 2000.

Shenhav, Yehouda. *The Arab Jews: A Postcolonial Reading of Nationalism, Religion, and Ethnicity*. Stanford: Stanford University Press, 2006.

Shepherd, Naomi. *Ploughing Sand: British Rule in Palestine 1917–1948*. New Brunswick, NJ: Rutgers University Press, 2000.

Shraybom-Shivtiel, Shlomit. "Mehayey halashon ha'aravit mul thiyat halashon ha'ivrit." In *Mehkarim be'aravit uvtarbut ha'Islam*, edited by Binyamin Abrahamov, 183–94. Vol. 1. Ramat Gan: Bar Ilan University, 2000.

Shtern, Marik. "Ben shney harim: Hakampus ha'ironi shel ha'universita ha'ivrit." In *Toldot ha'universita ha'ivrit birushalayim*, edited by Yfaat Weiss and Uzi Rebhun, 175–205. Vol. 5: *Medinat hale'om vehahaskala hagvoha*. Jerusalem: The Hebrew University Magnes Press, 2024.

Shur, Shimon. *Kivrosh basa'ar: 'Al hayav ufo'alo shel Dr. Shmaryahu Levin*. Haifa: The Herzl Institute for Study of Zionism–University of Haifa, 2007.

Sigalas, Mathilde. "Between Diplomacy and Science: British Mandate Palestine and Its International Network of Archaeological Organisations, 1918–1938." In *European Cultural Diplomacy and Arab Christians in Palestine, 1918–1948: Between Contention and Connection*, edited by Karène Sanchez Summerer and Sary Zananiri, 187–211. London: Palgrave Macmillan, 2021.

Snir, Reuven. "Arabic in the Service of Regeneration of Jews: The Participation of Jews in Arabic Press and Journalism in the 19th and 20th Centuries." *Acta Orientalia* 59, no. 3 (2006): 283–323.

Spuler, Bertold. "Oskar Rescher/Osman Reşer: Zum 100. Geburtstag 1. Okt. 1883/1983." *Der Islam* 61, no. 1 (1984): 12–13.

Stanton, Andrea L. *This Is Jerusalem Calling: State Radio in Mandate Palestine*. Austin: University of Texas Press, 2013.

*Stenographisches Protokoll der Verhandlungen des XI. Zionisten-Kongresses in Wien vom 2. bis 9. September 1913*. Berlin: Juedischen Verlag, 1914.

Stern, Rephael G., and Arie M. Dubnov. "A Part of Asia or Apart from Asia? Zionist Perceptions of Asia, 1947–1956." In *Unacknowledged Kinships: Postcolonial Studies and the Historiography of Zionism*, edited by Stefan Vogt, Derek J. Penslar, and Arieh Bruce Saposnik, 233–71. Waltham, MA: Brandeis University Press, 2023.

Stillman, Noam (Norman) A. "Islamici nil a me alienum puto: The Mindset of Jewish Scholars of Islamic Studies." In *Modern Jewish Scholarship on Islam in Context*, edited by Ottfried Fraisse, 181–98. Berlin: De Gruyter, 2018.

———. "Jews of the Islamic World." *Modern Judaism* 10, no. 3 (1990): 367–78.

Suwaed, Muhammad. "Cooperation between the Galilee Bedouins and the Yishuv during the 1948 War." *Israel Affairs* 26, no. 2 (2020): 213–23.

Szamet, Miriam. "Contested Pedagogy: Modern Hebrew Education and the Segregation of National Communities in Pre-State Palestine." In *Israel-Palestine: Lands and Peoples*, edited by Omer Bartov, 181–97. New York: Berghahn Books, 2021.

Tamari, Salim. *Mountain against the Sea: Essays on Palestinian Society and Culture*. Berkeley: University of California Press, 2009.

———. *Year of the Locust: A Soldier's Diary and the Erasure of Palestine's Ottoman Past*. Berkeley: University of California Press, 2011.

Tibawi, Abdul Latif. *Arab Education in Mandatory Palestine: A Study of Three Decades of British Administration*. London: Luzac, 1956.

Tidhar, David. "Avinoam Yellin." In *Encyclopedia leheker hayeshuv uvonav: Dmuyot utmunot*, Vol. II, 894–95. www.tidhar.tourolib.org/tidhar/view/2/894.

Tobi, Yosef. "Trends in the Study of Yemenite Jewry." In *The Jews of Yemen*, by Yosef Tobi, 267–78. Leiden: Brill, 1999.

Toledano, Ehud R. "The Arabic-Speaking World in The Ottoman Period: A Socio-Political Analysis." In *The Ottoman World*, edited by Christine Woodhead, 453–66. London: Routledge, 2012.

———. "Limudey hamizrah hatikhon beyisra'el beyameinu." MEISAI. Last modified July 10, 2007. www.meisai.org.il/.

———. "Review of *The Disenchantment of the Orient*, by Gil Eyal." *Ruah mizrahit* 5 (2007): 36–42.

Toynbee, Arnold J. *Civilization on Trial*. New York: Oxford University Press, 1948.

Trautmann-Waller, Céline. "Semites and Semitism: From Philology to the Language of Myth." *Philological Encounters* 2, no. 3–4 (2017): 346–67.

Tsur, Yaron. "Israeli Historiography and the Ethnic Problem." In *Making Israel*, edited by Benny Morris, 231–77. Ann Arbor: University of Michigan Press, 2007.

Turán, Tamás. "Academic Religion: Goldziher as a Scholar and a Jew." In *Modern Jewish Scholarship in Hungary: The "Science of Judaism" between East and West*, edited by Tamás Turán and Carsten Wilke, 223–70. Berlin: De Gruyter, 2016.

———. *Ignaz Goldziher as a Jewish Orientalist: Traditional Learning, Critical Scholarship, and Personal Piety*. Berlin: De Gruyter, 2023.

Turner, James. *Philology: The Forgotten Origins of the Modern Humanities*. Princeton: Princeton University Press, 2014.

Uhlmann, Allon J. *Arabic Instruction in Israel: Lessons in Conflict, Cognition and Failure*. Leiden: Brill, 2017.

Ullendorff, Edward. "Eugen Mittwoch and the Berlin Seminar for Oriental Studies." In *Studies in Honour of Clifford Edmund Bosworth*, edited by Ian Richard Netton, 145–58. Vol. I: *Hunter of the East: Arabic and Semitic Studies*. Leiden: Brill, 1999.

280 ::: BIBLIOGRAPHY

——. "H. J. Polotsky (1905–1991): Linguistic Genius." *Journal of the Royal Asiatic Society* 4, no. 1 (1994): 3–13.

Vilozny, Roy. "Levi Billig vehelko he'alum beheker hitpathut hashi'a." *Hamizrah hehadash* 60 (2021): 71–98.

Waardenburg, Jacques. "Louis Massignon (1883–1962) as a Student of Islam." *Die Welt des Islams*, New Series 45, no. 3 (2005): 312–42.

Wasserstein, Bernard. "'Clipping the Claws of the Colonisers': Arab Officials in the Government of Palestine, 1917–48." *Middle Eastern Studies* 13, no. 2 (1977): 171–94.

Weber, Max. "Science as a Vocation." In *The Vocation Lectures*, 1–31. Translated by Rodney Livingstone. Indianapolis: Hackett Publishing, 2004.

Weil, Gotthold Eljakim. "Bericht über meine Arbeiten im Weinbergslager (Wünsdorf) vom 10. November 1917 bis 5. März 1918." In *Sitzungsberichte der Preussischen Akademie der Wissenschaften*, Jahrgang 1918, Zweiter Halbband: Juli bis Dezember, 794–96. Berlin: Verlag der Akademie der Wissenschaften, 1918.

——. *Tatarische Texte: Nach den in der Lautabteilung der Staatsbibliothek befindlichen Originalplatten*. Berlin: Walter de Gruyter, 1930.

Weiss, Yfaat. "Ad Acta: Nachgelassenes in Jerusalem." *Naharaim* 13, no. 1–2 (2019): 99–115.

——. "Central European Ethnonationalism and Zionist Binationalism." *Jewish Social Studies* 11, no. 1 (2004): 93–117.

——. "The Golem and Its Creator, or How the Jewish Nation-State Became Multiethnic." In *Challenging Ethnic Citizenship: German and Israeli Perspectives on Immigration*, edited by Daniel Levy and Yfaat Weiss, 82–104. New York: Berghahn Books, 2002.

——. "'A Man with His Life at Both Ends of Time': Lea Goldberg, Paul Ernst Kahle, and Appreciating the Mundane." *Yad Vashem Studies* 37, no. 1 (2009): 1–42.

——. *Niemandsland: Hader am Berg Scopus*. Göttingen: Vandenhoeck & Ruprecht, 2021.

Wertheim, Suzanne. "Reclamation, Revalorization, and Re-Tatarization via Changing Tatar Orthographies." In *Orthography as Social Action*, edited by Alexandra Jaffe, Jannis Androutsopoulos, Mark Sebba, and Sally Johnson, 65–102. Berlin: De Gruyter, 2012.

*Who's Who in the Arab World 2007–2008*. 18th ed. Beirut: Publitec and K.G. Saur München, 2007.

Wiese, Christian. *Challenging Colonial Discourse: Jewish Studies and Protestant Theology in Wilhelmine Germany*. Leiden: Brill, 2005.

Wilkof, Shira. "An 'Ordinary Modernist'? Empire and Nation in Ariel Kahane's Large-Scale Planning." *Planning Perspectives* 35, no. 5 (2020): 805–26.

Winder, R. Bayly. "Four Decades of Middle Eastern Study." *Middle East Journal* 41, no. 1 (1987): 40–63.

Wright, J. C. "Obituary: Dr Tuvia Gelblum, 1928–2007." *Bulletin of the School of Oriental and African Studies* 71, no. 3 (2008): 555–56.

Wokoeck, Ursula. *German Orientalism: The Study of the Middle East and Islam from 1800 to 1945*. London and New York: Routledge, 2009.

Wust, Ephraim. "Tik mahane hasahar: 'Mu'askar al-hilal / Halbmondlager', yuli 1915—yanuar 1916." In *Sefer Rafael Weiser: 'Iyunim bekhitvey yad, be'arkhionim uvitzirat S. Y. Agnon*, edited by Gil Weissblei, 91–100. Jerusalem: Mineged, 2020.

Yadlin, Rivka. *'Amadot vede'ot bekerev 'arviyey hagada*. Jerusalem: The Hebrew University of Jerusalem, Institute of Asian and African Studies, Center for Research on Palestinian Arabs, 1973.

Yahuda, Abraham Shalom. "Die Bedeutung der Goldziherschen Bibliothek für die zukünftige hebräische Universität." *Der Jude* 8 (1924): 575–92.

"Yedi'ot hahevra: Hahevra hamizrahit hayisra'elit." *Hamizrah hehadash* 1, no. 1 (1949).

"Yedi'ot hahevra." *Hamizrah hehadash* 10, no. 3 (1960): 277–79.

*Yedi'ot hamakhon lemada'ey hayahadut*, no. 1 (April 1925).

*Yedi'ot hamakhon lemada'ey hayahadut*, no. 2 (August 1925).

Yegar, Moshe. "Moshe Sharett and the Origins of Israel's Diplomacy." *Israel Studies* 15, no. 3 (2010): 1–26.

———. "Moshe Shertok (Sharett) and the Jewish Agency's Political Department— Precursor to Israel's Ministry of Foreign Affairs (Part II)." *Israel Journal of Foreign Affairs* 11, no. 2 (2017): 227–34.

———. *Toldot hamahlaka hamedinit shel hasokhnut hayehudit*. Jerusalem: Hasifriya hatziyonit, 2010.

Yehoshua, A. B. "Hakdama." In *Yerushalayim hayeshana ba'ayn uvalev: Mivhar ktavim*, by Ya'akov Yehoshua, 7–18. Jerusalem: Keter, 1988.

Yeroushalmi, David. "Fischel, Walter Joseph." In *Encyclopædia Iranica* IX/6 (1999): 654–55.

Yogev, Gedalia, and Yehoshua Freundlich, eds. *Haprotokolim shel hava'ad hapo'el hatziyoni 1919–1929*. Vol II: *February 1920–August 1921*. Jerusalem: Hasifriya hatziyonit, 1985.

Zadoff, Noam. *Gershom Scholem: From Berlin to Jerusalem and Back*. Translated by Jeffrey Green. Waltham, MA: Brandeis University Press, 2017.

Zalashik, Rakefet. *'Ad nafesh: Mehagrim, 'olim vehamimsad hapsikhiyatri beyisra'el*. Tel Aviv: Hakibbutz Hameuchad, 2008.

Zander, Michael. "Dr. Walter Zander: 8 June 1898–7 April 1993. An Address by Michael Zander. Delivered at the Annual Dinner of the Friends of the Hebrew University, Glasgow Branch, May 8, 1994." www.walterzander.info/in_memoriam. html.

Zuccala, Alesia. "Modeling the Invisible College." *Journal of the American Society for Information Science and Technology* 57, no. 2 (2006): 152–68.

# INDEX

Abandoned Property books, 126–29
Abdul Haq, Maulvi, 90
Academy of the Hebrew Language, 241n74
Africa, 27, 124, 162, 208n214, 252n188, 257n23
African Studies, 163, 164, 165, 252n187. *See also* Institute of Asian and African Studies
Agnon, Esther, 55
Agnon, S. Y., 55
"agrarian romanticism," 12
Ahad Ha'am, 41, 80, 199n92
*Ahdut Ha'avoda* (Labor Unity Party), 170, 254n216
Albright, William F., 95, 201n119
Aleppo, Syria, 70, 114, 115
Alexander, Ernst, 166
Algerian War of Independence, 169
Aligarh, India, 14, 50, 81, 104
Allenby, Edmund, 34
Alliance of the Periphery, 250–51n171
Aman (Military Intelligence Directorate), 177–78, 246n117, 257n21, 258n32
American School of Oriental Research, 48, 95, 201n119
American University of Beirut (AUB). *See* AUB
Amit, Meir, 258n32
amity, intellectual, 102–17
Anglo-Oriental College, Aligarh, India, 50, 81
Ankara, Turkey, 136, 137
*Ansab al-Ashraf*, 59, 85, 128, 140, 207n200, 207n201, 209–10n227
ANT (Actor-Network Theory), 17–18
anthropology, anthropologists, 28,

62, 144, 185n6, 190n57. *See also* ethnography
anti-Semitism, 34, 36–37
Arab boycott, 161
"Arab Club, The," 224n107
Arab College (Dar al-Mu'allimin), Jerusalem, 72–73, 88, 94, 99, 117, 218n44, 223n93, 226n124, 230n1
Arab Higher Committee, 127
Arabic language, 5, 6, 11, 25, 28, 39, 43, 71, 100, 119, 134, 236n28, 238n51, 241n74; books and newspapers in, 17, 119, 127, 207n198, 233n3, 236n30, 244n103; classical, 51, 58, 75, 104, 112, 181, 194n41, 233n3, 241n76; colloquial, 112, 138, 240n70, 241n75, 241n76; dictionaries of, 90, 119, 130, 246n122; Fleischer and, 26, 27; Goldziher and, 36, 37, 38; Horovitz and, 103–17; at HUSOS, 1, 13, 51, 52, 81, 112; in Institute for Jewish Studies, 44, 46, 49; Jewish poetry in, 45, 47, 49; literary, 114–15, 117, 139, 140, 241n76; modern, 69, 104, 109, 114–15; as mother tongue, 55, 66, 112, 130, 139, 241–42n77; practical, 70, 134, 139; pronunciation of, 240–41n74; sight reading of as entrance requirement, 56–57; translated into Hebrew, 119, 241n75; in United States, 151, 247n136
Arabic Language Academies Conference, Cairo, 89
Arabic Language Academy, Cairo, 87
Arabic Language Academy, Damascus, 91, 92
Arabic Language and Literature Department, Hebrew University,

284 ::: INDEX

74, 160, 211n237, 233n3, 239n67, 241–42n77, 258n34

Arabic language instruction and studies, 3, 11–12, 66, 70, 73, 82, 97, 104, 112, 114–15, 194n41, 229n155, 232n207, 238n54, 240n70, 249n155, 250n163; HUSOS and, 82, 119, 133; practical, 114, 115; teachers of, 111, 240n73

Arabic literature and culture studies, 47, 50, 57, 59, 76, 186n12; historical, 51, 198n83. *See also* Concordance for Ancient Arabic Poetry

Arab-Israeli War of 1948, 19, 130, 177; recovery after, 125–51

Arab-Jewish affinity, 51, 80, 83–84, 215n12

Arab-Jewish conflict, 88, 169

Arab nationalist movement, 89, 95, 97, 100, 101, 127

Arabness and Arab-Islamic identity, 93, 202n124

Arab Question, 72

Arab Revolt (1936–39), 64, 92, 97, 99, 113, 115

Arabs, 11, 119, 170; Bureau of the Advisor on Arab Affairs and, 176–77, 236n30; culture of, 82, 84, 93; HUSOS and, 15, 49, 52–53, 78, 103–17, 226n124; Jews and, 2, 92–93, 116, 181, 184, 211n243, 225n118, 225n119; as minority in Israel, 123, 149, 158; in Palestine, 12, 197n73; as scholars, 19, 85, 207n201, 228n147, 232n207; as students, 102, 226n124, 256n16. *See also* Muslims; *and "Arabic language" headings*

Arab University, Beirut, 100

archaeology, 36, 41, 69, 94–99, 195n50, 230n178

area studies, 153, 164

al-Aref, Aref, 97–98, 224n107, 224n109, 224n110, 225n117

Arlosoroff, Haim, 89

Art and Archaeology of the Near East Department, Hebrew University, 211n237

art and architecture, 47, 52, 195n50, 223n93

Ashkenazi, Tuvia, 91, 220n64

Ashkenazi Jews, 70, 72, 111

Ashtor, Eliyahu (Eli; Eduard Strauß), 128, 144, 244n98; in second generation of HUSOS scholars, 142, 253n200, 258n34

Asia and Asian Studies, 24, 27, 51, 163, 164. *See also* Institute of Asian and African Studies

Assaf, Michael, 112, 114, 246n121, 254n211; as Mapai operative, 108–10, 120, 148–49

Assyriology, 3, 28, 51, 54, 95, 210n235. *See also* Syria

Athaminah, Khalil, 207n199

AUB (American University of Beirut), 100–101, 130–31, 138, 226n124, 227n133, 227n136, 228n147

Austria, 41, 45, 77, 142. *See also* University of Vienna; Vienna

Avnery, Uri, 171, 253n205, 254n214

Ayalon (Neustadt; Haglili), David, 137–38, 160, 175, 183, 227n133, 234n19, 238n48, 238n50, 238n51, 240n73; Arabic and, 130, 246n122; Foreign Ministry and, 132–33, 237n44, 258n32; Goitein and, 135–36, 173, 238n55; as HUSOS student in Beirut, 101, 130, 227n133; Institute of Asian and African Studies and, 167, 174, 178–79, 180; new HUSOS department and, 156, 168, 173, 238n55; in Political Department of Jewish Agency, 130, 131, 134, 227n136; in second generation of HUSOS scholars, 253n200, 258n34

al-Azhar University, 88, 117

Babylonia, 52

Bachi, Roberto, 131

Baer, Gabriel, 138, 197n76, 227n133, 246n123, 255n3, 256n8, 258n34; as director of Institute of Asian and African Studies, 174–75, 180; as

IDF intelligence officer, 174, 256n4; research of, 183, 240n69; in second generation of HUSOS scholars, 168, 180, 253n200; Trotskyites and, 239–40n69

Baer, Yitzhak, 39

al-Baladhuri, Ahmad ibn Yahya ibn Jabir, 57, 58, 75, 85, 91–92, 205n172

Balfour, Arthur James, First Earl of Balfour, 81, 101

Balfour Declaration, 101

Balochi language, 60

Baneth, David Hartwig Zvi, 13, 45, 84, 88, 93, 106, 120, 147, 173, 181, 182, 184, 200n103, 201n109, 203n140, 211n236, 221n85, 228n142, 231n189, 235n21; on Arabic language studies, 82–83; book reviews by, 258–59n37; character of, 21, 75; as department head, 241–42n77; as expert in philosophy, 64, 76; in founding generation of HUSOS scholars, 33, 135, 160–62, 253n200; Goitein and, 200n107, 201n113; Lektors and, 105–6; as teacher and faculty fellow, 64–66, 76, 98, 105, 134, 208n204

Baneth, Eduard Ezekiel, 45

Barak (Burak), Eliyahu, 227n133

al-Barghouti, Omar al-Salih, 95, 230n182

Barkat, Reuven, 169, 170, 171

Bar-Zakay (Bardaki), Nathan, 148

Becker, Carl Heinrich, 45, 59, 73; *Ansab al-Ashraf* and, 59, 209–10n227

Bedouins, 96, 97, 98

Beersheba, 97

Beilin, Asher, 98–99, 221n85

Beirut, 100, 101, 114, 117, 130, 227n133. *See also* AUB (American University of Beirut)

Beit Jala, 94

Ben-Gurion, David, 125–26, 164, 169, 170–71, 234n17, 251n182, 251n184, 254n217, 257n23

Ben-Horin, Uri, 255n227

Ben-Israel, Hedva, 252n187

Benor, Yehuda Leib, 149

Bentwich, Norman, 87, 199n92

Ben-Yehuda, Eliezer, 41, 42, 72, 80, 199n92, 214n10

Ben-Ze'ev, Israel, 71, 72–74, 129, 148–49, 213nn260–262, 213n264, 232n207, 236n30

Ben-Zvi, Yitzhak, 96, 113, 148, 149, 244n102

Ben-Zvi Institute, 244n102

Bergmann, Hugo, 41, 80–81, 117, 197n79, 201n109, 216n29, 221n85, 245n109

Berlin, 29, 45, 48, 50, 66; *Ansab al-Ashraf* fragment in, 59, 60. *See also* University of Berlin

Bhabha, Homi, 116

Bible, 18, 24, 25, 27, 30, 58, 65, 72, 74, 89–90, 128, 173, 236n28

Billig, Levi (Lewis), 64, 70, 77, 219n56, 223n96; Arabic language and, 66, 82–83, 106, 107, 113; Arabs and, 90, 99, 105; Baneth and, 83–84, 93, 208n204; death of, 22, 208n204; in founding generation of HUSOS scholars, 22; Horovitz and, 64–65, 67, 90, 104, 105; murder of, 113–14, 172, 208n204, 212n247, 230n182

Biram, Arthur, 202n127, 209n222

birth control, 174

Blank, Haim, 253n200

Blau, Yehoshua (Joshua), 160, 235n23, 253n200, 258n34

Bonne (Bonné), Alfred, 70, 131, 133, 135, 138, 238n54, 246n121, 253n200

book reviews, 150, 182, 258n37

Bourdieu, Pierre, 71

Bowman, Humphrey, 96

Brauer, Erich, 144, 243n95

Braun, Adam Noah (Bar-On), 65, 97–99, 204n156, 209n216

Bravmann, Meir Moshe (Max), 65, 209n218

British Empire and British imperialism,

286 ::: INDEX

15, 50, 69, 77, 81, 217n36; Palestine and, 85–86

British Mandate, 4, 125, 224n109; Arabic instruction under, 92, 218n44, 249n155; Arabs and Jews under, 79, 215n12; Department of Antiquities under, 41, 46, 67, 94, 223n97; Education Department under, 64, 96, 98, 125, 129, 225n118; government of, 96, 97, 214n10, 218n44; Hebrew University and, 46, 77, 80–81; High Commissioner of, 96, 97, 214n10, 224n104; knowledge transfer during, 9–15

British Orientalism, 65, 69, 110, 131, 162–64, 230n171

Brit Shalom association, 12, 84, 108, 216n27, 216n29, 217n30, 225n118

Buber, Martin, 144, 169, 204n150, 253n205

Budapest, Hungary, 30, 32, 36–37, 39, 91, 196n63

Burak, Eliyahu. See Barak (Burak), Eliyahu

Bureau of the Advisor on Arab Affairs and, 176–77, 236n30

Burma, 162

Butler, Nicholas Murray, 107

Caetani, Leone, 50, 220n65

Cairo, 87, 89, 90, 100, 117, 227n141; *Geniza* of, 15, 141–42, 151, 189n51, 242n84. *See also* University of Cairo

Cambridge University, 45, 64, 203n146, 252n187

Canaan, Margot Eilander, 95

Canaan, Tawfiq, 94–96, 144, 223n94, 235n21

Canada, 249n162

Carnegie Endowment for International Peace, 107

Catholic University of Budapest, 36

Center for the Study of Palestinian Arabs, 180

Central Europe, 21, 24, 65, 84; Jews in, 6, 9, 13, 23, 30, 152

Central Zionist Archives, 16

Central Zionist Office, London, 35, 39

Chair for the Modern Middle East, 136, 137

Chair in Near Eastern Art and Archaeology, 155

Chajes, Zwi Perez, 42, 198n79

Cherikover, Avigdor, 39

China, 161, 162

Chinese language and Sinology, 163, 165, 251n184

Christian Hebraism, 24

Christianity, Christians, 6, 24, 31, 34, 50, 100, 119, 223n97

Christian Orient and Orientalists, 6, 51

Classical Islam, 28, 154, 156, 158, 168

Clay, Albert, 95

Cliff, Tony (Yigael Glückstein), 239–40n69

Clyne, Eyal, 147, 185n6, 253n200

COGAT (Coordinator of Government Activities in the Territories), 16, 174–75

Cohen, Aharon, 149

Cohen, Uri, 125

Cold War, 152–53

Cologne, Germany, 130

colonial history, 252n187

colonialism and colonization, 6, 25; de-, 152–53; Germany and, 5, 13, 27, 28, 30; Orientalism and, 4–5, 9, 12, 13, 28. *See also* British Empire and British imperialism; imperialism

Columbia University, 48, 209n218

Concordance for Ancient Arabic Poetry, 57, 84, 100, 107, 235n27; index cards of, 18, 58, 74, 75, 89–90, 122, 128, 173, 236n28

Constantinople, 50, 203n145. *See also* Istanbul

Coordinator of Government Activities in the Territories. *See* COGAT

Creswell collection, 203n145
Crusades, 142

Damascus, Syria, 45, 89, 90–92, 114, 226n124
*Davar* (newspaper), 93, 112, 220n64
David, Percival, 67
Dayan Center, 179. *See also* Shiloah Center
de-Orientalization of Jews and Judaism, 6
de Sacy, Antoine Isaac, Baron Sylvester, 5, 25–26, 30, 31, 32
dialectology, dialects, 29, 180, 240n72; Arabic, 60, 194n41, 240n70, 241n76; Jewish, 25, 47, 142, 240n70, 241n74; Palestinian, 110, 138
diaspora university, 125
dictionary, dictionaries, 89–90, 119, 130, 246n122. *See also* Concordance for Ancient Arabic Poetry
diglossia, 139, 241n76
Diner, Dan, 10
Dinur, Ben-Zion, 131
diplomatic training, 133, 135
DMG (*Deutsche Morgenländische Gesellschaft*; German Oriental Society), 27, 31, 147–48
*Do'ar Hayom*, 72
doctoral dissertations, 59, 66, 73, 74, 121, 181; at HUSOS, 130, 138, 213n261, 256n8
Doegen, Wilhelm, 29, 60–62, 193n38, 206n192
Dotan (Lutzky), Alexander, 117–18, 146, 148
Dropsie College, 48, 209n218
Druzes, 119, 158

East Asian Studies, 161
Eastern Europe, 10, 243n93; Jews in, 30, 34, 60, 143, 206n181
Eban, Abba, 164
Efron, John, 6
Egypt, 40, 48, 50, 79, 90, 93–95, 104;
Arabic in, 89, 119; Israel and, 102, 179, 219n55, 258n32; Jews in, 142, 227n141. *See also* Cairo
Egyptian language, 68, 76, 160
Egyptian National Library, 214n6
Egyptians, 79, 87, 102, 108, 174, 202n124, 213n261, 214n6, 219n59, 220n65; at Hebrew University, 88–89, 100, 226n125; as scholars of Islamic studies, 87, 103, 118
Egyptology, 28, 54, 68, 210n235, 211n237
Einstein, Albert, 211n238
Eisenstadt, Shmuel Noah, 144–45, 165
Elath (Epstein), Eliahu, 101, 102, 131, 164, 222n92, 227n133, 251n180
England, 152, 154, 157, 164, 203n145, 239n69, 249n162; Germans flee Nazi persecution to, 200n100, 250n166; postwar Ottoman Empire and, 100; study of modern Middle East in, 157. *See also* Great Britain; *and "British" entries*
English language, 3, 17, 101, 117
Enlightenment, the, 4, 11, 24
Epstein, Eliahu. *See* Elath, Eliahu (Epstein)
Eshkol, Levi, 175, 178
ethics of research, 62–63
Ethiopia and Ethiopian languages, 44, 163, 250n171, 251n179
ethnography, 94–99, 143, 144, 206n181
Eurocentrism, 38, 142
Europe, 2, 4, 7, 17, 20, 41, 156; Jews in, 6, 145, 206n181. *See also* Central Europe; Eastern Europe; *and names of individual European nations*
Eyal, Gil, 11–12, 116, 188n35, 238n54
Eytan, Walter, 131–32, 135–36, 237n44, 239n61, 242n78

Far East, 3, 25
Fawzi, Hussein, 89, 102–3, 219n59
Fawzi, Mahmoud, 102, 219n59
*fellahin*, 96, 117

288 ::: INDEX

Ferdowsi, 228n143

Ferguson, Charles A., 139, 241n76

*Filastin* (Jaffa newspaper), 79, 230n182

first generation of HUSOS scholars, 124, 174, 180; German Orientalist tradition and, 15, 158; passing of, 18, 160; second generation and, 167–68, 172–73

Fischel, Walter Joseph (Yosef), 65, 84, 208–9n215

Fischer, Maurice, 169, 170, 254n214

Fleischer, Heinrich Leberecht, 25, 26, 27, 31, 32, 181, 194n43

Florence Conference (1958), 167–73, 253n204, 253n205, 253n206, 254–55n221

folklore, 10, 11, 76, 96, 190–91n58; Jewish, 76, 140, 206n181, 243n93; Palestinian, 95–96, 235n21

Foreign Ministry. *See* Israeli Ministry of Foreign Affairs

Foucault, Michel, 4, 9, 157

foundational memorandum of HUSOS, 15, 203n143; Mangold-Will on, 203n143

France, 5, 29, 100, 147

Frankfurt, 66, 74; Horovitz in, 50, 51, 52, 55, 57, 64, 106; natives of, 50, 65; Weil in, 67, 73, 182. *See also* University of Frankfurt

Freytag, Georg, 25, 31, 32

Friedmann, Yohanan, 231–32n197, 253n202

Friends of the Hebrew University, 69, 161

Fuad I, King of Egypt, 227n141

*Futuh al-Buldan* (al-Baladhuri), 75

Gad al-Mawla, Muhammad Ahmed, 90

Garbell, Irene, 241n74

Garidi, Shimon, 230n183

Gaza Strip, 97, 175, 181

Geiger, Abraham, 31–32

Gelber, Yoav, 9–10

Gelblum, Tuvia, 251n184

gender norms, 14

generation gap in Israeli Oriental Studies, 167–73

generations and cohorts: sociology of, 19–20, 167–68, 171–72, 180, 253n201. *See also* first generation of HUSOS scholars; second generation of HUSOS scholars; third generation of HUSOS scholars

*Geniza* of Cairo, 15, 141–42, 151, 189n51, 242n84

German Foreign Ministry, 60, 199n100

German-Jewish immigrants, 10, 14, 16, 34, 209n218

German-Jewish Orientalism, 6, 12, 16, 19, 33–34

German-Jewish scholars, 2, 34, 38–39, 189n49

German language, 1, 17, 182, 259n38

Germanness, 21, 184; of first generation of HUSOS scholars, 22, 23, 74, 76, 77

German Orientalism, 6, 7, 11, 22, 23, 28, 91, 110, 147, 163, 192n17; development of, 13, 18, 24–34; legacy of, 74–77; Marchand on, 8–9, 16, 27, 185n5

German Orientalist tradition and German Orientalists, 42, 102, 104, 111, 154, 159, 181; first generation of HUSOS scholars and, 15, 21; study of Asia and Africa and, 163–64; wartime mobilization of, 29–30, 193n38

German Oriental Society (*Deutsche Morgenländische Gesellschaft*; DMG), 27, 31, 147–48

German POW camp recordings, 17, 28–29, 193n33

German scientific tradition, 6, 10, 11, 33, 68, 74, 75, 144, 145, 237n41; *Ansab al-Ashraf* edition and, 58–59; standards of, 117–20

German universities, 25, 30, 46, 228n147; first generation of HUSOS scholars trained in, 1, 18, 19, 22. *See also names of specific universities*

# INDEX ::: 289

Germany, 5, 94, 192n17, 222n89; colonialism and, 27, 163; India and, 191n12, 217n36; Jewish immigration from, 9–10, 21, 67–68; knowledge transfer from, 2, 4, 9–15; during World War I, 8, 60–63, 193n38, 199–200n100. *See also* Berlin; Nazis; Prussia

Gershoni, Israel, 93, 214n8, 222n87

Gibb, Hamilton A. R., 228n142

Goitein, Shelomo Dov, 13, 15, 19, 75, 190n52, 202n124; Baneth and, 200n107, 201n113; Cairo *Geniza* and, 141–42, 151, 189n51, 242n84; as head of HUSOS, 19, 125–51; Mayer and, 45, 70, 92

Gökalp, Ziya, 131

Golan, Joe (Yosef), 169, 253n205, 253n206

Goldziher, Ignác, 40, 196n62, 198n83; as central German Orientalist figure, 31–32, 35; Levin and, 37, 39, 40–41, 196n62, 198n79, 198n80; network of, 32, 194–95n48; proposal of, 35–40; scholarly reputation of, 196–97n68; Zionism and, 17, 197n73

Great Britain, 5, 29, 130, 161, 214n10, 218n47; Oriental Studies in, 65, 69, 110, 131, 147, 162–64, 230n171. *See also* British Empire and British imperialism; British Mandate; England; London

Greek language, 41, 49, 52, 56

Grey Hill estate, Mount Scopus, 34

*Ha'aretz*, 149, 220n64

al-Habash, Hassan Amin, 117, 232n198

habitus, 13, 17, 21, 71, 75, 77, 172

Habsburg Empire, 41, 77

Haddad, Elias, 95

*hadith*, 73, 168, 202n124

*al-Hadith*, 114

Haganah, 128, 180, 219n55, 226n123, 241n75

Haglili, David. *See* Ayalon, David

Haifa, 117, 119, 209n222, 232n198,

245n107; libraries in, 127–28; natives of, 130, 160

Haifa Reali School, 45, 64, 66, 138, 209n222, 229n155

*Hakirya*, 176

Halbmondlager POW camp, 29, 193n37

Halperin, Liora R., 11, 216n25

*Hamashkif* (Revisionist newspaper), 100

Hamburg, Germany, 59, 65, 206n181, 243n93

Hamburg Colonial Institute (*Hamburgisches Kolonialinstitut*, HKI), 163, 251n177

al-Hamdani, Hussein bin Faydullah, 228n142

*Ha'olam* (World Zionist Organization newspaper), 41, 225n117

*Ha'olam Haze*, 171

Harari family, 87

Hareli, Shaul, 91, 99, 220n70

Harif, Hanan, 14–15

Harry S. Truman Research Institute for the Advancement of Peace, 180

Hartog, Sir Philip, 68–69, 211n240, 230n171

Hartog Committee, 68, 211n238; 1934 report of, 69–70, 110–13, 122, 135, 237n41

*Hashomer Hatzair*, 119

Hasson, Shlomo, 12

Hebrew culture and Hebrewness, 38, 83, 214n10

Hebrew Encyclopedia, 216n29

Hebrew language, 3, 28, 43, 64, 67, 100, 196n62, 216n25; Arabic and, 25, 71, 99, 241n75; Bible and, 24, 27; dictionaries of, 119, 130, 246n122; instruction in, 97, 229n155; publications in, 2, 17, 149, 182

Hebrew University, 16, 85, 86, 118, 125, 148, 150, 164, 171, 175, 180, 183, 232n207, 233n3; 1956 Sinai expeditions of, 174–75, 255n227; Academic Senate of, 113, 114, 167; administrative structure of, 69, 80; African Studies

290 ::: INDEX

Committee of, 165; Arabs at, 19, 97–100, 226n124; Board of Governors of, 54, 68; degrees offered by, 76, 126; departments of, 130, 133, 142, 144, 158, 160, 165, 177, 183, 210n234, 240n73, 252n187, 255n226, 258n30, 258n34; establishment of, 1, 34–35, 35–36, 181; Executive Committee of, 69, 99, 111, 113, 125, 133, 210n233, 234n11, 236n34, 237n45; faculty of, 87, 133, 217n30, 241n74; funding of, 122, 125, 150, 175, 233n6; Germanness of, 2, 22; Hebrewness of, 38, 93; Heyd on, 158–59; history of, 13–14; Humanities Faculty of, 129–30, 160, 167; Israeli government and, 132, 145, 175; modern Middle East at, 152–61; need for hybridity in, 116–17; opening celebration of, 51, 52, 78, 81, 102; Paris founding committee on, 43–44; president of, 125, 164, 166; Professors Committee of, 175–76; Shiloah Center and, 178–79; Standing Committee of the Senate of, 130, 133, 137, 166; students at, 152, 170, 171; Terra Sancta compound of, 126, 150; Zionist movement and, 111–12, 118. *See also* HUSOS; Institute for Jewish Studies; Mount Scopus; *and names of individual chairs and departments*

Hebrew University, Department for the History of the Jewish People, 142

Hebrew University, Department of Arabic Language and Literature, 183, 233n3

Hebrew University, Department of History, 252n187

Hebrew University, Department of Islamic Culture, 1, 85, 142, 158, 160, 211n237, 233n3, 239n67, 255n226

Hebrew University, Department of Linguistics, 160, 210n234

Hebrew University, Department of Modern Middle East, 139, 157–59

Hebrew University, Department of Muslim Culture, 158

Hebrew University, Department of Political Science, 240n73

Hebrew University, Department of Semitic Linguistics, 211n237, 241n74

Hebrew University, Department of Sociology, 144, 165, 177

Hebrew University, Department of the History of the Islamic Lands, 160, 258n30

Hebrew University, Department of Turkish and Iranian Studies, 136

Hebrew University, School of Oriental Studies. *See* HUSOS

*Hed Hamizrah*, 72

Heidelberg, 228n142

Hellenism, 51

Herzfeld, Ernst, 45

Heschel, Susannah, 6

Heyd (Heydt), Uriel, 19, 130, 173, 175, 227n133, 236n36, 238n59, 242n78, 244n103, 246n121, 248–49n151, 248n142, 249n153, 251n184, 252n190, 257n20; Ayalon and, 138, 139, 167, 177, 179, 183; death of, 249n157; at Florence, 170–71; Goitein and, 136–37, 154–55, 160–61, 184, 239n61; as HUSOS director, 151–52, 159–61, 255n3; Institute of Asian and African Studies and, 123, 124, 161–67, 177, 247n132; Israel Oriental Society and, 160; language studies of, 130–31, 238n57, 239n66, 248n147; Ministry of Foreign Affairs and, 19, 137, 161, 172; Plessner and, 171–72, 255n223; in Political Department of Jewish Agency, 131, 146, 161, 172, 227n136; in second generation of HUSOS scholars, 253n200; on Toynbee, 248n148; vision of, 153–54, 155–59

High Commissioner of British Mandate, 96, 97, 214n10, 224n104

Higher Institute of Jewish Studies

*(Hochschule für die Wissenschaft des Judentums)*, 32, 45, 76

Hindustani language, 60

Hirschberg, H. Z., 246n117, 246n121

Histadrut, 169

Hitler, Adolf, 67

HKI (*Hamburgisches Kolonialinstitut*; Hamburg Colonial Institute), 163, 251n177

Holland, 5

Holy Roman Empire, 24

Hopkins, James, 245n105

Horovitz, Josef, 13–15, 64, 70, 76, 84, 90, 92, 109, 174, 184, 205n163, 220n66, 221n74; Arabic teachers and, 104–5, 138; death of, 15, 67, 107, 110, 116, 124; as founder and first director of School of Oriental Studies, 1, 19, 22, 54, 57, 58, 104; Goitein and, 106, 140, 181; in India, 50, 60, 65, 90, 203n136; Magnes and, 51–54, 56, 65, 71, 77, 87, 102, 103, 107; Plan of, 49–57, 103, 104–5, 109, 114; research projects and, 57–63; at University of Berlin, 32–33, 50, 59; at University of Frankfurt, 51, 52, 55, 57, 61, 65, 66, 73; vision of, 55, 81, 82–83, 110–11, 122, 153; Weil and, 62–63, 74

Hoter Hacohen, Yehoshua, 55, 204n156

humanities: at Hebrew University, 69, 76, 87, 115, 125, 126, 129, 138, 143, 153, 160, 167; Jewish and Oriental Studies and, 40–44

Humboldtian university model, 26, 33

Humboldt Universität, 17. *See also* University of Berlin

Hungarian Academy of Sciences, 17, 194–95n48

Hungary, 31, 141; Minister of Culture, 87–88. *See also* Budapest, Hungary

HUSOS (Hebrew University, School of Oriental Studies), 78, 171; Abandoned Property books and, 126–29; *Ansab al-Ashraf* edition of, 59–60;

Arabic teachers and lecturers at, 103–17; Arabs at, 99–100, 113–14, 118, 226n124; "Basic Studies" program of, 240n71; Board of Directors of, 54; chronological and thematic expansion of, 19, 125–51; courses of, 70, 75, 100, 238n51, 240n70; departments of, 74, 112, 121, 160, 211n237; expansion of, 107, 124, 164, 166; first generation of scholars of, 15, 18–20, 22, 32, 124, 134–35, 148, 158, 167, 168, 172, 174, 252–53n200; founding of, 15, 16, 18, 19, 34–57, 203n143, 215n12; fourth and fifth generation of scholars of, 253n200; funding of, 107, 140; German heritage of, 13–14, 145; inauguration of, 1, 2; Israeli government and, 120, 121–73; mission of, 78, 109, 112; Muslim intellectual world and, 77–102; name of, 55, 165–67, 229–30n171; potential students of, 55, 56; recent literature on, 13–15; research enterprises of, 90, 91; second generation of scholars of, 115, 134, 142, 151–67, 168, 180, 183, 253n200, 258n34; student demands of, 115, 154; students of, 75, 76, 100, 101, 112–13, 134, 219n55, 225n114, 239n67, 240n74, 246n123, 249n162, 256n15, 256n16; third generation of scholars of, 175, 179, 249n162

HUSOS (Hebrew University, School of Oriental Studies) faculty, 66, 79, 80, 84; Hussein and, 88–90; lecturers on, 75, 103–17, 113; Lektors as, 49, 104–6, 115, 138, 228n147

Hussein, Taha, 74, 88, 111, 225n114, 227n137; Arabs and, 102–3; Hebrew University scholars and, 87–88, 93; Kurd Ali and, 90, 104, 220n62; visits Hebrew University, 88–89, 102, 119, 218n47, 218n48, 219n55; Zionism and, 227n139

al-Husseini, Hajj Amin, 97

292 ::: INDEX

al-Husseini, Ishaq Moussa, 88
al-Husseini, Kamil, 34
al-Husseini, Muhammad Yunis, 226n124
hybridity, 116–17
Hyderabad, India, 90, 203n136

Ihud association, 128, 170
immigration, immigrants, 9–10, 34,
    66, 175, 242n81; from Germany and
    Austria, 14, 21, 34, 142; Jewish, 12, 21,
    145; to Palestine, 2, 13, 16, 18, 34, 41,
    43, 45, 54, 64, 68, 70, 72, 74, 95, 120,
    128, 140, 241n74; to United States, 14,
    209n218, 226n126
imperialism, 6, 24, 85; anti-, 81, 84;
    British, 50, 81, 217n36; Orientalism
    and, 4–5
index cards of Arabic Poetry Concor-
    dance, 18, 58, 74, 75, 89–90, 128, 173,
    236n28
India, 5, 25, 29, 67, 69, 161, 166, 228n142,
    245n109, 251n184; British rule in,
    69, 81, 217n36; Horovitz in, 14–15,
    50, 60, 65, 90, 203n136; Israel and,
    162, 250n170; Muslims in, 60, 61, 161,
    189n49. See also Indology
Indo-European languages, 26
Indo-Iranian languages, 60
Indology, 25, 163–65, 191n12, 217n36
Institute for Further Studies (Hamosad
    Lehishtalmut). See School for
    Diplomats
Institute for Jewish Studies, 7, 63, 67, 142,
    144, 209n216, 244n98; Arabic studies
    at, 49, 111; establishment of, 44, 49–57,
    81–82; Jewish-Arab cooperation
    at, 49, 82; name of, 229–30n171;
    proposed structure of, 51, 54; research
    projects of, 57–63, 77, 84, 85, 92, 119;
    scholars of, 39, 45, 47, 49, 63–70,
    203n140. See also HUSOS
Institute for the Study of Oriental Jewish
    Communities, 244n102
Institute of Asian and African Studies,

18, 124, 161–67, 175, 178–80, 184,
    241n76; collaborates with COGAT,
    174–75; generations of HUSOS
    scholars and, 252–53n200, 258n34;
    naming of, 165–67, 252n196
intellectual amity: institutionalization
    of, 102–17
International Congresses of Orientalists,
    59, 90, 91, 242n78
"Invisible College" of Oriental expertise,
    86, 102, 217n37
Iran, 124, 136, 137, 161, 238n59, 239n61,
    250n171; study of, 124, 165. See also
    Persia; Persian language
Iraq, 141, 149, 257n23
Islam and Islamic world, 5, 6, 24, 31;
    archaeology and art of, 195n50,
    230n178; classical, 28, 154, 156, 158,
    168; Goldziher and, 37, 87–88; history
    and, 106, 222n89; Israel and, 153–54;
    Jews and Judaism and, 39, 47, 140–45;
    scholars of, 27, 182
Islamic Studies, 3, 7, 13, 14, 40, 45, 93;
    Arabic and, 22, 23, 30, 247n136;
    father of, 76–77; Hebrew University
    and, 43, 179; Islamkunde, 28, 192n29;
    Islamwissenschaft (scientific research
    on Islamic religion), 32, 104, 192n29,
    194n47; in Israel, 18, 238n48
Ismalis, 228n142
Israel, Ancient, 38
Israel, State of, 20, 197n78, 232n198;
    Africa and Asia and, 166, 252n188;
    Arabic language instruction in,
    11–12, 249n155; Arabs in, 123, 149, 158,
    241n77; Archives of, 16–17, 224n104;
    critics of, 128, 170; diplomacy of, 102,
    137, 153, 162, 164, 169, 250–51n171,
    250n170; establishment of, 4, 124, 146;
    Hebrew University and, 19, 122–23,
    246n119, 247n137; Institute of Asian
    and African Studies and, 167; Middle
    Eastern Studies in, 18; Oriental
    Studies in, 2, 4; President of, 219n55,

243n92; Prime Minister's Office, 123, 125, 164, 175, 178, 236n30, 250n163, 257n20. *See also* Israel Defense Forces; *and "Israeli Ministries" entries*

Israel Defense Forces (IDF), 148, 149, 174, 179, 180, 237n42, 246n117, 249n155

Israeli-Arab Conflict, 88, 169

Israeli Ministry of Defense, 180

Israeli Ministry of Education, 129, 141, 148–49, 150, 236n30, 250n163, 252n190

Israeli Ministry of Foreign Affairs, 121, 161, 164, 167, 169, 180, 234n19, 250n163; Ayalon and, 132–33; Florence Conference and, 169, 170; Hebrew University and, 151, 155, 165; HUSOS and, 19, 120, 121–73, 237n44, 237n45, 239n61, 242n78; Israel Oriental Society and, 148, 160, 177; *The New East* and, 149, 150; officials of, 18, 117

Israeli Ministry of Justice, 231n196

Israeli Ministry of Religion, 121

Israeli Oriental Studies, 16, 121, 147, 151, 159, 174, 188n35; biases of, 11; generations of, 167–73; Heyd on, 153–54; security establishment and, 10–11

Israeli security establishment, 123, 176; Israeli Orientalism and, 10–11; Shabak and, 177, 257n23

Israel Oriental Society (*Hahevra Hamizrahit Hayisra'elit*), 150, 151, 160, 173, 176, 245n107, 246n119, 257n20; council of, 148–49, 176, 246n117; founding of, 124, 146–48, 245n109; Shiloah Center of, 177–79; in Tel Aviv, 176, 245n105. See also *New East, The*

Israel Security Agency (Shabak), 177, 257n23

Istanbul, 59, 227n141, 242n78. *See also* Constantinople

Jacobson, Abigail, 11, 116

Jaffa, 95, 127, 226n124

Jaffa Gate, 97

al-Jahiz, 55

Japan, 161, 162

Jerusalem, 20, 34, 35, 97, 99, 139, 202n124, 205n171, 209n218, 219n55, 226n124, 240n72, 245n107; al-Aqsa Mosque in, 202n124; American School of Oriental Research in, 95, 201n119; Arabs and Muslims in, 52, 92, 95, 120, 221n85, 223n94, 225n123, 226n124; archives, repositories, and libraries in, 16–17, 127; East, 96, 181, 223n94, 224n106, 225n123; Egyptian Consul in, 97, 219n59; Grand Mufti of, 34, 99; Jewish-Arab relations in, 94, 225–26n123, 225n119; Jewish university established in, 34, 43, 78, 208n213; Jordanian, 97, 122; mayor of, 96, 97, 225n118, 230n182, 246n117; Mount Scopus in, 1, 122; natives of, 1, 21, 42, 45, 71, 72, 111, 139, 225n119; networked with Berlin and Frankfurt, 66, 67, 182; Old City of, 96, 120; radio in, 92, 131, 221n74; riots and violence in, 97, 113, 120, 122, 221n80; Sheikh Jarrah neighborhood, 92, 99, 139; Terra Sancta compound in, 126, 150; West, 122, 128. *See also* Hebrew University; Mount Scopus

*Jerusalem Calling* (Radio al-Quds), 92, 221n74

Jerusalem Citadel, 96

Jerusalem Governorate Office, 45–46

Jerusalem Riots (1920), 97, 120

Jewish Agency, 91, 99, 119, 148, 220n64, 227n136; personnel of, 70, 117, 135. *See also* Political Department of the Jewish Agency

Jewish-Arab affinity, 49, 81, 82, 162

Jewish-Arab conflict, during British Mandate, 79, 118

Jewish history and literature, 7, 36, 38–39, 197n78

Jewish National Council, 73, 115, 213n264

Jewish National Fund, 220n64, 257n21

294 ::: INDEX

Jewishness, 22, 153

Jewish Orientalists, 6, 7, 53

Jewish Studies, 22, 94; historiography of, 7–8; Oriental Studies and, 23, 40–44, 47, 76; Wiese on, 6–7. *See also Wissenschaft des Judentums*

Jews, 6, 11, 60, 100, 139, 158, 215n12, 216n25; Arabs and, 103, 116, 181, 184, 211n243, 225n119; in Central Europe, 23, 30, 41; in Eastern Europe, 30, 206n181; in Islamic world, 47, 87, 140–45, 145, 157, 244n102; as scholars, 1, 32, 66; Sephardi, 11, 71, 72, 116, 143, 212n255; Yemenite, 140, 141, 144. *See also* Judaism

Joel, Isachar (Bernhard), 65, 204n156, 209n217

Johansen, Baber, 5

Johnston-Bloom, Ruchama, 14, 15

Jordan, 100, 134, 175, 236n28, 238n51. *See also* Transjordan

*Journal of the Palestine Oriental Society* (JPOS), 95, 223n97

Judaism, 15, 44, 57, 94, 222n89; Europe and, 6, 7; Islam and, 31, 39, 47, 141; as legitimate field of knowledge, 33, 94; Orient without, 34–57; as theology, 7, 43. *See also* Jews

Ka'b al-Ahbar, 73

Kadima association, 100–101

Kapeliuk, Menehem, 225n114

*al-Katib al-Misri* (The Egyptian Writer), 87, 227n139

Katz, Shaul, 13–14, 22

Kedar, Aharon, 84, 216n26, 216n29, 234n17

Kedem association, 245n109

al-Khalidi, Ahmed Samih, 117–18, 230n182

al-Khalidi, Hussein, 230n182

al-Kinani, Ahmed, 221n85

King Saud University, 100

Kiryat Anavim (kibbutz), 219n55

*Kiryat Sefer*, 182, 258n37

Kister, Meir Jacob, 227n133, 250n163; Arabic and, 160, 183, 253n202; Concordance and, 74, 75; in second generation of HUSOS scholars, 75, 168, 183, 253n200, 258n34

Klausner, Josef, 41, 80, 199n92, 214n10

Klein, Menachem, 225n118, 225n119

Klein, Samuel, 144

Knesset, 170, 241n75; members of, 148, 230n183, 246n117

knowledge networks, 16–20

knowledge production, 26, 153

knowledge transfer, 1, 2; from Germany to Palestine, 9–15, 23; process of, 3–4

Koebner, Richard, 39, 131, 212n245

Kohn, Hans, 12

Kohn, Leo, 54, 64

Kollek, Teddy, 178

"Kol Yerushalyim" radio, 231n196

Kraus, Paul, 210–11n236

Kurd Ali, Muhammad, 104, 111, 220n62, 220n63, 220n65, 222n87; HUSOS scholars and, 90–93, 113; in Jerusalem, 92, 221n74

Kurdistan, 141

Kurdistani Jewish language, 242n83

Labor Unity Party (*Ahdut Ha'avoda*), 170, 254n216

Landau, Jacob M., 21, 147, 207n196, 240n73, 244n104

Landman, Amos, 227n136

Landman, Aviva Tourovsky, 101, 227n133, 227n136

language study, 157, 158

La Pira, Giorgio, 168–69

Latin, 26, 41, 52, 56; alphabet of, 62, 198n86, 206n186

Latour, Bruno, 190n57, 190–91n58

Lausanne Conference (1949), 169

Lavsky, Hagit, 42, 199n97

Layish, Aharon, 256n8

Lazarus-Yafeh, Hava, 13, 57

INDEX ::: 295

Lebanese visitors to Hebrew University, 88–89

Levantinism, 5, 71

Levi, Yitzhak (Isacco) Giuseppe, 227n141

Levin, Shmaryahu, 35, 196n61; Goldziher and, 37, 39, 40–41, 196n62, 198n79, 198n80

Levy, Kurt, 130–31, 236n36

Lewis, Bernard, 162–63, 165, 251n175

library, libraries, 126, 234n20, 235n20; Goldziher's, 40, 53, 55; Nimr al-Khatib's, 127–28, 129; removal of materials from, 235n27, 236n28

Libya, 141

Lichtenstadter, Ilse, 14

linguistics, linguists, 3, 25, 62, 102, 119, 130, 139, 196n65; comparative, 25, 27; diglossia and, 139; at Hebrew University, 210n234; Semitic, 100, 160, 211n237, 241n74; study in World War I POW camps, 28–29; tradition of, 156, 182

Livny, Adi, 71, 125–26, 233n6

Lockman, Zachary, 14

Loewe, Heinrich, 80–81, 198n81, 199n92

London, 64, 110, 131, 164; Hebrew University founding committee in, 43–44; Zionist Executive in, 54, 64

London University, School of Oriental and African Studies (SOAS), 65, 69, 110, 131, 162–64, 230n171

Lorch, Netanel, 165

Lord Plumer Prize, 144

Lurie, Joseph, 42

Lutfi al-Sayyid, Ahmed, 79, 102, 108, 214n6, 214n8, 227n137

Luther, Martin, 24

Lutherans, 94, 95

Lutzky (Dotan), Alexander, 117–18, 146, 148

Ma'ariv, 180

Magnes, J. L. (Judah Leib), 53, 71, 99, 105, 108, 199n95, 200n103, 201n121,

202n126, 209n222, 210n235; death of, 122, 152; Egypt and, 87, 90, 219n56, 219n59; Hartog Commission and, 69, 211n238; Hebrew University and, 43, 50; Horovitz and, 50, 51, 52, 54, 56, 65, 77, 102, 103, 106–7, 145, 202n127, 207n197, 215n14; Mayer and, 45, 200n103; as president of Hebrew University, 81, 96, 122, 183; study of Arabic and Islam and, 47, 49, 85, 108, 113, 117, 153, 215n12, 223n93, 228n142

Magnes Press, Hebrew University, 175

Mahboub, David Shalem, 55, 204n156

Maisler, Benjamin. See Mazar (Maisler), Benjamin

Mamluk period, in Palestine, 49, 130, 134, 142

Mangold-Will, Sabine, 5–6, 15, 25, 26, 192n14, 203n143, 205n163, 228n147

Mannheim, Karl, 168, 253n201

Mapam (United Workers Party), 148–49, 169–70

Marchand, Suzanne L., 16, 193n38, 228n147; on German Orientalism, 8–9, 16, 27, 185n5

Margolis, Max Leopold (Mordechai Yom-Tov Margaliot), 48–49, 201n121, 202n123; Plan of HUSOS founding of, 44–49, 52, 203n144

Maronites, 101

Massignon, Louis, 83, 92

Matalon, Emmanuel, 148

Mayer, L. A. (Leo, Leon; Ary, Aryeh), 41, 42, 45, 46, 49, 63–64, 67, 80, 84, 88, 99, 105, 111, 130, 135, 172, 173, 198n83, 198n86, 204n156, 213n264, 219n55, 219n56, 222n92, 228n143, 238n59, 242n78, 255n227; al-Aref and, 97–98; Arabic language instruction and, 113, 114, 115–16; British Mandate Antiquities Department and, 94, 223n97; Canaan and, 94–95, 96, 235n21; centrality of, to HUSOS, 77, 181; on committee to establish

296 ::: INDEX

humanities faculty, 41, 44; in first generation of HUSOS scholars, 15, 33, 160, 161, 252–53n200; founding of HUSOS and, 199n92, 200n103; Goitein and, 45, 70, 92, 133, 136, 146, 157, 161; government connections of, 98, 121, 123; Hartog Committee and, 110–11; as HUSOS director, 132, 152, 201n113; Institute for Jewish Studies and, 51–52, 55, 67, 68, 82, 125, 162, 210n233, 234n11; Israel Oriental Society and, 146, 148; Kurd Ali and, 91–92, 113; lectures and teaching of, 47, 52, 55, 65, 66, 75, 95–96, 133, 134, 155, 222–23n93, 223n99, 245n107, 246n121; Muslim art and archaeology and, 76, 94, 95, 121, 182, 195n50, 203n140, 203n145, 230n178; Palestine and, 47, 53, 94–95, 102, 110–11, 144, 146, 157. *See also* Mayer Plan for founding of HUSOS

Mayer Plan for founding of HUSOS, 44–49, 52, 54, 132, 200n103

Mazar (Maisler), Benjamin, 125, 164, 166, 254–55n221, 255n227

Mediterranean, 141

Mediterranean Conference (Florence, 1958), 168–69

Meir, Golda, 169, 253n206

*mekhina* (preparatory program), 66, 105–6, 114

Mendel, Yonatan, 11–12

Middle Ages, 82–83, 135, 141, 160

Middle East, 2, 28, 124, 192n17; contemporary, 133–34; decolonization of, 86, 152–53; modern, 69, 112, 124, 129–40, 133–34, 152, 248n150, 258n30; as term, 166

Middle East and Islamic Studies Association of Israel (MEISAI), 150. *See also* Israel Oriental Society

"Middle East Compilation" (*Yalkut Hamizrah Hatikhon*), 244n103

Middle Eastern Studies, 18, 249n152; German, 5, 7

*Middle East Record*, 178

Midrashic literature, 31, 45

Military Intelligence Directorate (Aman), 177–78, 246n117, 250n163, 257n21, 258n32

Milson, Menahem, 203n136, 241n76; on HUSOS's early years, 13, 22, 85, 252–53n200

*Mishnah*, 52, 100

Mittwoch, Eugen, 44, 54, 59, 70, 163, 196n61, 199n99, 202n127, 203n146, 220n66; as Ethiopian language expert, 44, 251n179; German Foreign Ministry and, 199–200n100; HUSOS steering committee and, 200n102

*Mizrahanim* (Oriental Studies scholars), 3

*mizrah* (East; Orient), as term, 3

*Mizrahan* (male expert in Orientalism), as term, 2, 185n4

*Mizrahanut* (Orientalism), as term, 2, 3, 185n4, 185n6

Mizrahi Jews, 11, 71, 72, 116, 140, 143

Mizrahi Teacher Training College, 55, 204n156

*Modern East, The*, 234n10

modernization of Oriental Studies, 172–73

Modern Middle Eastern Studies, 152–61

monotheism, 32, 36, 37–38, 39

Mossad (Institute for Intelligence and Special Operations), 179, 258n32

Mount Scopus, 227n139; demilitarized exclave on and displacement from, 122, 125 126–27, 233n4, 235n20, 235n27, 236n28; Hebrew University on, 78, 86; Hebrew University's opening celebration on, 1, 51, 78; land purchases for Hebrew University on, 34–35. *See also* Hebrew University

Moyal, Esther, 114

multilingualism, 11

*al-Muqtabas*, 90

murders and assassinations, 89, 99, 113, 128, 172

Muristan, 96

Museum of Islamic Art, 17

museums, 96, 224n104

Muslim culture, 75, 46, 69–70, 95, 174, 203n140; Mayer and, 76, 94, 121, 182, 195n50, 203n145, 230n178

Muslim epigraphs, 50

Muslim history, 43, 66, 79, 90, 112, 156, 244n98

Muslims, 6, 11, 34, 41, 100, 106, 107; as German POWs, 29, 61, 193n36, 193n37

Muslim scholars, 81, 189n49, 228n142; HUSOS and, 19, 77–102, 118, 119

al-Muzaffar, Jamal, 226n124

Myers, David, 7

Naor, Moshe, 11, 116

Nashashibi, Issaf, 92–93, 111, 221n80, 221n83, 221n85, 222n87, 224n107

Nashashibi, Raghib, 225n118

National and University Library (Jerusalem), 40, 68, 127, 142, 209n217, 236n30. *See also under current name:* National Library of Israel

nationalism, 38, 39, 131

National Library of Israel, 16, 193n37, 251n179, 255n227. *See also under former name:* National and University Library

Navon, Yitzhak, 219n55

Nazis, 142, 209n218, 210n229, 210n233; purge of Jewish scholars by, 122, 172, 236n36; refugees from, 2, 142; rise to power of, 67, 74, 130, 209n218

Near East, 67, 112, 117, 155

Nehru, Jawaharlal, 251n184

Neustadt, David. *See* Ayalon, David

*New East, The* (*Hamizrah Hehadash*), 124, 145, 146, 149–51, 178, 234n10, 246n121, 258n24

newspapers, 17, 72, 165

NfO (*Nachrichtenstelle für den Orient*;

Information Bureau for the Orient), 60, 61, 199n100

Niederland, Doron, 10

Nimr al-Khatib, Muhammad, 127–28, 129

Nitzan-Shiftan, Alona, 10

Nöldecke, Theodor, 71

Nordau, Max, 93, 221n83

North Africa, 5, 29, 124, 142; decolonization of, 152–53

Noy, Amos, 11, 194n41

al-Nubani, Hamdi Bakr, 99, 225–26n4, 225n123, 226n124

al-Nubani, Sheikh Bakr, 99

Occident, the, 4

ʿolim, 2

Olsvanger, Immanuel, 98–99, 221n85

Orient, the, 4, 158; Ancient, 51; aspects of, 3, 6; extent of, 24–25; as term, 3, 166; without Judaism, 34–57

"Oriental Communities" as term, 142

Orientalism, 20, 156, 159, 181, 185n5, 249n151; academic, 2, 13, 14; history of, in Palestine and Israel, 11–12, 17; Israeli, 10–11, 185n5; living, 108–9; modern, 25, 192n14; as term, 9; Western imperialism and, 159, 166; Zionist, 2. *See also Mizrahanut*

*Orientalism* (Said, 1978), 4, 30, 157

Orientalism, German (*Orientalistik*), 4, 5, 6, 14, 185n5

Orientalist critique of Said, 3, 4–5

Orientalists, 3; French, 25, 36–37; Jewish, 1, 14. *See also Mizrahan*

Oriental languages, 24; chairs of, 25–26

Oriental philology, 26, 38

Oriental Studies, 7, 43, 65, 121, 153, 191n59; conceptual infrastructure of, 152–61; expansion of, 129, 151–67; Jewish Studies and, 40–44, 42, 47, 76; modernization of, 172–73; statist, 123–24; as term, 2, 3

Orient-Occident dichotomy, 7

298 ::: INDEX

Oron, Yitzhak, 177–78, 257n21
Osmania University, 90
Ottoman Empire, 24, 41, 100, 154, 165;
during World War I, 8, 29, 85, 96
Ottoman period in Palestine, 10, 11, 12,
48, 55, 130, 177, 223n97
Oz-Salzberger, Fania, 10

Palestine, 1, 7, 14, 22, 47, 50, 94, 95, 100,
105, 113, 146, 177, 224n107; academic
immigrants to, 41, 43, 45, 53, 64,
67–68, 74, 211n236; Arabs in, 103,
197n73; British Mandate government
in, 86, 96, 97, 214n10; ethnography
of, 96, 144; history of, 47–48, 53, 158;
immigrants to, 9, 144; knowledge
transfer to, 2, 9–15; Mamluk period
in, 49, 64; Orientalist discipline in, 4,
13, 16, 17, 34; Ottomans in, 10, 11, 12,
48, 55, 130, 142, 223n97; violence in,
92, 100, 108. See also Israel, State of;
Jerusalem; Syria; Yishuv; Zionism
Palestine Broadcasting Service, 92
Palestine Folk Museum, 96, 224n104
Palestine Oriental Society, 95, 144,
146–47
Palestine Riots (1929), 108
Palestinian Heritage Museum, 224n106
Palestinian national movement, 97, 113
Palestinian Workers' Party (Mapai), 108
paradigm, Said's Orientalist, 5
Partition Plan, 137
Penslar, Derek, 12
Persia, 136, 228n143
Persian language, 26, 27, 47, 50, 51, 61,
143, 158; Goitein and, 76, 133; Heyd
and, 131, 136, 165, 238n57
Philippines, 162
philological Orientalism, 26, 30, 32,
36–38, 57, 63
philology, philologists, 8, 24, 48, 172,
182, 201n121, 203n136; Arabic and,
105, 139, 181, 194n41, 202n124;
classical, 26, 45, 76, 116, 143, 181, 183;

concordances and, 58, 63, 207n197,
207n200, 209n216; German tradition
of, 8, 11–12, 14, 65, 66, 70, 73, 75, 77,
106, 116, 154; HUSOS and, 69–70, 76,
77, 173; text-based, 26, 40, 116, 143. See
also philological Orientalism; Semitic
philology
philosophy, 26, 64
Piamenta, Moshe (Musa), 139, 240n73,
240n74, 241n75, 253n200
Plessner, Martin (Meir), 128, 169,
170, 182, 225n119, 235n23, 254n218,
255n226; Ben-Gurion and,
170, 254n217; Buber and, 169;
concordance and, 74–75; in first
generation of HUSOS scholars, 15,
252–53n200; Florence Affair and,
169–72, 254–55n221; Heyd and,
171–72, 255n223; as member of Ihud
association, 128, 170; National and
University Library and, 127–28
Poland, 45, 74
Political Department of the Jewish
Agency, 89, 91, 96, 113, 119, 120,
131, 138, 148, 149, 215n13, 230n182,
244n102; Arab Bureau of, 88, 117,
130; Ayalon and, 134, 136, 227n136,
238n50; Hareli in, 91, 220n70; Heyd
and, 131, 146, 161, 172, 227n136,
244n103; HUSOS and, 103, 115, 140;
School for Diplomats of, 131–32;
second generation of HUSOS scholars
and, 124, 150, 183; Shamosh and, 88,
231n189, 231n196; students and, 101–2.
See also Israel, State of: Ministry of
Foreign Affairs
politics, 16; academia and, 9, 13, 110, 111;
of Oriental Studies, 8–9; science and,
2, 33–34, 111, 147, 158, 181, 237n41
Polotsky, Hans Jakob (Hayim), 68, 75,
76, 160, 210n234, 211n237, 253n300,
255n227
polytheism, 36, 37
Popper, Tess Magnes, 53

Popper, William, 53, 54, 203n146, 204n147
Porath, Yehoshua, 246n123
Poznan, 12
Poznansky, Edward, 161
Princeton University, 151, 247n136
prisoners of war (POWs): Egyptian, in 1956 Sinai War, 174–75, 255–56n4; German Orientalists' interviews of, in World War I, 28–29, 60–63, 193n36, 207n196
Prophet Muhammad, 31, 59
Protestant Reformation, 24
Protestant theological research, 6
Prussia, 12, 24, 147; Ministry of Education and Culture (*Kultusministerium*), 28, 29, 45, 59, 73; Royal Phonographic Commission of, 29, 60; State Library of, 32, 41, 45, 54, 59–60, 62, 193n33, 193n37. *See also* Germany; *and "German" entries*
Prussian Academy of Sciences, 61

*qadis*, 202n124, 232n198
*Quarterly of the Department of Antiquities of Palestine* (QDAP), 223n97
Quran and Quranic studies, 51, 91, 140; Rivlin and, 66, 67, 76, 226n124

Rabbi Binyamin (Yehoshua Radler-Feldman), 204n156, 216n29
rabbinical training, 6, 30, 31, 41, 42, 43, 142
race laws of Nazis, 67–68
radio stations and broadcasts, 88, 92, 131, 218n47, 221n74, 231n196
Radler-Feldman, Yehoshua. *See* Rabbi Binyamin)
Ramadan, 92
al-Rashdan, Salim, 100, 226n129
Raz-Krakotzkin, Ammon, 7
Reali High School, Haifa, 45, 64, 66, 138, 209n222, 229n155
recordings made in German POW

camps, 28–29, 60–62, 193n33, 206n180
Reichmann, Shalom, 12
Reiss, Golda, 204n155, 204n156
Renan, Ernest, 36–37
Rescher, Oskar (Osman Reser), 203n146, 204n147
*al-Risala*, 93
Ritter, Hellmut, 220n66
Rivlin, Yosef Yo'el, 77, 98, 110, 216n29, 218n48, 225n118, 240n73, 242n83; Arabic language and, 111, 233n3; in first generation of HUSOS scholars, 15, 160, 252–53n200; Quran and, 67, 76, 91, 226n124; as student of Horovitz's, 33, 66, 106
Rockefeller Foundation, 165, 252n187
Romantic movement, 26
Rome, 169
Rosenblum, Saul (Shlomo), 42, 43, 199n92
Ruppin, Arthur, 12, 84, 144, 216n29
Russia, 5, 29, 35, 39, 40, 48, 60–61, 111, 130, 166, 206n186, 234n17

Sachau, Eduard, 59, 60, 61, 76, 181, 202n126, 220n66
Sa'd, Ibn, *Kitab al-Tabaqat al-Kabir*, 59
Said, Edward W., 7–9, 12, 159; *Orientalism* (1978), 4, 30, 157; Orientalism and, 3; Orientalist critique of, 4–5
Saint Catherine's Monastery, 255n227
Saint Joseph University, Beirut, 114
Salaymeh, Lena, 6
Salt, Transjordan, 100
Salzberger, Eli, 10
Sanskrit language, 25, 26, 27, 165, 251n184
Sapir, Adi, 125
Sasson, Eliyahu, 88–89, 99, 137, 169–71, 219n55, 254n211
Saudi Arabia, 100
Schiff, Jacob, 50
Schiffrin, Zvi Harold, 251n184
Schlegel, Friedrich, 25

300 ::: INDEX

Schocken, Gershom, 149

Schocken, Shlomo (Salman), 99, 199n92

scholarly archives, 16–20

scholarly networks, 17, 190n58, 194–95n48

Scholem, Gershom, 201n109, 216n29

School for Diplomats (Institute for Further Studies; *Hamosad Lehishtalmut*), 131–32, 137

School of Oriental and African Studies, London University (soas), 65, 69, 110, 131, 162–64, 230n171

Schorsch, Ismar, 7, 222n89

*Schriftarabisch* (modern Arabic), 104, 114–15

Schrire, Dani, 10, 190–91n58

science, 17, 46, 103, 154; German Orientalism and, 24–34; in Germany, 5–6; politics and, 2, 33–34, 111, 147, 158, 181, 237n41; Weber on, 111

second generation of HUSOS scholars, 168, 180; first generation and, 167–68, 172–73; relationship of, 19–20; rise of, 151–67

Second Oriental Renaissance (Marchand), 27

secularization, 154

security establishment, 13, 176, 181, 183

Seminar for Oriental Languages (*Seminar für Orientalische Sprachen*, sos), 8, 69–70, 110, 163

Semitic languages, 25–28, 32, 36, 44, 45, 160; chairs in, 30, 51; Oriental Studies and, 5, 43; scholars of, 50, 53, 58, 65, 68, 88, 163, 185n4, 208–9n215, 236n36

Semitic philology, 26, 45, 46, 163

Senator, David Werner, 117, 231n189, 237n44; Heyd and, 152, 155

separation principle (Weber), 33–34, 111, 237n41

Sephardicness, Sephardi, 11, 71, 72, 116, 143, 212n255

settler colonialism, 188n39

Shabak (Israel Security Agency), 177, 257n23

Shai (Information Services, Haganah intelligence arm), 180

Shaki, Avraham Shalom, 55, 204n156

Shamir, Shimon, 226n125, 258n30

Shamosh, Isaac (Yitzhak), 130, 139, 212n247, 218n47, 218n48, 219n55, 231n189, 231n192, 231n196, 253n200; as Arabic teacher, 70, 114–17, 133, 138, 232n197, 233n3, 238n54, 240n70; Arabs and, 88–89; students on, 231–32n197

Shapira, Israel, 185n4

Sharett, Moshe. *See* Shertok (Sharett), Moshe

*Sharq al-Adna* (Near East Broadcasting Station, NEBS), 88, 218n47

Shazar, Zalman, 243n92, 246n117

Shenhav, Yehouda, 116, 143

Sherf, Zeʾev, 148, 245n107

Shertok (Sharett), Moshe, 89, 99, 131, 137, 146, 231n189, 244n103, 253n205

Shiloah (Zaslani), Reuven, 169, 170, 177, 254n214

Shiloah Center (Reuven Shiloah Research Center of the Israel Oriental Society), 176, 177–80, 258n30

Shimoni, Yaacov, 149, 246n121

Shinar, Pessah, 149, 198n83, 246n122, 253n200, 258n34

Sinai Peninsula, 255n227

Sinai War, 162, 174, 255n227

Six Day War, 180

Slavs, 41

soas. *See* School of Oriental and African Studies, London University

social sciences, 14, 157

Society for Jewish Folklore (Hamburg), 206n181, 243n93, 246n117

sociology, 144, 145

Sorbonne University, 220n64

sos (*Seminar für Orientalische Sprachen*). *See* Seminar for Oriental Languages

Spain, 142

Stalin, Joseph, 206n186
state, the: academia and, 2; institution-
    alizing collaboration with, 129; Israel
    Oriental Society and, 147. *See also*
    Israel, State of; security establish-
    ment; statism
statism (*mamlakhtiyut*), 126, 148, 184,
    234n17; of Ben-Gurion, 170; in
    German tradition, 184; at HUSOS, 159;
    Israel Oriental Society and, 148
statist Orientalism, 18
statist utilitarianism, 5
Stephan, Stephan Hanna, 95, 223n97
Strauß (Strauss), Eduard (Eli). *See* Ash-
    tor, Eliyahu
students, 101, 205n161; at Hebrew
    University, 170, 171, 226n124; at
    HUSOS, 99, 177
Sufi Islam, 55
supremacism of Protestant theological
    research, 6
*Suriya al-Janubiyya* (newspaper), 97
Survey Committee of the Hebrew
    University of Jerusalem. *See* Hartog
    Committee
Swedish Consulate, 235n27
Syria, 97, 101, 104, 114, 142, 203n145,
    220n62, 223n97, 224n107, 242n78;
    Aleppo, 70, 114, 115; Horovitz in, 50,
    220n65, 242n78; Muslim culture in,
    95, 96; political situation in, 149,
    257n23. *See also* Palestine
Syriac language, 43, 45
Syrians: as Arab and Muslim scholars
    as, 85, 87, 88, 90–93, 110, 118; visit
    Hebrew University, 88–89
Syrian University of Damascus, 114
Szamet, Miriam, 10

Talbiyeh Leprosarium Jesus Hilfe, 95
Talmudic literature, 31, 45, 50, 52
Tamari, Salim, 96, 224n107
*Tarbitz*, 182
Targum, 50

*Tatarische Texte* (Tatar Texts; Weil, 1930),
    29, 62, 206n190, 207n196
Tatar language, 60–62, 175, 206n186
Tehran, Iran, 136, 137
Tel Aviv, 204n155, 257n21; Israel Oriental
    Society in, 148, 176, 179, 245n107
Tel Aviv University, 179, 180, 188n35,
    258n30
Terra Sancta compound, Jerusalem, 126,
    150
textual circle of Jewish-Arab network of
    connections, 87–94
textual studies, 13; as shared interest of
    Arab and HUSOS scholars, 87–94
Thailand, 162
theology, 30, 43, 104
Thirty Years War, 24
"Thousand and One Nights, A," 203n136
Toledano, Ehud, 188n35
Totah, Khalil, 95, 96
Tourovsky, Aviva. *See* Landman, Aviva
    Tourovsky
Tower of David, Jerusalem, 96
Toynbee, Arnold, 248n148
Transjordan, 97, 100. *See also* Jordan
translation gap, 3
transnational knowledge transfer, 18
Trotskyists, 239–40n69
Turkey, 124, 136, 161, 163, 165; Heyd in,
    242n78, 252n190; Israel and, 137,
    250n171; study of, 124, 165.
    *See also* Ottoman Empire
Turkish language and literature, 27, 44,
    47, 49, 51, 60, 61, 78, 158, 220n70,
    223n97; Fleischer and, 26, 238n57;
    Heyd and, 130–31, 136–37, 165, 238n57,
    239n66, 252n190; Weil and, 61–62, 68,
    75, 133, 138, 182, 206n188

Ukraine, 41
Ullendorff, Edward, 251n179
Umayyad period, 57
United Arab Republic, 257n23
United Nations, 137

302 ::: INDEX

United States, 20, 43, 49, 53, 125, 137,
209n218, 247n136; area studies in, 157;
Department of State, 220n64; Fischel
in, 208–9n215; Goitein in, 15, 151, 160,
190n51, 226n126, 247n131; Hebrew
University founding committee in,
43–44; immigrants to, 14, 15, 48,
209n218; Israeli Ambassador to, 131,
152, 164; Magnes returns to, 50, 122;
Middle East and, 152–53; Said on
Orientalism and, 5; study of Arabic
and Islam in, 247n136
United Workers Party (*Mapam*), 148–49,
169–70
University of Alexandria, 87, 89
University of Berlin, 1, 2, 17, 20, 23, 29,
32, 33, 46, 69, 122, 193n33, 202n127,
209n222, 228n142, 241n74; doctorates
from, 45, 50, 59, 152; SOS in, 69–70,
249n153
University of Bonn, 31, 236n36
University of Breslau, 30, 65, 74, 203n146,
204n147
University of Cairo, 38, 73, 79, 227n137
University of Calcutta, 69
University of California Berkeley, 53,
209n215
University of Dhaka, 69
University of Frankfurt, 1, 2, 17, 20, 23, 33,
46, 66, 67, 122, 140, 152
University of Göttingen, 25, 68
University of Hamburg, 29, 65, 163,
251n177
University of Heidelberg, 31, 65, 202n126,
228n142
University of Leipzig, 25, 26, 27, 31, 181
University of London, 69, 88, 228n142
University of Madrid, 72
University of Strasbourg, 71
University of Vienna, 33, 41, 46, 52, 55,
77, 121, 142, 152, 204n155; doctorates
from, 142, 152
Urdu language, 131

al-'Uri, Sa'ud, 202n124
Ussishkin, Menahem, 42, 80, 99, 199n92

Vienna, 1, 24, 30, 33, 41–42, 46, 142,
210n235. *See also* University of
Vienna

Wauchope, Arthur, 96
Weber, Max, 33–34, 111
Weil, Gotthold Eljakim, 15, 54, 59, 62,
75, 131, 133, 181, 210n229, 210n233,
242n78, 246n121, 246n125; *Ansab
al-Ashraf* and, 59, 67, 209–10n227; at
Berlin, 54, 62, 73, 199n99, 202n127,
203n146; as director of National and
University Library, 68, 138, 193n37,
207n196; at Frankfurt, 67, 68, 73, 74,
182, 207n196; as head of HUSOS, 67,
209–10n227, 251n179; Horovitz and,
59–60, 62, 67, 110, 174, 176, 251n179,
252–53n200; in Palestine, 68, 182,
211n237; retirement of, 138, 155, 160,
239n66, 248n142; Tatar language
and culture and, 61–63, 175, 206n188,
207n196; World War I German POW
camps and, 60–63, 207n196
Weil, Gustav, 31
Weinbergslager POW camp, 29, 207n196
Weiss, Yfaat, 10, 12
Weizmann, Chaim, 71, 78–80, 99,
197n79, 212n256; universalist vision
of, 78–79
West Bank, 175, 176, 180, 181
Western imperial powers, 162
Westernization, 154
Wiese, Christian, 6–7
Wilhelm II, Kaiser of Germany, 28, 29
Wilkof, Shira, 10
*Wissenschaft des Judentums* (lit. "science
of Judaism"), 6–7, 32, 33–34, 45;
expansion of, 30; German influence
on, 6, 22. *See also* Jewish Studies
Wokoeck, Ursula, 7–8, 9, 17, 26, 28,
192n17, 201n112

women, 55, 241n74
World Jewish Congress, 169, 253n205
worldviews of Orientalists, 16
World War I, 6, 8, 28, 34, 45, 133, 174, 243n93; end of, 35, 226n124; German POW camps in, 60-63, 174, 193n38; Mittwoch in, 44, 251n179; Ottoman Empire in, 85, 96; outbreak of, 59, 60
World War II, 20, 116, 125, 130, 152, 157, 200n100, 247n136, 248n150, 249n151
World Zionist Organization, 41, 215n12, 220n64, 225n117
Wormann, Curt, 127

Yadin, Yigael, 148, 149, 246n121
Yahuda, Abraham Shalom, 70-74, 108, 212n253, 212n256
Yehoshua, A. B., 21, 246n117, 246n121
Yehoshua, Yaakov, 21, 246n117
*Yekim* (German-Jewish immigrants), 21
Yellin, Avinoam, 45, 64, 77, 113, 201n110, 204n156
Yellin, David, 41, 42, 43, 45, 66, 72, 199n92, 203n140, 208n205, 214n10; Mayer and, 46, 201n113
Yemen, 76, 228n142
Yemenite Jews, 73, 140, 141, 144, 240n70, 242n81
Yiddish language, 60
*Yishuv* (Jewish community in pre-1948 Palestine), 11, 12, 19, 66, 98, 103, 108, 116, 119, 126, 216n25, 224n109; Gelber on, 9-10; Hebrew University and, 111-12, 118
YMCA, 95, 96

Zahiriyya Library, Damascus, 92
Zaki Pasha, Ahmed, 49, 202n124
Zalashik, Rakefat, 10
Zander, Walter, 161-62, 164, 250n166, 251n175, 251n182
Zaza, Hassan, 100, 226n126
ZDMG (*Zeitschrift der Deutschen Morgenländischen Gesellschaft*), 31
Zimmerman, Moshe, 10
*Zion*, 182
Zionism, 20, 22, 35, 66, 72, 79, 108, 117, 227n139; context of, 19, 77, 80; Goitein and, 15, 151; Goldziher opposes, 37, 197n73; Hebrew University and, 118, 119; opponents and critics of, 89, 95, 128, 223n94, 224n107; reality of, 117-20; as settler colonialism, 188n39
Zionist activists, 42, 43, 80, 245n109
Zionist Congress of 1913, 34, 78
Zionist consciousness, 83, 89
Zionist discourse and ideology, 18, 48, 118, 143
Zionist enterprise, 12, 13; Horovitz and, 14-15
Zionist Executive in London, 54, 64
Zionist General Council, 41, 198n85
Zionist movement, 34, 81, 84, 102; Hebrew University and, 111-12, 126; opponents to and critics of, 95-96
Zionist Orientalism, 2, 7, 18
Zionist Oriental Studies, 15, 16
Zionist project, 183
Zionists, 85, 95, 100, 172
Zionist theological view, 7